Internet Business Intelligence

Internet Business Intelligence

How to Build a Big Company System on a Small Company Budget

David Vine

CyberAge Books

Medford, New Jersey

Internet Business Intelligence:
How to Build a Big Company System on a Small Company Budget

Library of Congress Cataloging-in-Publication Data

Vine, David.
      Internet business intelligence : how to build a big company system on a small company budget / David Vine.
          p.   cm.
      Includes bibliographical references and index.
      ISBN 0-910965-35-8
      1. Business intelligence—Computer network resources.
2. Internet (Computer network)   I. Title.
      HD38.7 .V56 2000
      658.4'7'02854678—dc21   99-057389

Printed and bound in the United States of America.

Publisher: Thomas H. Hogan, Sr.
Editor-in-Chief: John B. Bryans
Managing Editor: Janet M. Spavlik
Copy Editor: Pat Hadley-Miller
Production Manager: M. Heide Dengler
Cover Design: Bette Tumasz
          Adam Vinick
Book Design: Jeremy M. Pellegrin
Indexer: Laurie Andriot

The author invites you to visit his Web site at
www.davidvineassociates.com

DEDICATION

For my loving wife Mar-Lee, whose
unswerving support, essential criticism, and
intellectual input made this book possible

TABLE OF CONTENTS

Introduction . . . . **xv**

Knowledge Management xv
Business Intelligence xvi
Internet Business Intelligence xvii
How to use this book xix

**1. What Is Business Intelligence and
Why Do You Need an Internet System?** **1**

The need for a system 2
History of business intelligence 3
Modern management 4
Business intelligence in contemporary
   management practice 6
IBIS fits into the big picture 9
Spy vs. spy? 11
Intelligence meets the Internet 13
Strategic planning models 14

**2. What Are the Characteristics of
Internet Business Intelligence?** **19**

Technical 19
World Wide Web 20
Psychological aspects of IBIS 23
   Synergistic power of sharing information 23
Selecting people for IBIS 25
Cataloging the personalities 27
Editorial content available for IBIS 29

3. IBIS for Top Management **39**

Seizing the knowledge advantage 41
Maximizing resources 44
   Time expansion 44
   Developing contacts 45
IBIS for strategy development 46
   Vision 47
   External environment 48
   Mission 49
SWOT 50
Business planning 50

Non-Internet information for business planning 52
Defining the competition 53
Internet information sources for due diligence 57
Peering into the future 58
Summary of the information requirements of executives ... 59
Representative sources (Internet and non-Internet)
   by executive function 61
Putting it all together............................... 63
Mini Case: Who really owns the company? 64
Mini Case: Is there a threat to our
   executives or employees? 66
Mini Case: Who's stealing our
   proprietary information? 67

4. IBIS for Marketing **69**

Rapid identification of new markets.................... 71
Replacing or augmenting costly market
   research reports 72
New product development.......................... 75
Sales support 77
Customer intelligence................................ 78
Gathering background information 80
Developing marketing strategies...................... 82
Marketing management 83
Mini Case: Geographic and demographic
   targeting in consumer marketing 85
Mini Case: Geographic targeting in business-
   to-business marketing.............................. 86
Mini Case: Defining BI process in a newly
   deregulated industry............................... 87

5. IBIS for Finance **89**

Risk and reward 89
Maximizing profitability 91
Sources of information 92
Free software 94
Strategic financial management 95
Strategic metrics.................................... 97
Economic data 98
Internet and accountants........................... 103
Strategic company audits, due diligence
investigations, and business valuations................ 103
Mini Case: Shall we extend our contract
   with a particular vendor? 108

**6. IBIS for Small-Business
Owners and Entrepreneurs** **111**

Small-business financing 113
    SBA financing programs 114
    Financial staging 115
    Venture capital 116
Research and planning 116
Finding customers 118
Marketing organization for small business 120
Mini Case: Entrepreneur-investor's
study of temporary staffing industry 122

**7. A Framework for
Internet Business Intelligence** **129**

The PROACtive methodology 130
Scoping out the system 131
System cost 134
Categorizing tools 135
    Level I—Basic IBIS 136
    Level II—Intermediate IBIS 138
    Level III—Advanced IBIS 140
Planning—What do we want to know? 142
Essential elements of information 142
Information quality 143
BI Focus 145
    Template example: Target organization focus 145
    Template example: Key business issues focus 145
    Template example: Customer focus 146
    Business plan template 146
    New product plan data requirements template 147
    Competitive analysis template 148
    The general survey outline 149
Organizing a BI team 150
Business intelligence program implementation 152
System features 153
Knowledge building 154

8. Access **161**

Historical background 161
Enabling the Web 162
Technicalities 163
Traffic routing 164
Internet Service Providers 166
    ISDN 167
    "Cable modem" service 168

Digital Subscriber Line.............................. 169
Digital satellite service 170
Biggest and oldest ISPs 172
AOL's many facets 173
AOL's networked neighborhood. 174
IBIS features of AOL.................................... 175
AOL's News Profiles 176
Fine-tuning News Profiles 178
CompuServe 180
The unplugged future of Internet access 181
Meeting various needs 182
Various methods of operation...................... 183
Big and Little LEOS 184
Telecom deregulation 185

9. Collection Tools to Rapidly Obtain Required Information

**9. Collection Tools to Rapidly
Obtain Required Information** **187**

Netscape Communicator suite 188
Browser mechanics 188
Bookmarks 189
Drag and drop 190
Netscape power tips 191
Automatically download, store,
and locally search Web pages....................... 192
Data sculpting 195
From text to database 197

10. Searching the Internet for Business Intelligence ... **199**

Search engines become mini online services 200
Search engine personalities 201
Hierarchical 203
Keyword search 205
Other major search engines........................... 207
Content ratings....................................... 209
Metasearch resources 210
Search engine features 212
Other types of searches............................... 215
Browser search features 216
Link sites 217

**11. Business Intelligence Use of
Newsgroups and Mail Lists** **219**

Electronic Communications Privacy Act 219
Newsgroup basics 220

Newsgroup categories............................221
Finding specific Newsgroups.......................221
Newsgroup information 224
Free Agent......................................225
News Rover......................................225
Mail lists 226
Mailing list basics with LISTSERV...................227
Public vs. private 228
Locate lists 229
How to join and leave a mailing list 230
How to send mail to a list.........................231
How to see who is on the list 232
Options that may be set 232
Topics..233
Other LISTSERV software uses......................234
Knowledge development 234

12. What Else Is Available via the Internet? **237**

Subscription services (free and commercial)
    via the Internet..............................237
Free and low-cost communications 238
News now 239
Public company information.......................241
International news................................245
Listen in live 248
Industry-specific resources 251
Corporation-provided information..................252
Government documents
    (federal, state, county, and local)...............253
Downloadable software 254
Freeware and shareware categories 256
    Personal information managers 257
    Primary research...........................257
    Quotes, bids, and estimating...................258
Online courses 258

**13. Other Information Sources
    to Supplement the Internet** **261**

CD-ROM databases..............................261
Low- to medium-cost CD-ROMs....................262
High-cost library CD-ROMs........................265
Premium databases..............................273
Premium online databases at libraries................275
Smaller online business information providers 277
Directory publishers 278
Books that serve as directories.....................279

Magazines to help you find information 280
Business directories. 280
    Representative directories: Company information 281
    Representative directories: Specialized 281
Sources of exotic BI 282
Picking your source(s). 289

14. Organizing Information
    to Produce Intelligence. 291

Information architecture 292
Micromanagement methods 293
Find Fast 295
Contact management with Netscape Communicator 296
Organizing e-mail into categories 296
Using Netscape's e-mail features to organize Web pages. . 298
Filter and file e-mail messages 300
Manage information with Microsoft Outlook 300
Organizing information in CorelCENTRAL 301
    Card File in CorelCENTRAL. 302
    Linking information 303
Organizing bookmarks 304
    Internet Explorer. 304
    Netscape Navigator. 305
Bookmarks and delegation. 307
Auxiliary software to manage bookmarks 307
Organizing information with hyperlinks 309
    Creating HTML-linked documents 309
    Using Netscape to create HTML documents 312
    Using Microsoft Word to create HTML documents 313
Building the IBIS database 313
    Free-text databases with askSam 314
Scanning and storing documents 316
Capture and manage all required information 318
Lotus Notes groupware 319
Managing the fire hose flow 321
    Screening with LMDS. 321
    Organizing and retrieving information 323

15. Analyzing Data and Information
    to Create Intelligence. 325

AutoSummarize in Microsoft Word. 327
Evaluation of subjective judgments 328
Market analysis 329
Patent analysis 329
Benchmarking 330
Ratio analysis 330

Liquidity ratios. 331
Leverage ratios. 332
Income statement ratio analysis. 332
The 80/20 rule applied to spreadsheets 333
Excel database and list management functions 334
Statistical analysis 336
Relationship analysis. 337
Data mining with DB2. 338
Competitive analysis 339
Visualizing relationships with graphic representations. . . 341
Relationship analysis with OrgChart 344
Geographic analysis 346
High-performance text analysis 348

16. Communicating Business Intelligence 353

Persuasion. 354
First step: Organizing information
 to be communicated 356
Formats and templates. 357
Formal report format 358
Template Wizards 359
Microsoft Word features for communicating
 business intelligence 361
Annotating, finding, and opening text files. 361
Collaboration. 362
Simplifying complex functions 363
Other tools in Word. 364
Communicating via Newsgroups and mail lists 365
Publishing presentations on the Internet 366
Lights, camera, action! 367
Powering up PowerPoint. 367
Adobe Acrobat 369
Netscape Composer 370
Free classes on communication 371
Communicating Business Intelligence via CD-ROM 372
Reports on diskette 374
Fax broadcasting 374
Windows native communications capabilities 377
Exchange. 378
Networking 379
Sharing corporate knowledge 380
In-person briefings 382
Live conferencing. 383
Microsoft NetMeeting. 384
Conference ware 385
Business intelligence briefing procedure. 385
Wireless communications 386
Wireless Internet video 388

17. Potential Problems and Pitfalls 391

FBI's ANSIR 394
National security threat list 395
Economic espionage 396
Information security 398
Codes and ciphers 399
Rules of conduct 400

18. Reflections 403

Glossary 407

About the Author 421

Index 423

INTRODUCTION

The world of business changed drastically during the latter part of the 20th century. Business success today increasingly requires the best possible Business Intelligence (BI) to compete in a global marketplace, where faster moving competitors are a constant threat. Fortunately, we have the Internet. However, this resource also is available to your competitors on a global basis. You must be better at using the Internet for a competitive advantage. This book shows you how.

Internet Business Intelligence presents a new paradigm for business. "Work smarter not harder" is a cliché, but it takes on new significance when you consider the present situation. Businesses large and small, as well as professionals, are faced with rapid change in their markets as well as increasing competition. The need to know has never been greater. *Internet Business Intelligence* fits right into this need, reflected in the realities presented by a global information economy.

Knowledge Management

The term "information economy" surfaced in the later part of the 20th century. This term acknowledges that manufacturing has declined as a percent of Gross Domestic Product while all other activities have increased. Bureau of Labor Statistics surveys of specific managerial occupations reveal that less than 12 percent of all line and middle managers are employed in the field of industrial production. This means that instead of making things, we are processing information. Because it takes "know-how" to make things or process information, the importance of knowing how to do it becomes an asset.

The raw materials of the information economy are intangible—theories, ideas, computer programs, laboratory test results, documents, financial transactions, and the like. A large measure of the success of the mega-retailers is a result of their inventory control and tracking systems. While retailers are selling a tangible item, the intangible knowledge they manage helps them get bigger and more profitable. Today e-commerce is the current trend. Then there's the entertainment industry and its myriad information products. All this means that successful companies will fully understand their potential in terms of intellectual capital so they can compete in the information economy.

"We have entered an era of total competition. No matter your industry, company or nationality, there is a battle-ready competitor somewhere who is busy thinking how to beat you. There are no safe havens," according to Mark B. Fuller,[1] co-founder of Monitor Company, one of the world's leading strategic consulting firms. "The key objective in competition—whether business or war—is to improve your organization's performance along these dimensions:

- To generate better information than your rivals do

- To analyze that information and make sound choices

- To make those choices quickly

- To convert strategic choices into decisive action."

Business Intelligence

Business Intelligence (BI) is an umbrella term that encompasses a variety of information functions in business. Recently, competitor intelligence, also known as competitive intelligence, has come to the forefront of management literature, but market research and financial analysis are examples of other areas that fall under the umbrella. Complexity of the marketplace has driven the need to partner with other businesses. Understanding the threats and opportunities in the market as well as the strengths and weaknesses of one's own business and those of potential partners or competitors is another driver.

Product development cycles have been shortened from years to months. Rapidly changing technology and consumer preferences drive unending change, which requires a whole new area of concern. Monitoring technological developments and forecasting potential impacts to position the business for growth are other relatively new requirements served by BI. The entire process of management decision making now moves at a more rapid pace that demands more and better information, faster.

Internet Business Intelligence

Internet Business Intelligence is unique. There are many books that tell you what's available via the Internet or how to use the Internet generally. There are a few good books on competitor intelligence (see *Millennium Intelligence* by Jerry Miller, et al.), but this is the only book that proposes a complete, low-cost, Internet-based business intelligence system for overcoming real-world business problems. The principles and methods in this book will serve you well as technology continues to advance and new capabilities become available.

The Internet is a mirror of the world, but unlike a mirror's two-dimensional image, this global system of interconnected networks allows you to reach into cyberspace and pull out needed information or make business contacts and connections. These capabilities are available 24 hours a day, seven days a week, from anywhere to anywhere. While the Internet is not a cure-all for information desperation, it's rapidly becoming a universal source of much of the data we need for a variety of business activities.

If you are an entrepreneur, an owner of a small- to medium-size business, or a manager or executive employed with a larger organization, you need this book. It shows you details about Internet use that you will find nowhere else. It sets up the PROACtive process of business intelligence I've developed to help clients and seminar attendees. It treats Internet and business intelligence in an integrated way to solve everyday business problems. The problems of both small and very large businesses are presented. You can pick and choose solutions or illustrative scenarios that best fit your business needs to build an integrated system for your personal use or for use within a large organization.

This integration is important because of the increasing emphasis on multimedia via the Internet and electronic commerce. Netscape's voice mail in Communicator is just one example of how the function of our most basic intelligence gathering instrument, the telephone, is being integrated with the Internet. Distributing audio-visual communications and the means to find specific portions of video using keyword searches is now commonplace. Shopping on the Net is an accepted practice for millions of consumers. Integration of the Internet with many aspects of our lives is well underway.

The wisdom of a "holistic" approach to using the Internet as the core of a comprehensive business intelligence system should be self-evident. This book will help you achieve your goals in obtaining and using business intelligence for competitive advantage. There are separate chapters for the major functions of business management, addressing specific business intelligence needs. Outlines and graphics throughout the book highlight important points.

Technological advancement in our ability to obtain and use this information continues to accelerate. Each innovation yields a new capability, and that becomes yet another stepping stone on the path of enhanced knowledge management. While there are many forces beyond our control in business and life itself, better knowledge and heightened abilities to put that knowledge to work yield an advantage. Coping with ever-changing conditions is a little easier when you're more knowledgeable about what's going on. Better knowledge can make you a winner.

In an era when access to financial resources and business know-how worldwide is virtually unrestricted, those with superior knowledge management and business intelligence capabilities will have a competitive edge in a brutally competitive world. Information is key to success today, just as it has been throughout history.

"Knowledge is power" are the words of Lord Chancellor Francis Bacon.[2] These three words are truer today than when first spoken more than 350 years ago. Bacon's timeless contribution enhances our technologically advanced sources and methods. He proposed induction as the logic of scientific discovery and deduction as the logic of argumentation. Both processes are used together regularly in the empirical sciences. By the observation of particular events (induction) and from already known principles (deduction), new hypothetical principles are formulated and laws are induced.[3]

The nature of competition and the complexity of the business environment, coupled with advancing information technology, will continue to evolve. Business intelligence tools, techniques, and management methods are becoming permanent features of the business landscape. The Internet has taken center stage, and this book provides the processes and tools you need to harness its power.

Each day brings technical advancements in the way information is presented via the Internet. Modes such as Java-enabled programs,

Virtual Reality Modeling Language, more and more sophisticated audio and video programming, and other variations of Internet media are becoming commonplace. Vast new libraries of content are replacing traditional sources of information. In just one example, costly subscription-based custom news-clipping services are being supplanted by no-cost services that provide access to respected sources of editorial content and the tools needed to deliver specific items to the end-user. All of this richness and capability provides to the business user an enormous resource.

From understanding the basics to knowing about search engine personalities, we'll show you how to find answers to critical questions in all of these important categories. But we'll do much more in this book. We'll provide a framework, a methodology, and the tools you'll need to execute the process so you can create a true Internet Business Intelligence System (IBIS). Without much of a need to incur new expenses, this system can be scaled up from a one-person operation to a system that supports hundreds of people all over the world, assuming all have Internet access. The scale-up is less dependent upon funding than it is on the imagination, creativity, resourcefulness, and enthusiasm of the people who use it.

The Internet is the fastest growing and most powerful information technology ever placed into the hands of virtually anyone who wishes to make use of it. Anyone who uses this limitless treasure trove of information may partake at home or work, in school or office, and if need be, at the local library. With rapidly advancing satellite transmission technology, you soon will be able to tap into the Net from anywhere on earth. Elsewhere in the world not everyone is as fortunate as we Americans are, but as time goes on Internet access will become as commonplace as our telephones and televisions. Right now we have the advantage of a head start. This book will show you how to transform Internet resources into business success.

How to use this book

Some readers may wish to read this book cover to cover while others may want to focus on certain chapters pertinent to their interests. If you'd like to explore the historical underpinnings of BI, read Chapter One. Chapter Two examines Internet Business Intelligence from a characteristic perspective. Chapters Three through Six explore the relationship of Internet Business Intelligence to executive management, marketing, finance, and small business, respectively. Chapter Seven is important for all readers, because it outlines the PROACtive process that serves as an important framework for Internet Business Intelligence.

If you are thoroughly familiar with the Internet, you might consider skipping Chapter Eight. Chapters Nine through Thirteen will help you develop a keener sense of how to get the information that will serve as the raw material for IBIS. Chapter Twelve also offers insights on where to obtain free, specialized software that can support IBIS.

Chapter Fourteen helps you organize the plethora of information you'll gather, while Fifteen provides a brief overview of analysis. Chapter Fifteen should spark ideas on how to add value to your data in specific ways that are tailored to your requirements. Communication of BI is an essential part of the PROACtive process, and this subject is treated as fully as possible in Chapter Sixteen. Finally, Chapters Seventeen and Eighteen address concerns about various issues you'll need to consider to understand some prudent limits and cautions.

Endnotes

1.   Mark B. Fuller, *Business as War*, Fast Company, November, 1993, Vol. 1 No. 1.44-5.

2.   *The Columbia Viking Desk Encyclopedia.*

3.   **http://www.encyclopedia.com/articles/06344.html**.

CHAPTER 1

WHAT IS BUSINESS INTELLIGENCE AND WHY DO YOU NEED AN INTERNET SYSTEM?

An early definition of business intelligence (BI) stated that it is the activity of monitoring the environment external to the firm for information that is relevant for the decision-making process in the company.[1] While the basic concepts are timeless, their application to commerce has intensified recently. Business intelligence has been practiced for quite a while but the intensity has reached higher levels. In 1981 a report stated that the Japanese had spent three years staffing listening posts in Silicon Valley.[2] Over the years there have been numerous reports of foreign intelligence gathering targeted at U.S. businesses. See Figure 1.1 for a sampling of headlines, including one that could have presaged the Chinese Nuclear Secrets Scandal of 1999.

Figure 1.1

1

An Internet Business Intelligence System (IBIS) can provide a competitive advantage in any size business. Although it's more than just competitor intelligence, knowing more about all of your competitors (known and unknown, around the corner or across the globe) faster and in a way that makes the information more useful is just the start. Beyond competitor intelligence, one can develop a comprehensive system for defining new markets, assessing financial and economic conditions, finding technology or investment partners, and more.

The need for a system

Today you must deal with ever-greater complexity—new government regulations, changing financial and market conditions, and even unexpected events such as natural or manmade disasters and other factors that could affect your business—positively or negatively. In addition to providing an overview of business intelligence, we will explain how to use business intelligence on Internet to achieve the following goals:

- Earlier awareness of threats and opportunities

- Rapid identification of new markets

- Better, more useful information to improve decision making

- Easier discovery of joint-venture partners
  and new technologies

- Direct access to new capital markets
  and other funding sources

- Instant international connections to people,
  companies, organizations, and governments

Enhanced business intelligence operations can be an important driver of future profitability. Information systems in general are viewed as "critical success factors" by some executives, and others view them as "strategic arsenals supporting the core business." Another important focus is understanding emerging opportunities for growth. By their very nature, "emerging opportunities" involve investigation into non-routine topics, possibly on a high-intensity basis during a short period. The value of better, more timely BI could tip the delicate balance between success and failure in seizing the right opportunities. Solid business know-how must be combined with upgraded BI and supported by computer technology. People involved with BI want to know more about:

- Useful information that is readily available

- How to evaluate various information products

- Information on joint-venture partners, particularly private companies

- How to develop a competitive intelligence network

- Planning a collection process

- Getting more and better information at an earlier point

- Finding accurate and comprehensive data in the easiest to use format at the lowest cost

- An effective method for monitoring specific targets

History of business intelligence

Like war, business is a competition between organizations. Strategy is the art and science of managing organizations in competitive situations. People, organizations, and management systems win wars and capture market share. In business today, the global marketplace is the battlefield. To win, people and systems must deliver quality products and services to remain competitive.

Management thought continually evolves, and it has become fashionable to cite the philosophies of ancient warriors. Levinson (*The Way of Strategy*, 1994) unites the legacies of teachers such as Sun Tzu (*The Art of War*), Miyamoto Musashi (*The Book of Five Rings*), Niccolò Machiavelli (*The Prince*), Carl von Clausewitz (*On War*), and others. He describes how their strategies and leadership principles produced military victories.[3]

From China's legendary Sage Emperor era of 2852-2255 B.C. through the Ch'Ing dynasty of A.D. 1644-1911, the Eastern tradition of strategic thought has emphasized outwitting one's opponent through speed, stealth, flexibility, and a minimum of force. This is an approach very different from that stressed in the West, where the advantages of brute strength have overshadowed more subtle means. Military thought is a complex product of both violent war and intellectual analysis. Ancient Chinese military intelligence has evolved from the predefined battle tactics of T'ai Kung, which included mounting intensive efforts to gather intelligence, to Sun Tzu's definitions of the five types of spies. This lore is rich with methodologies.[4]

The theoretical foundation of business intelligence can be traced back to the ancient philosophies of Sun Tzu who wrote about laying plans, tactics, maneuvering, the use of spies, etc. circa 300 B.C.[5] The collected writings have been rediscovered, lending credence to the assumption that warrior philosophies embracing an age-old form of business or competitor intelligence have been embodied in *The Art of War* for centuries. Students of strategy development cite figures such as Niccolò Machiavelli (the shrewd philosopher and observer of the affairs of state circa A.D. 1500 who eyed the world with practical realism[6]), Hannibal (one of the great military geniuses of all time, circa 200 B.C.[7]), and Maj. Gen. Carl von Clausewitz (another practicing theoretician). These "philosophies" and many, many others are part of a continuum of management thought.

Since the dawn of the Industrial Revolution, management trends have altered the course of events and left their mark on the business landscape. Frederick W. Taylor's "Scientific Management" methods circa 1900 developed a new philosophy and approach to management.[8] Scientific Management evolved from a "shop system" to "principles of management," which promoted disciplined investigation to determine the most effective method for performing a specific task, such as shoveling coal into a furnace. Taylor's work pioneered the development of business processes.

Modern management

The post-World War II economy spawned improved market research (along with pent-up demand fomented during the war years) and, as early computer systems programmed with punch cards played a role in the analysis of data, more and more was known about consumers, customers, and clients. The threat of Soviet spies and nuclear war during the 1950s and 1960s undoubtedly had a significant impact on the national psyche. Nuclear-tipped missiles and the possibility of instant destruction broadened our awareness. Herman Kahn, a nuclear physicist and an acknowledged expert in national security planning, in a chapter titled "In Defense of Thinking," wrote: "Social inhibitions which reinforce natural tendencies to avoid thinking about unpleasant subjects are hardly uncommon. The psychological factors involved in ostrich-like behavior have parallels in communities and nations."[9]

During the 1970s and early 1980s, databases and easy access to information via desktop computers became commonplace in the business world. These activities were focused mainly on the consumer, but strategic thinkers expanded their concerns to include competitor information as well. A body of business intelligence began to form.

Simultaneously, W. Edwards Deming's "Quality Improvement" (QI) philosophy, which used various statistical techniques and an approach to making better products, was adopted in post-World War II Japan.[10]

Deming and several others had pioneered the QI field, which originated with the need to connect hundreds of local telephone companies during the early 20th century. The Bell System needed absolute reliability and this gave rise to a methodology that became known as statistical quality control. Quality is just one management trend that has shaped the business world, probably since the time of money-changers of ancient times. Various types of operational and philosophical approaches have been adopted over the years.

Dr. Deming, a statistician and consultant, was so successful in his mission that in 1951 the Japanese government established the Deming Prize for innovation in quality management. He brought these mostly unrecognized American management techniques (which were pioneered by the Bell System when that telephone company pieced together many local companies to go national) back from Japan. Deming's techniques were widely adopted here during the 1980s. Benchmarking, now a commonly used quality improvement tool, is an allied form of BI.

During the 1980s, American business faced much greater competition in an increasingly global marketplace, particularly with Japan and other rapidly emerging economies. This led to increased emphasis on knowing more about competitors. These trends, coupled with the increasing availability of information, particularly in an electronic format, may have hastened the growth and formalization of BI. The business climate in the U.S. simultaneously has grown increasingly complex and competitive, especially during the past decade, and with it the "need to know" more about competitors and other commercial factors has grown.

There has been no dearth of business books providing "management musts" throughout the 20th century. *The Economist*, a venerable British business periodical with a distinctive worldview, published *The Good Book Guide for Business: An Indispensable Guide to More than 600 Essential Business Books for Today's Managers* in 1984. The subtitle alone indicates the wide range of literature in the popular realm. Broad categories covered in the *Guide* include The World Business Environment, The Management of Organizations, The Individual in Business, Business as It Happened, and Reference. Business intelligence as a specific discipline has only recently emerged.

Business intelligence in contemporary management practice

Motorola is credited with developing one of the first formal Competitor Intelligence functions in the mid-1980s. Robert W. Galvin, Motorola's chief executive, served on the President's Foreign Intelligence Advisory Board and recognized the value of intelligence. A highly successful world class company, Motorola was the first large-company winner of the Malcolm Baldrige National Quality Award in 1988. The award emphasizes the acquisition and use of certain types of BI—both internal and external.

While other companies (Corning, Eastman Kodak, Southwestern Bell, and others[11]) have been cited, Motorola seems to have the longest lasting and most successful program amongst big American businesses today. However, given the nature of this type of activity, we should assume that there are other, possibly more successful, BI operations at work here and abroad. It would be wholly consistent with *The Art of War* to keep rivals in the dark about a strategic capability.

The types of information needed in a competitive business environment are not secret. Some examples are shown in Table 1.1, from a 1989 article about The Conference Board's research on this topic.[12]

This early work helped to raise awareness of competitor intelligence and what top management needed. The popularity of electronic information sources, particularly the Internet, has given rise to a collection mentality, although many practitioners work to provide useful intelligence products. In general, business intelligence usually encompasses the following:

- Retrospective print searching by an information broker for background

- Early warning alerts provided by consultant(s) on a continuous basis

- Ad-hoc searches of computer databases to answer pop-up questions internally

- Monitoring Internet Web sites for alerts and background

- Field reports on breaking developments from reps to HQ

- Archival database in a format such as Lotus Notes as the central source of BI products

Table 1.1

EXAMPLES OF COMPETITOR INFORMATION (RATED AS USEFUL BY RESPONDENTS FROM 158 COMPANIES)	
Present status	**Costs**
Pricing. 99%	Manufacturing 88%
Key customers. 94	Marketing 66
Sales statistics. 94	Advertising 32
Market share changes 90	
Prospects	**Organization and operations**
Strategic plans 95%	Manufacturing processes. 81%
Expansion plans. 92	Service capabilities 77
New product programs 91	Operating style 75
M&A prospects/plans. 86	Organization structure. 58

This emphasis on business intelligence in corporations led to the formation of the Society of Competitive Intelligence Professionals[13] (SCIP) in 1986. Twelve years later SCIP had grown to include more than 5,000 members. Membership includes many people in corporations who perform or supervise business intelligence functions. Consulting firms of all sizes and various vendors also are members.

SCIP has made a concerted effort to become a global organization. Association management executives in SCIP's Alexandria, Virginia headquarters have invested considerable time and energy to pull together various smaller country-based groups with similar purposes including several that had unofficially used the SCIP name. In addition to several Canadian chapters, there are local groups in Belgium, Italy, Mexico, China, South Africa, Sweden, Switzerland, and the U.K. There are 29 U.S. chapters.

Other organizations like the American Marketing Association,[14] Strategic Leadership Forum,[15] and the Special Libraries Association[16] have members who are involved in formalized BI programs.

The American Marketing Association (AMA) dates back to 1937 when the National Association of Teachers of Marketing merged with the American Marketing Society. In 1940 it had 817 members in 11 chapters. This has grown to 400 professional and collegiate chapters. Today, AMA members are involved in a wide range of marketing activities. AMA members include marketing specialists in agribusiness, business-to-business, consumer, global, healthcare, and services, as well as marketing research and education.

There is some overlap with SCIP membership, particularly in the area of market research. When you consider that, according to their literature, the AMA "has consistently focused on representing state-of-the-art thinking as the marketing field has grown and continues to evolve," you can see that its members will more fully embrace business intelligence sources and methods as they permeate management thinking.

The Special Libraries Association (SLA) is in transition from being an organization of business librarians to one in which members strive to be corporate knowledge managers. Considerable emphasis is placed on electronic information and Internet skills, particularly in SLA conference, seminar, and chapter meeting programs.

"SLA is a very special network of people," according to its literature. "Through SLA, members are in contact with people who can make that special difference in the quality of their professional lives." Now 15,000 members strong, the organization was founded in 1913 by "information pioneers." It is well represented geographically (56 regional chapters), and its 25 divisions serve to channel members with similar special interests.

All of these organizations overlap in their areas of interest. Judging from membership totals and percent representation of members versus total employed in each field, a rough guess of 50,000 to 100,000 people functionally concerned with business intelligence might be a good estimate. There are others who are concerned with business intelligence from a different perspective. Some members of the private security and law enforcement community are concerned about protection of intellectual property, trade secrets, and the like. The latter are taking more responsibility in this field, as knowledge becomes a more important company asset.

IBIS fits into the big picture

In the later 1990s corporate executives began to address the newest "management must" concept—Knowledge Management (KM). Most would agree that we are in a post-industrial information economy. All organizations must efficiently utilize their intellectual capital, an increasingly scarce resource. KM is an overarching concept that includes business intelligence. BI, in turn, is broader than Competitor Intelligence (CI). CI encompasses mostly external knowledge. KM seeks to tap the intellectual capital of a corporation. This intellectual capital is, to a lesser or greater degree, locked inside the minds of employees. The PROACtive process, detailed in Chapter Seven, provides a method for utilizing this asset.

How do we transform the abstract notion of "knowledge management" into a practical methodology? First, we can look at Rigby's[17] description. "Knowledge Management develops systems for acquiring and disseminating intellectual assets, and for increasing the outputs they generate. It seeks to increase both individual depth and team learning. Knowledge Management maintains that successful businesses are not a collection of products but of distinctive knowledge bases. The key to success, therefore, is developing intellectual capital in areas that will give the company competitive advantages with its targeted customers. Knowledge Management seeks to build the intellectual capital that will create unique core competencies that will then enable distinctive products that will build superior results and shareholder value."

Further, Rigby outlines the methodology. He says that Knowledge Management requires managers to:

- Catalog and evaluate the organization's current bases of knowledge

- Determine the competencies that will be key to future success, and identify the knowledge bases that can build sustainable leadership positions in these competencies

- Invest in systems and processes to accelerate the accumulation of knowledge

- Codify new knowledge and turn it into tools
  and information that will improve business profitability

- Improve the dissemination of knowledge
  throughout the organization

- Apply new knowledge to improve behaviors

Second, we can examine another approach to understanding this subject. Don Tapscott, chairman of the Alliance for Converging Technologies, a Toronto-based think tank that conducts studies of new media's impact on business strategy, has outlined Twelve Themes of the New Economy.[18] These twelve themes are an appropriate foundation for a broad understanding of Internet Business Intelligence and how it fits into the "New Economy":

- **Knowledge**—The new economy is a knowledge economy
  based on human capital and networks

- **Digitization**—The new economy is a digital economy

- **Virtualization**—As information shifts from analog to digital,
  physical things can become virtual—changing the metabolism
  of the economy, the types of institutions and relationships
  possible, and the nature of economic activity itself

- **Molecularization**—The new economy is a molecular
  (clusters of individuals and entities) economy

- **Integration/internetworking**—The new economy is a
  networked economy, integrating molecules into clusters that
  network with others for the creation of wealth

- **Disintermediation**—Middleman functions between producers
  and consumers are being eliminated through digital networks

- **Convergence**—The dominant economic sector is being
  created by three converging industries (computing,
  telecommunications, and content creation), which, in turn,
  provide the infrastructure for wealth creation in all sectors

- **Innovation**—The new economy is an innovation-based economy

- **Prosumption**—In the new economy, the gap between
  consumers and producers blurs

- **Immediacy**—In an economy based on bits, immediacy becomes a key driver and variable in economic activity and business success

- **Globalization**—The new economy is a global economy

- **Discordance**—Unprecedented social issues are beginning to arise, potentially causing massive trauma and conflict

Technological advancements in business information (specifically the wealth of Internet-accessible information and tools to manage it) can be married with the traditional approach in the use of management tools and techniques.[19] Such tools as Activity-Based Costing, Balanced Scorecard, Competitive Gaming, Portfolio Analysis, and Scenario Planning are intended to improve organizational decision making in the larger organization. Less formal techniques are used in smaller businesses. All of the many and varied management tools and techniques require input. Whether a column of numbers for spreadsheet calculation or officers' biographies to determine strengths and weaknesses, input from external sources almost always is required. That's where the Internet can play a significant role.

Spy vs. spy?

Today's practice of BI draws from the experiences of former members of the government intelligence community, indicated by the CIA's Intelligence Cycle. This is a generic process that serves as a process model for the various civilian and military intelligence organizations within the government as shown in Figure 1.2.

Important similarities exist among intelligence cycle models used for national security, law enforcement, and business purposes. In all cases the process is driven mostly by the needs of its masters. Collection methods differ somewhat. For example, national security might rely on space satellite systems, while law enforcement might rely on wiretaps, and business might rely on open source or publicly available information. Increasingly, all are using relatively similar analysis and communication methods. It is useful to examine this model to better understand the nature of business intelligence.

Civilian and military intelligence often overlap, and that is why we have a Director of Central Intelligence (DCI). Because military force is a tool of governments and governments are the focus of civilian intelligence, the two are intertwined. There are unique characteristics of either wing of the Intelligence Community (IC), sometimes referred to simply as "the community." Civilian intelligence focuses on economics, science and technology, and government policy. Military intelligence is shaped to support war fighting.

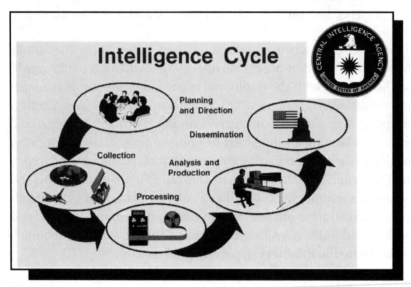

Figure 1.2

Some in the military call it Dominant Battlespace Knowledge.[20] They distinguish between battlespace vision (the ability to see anything worthwhile) and the knowledge needed to understand all of the input and act decisively. There have been many technological breakthroughs in the military setting. Broadly these include advances in (1) intelligence, surveillance, and reconnaissance, (2) command, control, communications, and computer applications, and (3) precision force. These three categories parallel capabilities on the economic battlefield of business. Just as opponents in war fight back, so do business competitors. Winning or losing in the global marketplace, while not as deadly a proposition as military battles, still carries significant consequences.

Some contemporary examples of wars in business battlespace illustrate the need for, at the very least, a "distant early warning" system that could be likened to the DEW Line of the Cold War era. Motivation for better, earlier, more predictive business and competitor intelligence can be garnered from the following situations:

GM and other U.S. automakers and fuel-efficient imports, primarily from Japan; IBM and the PC revolution, including the distribution of desktop computing; Apple and its battle to preserve its proprietary architecture; Long Island Lighting Co. and the government intervention in its nuclear power plant start-up; AT&T and the impact of stored value phone cards.

Although the most dramatic growth has been in the area of Competitive Intelligence, it still is a rather small part of the overall business. It is perceived to be glamorous and possibly even exciting but the tough work, like classic intelligence efforts, yields the best results in the long run. This tough work consists of diligent, consistent efforts to absorb every relevant (and sometimes not so apparently relevant) scrap of information and to piece together these scraps to form hypotheses, which are tested and transformed into business insight. These insights are part of knowledge management needed to operate a business.

Intelligence meets the Internet

Even though the number of households online in the late 1990s doubled, business still looked at the Internet more as a marketing tool (pushing information outward and taking orders inward) rather than as a tool for intelligence gathering. This was despite polls showing that more than half used the Internet for work and 41 percent used it for business research.[21] Individual users took it upon themselves to use the Internet at home and work. One reason for this might be that premium business database providers continue to deride the "quality" of the Internet information in their marketing communications. This is a desperate attempt to deny, for as long as possible, the revolutionary aspects of the Internet and its ability to eliminate the markup charged by the middleman.

The growth of the Internet and other forms of information transmission capability may be another reason why there is strong emphasis on Knowledge Management. See Figure 1.3.

Consider that more and more corporations are competing on the basis of information advantages. For example, had AT&T been more attuned to the threat of stored value phone cards for long-distance calling, it might have been able to counter the erosion of market share in that product line. On the positive side, Federal Express (FedEx) held a competitive edge for a short while after instituting customer access to its package-tracking system so that customers could use a personal computer to access up-to-the-minute data about their shipments. This is an example of an information advantage in a competitive market-place. Some say that FedEx is really an information company with the systems and know-how to move packages as opposed to the common perception that it is a global delivery service.

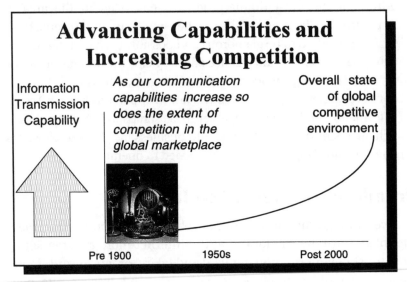

Figure 1.3

Strategic planning models

Business intelligence is a critical component of successful business strategy. Broadly speaking, business strategy considers the past, present, and future. Knowing your own capabilities and the needs of the market, now and in the future, carry one further toward a successful business strategy. A classic business strategy tool is SWOT, an acronym for Strengths, Weaknesses, Opportunities, and Threats. BI is used to achieve earlier awareness of threats and opportunities, while a companion tool (frequently used in quality improvement programs) called benchmarking is used to clarify strengths and weaknesses.

A part of the management continuum outlined earlier, these are some of the evolving management tools that are being adopted. Over the past decade, executives have witnessed an explosion of management tools. The demands of increasingly competitive global markets and the supply of ideas and information have driven this explosion at much faster speeds and lower costs.[22]

Any formalized intelligence process relies on the fitting together of many small pieces of relevant information to understand the "big picture" or to answer strategic questions. Various software tools and systems, such as those in the category of "data mining," are helping to organize and analyze myriad information.

Doing business in a global marketplace has recently presented new opportunities and threats. A large global player often has competitors that are simultaneously vendors and joint-venture partners. These similar relationships can be found in other industries, including pharmaceutical giants that have "teamed" in certain areas while fighting it out in other markets. Major development projects have become so costly that even mega-corporations see an advantage in risk sharing through all types of business relationships.

But what about the knowledge gained from such relationships? It certainly would be unethical for Corporation X's project team member to pry information for competitive advantage from their opposite number in Corporation Y. However, the experience serving on the project team does provide valuable insights into the opposite number's organization. Similarly, a purchasing agent who has intimate knowledge of a supplier, which happens to be a competitor in another arena, holds valuable BI. The proliferation of groupware, and more recently corporate "intranets," is facilitating exchange of this sort of intellectual capital.

There is a clear imperative to deal with this massive shift from making things to making information and the key is an organized approach to the Internet. Simply put, business needs process and tools to create a business intelligence system that will support the business in ways that are specific to the individual business need. See Figure 1.4.

The process is a methodology derived from centuries-old warrior strategies but updated for the new millenium. This update encompasses technology and ever-greater flows of digital information. The PROACtive process involves age-old principles similar to those of the Intelligence Cycle. However, the PROACtive process is geared toward the needs of business and is structured around computers and the Internet. See Figure 1.5.

This process includes Planning; Rapidly obtaining required information; Organizing the information and Analyzing it; then Communicating it by translating, interpreting, verifying, and evaluating information throughout the process. Planning can be performed to address either the overall Internet Business Intelligence System (IBIS) or for a specific project. Rapidly obtaining required information involves understanding how best to utilize the Internet and other supporting resources to efficiently gather information from which intelligence products will be derived. Organizing involves storage and retrieval of information to provide a raw material by Analyzed methods appropriate to each situation. The IBIS Knowledgebase uses information from various Internet sources, and pulls it into software tools that are used by individuals and groups under the direction of management. Finally, information is not intelligence unless it is Communicated in a way that has the desired impact. See Figure 1.6.

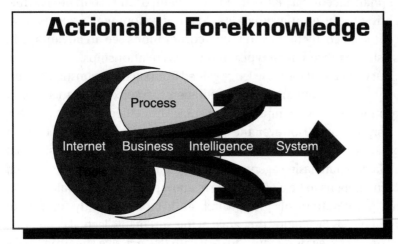

Figure 1.4

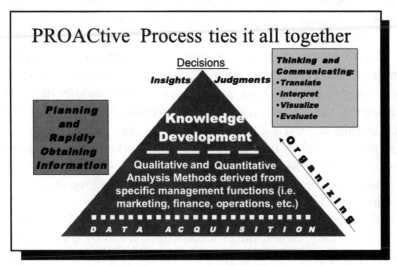

Figure 1.5

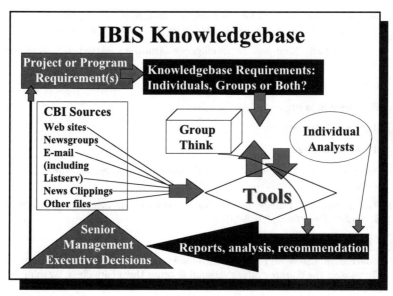

Figure 1.6

Endnotes

1. Benjamin and Tamar Gila, *The Business Intelligence System* (AMACOM, New York, 1988).

2. Leonard M. Fuld, *Monitoring the Competition* (John Wiley & Sons, New York, 1988).

3. William Levinson, *The Way of Strategy* (ASQC Quality Press, Milwaukee, WI, 1994).

4. Ralph D. Sawyer, translator, *The Seven Military Classics of Ancient China* (Westview Press, Boulder, 1993).

5. James Clavell, editor, *The Art of War* (Dell Publishing, New York, 1983).

6. Claude S. George, Jr, *The History of Management Thought*, chapter six, second edition (Prentice Hall, Englewood Cliffs, NJ, 1972:43-47).

7. *The Columbia Viking Desk Encyclopedia* (Viking Press, New York, 1968).

8. George.

9. Herman Kahn, *Thinking About the Unthinkable* (Avon Books, New York, 1962:19).

10. Norman Gaither, *Production and Operations Management*, fifth edition (The Dryden Press, Orlando, FL, 1992:638-639).

11. "Motorola: A Case in Point for Competitive Intelligence," from articles compiled by LEXIS-NEXIS Services in recognition of the 10th Anniversary of SCIP.

12. Tom Eisenhart, "Competitive Intelligence" (*Business Marketing*, November 1989:42).

13. SCIP (**www.scip.org**).

14. AMA (**www.ama.org**).

15. SLF (**www.slfnet.org**).

16. SLA (**www.sla.org**).

17. Darrell K. Rigby, *Management Tools and Techniques: An Executive's Guide* (Bain & Company, Boston, 1997:34).

18. Don Tapscott, "Strategy in the New Economy" (*Strategy & Leadership*, November/December 1997:8-14).

19. Rigby.

20. Stuart E. Johnson and Martin C. Libicki, editors, *Dominant Battlespace Knowledge: The Winning Edge* (National Defense University Press, Washington, DC, 1995).

21. "It's a Wide, Wired World, The Web: Infotopia or Marketplace" (*Newsweek*, Jan. 27, 1997).

22. Rigby.

CHAPTER 2

WHAT ARE THE CHARACTERISTICS OF INTERNET BUSINESS INTELLIGENCE?

Understanding what the Internet is all about entails at least three tracks of knowledge: technical, psychological, and editorial. It's important to have a basic understanding of the technicalities of how the Internet works, but when it comes to serious business use of the medium for IBIS, you also should understand something about who uses the Internet and why they use it. Finally, a general overview of the editorial content of the Internet also must be considered. Let's tackle the technicalities first.

Technical

The Internet is a vast INTERconnected NETwork of millions of computers communicating via the Transmission Control Protocol/Internet Protocol (TCP/IP) and connected via the telephone system (copper cables, fiber optics, microwave, and satellite links). Formerly funded by the National Science Foundation, it was privatized in April 1995, and major telephone companies now carry the bulk of traffic.

To find a particular computer, a user types an Internet address that ends with two- or three-letter designations representing such top-level domains as .com (commercial), .edu (educational), and .mil (military). The other part of the Uniform Resource Locator (URL) is assigned after registration with government contract holders that register domain names in the U.S. The URL is the standard address of any resource on the Internet. An example of a complete domain name is davidvineassociates.com, and additional pages are added to that assigned URL by adding identifiers separated by slash (/) marks.

An arcane bit (no pun intended) of possibly useful information is the understanding of the concept of packet-switched data.

The Internet Protocol (IP) is the method or protocol by which data is sent from one computer to another on the Internet. Each computer (known as a host) on the Internet has at least one address that uniquely identifies it from all other computers on the Internet. When you send or receive data (for example, an e-mail note or a Web page), the message gets divided into little chunks called packets. Each of these packets contains both the sender's Internet address and the receiver's address.

Any packet is sent first to a gateway computer that understands a small part of the Internet. The gateway computer reads the destination address and forwards the packet to an adjacent gateway that in turn reads the destination address and so forth across the Internet until one gateway recognizes the packet as belonging to a computer within its immediate neighborhood or domain. That gateway then forwards the packet directly to the computer whose address is specified.

A packet is the unit of data that is routed between an origin and a destination on the Internet or any other packet-switched network. When any file (e-mail message, GIF file, URL request, and so forth) is sent from one place to another on the Internet, the Transmission Control Protocol (TCP) layer of TCP/IP divides the file into "chunks" of an efficient size for routing. Each of these packets is separately numbered and includes the Internet address of the destination. The individual packets for a given file may travel different routes through the Internet. When they have all arrived, they are reassembled into the original file (by the TCP layer at the receiving end).[1]

World Wide Web

Perhaps the most compelling aspect of the Internet is the click-through capability of the World Wide Web. Pages are based on HyperText Markup Language (HTML). Instead of reading text in a linear structure (such as you would a book), you can jump from one point to another, go back and forth between pages, jump to other topics, and navigate based on your interests.

HTML has its roots in the older Standardized General Markup Language. It is used to program a structured document with headings, bulleted lists, and embedded graphics plus the all-important links to other documents and graphics. Today it is simple to create HTML pages in most word processors or programs designed for Web page creation. A simple File Transfer Protocol method is used to place the finished document on the server for access to others.

Getting connected to the Internet will be thoroughly covered in Chapter Eight, but you might want to know at this point that most individuals and organizations use either a commercial online service (America Online, CompuServe, etc.) or an Internet Service Provider (ISP). Many variations of ISPs exist, ranging from former online services (like Prodigy), which now just provide Internet connections via local telephone numbers, to fast-growing ISPs like @Home, which provides high-speed access via cable modem. Large organizations typically deal with non-retail ISPs such as the local phone company (aka Regional Bell Operating Company), which provides a high-capacity connection.

According to the Internet Society[2] there were 130 Web servers in June of 1993. It took about 18 months to reach the 100,000-site mark. Another 18 months brought the total to 1,117,255 sites, and that number doubled in less than a year. From the April 1998 total of 2.2 million, the figure grew to 3.7 million by the end of that year, just eight months later. At the turn of the century there were almost nine million Web servers worldwide according to Netcraft (**www.net craft.com/survey**).

Because nearly all of today's documents are created on a word processor, they can be quickly transformed into Web pages and posted to an Internet-accessible server. Given a few hundred dollars worth of software and Internet services, anyone can publish comprehensive information that will be available worldwide. The World Wide Web has proliferated very rapidly, and with it various cultures have flourished.

In addition to published information available via Web pages, Newsgroups, and mailing lists, various forms of real-time online "chat" via computer keyboard have been around since the early 1980s. CompuServe's "CB simulator" was perhaps the forerunner of this type of live keyboard-to-keyboard communication. Today, however, chat is increasingly embellished with sound, graphics, and even live video. These bandwidth-intensive transmission modes are in constant use supporting many interests. Also, there is widespread access to other types of textual, numeric, and graphical data. You can quickly and very easily download entire spreadsheets full of data or complete slide shows or other multimedia presentations for use on your own computer or for integration into your own project (with appropriate credits, of course). Many organizations all over the world are providing sophisticated multimedia offerings. See Figure 2.1.

All of this comes at a time when the cost of access is dramatically falling at the same time that information transmission speed is dramatically increasing. In 1982 a 300 bits-per-second modem for connecting the computer to a telephone line cost about $400. By 1990 a much smaller unit about 100 times faster was selling for half the price. Soon, 1.5 million bits per second (T1 speed) hardware and connections for the individual computer (home, office, or mobile unit) will be commonplace. The "chicken and egg" riddle can be used to consider this situation. Does more complex computer data drive the demand for ever-faster transmission speed or does the faster speed allow for more complex data streams?

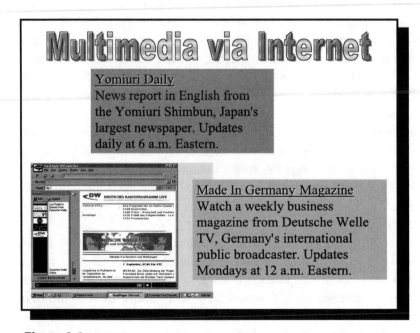

Figure 2.1

This enhanced capability has made possible lower-cost transmission of data-intensive multimedia information with audio and video accompanying Web pages.

Psychological aspects of IBIS

Creating an Internet Business Intelligence System (IBIS) involves technology, information, and people. The technology gets you to the information. The information represents people. People populate the Internet. To fully utilize the Internet as an information source, it helps to know something about the people.

Consider the growing Net culture and you begin to think of psychological and sociological aspects of the Internet. Hackers, punk rockers and GenXers make the news, but scratch deeper and you'll find the bedrock. It consists of tens of millions of "average users" young and old. For business purposes, let's consider the Internet users between the ages of 20 and 40. What's happening on the Internet and some of its enablers facilitate the following:

- Ability to target niches or easily create ad-hoc assemblages

- Contribution to mobility

- Internationalization

Synergistic power of sharing information

One of the segments of Internet society that has received a lot of attention is the Hacker culture. *Mentor's Last Words* is a cult text that seems to capture the emotion of hackers. It speaks of young people's frustration with wanting older people (read "authority") to understand them. This age-old yearning is voiced in the context of the computer. *Mentor's Last Words* carries the frustrated youth into a fourth-dimension world of computer connections. "This is our world now…the world of the electron and the switch, the beauty of the baud" the anonymous writer proclaims. Mentor, whoever he is or was, presents the timeless psyche of the teenager in the context of computers and the Internet.

Lest you think he's a lone voice in the wilderness, check out a few hacker pages. They run the gamut from the well-established (**www.2600.com** for the leading hacker magazine) to others that weld hacking onto radical politics. Phreaking (telephone system manipulation) and e-zines (grunge publishing for the most part) proliferate in hacker space as do "anti-online" archives of "documentation on all topics relating to computer security…putting hackers and system administrators on level playing ground." Software for hacking is enthusiastically distributed free of charge and cryptography is a popular subject. Let's hope that most of it is just educational, satisfying the typically overactive imagination of younger folks.

With all of the possible approaches to using the Internet (exploring, random thinking, alternatives, independence), just what kind of people are using it and for what specific purposes? Statistics and demographics Web pages accessed via Yahoo! address a variety of aspects of this topic. Some proffer insights into how "changes in digital communications are going to affect the way we think about the world we live in." Others are much more specific but also narrow in scope.

As the new century begins, we will likely have more than 50 million hosts advertised in the Domain Name System. This is inferred from a survey produced by Network Wizards (**www.nw.com**). An "educated guess" of how many people are online exceeds 150 million, according to data by NUA Internet Surveys (**www.nua.net/surveys**).

Forrester Research, Inc. (**www.forrester.com**) has predicted that Internet commerce sales will reach as high as $3.2 trillion in 2003. Astute observers of the Internet know that it is more than just a new technology. It's more than a new communications medium or information-gathering tool. It's even bigger than just electronic commerce because it represents a convergence of user-accessible media and knowledge transfer. The Internet is a new approach to life, the world, business responsibilities, and personal and family interests for many millions of people the world over. Knowing more about this new approach to life in the 21st century will help the business user to fully understand the potential of Internet Business Intelligence.

The basic concept of hypertext-linked Web pages is easy to understand, but the notion of who might be best suited to using this type of information-seeking method is not as apparent. It's easy to pursue Internet information in two dimensions, that is, clicking on a hypertext link from a home page to get to another page on the same Web site. It becomes more complicated when one decides to pursue additional or related information. By what process does one decide when to stop searching or where to go for additional information? Understanding the decision-making process might be able to help us "fit the round peg into the round hole." Doing this could lead to more effective use of the Internet for business intelligence purposes and to happier users, since someone with less aptitude might be better suited performing another function.

Selecting people for IBIS

Following the axiom of not putting a square peg into a round hole, executives staffing an IBIS function within an organization might want to consider using the Myers-Briggs Type Indicator to select people who are best suited for the function. It's safe to assume that certain types of people would be best suited to the abstract work required and assertively dealing with the Internet to find what they need.

According to the Association for Psychological Type,[3] "The Myers-Briggs Type Indicator (MBTI) is a self-report personality inventory designed to give people information about their Jungian psychological type preferences. Isabel Briggs Myers and Katherine Cook Briggs began developing the MBTI in the early 1940s to make C. G. Jung's theory of human personality understandable and useful in everyday life. MBTI results indicate the respondent's likely preferences on four dimensions:

- Extraversion (E) OR Introversion (I)

- Sensing (S) OR Intuition (N)

- Thinking (T) OR Feeling (F)

- Judging (J) OR Perceiving (P)

"Results on the Indicator are generally reported with letters representing each of the preferences as indicated above." There are 16 possible ways to combine the preferences, resulting in the 16 MBTI types listed in Table 2.1.

"Though many factors combine to influence an individual's behaviors, values, and attitudes, the four-letter type descriptions summarize underlying patterns and behaviors common to most people of that type.

"After more than fifty years of research and development, the MBTI is the most widely used instrument for understanding normal personality differences. It is used in: Self-understanding and development; Career exploration, development, and counseling; Relationship and family counseling; Organization development;

Team building; Improving problem solving Management training; Leadership development; Education and curriculum development; Diversity and multicultural training."

Table 2.1

ISTJ	ISFJ	INFJ	INTJ
ISTP	ISFP	INFP	INTP
ESTP	ESFP	ENFP	ENTP
ESTJ	ESFJ	ENFJ	ENTJ

Choosing the right personality type for important business functions is commonplace. We might want to consider an MBTI personality type, such as ENTJ, when staffing a business intelligence function. Perhaps an extraverted person is best suited to understanding the business intelligence requirement through repeated contacts with others in the organization. Intuitively, this person understands what is required and where the information might be found. The three-dimensional nature of Internet information adds another aspect to matching the person to the task. See Figure 2.2.

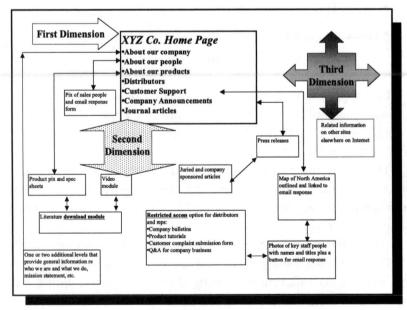

Figure 2.2

Thinking this through and making small but constant judgments as to how each item of information fits the requirement, this person may be able to complete a business intelligence assignment more easily than another person who is less suited to this particular task. This example illustrates how the MBTI might be employed.

Cataloging the personalities

One organization that is looking into psychographic issues is SRI International, a nonprofit research organization in Menlo Park, California. Their iVALS survey[4] is being conducted online to better understand the Internet population and to guide the creation of new, Internet-specific research tools. SRI investigated how psychographic systems such as VALS can be relevant to helping online users identify content of interest and how content providers can better understand their potential audiences. iVALS is the basis for affinity-mapping software that makes smart connections—connecting people with content of interest and businesses with customers of interest (and vice versa). The point is to create an environment with more signal and less spam for everyone.

According to SRI, "The VALS questionnaire is based on a $1.5 million development effort and several large national surveys of consumer opinion, conducted between 1987 and 1992 by SRI. These surveys allowed SRI to identify the specific attitude statements that had a strong correlation with a large range of consumer preferences in products and media. The current questionnaire is the third version based on this kind of extensive empirical research.

"The motivations and demographic characteristics their questionnaire asks about are very strong predictors of a variety of consumer preferences in products, services, and media. The main advantage, therefore, is predictive power: to understand your individual preferences and likely reaction to new products or services, we can ask this relatively short list of questions in place of a very long list of questions about your current product, activity, and media choices."

iVALS personality type groupings called Segment Profiles include the following:

Wizards: The most active and skilled Internet users. Computers are a key aspect of their lifestyles, and mastery of technology figures prominently in their identities.

Pioneers: Generally positive and active user segment. They spend a lot of time on the Internet, read and post to conferencing systems such as Usenet frequently, and are high users of WWW retail sites. Solitary voyagers, they don't get much Internet-related information from others, yet most Pioneers have a comfortable technical mastery of the Net and think of themselves as "power users."

Upstreamers: Internet generalists. Like Mainstreamers (see below), they approach the Net as a resource for the pursuit of personal and career interests, although these interests can vary widely from one individual to the next. However, Upstreamers differ from Mainstreamers because they are significantly more involved in and enthusiastic about Internet use.

Socialites: Strongly oriented toward the social aspects of the Internet and often are among the senior members of recreational social venues. As such, they tend to be prominent participants in online discussions, and they often have multiple, well-developed online personae.

Workers: Take a very utilitarian view of the Internet. With the lowest average per-month personal online charges, Workers bill almost all their online activities and computing to their schools or employers. Most have more than two personal e-mail accounts and read and post to conferencing systems such as Usenet several times a week.

Surfers: A rapidly learning but technically modest segment: comfortable online, active on the Internet, and very much leisure oriented. Overall, they rate the Internet positively—so much so that they are willing to pay more money out of their own pockets for Internet services than will any other segment—probably because much of their activity is clearly recreational in nature.

Mainstreamers: Have evolved a pattern of Internet usage that just fits their work and personal requirements online, and goes no further. Although they frequently connect from work, Mainstreamers are not entirely work focused. Indeed, many spend significant time just surfing the Internet. But they feel relatively comfortable on the Internet already, so they aren't motivated to invest a lot of effort to expand their online skills or Web exposure.

Sociables: Strongest orientation is toward the social aspects of the Internet. Compared to the group most similar to them (Socialites), Sociables gravitate toward less-structured venues—for example, showing higher interest in chat rooms than conferencing systems, although they still frequent the latter.

Seekers: A very work-focused group. Productivity is their principal reason for using computers. Becoming power users or wide-ranging Net explorers are not priorities. Accordingly, Seekers focus their time online to specific work tasks—information searches, communications, and document sharing among them.

Immigrants: Tend to be relatively recent arrivals to cyberspace, and they are familiar with only very specific parts. In most cases, they were drawn online—or were put online—for purposes relating to work (including schoolwork). They are one of the most subsidized segments, and most Immigrants would not pay for Internet access if it did not come free with work or school.

While SRI is quantitatively characterizing Internet users through the use of an online survey form system, other organizations are qualitatively characterizing it from different perspectives.

For example, Zona Research, Inc.[5] (an IntelliQuest company) provides qualitative and quantitative information and advice to the Internet industry. Among their many products and services are research reports, such as one titled "Emerging Info-Keiretsu." With the emergence of the Internet as a new infrastructure for information creation, delivery, and consumption, formal and informal relationships between the organizations creating, delivering, and facilitating the consumption become more synergistic.

We have reached a stage in the evolution of the information processing industry where access to information is more important than processing information. This shift toward access-based computing places information delivery and those facilitating delivery at the vortex of emerging global relationships and alliances. The Internet represents the new information infrastructure at the root of these emerging info-*keiretsu.*

Editorial content available for IBIS

The Internet is now considered to be the primary conduit for input to the BI process. Since 1992 the phenomenal growth of this channel of communication is particularly apparent in the form of corporate "home pages" and World Wide Web sites. The challenge expressed by all participants is finding the right information at the right time. Also, many early adopters express intense interest in acquiring tools and techniques for better managing Internet-derived data. A very short list of representative business information resources now commonly used includes the following:

- FedWorld: **www.fedworld.gov** (one of many general gateways to USG information)

- Financial Times Group: **www.usa.ft.com** (substantial amount of "teasers" that likely will satisfy many short of purchasing)

- Global Business Network: **www.gbn.org** (information about an elite enclave of international strategists)

- Hoover's Online: **www.hoovers.com** (lots of basic information about many businesses, more for subscribers)

- SEC: **www.sec.gov/index.html** (full text of most filings required of public companies)

The Internet has had a tremendous impact on "traditional" commercial providers of information services. It has helped America Online to grow from a few hundred thousand subscribers to many millions. But it has also forced companies like Dow Jones, Knight Ridder, and LEXIS-NEXIS to completely rethink their business strategies. Traditional providers of "premium" business information include:

- Associated Press (association of newspapers operating 237 bureaus worldwide)

- Bloomberg (private business information services oriented to financial professionals)

- Business Wire (press release distribution service)

- Derwent (international provider of technical information, mostly patents)

- Dialog Corporation (international provider of general business information)

- Dow Jones (business information, publishes *The Wall Street Journal*)

- Dun & Bradstreet (business data, known for 50-million-company global database)

- McGraw Hill (broad-based publishing conglomerate with several lines of business)

- PR Newswire (press release distribution service)

- Reed Elsevier PLC (Reed International and Elsevier, publishes trade, scientific, and professional journals and magazines, owns and operates LEXIS-NEXIS)

- Reuters (international news and financial information)

- Thompson Corporation (international legal and regulatory publisher with 85-percent U.S. sales, owns and operates Westlaw and Information America)

These and many other national and international publishers have embraced the Internet as a low-cost, universal medium for marketing and distribution of information product. The predominant model seems to be to give something away to attract buyers. For example, Bloomberg and Dow Jones give away bits and pieces of their valuable business information, but you must subscribe to their various services to obtain complete access to all of their features.

The pay-per-view model also seems to be gaining acceptance. This is particularly true of newspaper publishers that provide free searches of the archives of major daily newspapers. However, if you find articles that you want, you must pay a modest ($1 to $4) per-article charge, usually via a secure page with credit card charge facilities. The screenshot in Figure 2.3 represents one such pay-per-view site.

Most progressive businesses have Web sites, and most of those provide a wealth of information that can be used to develop business intelligence. But what about the secretive private company that doesn't have an extensive Web presence? Often one can find relevant public record information.

Little by little we see more and more public records available via the Internet. This is the investigator's dream come true. No more bored, underpaid, slow, and surly "civil" servants standing behind the glass doling out dribs and drabs of public record information at their pleasure. Smart and forward-thinking government agencies at all levels are providing direct access to many of the public records for which your tax dollars already have paid. Using the Internet they're doing it faster, better, and at lower cost too!

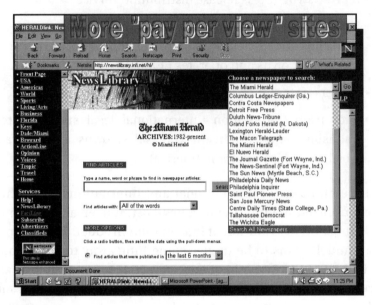

Figure 2.3

A classic example of the power of public records is the *Get to Know Perot* collection of "government documents revealing the good, bad and ugly of presidential candidate H. Ross Perot." Published by Information USA in 1992, this fascinating catalog of public documents revealed much about his personal life, business practices, violations of EEOC and labor laws, charitable contributions, and much more. The entire book, 348 pages, consists of reproductions of various documents in the public domain. It is the best catalog of available types of public records I have ever seen.

A review of this category of Internet resources will uncover free or low-cost access to corporate filings, court documents, DMV records, laws and statutes, real property data, regulatory filings, state archives, UCC filings, and a wide variety of other public records and documents. These documents and much more are becoming available because of the low cost of creating and maintaining a Web site on the Internet. No longer does the content creator require a "middleman" to make the content available to end-users via an elaborate proprietary network.

The National Association of State Information Resource Executives (NASIRE) represents state chief information officers and information resource executives and managers from the 50 states, six U.S. territories, and the District of Columbia. State members are senior officials from any of the three branches of state government who have executive-level and statewide responsibility for information resource management. Representatives from federal, municipal, and international governments, and state officials who are involved in information resource management but do not have chief responsibility for that function participate in the organization as associate members.

According to NASIRE (Figure 2.4), "Public access to government is an increasingly important issue for states; it has come to mean more than the Freedom of Information Act and similar state statutes which give people the right to request records kept by government agencies. Today, it also means providing electronic access to databases, disseminating information over the Internet, transacting business electronically, and providing an information infrastructure, which makes government accessible from almost anywhere."

STATE SEARCH

2130 entries in 23 categories

http://www.nasire.org/ss/index.html

Auditors	Judicial
Criminal Justice	Libraries/Records Mgt
Economic Development	Lieutenant Governors
Education	Procurement
Employment Services	Regs and Licensing
Energy/Environment	Revenue
Executive Branch	State Homepages
Finance and Admin	State Legislatures
Governor's Offices	Tourism
Health/Human Svcs/Welfare	Transportation
Information Resource Mgt	Treasurers
	Y2K Problem Info

Figure 2.4

The proliferation of information has democratized BI and made it easier and less expensive for smaller businesses with limited resources. Broward County (Florida) is making court records available to the public at no charge, and this will undoubtedly impact commercial providers of these records. Public records are sometimes used as a source of information about privately held companies. Private companies (or smaller units of large publicly traded companies) pose a particular challenge in the gathering of information for BI purposes because they are usually "closely held." Available public records (not all types available in all jurisdictions around the country) and their uses are shown in Table 2.2.

Table 2.2

PUBLIC RECORD TYPE	BUSINESS INTELLIGENCE USE
UCCs	Estimate leverage
Corporation records	Determine ownership
Real estate/Assessor	Detect expansion plans
Executive affiliation	Understand relationships
Professional licensing	Check veracity
Litigation records	Uncover liabilities
Bankruptcy filings	Explore financial history
Motor vehicle records	Check background
Criminal records	Perform due diligence

Internet content is the contemporary source of BI and in many cases the conduit through which commercial databases of open-source information is available. Hundreds of thousands of substantial business and editorial Web page content, and millions of pages of academic and government documents are available instantly, at no cost. This is forcing down the price of premium business information sources (commercial databases) and giving rise to other information providers because the cost barrier to entry has been lowered. As time goes by information will continue to decline in value as it becomes more plentiful. The tools, techniques, and people who can transform information into valuable, actionable business intelligence will correspondingly increase in value.

Looking at the Internet broadly, in the context of knowledge management, it's clear that there is an overall technological facilitation of knowledge transfer as represented in Figure 2.5. As personal communication devices become smarter and more capable, as television becomes more of a pathway for interactive knowledge building instead of a pacifier for the intellectually infantile, and as computer communications are facilitated in public and private settings, our overall appetite for useful information will increase. To paraphrase a cultural icon, "it's a good thing" for the business person who wants to establish an effective IBIS.

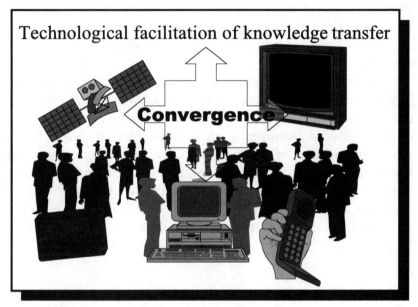

Figure 2.5

Local information sources increasingly are on the Internet. Newspapers, chambers of commerce, and community organizations, as well as local government and schools, all have a presence and are stimulating further use. This means that, after a period of adjustment and learning, we should be able to accomplish service functions more efficiently. Long term, as more of our daily lives become "Internet accessible," independence and mobility are supported.

The availability of Internet resources may shape society in ways we can only imagine today. For example, water rights are important factors in the valuation of real estate in Western states. Could it be that availability of high-speed Internet service with fiber-to-the-curb will, in the long run, have more of an impact on real estate values in these areas? If computer-based training and distance learning become widely accepted, could high-speed Internet access have more of a bearing on tax ratables than the quality of local schools?

New Internet technologies will hasten these types of changes. Rich interactive media with video conference capabilities, enhanced security with encryption standards, full integration of personal digital assistants via wireless networks, and more sophisticated finding aids all will contribute to the already-in-progress Internet information revolution. These technologies will drive the development of infrastructure, which may dominate the Internet's current landscape and positioning of the players.

Creation of editorial content will, for the foreseeable future, not be affected by the commoditization trend forcing down prices on repackaged information. It still takes a creative mind to produce original material. However, as the need for speed increases in the future, the balance of power in the commercial world may shift from development and sale of software (for individual use on tens of millions of computers) to provision of Internet infrastructure (and user-selectable access to hundreds of millions of, or even billions of, individual resources) in a truly networked world. See Figure 2.6.

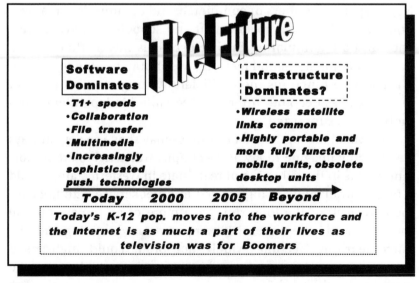

Figure 2.6

Endnotes

1. www.whatis.com/IP.htm.

2. http://info.isoc.org/internet/history/.

3. www.aptcentral.org/.

4. http://future.sri.com/vals/iVALS.index.html.

5. http://www.zonaresearch.com/.

CHAPTER 3

IBIS FOR *TOP* *MANAGEMENT*

In Chapters Three through Six, we will focus on the needs of specific strategic and tactical functions within business and how the Internet Business Intelligence System (IBIS) can support these functions. From the small business owner who wears several hats to the senior executive who oversees a single large department or corporate function (e.g., strategy, finance, production, operations, and marketing), all need a way to keep up with developments in one or more specialty areas.

In a simpler time, competitive advantage meant that your indigenous climate might support a specific type of crop. When water power was important, competitive advantage meant a good riverside location upon which a water wheel could be mounted to create machine power from water flow. Having good retail locations as well as an appropriate network of transportation and distribution facilities might claim recent competitive advantage. During the later part of the 20th century, competitive advantage was gained by the best in class of those companies that knew what their far-flung operations were doing at any given instant, via internal computer networks. Competitive advantage in the 21st century will be garnered by best-in-class organizations of any size that can better utilize external knowledge.

The 21st-century Knowledge Management Challenge involves dealing with the torrents of information—print, electronic, interpersonal, and environmental—in a constructive way to maximize the value of the information. See Figure 3.1.

Many consider this information to be intellectual capital worthy of corporate resources to manage and utilize a valuable asset. One of the most potentially anxiety-producing aspects of this challenge is the awareness that "we don't know what we don't know." After proceeding through the stage of recognizing and placing a value on corporate knowledge, some will ponder what they don't know. This concept often is extended to worrying about whole classes of information that the individual is unaware of but should know about.

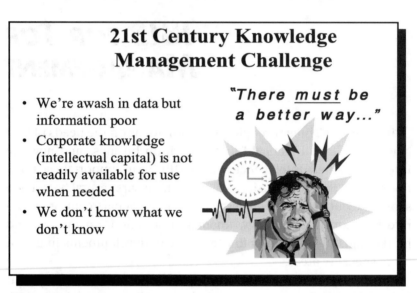

21st Century Knowledge Management Challenge

- We're awash in data but information poor
- Corporate knowledge (intellectual capital) is not readily available for use when needed
- We don't know what we don't know

"There must be a better way..."

Figure 3.1

The Internet is the conduit through which this external knowledge flows. Top management may expect that someone else within his or her organization (large or small) will use the Internet to dip into this vast reservoir of external knowledge. The dilemma of management, particularly owners of small businesses, is how much to delegate. Delegation is imperative in growing businesses, but too much delegation means that management becomes disconnected from important realities. This same dilemma exists with top management's use of the Internet.

Many solo professionals and small-business owners rely on the Internet and other technologies to manage their businesses efficiently. However, many more do not. Some businesses naturally lend themselves to Internet and computer technologies while others do not. However the common denominator is external information. All business needs to understand its customers, suppliers, and economic forces to name just a few of the categories of external information.

Top management will do well to spend some time using the Internet for access to external information. The amount of personal, hands-on use versus delegated Internet use will vary, but all top management will benefit from an appropriate level of personal use of the medium.

Seizing the knowledge advantage

For top executives who must exploit every possible advantage in their business, there is a unique area between strategy development and operational tactics. The Internet Business Intelligence System (IBIS) encompasses a wide range of information sources and methods, providing a tool for the exploitation of information to create a knowledge advantage. Business intelligence is a central management discipline that is at the core of management decision making. It fills the void between long-term strategy development and tactical decisions. See Figure 3.2.

Depending on the size of the organization, this space could expand to include nearly all of the decision-making elements, including coordinators that facilitate the process. In smaller operations fewer people with more, perhaps overlapping, responsibilities will be involved. In any case, top management, whether a division vice president and associated "mahogany row" executives in a very large corporation or the small-business owner, need to make decisions, sometimes hourly. The flow of excellent business intelligence (BI) is invaluable.

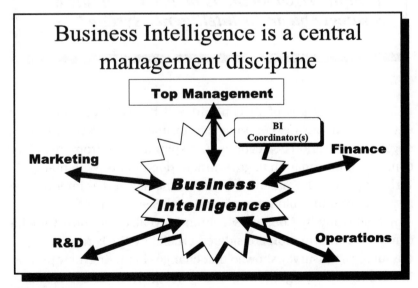

Figure 3.2

Just what constitutes excellent business intelligence? That depends on the needs of the people involved. For example, in a large organization top management may be most desirous of strategic information. This type of BI must be relevant and timely and, by definition, used to support strategic goals. A strategic intelligence system doesn't have to cost millions or even thousands of dollars. IBIS provides a knowledge advantage if implemented and utilized in a serious way. The ever-growing sources of information on the Internet, combined with more sophisticated tools available at little or no cost, put IBIS within the reach of anyone who wants to implement a system for knowledge advantage. See Figure 3.3.

Strategic Information For Competitive Intelligence Is...

❶ **Relevant and timely**
❷ **Used to support strategic goals**

Can a combination of Internet sources and computerized methods be used to create a strategic business intelligence system?

Figure 3.3

Many other types of BI can and will be used for competitive advantage in business. Strategic information however must be developed in various categories that span a range from anecdotal competitor information to government documents. With many and varied types of information, a system to manage it is as important as a system used to exploit the raw material. See Figure 3.4.

A 1996 study by Coopers & Lybrand revealed the most valuable competitor information considered crucial by CEOs responding to the survey. This survey showed that changes in pricing, new product initiatives, and changes in corporate strategy were ranked crucial by more than 80 percent of respondents. See Figure 3.5.

What would you need to do it?

- Competitor information
- Industry specific developments
- Current news and financial data
  - Local, regional, national & international markets
- Government documents
  - Public records, particularly re private companies
  - Policy and position papers
- *System to manage all of this information*

Figure 3.4

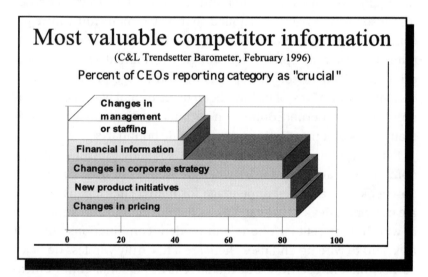

Most valuable competitor information
(C&L Trendsetter Barometer, February 1996)

Percent of CEOs reporting category as "crucial"

- Changes in management or staffing
- Financial information
- Changes in corporate strategy
- New product initiatives
- Changes in pricing

0   20   40   60   80   100

Figure 3.5

This study can help focus the resources needed to implement a system that will serve the needs of top executives in larger organizations. Information identified as most valuable can be developed through the available sources cited above. In some cases it will be obvious from monitoring news releases distributed via services or published somewhere on the Internet. In other cases it will require collection over a longer period and a good dose of intuition to understand market activity and competitor behavior.

Maximizing resources

All of us are concerned about two resources that can be addressed through the use of IBIS—time and talent. As our daily lives get more complex, the fixed amount of time we have to deal with ever-growing responsibilities seems more and more deficient. As the pace of change quickens we must deal with more unique situations that demand specialized expertise. IBIS can help you make better use of your time and expand your range of professional contacts.

Time expansion

On a very simplistic level, e-mail is helping many executives to avoid the frustration of voice-mail telephone-tag. Less intrusive than a desktop noisemaker that demands your attention, e-mail waits patiently for your examination and immediate (if you choose) response. E-mail is more detailed than voice mail. You can really communicate back and forth. Also, you can attach relevant computer files such as spreadsheets, highly formatted text, and now even audio and video. This speeds up knowledge production and dissemination. Many of us have been using e-mail within organizations, but the Internet connection permits sending and receiving e-mail across organizational and geographic boundaries.

For some of us, mobility is important. Mobility provides the freedom to move about and work when we want to or need to. Today's notebooks are a virtual appendage for many. That means that we are carrying a device that can link us to information and knowledge at will. Today's cellular phone and modem combinations are a bit awkward to wire up and use. There are a few truly wireless dedicated networks in use now, but the advent of personal communications systems and computing products crafted for them will soon yield higher levels of mobility. In a few years we will make even greater advances with the introduction of low earth orbiting satellites for unfettered mobile computing.

All of us would like better and earlier warnings of threats and opportunities through improved environmental scanning. We need a system that will scan, filter, and transmit the essential elements of information faster and more comprehensively. Dozens of news-monitoring services are available. To one degree or another, the decision-maker who wants to avoid unpleasant surprises and stay abreast of daily developments can do so—quickly scan, make selective inferences, and employ intuition to maximize the effort.

In certain cases you will need to access additional relevant archived external data to help resolve a situation. New, easier-to-use databases that fuse a wider range of information sources into a single service provide the information from which to formulate your response. Much of this information is available at no cost via the Internet. Also, most commercial information providers are accessible via the Internet.

The data market has been, and will probably continue to be, very imperfect. You could pay $2 per minute or more for the same information that you can get at no charge elsewhere in cyberspace. As more sophisticated users populate the online world, the situation is getting better. A variety of Internet search engines (Lycos, Yahoo!, etc.) are available. They help you search through the seemingly endless information haystacks to find the desired needle.

When our early warning system alerts us to a threat or opportunity and we have gathered relevant external data, we need to evaluate the threat or opportunity in relation to our strengths and weaknesses. The Internet is making this possible through enhanced communications both internally and externally.

Developing contacts

Fluid social attitudes and roles, tectonic political shifts, advancing technology, and a host of other factors present problems and opportunities that demand specialized expertise. Today, we can reach out to find talent, with great precision, worldwide via the Internet.

The Internet's common computer communications protocol (TCP/IP) enables hundreds of millions of disparate computers to talk to each other. Local Internet access providers as well as national and international online services provide the local entry points for individuals to tap into the Net. Many sites that permit connections to the Internet have developed "cyberplaces." Cyberplaces (aka forums, roundtables, mailing lists, and newsgroups) help you locate and communicate with other people who have similar interests.

First, become acclimated to traveling the Internet. It's easier than you think. It just takes practice. Then you will begin to develop an intuitive sense of direction that helps you "surf the Net" and link up with like-minded people in cyberspace.

Using the Internet to link up with talent is perhaps one of its most powerful features. Sure, you can use it as a global early warning system. Certainly it is extremely powerful for uncovering facts and opinions through concerted or casual research. The ability to find and connect with experts, virtually anywhere on the globe, is truly amazing. It could very well save the day in certain circumstances.

IBIS for strategy development

An Internet Business Information System (IBIS) can help get fast answers to ad-hoc questions. It also enables the organization to build a knowledgebase for long-range planning in each area of specialization. IBIS can provide many aids to top management. These aids could include the latest news, or a database of internal expertise and outside contacts so they can draw on a virtual network of experts, worldwide. IBIS also can contain specialized information that is quickly and easily accessible.

Let's start with the needs of top executives and managers, management analysts, operations/systems analysts, and economists who are especially concerned with the "big picture." Formally this operation is called strategic planning, but in practice it is a wide view, a sort of holistic approach to business that views the business as a whole and as various markets or market segments. While managers and functional executives in large organizations focus on doing a better job at executing departmental tasks, they usually are not concerned with all of the facets of running a business. That's not to say that big-picture people are micromanagers. No, big-picture people see the overview.

The information needs of these people are quite varied. They are especially interested in seeing important trends that could affect their businesses. These trends can create threats and opportunities. The organization's strengths and weaknesses are considered in light of these threats and opportunities, and a business plan emerges. What information is needed, and what is the best way to manage "big-picture" business intelligence?

As previously mentioned, top management needs business intelligence that is relevant and timely. It will be used to support executive decision making directed toward strategic goals. The right combination of Internet sources and computerized methods can be used to create a strategic business intelligence system. Here's a summary of big picture information needs:

- Industry-specific developments
- Current news and financial data
- Competitor information
- Government policy and position papers
- Economic data

Strategic information is relevant and timely, and it is applied to a long-range planning horizon. Tactical information is used to solve a problem at hand. These are two extremes, and in practice, they usually merge. MBA schools teach a strategic planning process that includes "environmental scanning." This corporate radar should pick up the faint blips that will become important in the future. In that regard, it is something of a crystal ball.

Environmental scanning monitors several broad areas of concern to business. Competitor actions, industry developments, financial conditions, and government regulatory affairs are some of the major aspects of the environment that concern us. The environment can be extended to the market for our goods or services and includes buyer behavior and trends that affect purchases.

Corporate strategy begins with vision and mission. While vision describes a succinct image of what the company is and how it fits into its marketplace, corporate mission sets forth the goals, in a very broad sense, that the organization should strive for within its marketplace. The business plan is based on both vision and mission.

Vision

A generic corporate vision statement might say, "We are world leaders in the ABC Industry with a premier position in the XYZ market. We are an organization that provides 1, develops 2, and serves 3. We are at the forefront of technology in our industry. We are committed to excellence, innovation, and flexibility."

The creation of an organizational vision requires full strategic understanding of the internal and external environments. The first requirement is a realistic self appraisal of the organization's internal situation. This includes an inventory of capabilities including human resources, financial strength, and production or operational aspects of the business. As simple as these may be to catalog, this inventory of critical elements must then be factored into the framework presented by the organization's external environment. Successfully factoring these critical elements allows an accurate "positioning" of the organization and helps define its distinctive competencies.

External environment

- Demand for the organization's product or service

- Supply of resources needed to produce the product or service

- Value adding process or technology vis-à-vis the "state of the art" of the industry

- A myriad of details about the competition

- Various aspects of finance

- Demographics

- Econometrics

- Regulatory factors

How does a corporate strategist understand the organization and the environment in which that organization operates? In many cases there is significant personal experience on the part of the senior executive that helps the evaluation of an organization's capabilities (present or future). However, with a rapidly changing work environment, which can include work teams that often temporarily constitute virtual organizations, the traditional expectation of having senior management may be faulty. Rapidly changing industries and the emergence of entirely new ones also complicate the notion of "senior management."

To some degree the experienced strategist can mentally juggle these factors to create the vision statement, but he or she would do well to rely to some extent on computer intelligence support. Today this includes the vast array of information sources and IBIS tools to collect pertinent information, analyze it, and present an executive summary in a convincing fashion.

Mission

Once a clear "self-image" (vision) is formulated, the general direction of motion in the marketplace is established and the mission statement is developed. A mission statement can be broad or narrow. It can encompass a specific purpose for the organization's activities, or it can broadly outline general direction. The mission statement provides a common, shared perspective for all members of the organization. It starts them rowing together in a way that takes advantage of human resources and maximizes the efficient use of finances and other resources. Short- and long-term goals follow from the organization's mission statement.

Although it is a broad statement of direction and purpose, the mission statement is more specific than the vision statement. The mission statement clarifies what business the organization is in and what its objectives are for the three- to five-year term. For example, if the mission of the Acme Office Supply Corporation is to be the "dominant office-supply business serving all medium-sized businesses in its region," then the goal may be to achieve 20-percent market share in that segment of the office-supplies market of five Northeastern States.

Certain action steps must be taken to clarify the many facets of that simple statement. The clarification provides a series of benchmarks or targets that guide Acme's spending to achieve the goal. The challenge to management is to make the mission statement a worthy overall achievable goal that is not too broad nor too narrow in its definition.

Developing Acme's mission statement should include some activity involving an examination of its competition in the Northeast to compare and contrast mission statements.

Internet Business Intelligence can be used to determine what the competitors primary and other activities are, the kinds of customers the competitor sells to, what the competitor can and cannot do, and what it is likely to do three to five years hence. In a competitor analysis mode, the strategist using IBIS will locate published mission statements or find knowledgeable people to interview. Failing that, the competitor's mission may have to be inferred from its actions and policies as reported in news releases transmitted via such services as PR Newswire (**www.prnewswire.com**) or Business Wire (**www.businesswire.com**). Determining a key competitor's strategic intent may be more or less difficult depending on the size and diversity of the competitors being analyzed. All of this will serve to shape a unique, highly competitive mission statement.

SWOT

Strategic management and business intelligence gathering and analysis are intertwined now more than ever before. Today, an unprecedented but still growing collection of tools for BI, including the new methods of computer harvesting, is available to the strategist. IBIS helps the strategist to create a plan to guide the organization. Strategic management integrates such various business disciplines as finance, marketing, operations, and human resources and relies heavily on intuition and judgment. This process is fed with external information. While the strategist has a basic understanding of an organization's Strengths and Weaknesses, environmental scanning via IBIS reveals Opportunities and Threats (SWOT). It further illuminates the strengths and weaknesses through benchmarking. This is the classic business school SWOT approach to strategic management.

Once an organization has a highly developed sense of vision and mission, it is ready to transform these broad abstract statements into specific activities, which are contained in a business plan.

Business planning

Vision and mission are the heart and soul of the business plan. The plan starts with an executive summary that presents an overview of the company, a description of the business, current position and future outlook, management and ownership, the company's unique selling proposition, the funds sought and how they will be used, etc. Overall the business plan sets forth the actions that need to be taken for the organization's strategic thrust—its competitive position. This might be price or cost leadership, uniqueness of its product or service, etc.

In developing a comprehensive business plan (or refining/ updating an existing one), the strategist will need lots of external information. It's impossible to say that the company's product or service is unique unless a thorough search has been performed to determine whether this is really true. Further investigation must be made to determine pricing of competing products, other value added by competitors, and even whether there might be patent, trademark, or copyright issues involved.

A strong business plan presents an extensive section on market research including an overview of the size, growth potential, customer and competitor profiles, pricing details, geographic and other factors. Operations plans detail just how the business actually will be conducted, covering such key issues as technical details, employment issues, etc. The financial section presents historical and/or projected cash-flow statements, income statement and balance sheet, and important financial ratios (sales per employee, return on investment, etc.), which are used to measure performance or compare the business to its competitors.

Much of the external information for the business plan can be gathered from the Internet and various online databases, CD-ROMs, and purchased data files. The U.S. Commerce Department's Bureau of Economic Analysis (BEA) Survey of Current Business as well as data from various Federal Reserve System reports can be utilized in spreadsheet software. The better packages permit the user to do statistical analysis. Excel's Analysis Toolpak is a particularly useful statistical analysis add-in included in that software. Most of these types of data files are relatively inexpensive and some can be downloaded at no charge from the Internet.

Once the strategist has compiled the necessary business intelligence and other information garnered from interviews or other research, the process of building (or rewriting) the business plan begins. This process compiles all of the pertinent information required to establish or expand the business. Smaller firms that need to raise funds often use a business plan to show private investors, bankers, investment organizations, and venture-capital firms that they are a worthy risk. Larger firms may create or periodically update a strategic plan that serves a purpose similar to the business plan. Public companies may use a variation of the business plan (perhaps in concert with a detailed strategic plan) to guide the creation of the Securities and Exchange Commission mandated 10K annual report.

Measurable objectives are set forth in the business plan. Objectives may be measured by any combination of business indicators—all of which should be benchmarked against similar companies in the same field. For example, if a public corporation determines that its basic mission is to be the most profitable company in an industry, then it must ultimately achieve an earnings-per-share ratio that compares favorably with its competitors. Another example might show four or five private companies in the same region of the country doing the same work with roughly similar numbers of employees. The profitability per employee might be a key indicator of having achieved the highest profitability in the field.

Non-Internet information for business planning

In larger organizations, functional executives and staff are responsible for their respective areas. In the case of "Acme," market share is broadly addressed in the mission statement. The marketing department would be responsible for determining the market size and what percent the organization controls. BI is employed to help marketing scope out the big picture and fill in the details. In addition to Internet, they may use a CD-ROM system to locate articles in national office-supply trade magazines that provide statistics relating to what quantity of office supplies are purchased by all categories of businesses. The categories are broken down by Standard Industrial Classification (SIC) code, and average purchases may be given for several size categories of businesses within each SIC code.

Another CD-ROM that can be used is the MarketPlace Information Corporation CD-ROM. For less than $1,000, Acme's marketing department can take advantage of this product that is based on Dun & Bradstreet data. Mailing information, phone numbers, and full demographic records for over 10 million businesses are contained in MarketPlace. MarketPlace offers state-of-the-art sort capabilities and the resulting output can be standard mailing labels, telemarketing data, or full demographic data for each company or the industry as a whole. The latter is perfect for business-planning purposes while the former can be used for backup data or actual sales campaigns.

Using the CD-ROM, which contains numerous fields of data on each business, allows the compilation of a report on the number of businesses in Acme's market area, listed by SIC and size. Using these data, they determine the total market. Acme's sales give them a percent of the total market share they presently command. That's the easy part. Now comes the time-consuming market and competitor analyses required to determine who owns the rest of the market.

Information to answer this question also comes from BI sources though it probably would be supplemented with personal interviews and perhaps focus group discussions.

The corporation's finance experts compile and monitor financial data. An outside accounting firm also audits larger organizations. In the smaller organization an outside accounting firm might be used to gather and report the internal numbers (within the company) and reference published data on other organizations for comparison. Similarly, a variety of data files are available to support the finance portion of business planning. For example, the Department of Commerce's Bureau of Economic Analysis sells a historical database of financial ratios on disk, updated quarterly, for under $100. More expensive data file subscriptions can be obtained from value-added resellers of such traditional data as that compiled by Robert Morris Associates, a banking trade association.

Finding and developing business relationship candidates may form a critically important part of a new or existing business plan. Applying the power of BI will help the strategist to identify and understand (before initial contact) likely candidates. These business partners could include original equipment manufacturers, wholesalers and distributors, companies that engage in joint marketing arrangements, and third-party suppliers, as well as joint-venture development partners sharing financial and technical responsibilities.

Defining the competition

Management at the highest levels in an organization must make strategic decisions regarding the landscape of the marketplace after sorting out all the players. The scope and complexity of competition in big business is illustrated by the following list of potential and actual competitors compiled for a telecommunications research organization. In the following case, strategic planners wanted to know more about their competitors. But first, they were interested in the opinions of consultants as to just who those competitors were. A list of their competitors follows:

Advantis

ALC Communications

Alcatel

Ameritech Corp.

Andersen Consulting

AT&T Bell Labs

AT&T Network Systems International

Australian Telecom

Battelle Memorial Institute

Bell Atlantic

Bell-Northern Research, Ltd.

Bell South

Booz Allen & Hamilton

British Telcom

Cable & Wireless

Cable Television Laboratories, Inc.

California Institute of Technology

Cap Gemini Sogeti

Cellular Vision of New York

Century Telephone

Columbia University Computer Science Dept.

Columbia University Institute for Tele-Information

Comcast

Communication Intelligence Corp.

Compania de Telefonos de Chile

CompuCom Systems

Computer & Communications Labs Taiwan(Government's Computer Research Lab)

Computer Sciences

Contel Cellular

Continental Cablevision

Continuum

Coopers & Lybrand

Corning Corp.

Cox Cable

CSC Consulting

David Sarnoff Research Center (a unit of SRI)

Defense Advanced Research Projects Agency

Deloitte & Touche

Deutsche Telekom

Electronic Data Systems Corp.

Ericsson

French Telecom

Fujitsu

Gemini Consulting

General Magic, Inc.

GTE

Hitachi

Hughes Aircraft Co.

IBM Thomas J. Watson Labs

Institute for Advanced Studies, Princeton

Integrated Network Corp.

Intel Corp.

Intelligent Electronics

Kurzweil Applied Intelligence

Matsushita Electric Corp. of America Business & Engineering Center

MCC Ventures

MCI

Metromedia

MFS Communications

Microelectronics & Computer Technology Corp.

Microsoft Corp.

MIT Lincoln Laboratory

MIT Media Lab

Mitsubishi Electric Research Laboratories, Inc.

Motorola

National Institute of Standards & Technology

NEC Corp.

Newbridge Networks

Nippon Telegraph & Telephone Corp.

Nonvolatile Electronics, Inc.

Northern Telecom, Ltd.

Nynex

Oki

Pacific Telesis

Perot Systems

Philips Electronics

Rogers Communications

Siemens Rolm Network Systems Group

Southwestern Bell

Sprint

SRI International, Inc.

Telephone and Data Systems

Terisa Systems

Time Warner

Toshiba

U.S. West

United Research Co.

Unitel Communications

Viacom

Xerox Palo Alto Research Center

Resources are always limited and management must focus on key competitors. The short list for the telecommunications research organization included these companies:

Andersen Consulting

AT&T Bell Labs

Battelle Memorial Institute

Bellcore

Bell-Northern Research, Ltd.

Booz Allen & Hamilton

British Telcom

Cable & Wireless

CSC Consulting

David Sarnoff Research Center (a unit of SRI)

IBM Thomas J. Watson Labs

MIT Media Lab

Mitsubishi Electric Research Laboratories, Inc.

Motorola

Nippon Telegraph & Telephone Corp.

United Research Co.

Xerox Palo Alto Research Center

Defining the competition through environmental scanning or monitoring with an Internet Business Intelligence System can serve multiple purposes for top management. Every one of the above listed companies has a Web site from which various quantities of relevant information can be extracted. Whether the Web pages are printed and stored in a three-ring binder or managed in a sophisticated computer system, having the information at hand, in a convenient format, helps make decisions more accurate and less frustrating.

The pace of change affects all of us, some more harshly than others. A telecommunications research organization had many peripheral competitors and some direct competitors, and management wanted to grow the organization. Should this company go public? Should they consider joint ventures, a merger, or an acquisition? One very large and successful company[1] uses the M&A/Joint Venture/Strategic Alliance decision methodology contained in Table 3.1.

Table 3.1

	DECISION	**YIELDS KNOWLEDGE FOR**
Is it real?	Is the opportunity the right size?	Deciding if we have picked the right candidates and product/service/market
Does it fit?	Can we live with the personnel, culture, and integration plan?	Understanding the integration plan before considering closing the transaction
Can we win?	Does it yield a competitive or strategic advantage?	Setting market share and profitability goals for the new enterprise

From this top-level matrix, several lower levels of data gathering and analysis expanded upon the basic questions. For example, the "Is it real?" question is fleshed out in another matrix used for ranking potential markets on a global basis. The "Does it fit?" question is addressed in another matrix that evaluates all of the pertinent dimensions including engineering and technology, manufacturing and marketing, distribution channels and sales, manufacturing support, training, product technology, and competitor response. "Can we win?" is addressed by a matrix that organizes such quantitative factors as competitor shares, market position, and other situation-specific factors. Finally, all of the items of information are synthesized into a ranking matrix with the output being attractiveness scores.

Internet information sources for due diligence

The Internet is changing the landscape of executive decision making. Direct access to timely information and historical data is a two-edged sword. On one hand it enables more thorough research. On the other hand it raises the bar of what can be accomplished in terms of due diligence. This puts pressure on management to take all reasonable steps to "know what they don't know," particularly inside public companies where shareholders sometimes take legal action against top management and boards of directors following unfavorable business developments.

Although not strictly limited to buying and selling of businesses, due diligence can encompass three areas of investigation: business, legal, and accounting. The business review should cover products, markets and marketing, sales, management, industrial relations, facilities, equipment, etc. Legal investigations, performed primarily by lawyers, would include reviews of such legal documents as incorporation papers, regulatory filings, contracts, judgments, and the like. Accountants experienced in auditing usually handle the accounting investigation.

In these situations, early-stage executive decision making requires both objective data and subjective information. All of this input must be factored into the various stages of the process up to the ultimate decision. Fortunately, the Internet provides plentiful input for due diligence. A good example of this is the availability of regulatory compliance data, now accessible at **www.oshadata. com**. This private service provides aggregated history violations databases updated quarterly. Data presented include:

- Employment Standards Administration Wage and Hour Division violations

- National Labor Relations Board Unfair Labor Practices

- Equal Employment Opportunity Commission Equal Pay Act and Age Discrimination violations

- Immigration and Naturalization Service work-site enforcement records

- Federal Trade Commission complaints, consent agreements, and external court cases

- Health and Human Services cumulative sanctions

- Environmental Protection Agency National Emission Standards for Hazardous Air Pollutants, Asbestos

- Federal General Services Administration Excluded Parties List

- New Jersey General Services Administration Debarment List

The Internet provides inexpensive access to a vast information network. Anyone who wants to present a data product to the consuming public now can do so at incredibly low cost. Making it a profitable business is another story. But as the Internet evolves, more of the marketing will shift from costly traditional channels (print advertisements, direct mail with ever-increasing postage costs, etc.) to more sophisticated methods of marketing via the Internet. In the monitoring of technology markets and companies, the Internet often plays a bigger role as these companies conduct most of their activity on the Internet.

Company news releases over time are easier to retrieve. Public records, including secretary of state filings, court records, regulatory agency reports, and many other types increasingly are available via the Internet. Ongoing monitoring using free or fee-based services can be accomplished at low or no cost. All of this information and many other bits and pieces of data must be collected, analyzed, and reported individually and as a whole. This is why an integrated Internet Business Intelligence System is called for in many cases.

Peering into the future

2025: Scenarios of U.S. and Global Society Reshaped by Science and Technology, by Coates, Mahaffie, and Hines, is an intriguing topic for discussion. It promises a view of the future from which decisions can be made to steer the business in a direction that will enhance future profitability. There are some that make predictions for a living. This type of information can't be called "intelligence," but it is a valuable commodity.

Joseph F. Coates, president of Coates & Jarrett, Washington, DC, is one of several noted professional futurists. According to Coates, developments in the technologies of energy, information, genetics, materials, the environment, and the brain will offer great business opportunities. Business people want to know how to translate the opportunities into sales. Such technologies will separately and together alter the structure and organization of the workforce and its management. Each of these areas carries the potential for effects as profound as the introduction of the automobile or the electric light in the last century.

Futurists like Coates identify primary developments in these fields and link them to social, economic, political, and demographic trends. The best of these observations can lead top management to conclusions that may benefit them and their organizations. A recent search via AltaVista turned up 33,000 pages using the keyword "futurist." Other organizations, like the Strategic Leadership Forum, are excellent resources for strategic thinkers. What are the critical issues facing business leaders? What trends create these issues? What are the strategic implications of the issues? What actions are recommended? These are some of the concepts dealt with by business futurists[2] and top management. IBIS is no crystal ball but it is a systematic, state-of-the-art approach to creating a knowledge advantage in a world of uncertainty.

Summary of the information requirements of executives

Collection of information provides the critical input to the strategist's thinking. This could be as simple as logging onto America Online once a day to monitor business trends in general and industry developments in particular. A more sophisticated approach is to establish electronic clipping files that automatically scan newswires and save items that relate to a topic of interest. Targeted research often is conducted by an in-house librarian using one or more specialized online databases or CD-ROMs to find pertinent information on a specific topic. All this information eventually becomes intelligence as it is processed and analyzed. The intelligence product assists the strategist to create a framework in which to place his organization for the development of a corporate vision.

The following lists show typical management functions and business intelligence requirements as well as sources available to fulfill some of the requirements.

President/CEO: Synthesis of intelligence from functional units presented in summary fashion, overview of organizational politics. Fusion of appropriate data from functional units presented via Executive Information Systems (larger organizations) or via customized groupware in smaller organizations. Broad tracking of business and industry trends and market opportunities, economic, regulatory, and demographic trends as they affect the industry. Real-time news feeds, online forums to communicate with other executives, executive information systems, groupware, and analysis systems.

Finance: Financial statements, risk and return on projects, cash flow analysis, and capital structure. Accounting system (subsystem of large corporate network or feed to groupware in smaller organization). Industry financial ratios, cost of capital, customer credit ratings, economic trends, tax law changes. Subscription services or specialty databases, data files, forums to communicate with other executives.

Marketing: Marketing strategy and program planning, budgeting and expenditures, results of marketing programs. Marketing system (subsystem of large corporate network or specialty software feed to groupware in smaller organization). Market dynamics and trends, pricing, competitor analysis, customer feedback. Lotus Notes or Microsoft Exchange for sharing information, sales contact management system and forums.

Research & Development: Basic and/or applied research (larger organizations), new product or service development. Project tracking system (subsystem of large corporate network or specialty software feed to groupware in smaller organization). Benchmarking of competitor product or service, reverse engineering of products, closely related to marketing and production operations functions, status of competitor research. Subscription services or specialty databases, data files, downloading from specialized dial-up bulletin board systems (BBS), and online forums to communicate with other executives.

Production or Operations: Input/output measurements of organization function, productivity measures, inventory and quality control, short- and long-range forecasts. Operations monitoring system (subsystem of large corporate network or specialty software feed to groupware in smaller organization). Developments affecting state of the art or economics of organization's production or operations functions, new processes of competitors. Subscription services or specialty databases and CD-ROMs, online forums to communicate with other executives.

Human Resources: Current and projected staffing, compensation and benefits details, performance ratings, and motivational factors. HR system (subsystem of large corporate network or specialty software feed to groupware in smaller organization). Labor market price and supply details, state and federal regulations, societal trends, workplace issues. Subscription services or specialty databases, online forums to communicate with other executives.

Representative sources (Internet and non-Internet) by executive function

President/CEO

ABI/Inform

Business Database+

Business Dateline

Business NewsBank

Business Strategies

Business Week

Dow Jones

Electronic Newsstand

Executive News Service

Individual, Inc. Newspage

Infotrac General Business File

IQuest

M&A Database

Magazine Database+

News Source USA

Nightly Business Report

U.S. Government

U.S. Industrial Outlook

Venture Capital Networks

Finance

AICPA

Bloomberg

National Association of Business Economists

Credit information networks

Disclosure

Federal Reserve System

Finance Industry News

Financial Economics Network

Financial Services. Tech. Consortium

I/B/E/S Earnings Estimates

Investor and Financial forums

Investor's Business Daily

Investor' s Network

IRS

Moody's domestic and international companies

Morningstar

S&P public and private companies

SEC EDGAR

StockLink

Tax Forum

TRW Business Profiles

Worth Online

WSJ Money & Investing

Marketing

Ad Age

American Marketing Association

Association for Public Policy Analysis

Business Demographics

Capital Connection

CENDATA

Commerce Business Daily

Cowles/SIMBA Media

D&B MarketPlace

Economic Census

Economic Social

Federal Information News Syndicate National

Hoover's Company Database

List of Marketing Lists

Media Services

PR & Marketing Forum

Sales Automation

Society of Competitive Intelligence Professionals

Tenderlink

International Operations

BBC

European Union

International Business Opportunities Service

International Company Information

International Trade Forum

Intl. Chambers of Commerce

Intl. Import Export Exchange

Japan Forum

Mexico or European business telephone directories

National Trade Databank

Global Trade Network

Trade Compass

Trade Fair International

UK Marketing Library

World Access Corp.

Research & Development

Adis

Boston Computer Society

Compendex Engineering Index

Dissertation Abstracts

Electronic Engineering Times

Engineering and Research Councils

Knowledge Index

National Academy of Science

National Institute of Standards and Technology

R&D Insight

Scientific American

UNCOVER

Production/Operations

Computer and Software Support Forums

Consumer Product Safety Council

Industry Connection
(computer and software
support)

Intelliseek

IQuest Engineering Info
Center

Online

Product Registry

Programming Forums

Reuters Business Briefing

SafetyNet

Thomas Register

Human Resources

Adult Literacy

American Bar Association

Career Center

EAASY SABRE Travel Service

European Community
Telework Forum

Job Listings

Jobs Online

Labor Department
(numerous)

Occupational Outlook

Online Career Center

PsycLIT

SeniorNet

Travel disABILITIES Forum

Working from Home Forum

Putting it all together

Today's business environment demands rapid and sophisticated production of knowledge for competitive advantage. As shown, this involves a great many sources generating all types of information. How can one possibly manage the individual pieces, let alone infer a big picture from the many pieces of the puzzle? New software, previously used only by government and military intelligence organizations, is coming onto the commercial market (see Pathfinder in Chapter Fifteen). These high-value packages allow the user to manipulate data to create flexible and dynamic intelligence products.

Discussed in greater detail later, you will see how systems allow the user to effectively manage enormous volumes of relevant information. Management includes sorting, selecting, and summarizing but, most importantly, analysis and communication. For example, today's large organizations have competitors who are, at the same time, suppliers and joint-venture partners. Complex relationships can be portrayed graphically from large amounts of external information. In addition to relationship visualization, temporal analysis tracks changes over time. Powerful presentation capabilities, among other features, help intelligence consumers to gain a Knowledge Advantage.

Business intelligence is about using information and a variety of methods as a powerful competitive weapon. Personal or corporate IBIS is the boundary area between strategy and tactics on the road to the Knowledge Advantage.

■ **MINI CASE: Who really owns the company?**

Top management often grows the business through acquisition of other businesses. Before the investment bankers get involved there is a need to initially research the takeover target. This phase is called "pre-acquisition due diligence."

An assignment to research a very secretive private holding company that had nearly $1 billion in total annual sales used the Internet as well as other resources. The client was a very large international company that was interested in acquiring a relatively small unit of the private holding company. In this case you'll see that other types of research sources are just as important as the Internet. However, the power of Internet searching and its ability to find the proverbial "needle in the haystack" via search engines is also illustrated.

The first challenge was to find something beyond the standard D&B report about the subsidiary as well as the holding company. One of the first pieces of information that gave us some insight into the thinking of the founder of this company was a *New York Times* article, which we found through a CD-ROM in the local public library.

Other CD-ROMs provided a good framework of basic business information. For example, Standard & Poor's private company database as well as American Business Information's CD-ROMs provided information on the various physical locations (plants, warehouses, sales offices) of the target company. The Standard & Poor's private company database has an executives database. It contains data and search tools to research people on boards of directors across all 40,000-plus companies in the database, giving basic background on each of the executives, including those on the board of the holding company.

We also conducted field research for corporate records at the Secretary of State's office and for articles at the local newspaper in the rural town where the main manufacturing plant was located. The latter yielded some excellent articles on the subsidiary providing unknown (to us) labor troubles. Had this project been assigned two months later, we'd have been able to find this information via the Internet, according to the paper's librarian. More and more local newspapers offer complete archives of article text.

We were first able to determine the actual ownership of the company through an article that we found simply by searching the company's name in AltaVista. Within seconds we found a relatively obscure item in an upscale magazine that provided the name of the actual owner plus some interesting background. This was the only reference to the actual owner that was uncovered in the course of the project.

The target company had a number of distributors throughout the country, many with Web sites. Each distributor listed the lines carried, which included the target company as well as other aspects about which we were interested in learning. A number of trade magazines have established a presence on the Web, and those covering our target's industry listed various types of industry-specific data. In some cases, pricing is given. For example, one distributor was located using the Internet and it was determined that a jobber cost of approximately one-half the retail price was given along with a list of all the products that this distributor carried.

The EPA's Envirofacts Toxics Release Inventory database on the Internet provides detailed filings of hazardous waste and air releases. The listings contain chemical name, year, release amount, transfer site name and address, and type of treatment. This provides some insight into the manufacturing processes used, as well as an indication of the amount that they're using. One can plot the amount of these chemicals and determine activity over a period of several years, although waste minimization could be a factor in declining numbers. In this case, we plotted five years of data from 1991 to 1995, which showed the amount of a particular compound disposed by the company had increased steadily, but from 1994 to 1995 had basically flattened out.

Another type of business intelligence was obtained by patent search. We used the United States Patent and Trademark Office Internet site to search for the assignee (the target company) and found two patents.

Finally, another Internet-derived piece of the information puzzle was the discovery of a home page for a Board Certified Ergonomist. This individual wrote a research paper on early workplace assessment for the prevention of certain types of injuries for the target company. This individual was not interviewed, but potentially could be an interview source if needed.

Another interesting bit of detail from the Internet was a listing of electronic data interchange, or EDI, formats supported by the target company. The listing provided the types of EDI documents that they can transfer, such as purchase orders, acknowledgements of purchase orders, shipping notices or manifests, planning schedules with release capability, invoices, and formats supported, as well as the networks used. It also listed planned EDI implementation at the company. This type of data, widely available via the Internet, has information security implications. A voluminous briefing book was prepared for the client.

■ **MINI CASE: Is there a threat to our executives or employees?**

Considering the various aspects of threat assessment, the Internet can play a role in the process by providing a means to quickly gather together required input for evaluation. This input is used within a model. For example a U.S. Army terrorist threat assessment model includes the following factors: existence, history, capability, intentions, targeting, and security environment. Security environment is considered separately as a modifying factor and will influence the assigned threat level. Threat levels include critical, high, medium, low, and negligible. Each element of the threat-assessment model is broad, but given a few specifics, the appropriate subject area can be researched via the Internet.

In a recent corporate assignment, a large portion of the Internet was surveyed using various search engines. Several specific groups were identified, each of which had ongoing activity in the general area of our interest. However, only one was judged to be of concern because of the wording and tone of its Web page text. Also, all other groups were identified with a street address or phone number, but this group solicited funds to a post office box and gave no phone number.

Search engines are critical to the success of most Internet research projects, but the browser software (usually Netscape Navigator or Internet Explorer) also plays a role. With a Web site loaded into the browser, the user may be confronted with a very large amount of text, sometimes several thousand words. Both software packages have a "find text string" feature (control-F) that permits the user to quickly locate a specific string within the entire text of the Web page once it has been loaded into the browser. Other simple functions, Save Text (or save individual graphic on a Web page with right-button mouse click) or Cut and Paste allow the user to work with text and graphics to construct a report incorporating the material found on the Web site. Netscape Communicator and Internet Explorer have many other productivity enhancements useful for investigations on the Internet.

Knowing which search engines to use and how to use them effectively are important. For example, most of the dozens of major search engines enable the user to locate World Wide Web pages. Only a few can be used to reliably pinpoint Usenet newsgroups (where fast and furious free-flowing text messages are sent back and forth for public viewing). Deja News is preferred for newsgroup searching. Using search engines, one can easily locate Web pages, newsgroup messages, newspaper articles, lists of people or organizations and statistics—worldwide—which can be useful in building the threat assessment.

■ **MINI CASE:**   **Who's stealing our proprietary information?**

One forward-thinking director of corporate security in a very large service business had his hands full with a variety of security problems. He instinctively knew that the Internet was a vast, uncovered area where wrongdoing involving business' intellectual property might be discovered. In addition to bringing his staff up to speed on the Internet, he wanted to conduct a broad sweep of the Internet to uncover examples of this type of threat—real or potential detrimental activities relating to his company's intellectual property.

Several of the client's intellectual property assets had unique names. Searching these produced mostly relevant results. Simply by weeding through 100 to 200 references we were able to find the few items of interest. But where the asset name is more like a common phrase one must fully utilize the powerful search capabilities of a major search engine.

According to their promotional literature, "You can search through AltaVista's entire Web index—approximately 200 Gigabytes of data—in less than a second. With the help of sophisticated software, robust Internet connections, and state-of-the-art Digital Equipment Corporation Alpha technology, your AltaVista search can take less time than it takes you to find a file on your personal computer (or anything on your desk!)." A variety of advanced search capabilities can yield highly relevant hits from an AltaVista search.

Founded in May 1995, Deja News, Inc. claims to have provided the first search engine capable of organizing, indexing, and archiving the content of "the most powerful, and two-way communications medium of all time—Usenet newsgroups." The Deja News user interface provides users with an easy, powerful, and free Web interface for searching the more than 20,000 active discussion groups, 180 gigabytes of information, and 138 million articles in the Deja News database. Deja News provides four search methods: quick search; power search; interest finder; and browse groups.

Endnotes

1. "Competitive Intelligence Evolution at Pillsbury." Presentation at SCIP, Minnesota Chapter seminar, October 2, 1998.

2. "A Forum of Futurists" (*The Planning Review*, November/December 1995:10-18).

CHAPTER 4

IBIS FOR **MARKETING**

For many managers, Internet and marketing are synonymous because of the immense rise in online shopping. This means that the Internet is considered to be a primary marketing channel or sales tool. The security of credit-card orders via the Internet has ceased to be an issue. Today, most Internet-savvy consumers consider an online purchase to be rather routine. The Internet Business Intelligence System (IBIS) for marketing is not about selling via the Internet—it's about supporting the marketing function with business intelligence (BI).

The following definitions were approved by the American Marketing Association Board of Directors and published in *Marketing News*, March 1, 1986. "Marketing is the process of planning and executing the conception, pricing, promotion, and distribution of ideas, goods, and services to create exchanges that satisfy individual and organizational goals." Also, "Marketing research is the function that links the consumer, customer, and public to the marketer through information—information used to identify and define marketing opportunities and problems; generate, refine, and evaluate marketing actions; monitor marketing performance; and improve understanding of marketing as a process. Marketing research specifies the information required to address these issues, designs the method for collecting information, manages and implements the data collection process, analyzes the results, and communicates the findings and their implications."

It's clear that today, Internet and marketing go hand in hand. Marketing seeks to understand the needs of buyers and fulfill those needs while making a profit. Marketing people may be the people who can best utilize Internet Business Intelligence because they must understand a variety of external factors to offer products and services that meet customer needs. Marketing people must understand competitors to help plot future direction with regard to this and a variety of other market factors.

Business intelligence is something that all marketers recognize that they need. Disagreements may arise from how to get it or how to use it. This book presents a framework in which all businesses, large and small, can structure IBIS to fit their specific needs. In many cases however, the marketing people will be in charge of their company's IBIS. This should come as no surprise because the Internet itself has become an extension of the traditional marketplace. Today's complex relationships among large companies that have units or divisions that simultaneously are vendors, alliance partners, and competitors, also share marketspace with Internet users who are customers at the retail and business-to-business levels. "Cybertribes" are extensions of trade and professional associations and social and hobby clubs, as well as other groups of people who previously met in home, offices, hotels, and other public meeting places located in physical space as shown in Figure 4.1.

Figure 4.1

Rapid identification of new markets

Let's assume that we sell domestic appliances and we want to begin a marketing program in a new country. Our first step would be to obtain such statistical data as population, gross domestic product, and exchange rates. A summary of the industry sector might include information on competitors and their production rates, market size including spending on domestic appliances in general, and types of appliances purchased. Import and export data also would be useful. Soft information on trends and predictions would round out this market research package.[1]

This suggests an organization of BI gathered via the Internet to form a broad-scope market research project from which a standardized template could be modeled:

- Summary and highlights

- Introduction

- Production

- Size of market

- Consumption patterns

- Leading companies and brands

- Company profiles

- Distribution

- Prices and margins

- Advertising and promotion

- Information sources available

- Statistical appendices

Examining these categories reveals that much of this information can be gathered via the Internet. In Chapter Ten we'll explore search engines in detail. To address broadly the issue of how we might gather information to compile a market research report, it should be understood that there are basically two ways to search the Internet. The first is by keyword, and the second is by following the hierarchical approach.

In the keyword approach, one searches for a combination of words that is likely to return Web pages that contain information closely related to what you seek. The specific methods of focusing a keyword search are outlined in Chapter Ten. The hierarchical approach takes you from broad topics down to more specific topics until you reach the information you are seeking. In either case, eight to ten hours of searching over a two- or three-day period should turn up enough basic information to help the marketer to begin piecing together the report.

Replacing or augmenting costly market research reports

Market research consultants have specialized in knowing what information is needed, where to get it, and how to package and sell it. The better consultants add value to market research reports by shaping them through the application of their judgment and experience. How much of this can be performed by the non-consultant? That question is best answered by an observation concerning the use of consultants. Recognizing that their best use may be for the added value of judgment and experience, perhaps that's all you need to purchase. Rather than hiring a consultant to create and package the entire product, the Internet allows one to put most of the information together very rapidly. An expert review will reveal gaps, and from that point forward the expert's advice, guidance, and evaluation is a bargain.

Many of us have seen the phrase "Researchers Frost & Sullivan predicts sales will jump from $1.6 billion last year to more than $5 billion in 2005…" There's a lot more detail underneath that top-line figure. Market research report prices commonly range from $500 to $5,000 and more. The statistics, analyses, and forecasts contained in such reports can play important roles in marketing decisions that drive product development and marketing programs. Sales trends and projections for products and services, including potential entrants with new products or technologies, along with background on current players all are important factors that must be considered in developing a marketing program. This suggests the following categories that can be used to create a template for more in-depth stage II industry studies:

- Consumer preferences

- Competitor profiles

- New products

- Market segments, share, and growth potential

- Pricing

- Distribution channels

- Marketing strategies

- Advertising budgets

- Industry economics

- Foreign trade

Some market research companies offer portions of a complete market research report for a fraction of the cost of the whole report. To customize your market research you may want to consider carefully what information you can gather via the Internet and what it costs to purchase. It may take very little time and effort to compile certain facts, while other facts may be very difficult or time consuming. If you can derive 60 percent of a $3,000 market research report in two days and purchase the remaining portions for $1,000, the choice is clear.

To give you an idea of the elements of a full-scale industry market research report and what goes into creating it, the following table of contents for a Mediamark Research, Inc. report distributed by Business Trends Analysts (**www.businesstrendanalysts.com**) is presented:

THE MARKET FOR OPHTHALMIC GOODS

Section I: Overview of the U.S. Ophthalmic Goods Industry

Section II: The U.S. Market for Ophthalmic Goods

Section III: The U.S. Contact Lens Market

Section IV: The U.S. Contact Lens Care Solutions Market

Section V: The U.S. Market for Frames And Lenses

Section VI: The U.S. Sunglasses Market

Section VII: The U.S. Market for Safety and Sport Glasses and Goggles

Section VIII: The U.S. Market for Eye Care Products

Section IX: Factors Affecting Demand in the Ophthalmic Goods Industry

Section X: Foreign Trade of Ophthalmic Goods

Section XI: Structure of the U.S. Ophthalmic Goods Industry

Section XII: Consumer Advertising in the Ophthalmic Goods Industry

Section XIII: Competitive Analysis of Selected Ophthalmic Product Companies

Section XIV: Directory of Selected U.S. Ophthalmic Goods Manufacturers and Retailers

To give you a better idea of the detail contained in this report, here is a section with its contents listed:

Section VI: The U.S. Sunglasses Market

Summary and Analysis, 118-121

U.S. Manufacturers' Sales of Ready-Made Sun or Glare Glasses and Sun Goggles and Accessories: Total, 122

Graph: Total, 123

Producer Price Trends for Sun or Glare Glasses or Goggles, Ready-Made, 124

U.S. Retail Sales of Sunglasses, 125

U.S. Retail Sales of Sunglasses Through Primary Retail Channels, 126

Operating Statistics for Sunglasses Sold in Department Stores, 127

U.S. Retail Sales of All Women's Accessories, 128

Top Seasonal Sundries Sales, 129

Demographic Profile of Sunglass Consumers, 130

Graph: Profile of Sunglass Consumers, by Region, 131

Demographic Profile of Sunglass Consumers, by Amount Spent, 132

Distribution Channels for the Plano Sunwear Market, 133

Material Types and Distribution of Sunwear Lenses, 134

Average Plano Sunwear Sales per Patient, 135

Motivation for Purchasing Sunglasses for $50 or More, 136

Selected Brand-Name High-Performance Rx Sunglasses, 137

Selected Effects of Harmful Rays and Light, 138-139

Selected Sunglass Lens Materials and Coatings, 140

Benefits of Selected Sunglass Lens Colors, 141

Selected New Product Introductions: Sunglasses and Sunwear Accessories, 142-146

Obviously, the expertise and cost to produce a comparable report far exceeds the retail purchase price. In many cases this build or buy decision will weigh in favor of the faster and lower cost purchase option. However, an examination of the framework is useful for those lacking the budget to purchase such a report.

New product development

Product development often means incorporating new technology into an existing product or process. The process of locating new technology previously took months of reviewing journals, attending meetings, and making phone calls. Now using the Internet this can be accomplished in days. Finding the right technology is less time consuming now because of the research community's long-standing affinity for the Internet. This means that most researchers are well represented in cyberspace. IBIS can be used for product development collaboration too.

One way to demonstrate quickly the value of the Internet is to showcase its ability to locate people and resources important to the company. An action plan to accomplish this includes creating a matrix with desired areas of technology represented in one direction and prospective facilities where that type of research is conducted listed in the opposite direction. The name of the researcher and pertinent notes (or hyperlinks to an illustrative Web page embedded in the document) are contained in the cells. See Figures 4.2 through 4.4.

Product Development Collaboration

Use the Internet for rapid identification of R&D assets or new technology (globally) that can be acquired or utilized to strengthen competitiveness of existing products.

Figure 4.2

Action Plan

1. **Search/browse the Internet to complete matrix**
2. **Build database of researcher and vendor contacts**
3. **Provide orientation sessions for key execs to develop contacts**
4. **Establish relationships with selected researchers and firms for technology transfer**

Figure 4.3

Using a combination of search engines and site-to-site Web surfing, one can locate researchers and facilities engaged in work coinciding with the type of technology needed for new product development. As you locate these resources, fill in the cells with data about individual researchers who are developing or offering technology that fits into the strategic plan for your company. A database of research and vendor contacts is built up and presented to senior management for consideration. Once specific researchers or vendors are evaluated and found to meet the screening criteria, personal contact is initiated. Again, the Internet can be used. Skipping potential telephone tag, contacts and exchange of information are facilitated by e-mail, although telephone and finally face-to-face contacts also, of course, are required.

Pinpoint Internet R&D Resources

	Technology 1	Technology 2	Technology 3	Technology 4	Technology 5
Facility 1	Researcher A	Researcher A	Researcher B	Researcher C	Researcher C
Facility 2	Researcher D	Researcher D			Researcher E
Facility 3	Researcher F		Researcher F		
Facility 4		Researcher G		Researcher H	Researcher H
Facility 5			Researcher I	Researcher I	Researcher I

(Hyperlink Embedded Document)

Figure 4.4

Sales support

While marketing seeks to connect with buyers on a more complicated level (market studies, advertising and public relations programs, etc.), sales people and their management often are attempting to directly communicate with individuals who can purchase a product or service. There are two distinct categories of sales. The first is consumer sales, which is usually a mass-market approach. The second is generically called "business to business," and generally is highly targeted to specific individuals and groups. IBIS can be particularly helpful in business-to-business sales.

Crude attempts at marketing using the Internet include the e-mail blitz, which usually is highly ineffective and very annoying to recipients. Smarter IBIS marketing efforts are used to build a highly targeted list of potential buyers. As it gets more and more difficult to identify buyers and communicate with them directly, the Internet is emerging as a communications medium highly suited to this purpose. Mailing lists and newsgroups carry hundreds of thousands of individual communications each day. The user has the ability to select a few pertinent lists or newsgroups and monitor these channels of communication to understand market segments and to identify buyers.

Internet-accessible databases ranging from many Yellow Page-type directories to those presented to users by such businesses as Dun & Bradstreet (**www.companiesonline.com**) and CorpTech (**www.corptech.com**) often provide leads free of charge. The best business listings can be selected by geographic location, line of business, and business size. Sometimes these free listings contain names of executives that make targeting possible in certain cases. Often there will be a link to a company's Web site that can be rapidly scanned to identify a potential need for products or services being sold. You will always find at least one "mail to:" button, and often you will find a contact person's name and e-mail address on the Web site to contact them directly.

Customer intelligence

Account executives selling to larger businesses need intelligence at the corporate level and the business unit or department level to which they are selling. As search engines become "portals" and offer more and more aggregated content, a tremendous amount of information on public companies is presented on a single screen. In addition to stock quotes and financial data this can include analyst reports and news articles. Information from both of these categories can be used to understand the strategic direction of the prospect company. While this probably is not important for people selling commodity products, it can be critical for big-ticket sales involving real estate, company-wide computer or telecommunications systems, and other products and services that would be required given a shift in corporate strategy.

For example, let's say that a broker selling corporate jet charter services learns that one of the 20 or so public companies head-quartered in his territory has announced negotiations to acquire a company 500 miles distant. There probably will be an initial flurry of travel activity related to the acquisition during and after negotiations, which could last several months. Given the right set of circumstances, jet charter might be the right choice for executive transportation, and after the initial travel a shuttle service using private aircraft might be very cost-effective. Close monitoring of developments within these 20 companies would have paid off for the broker.

Templates are an important part of business intelligence gathering in all areas of business. This also is true in marketing. The prolific no-nonsense author Harvey Mackay has produced several business books that deal with practical subjects. In *Swim with the Sharks Without Being Eaten Alive,* Mackay presents a template that can be used to guide information gathering for big-ticket sales efforts. His "66-Question Customer Profile" is quite detailed, but it provides a valuable starting point for selecting relevant items of information required for successful relationship marketing efforts in big-ticket sales. Broad subject areas, each of which has about six questions about the specific customer, include the following:

- Personal statistics (name, nickname, birth date and place, height and weight, etc.)

- Education (schools, sports, military service, etc.)

- Family (marital status, spouse's name, wedding anniversary, children, etc.)

- Business background (previous employment, status symbols in office, honors, etc.)

- Special interests (clubs, politics, religion, confidential items not to be discussed, etc.)

- Lifestyle (medical history, drink/smoke, favorite places for lunch/dinner, hobbies, conversational interests, personal goals, etc.)

- The customer and you (moral or ethical considerations, obligations to you or competitor, his management's priorities, how you can help, etc.)

This type of one-on-one business intelligence can be used to build a solid relationship with an important customer. As Internet broadens in scope of information available, more of the items listed above can be obtained from online sources. The most obvious sources are biographical databases (if the individual is of great stature or a senior executive at a large company), but other sources can include the company's own Web page (if they list bios or news releases) and newspapers that cover the individual's home or office location. Other Internet sources could include Usenet newsgroup postings or even a personal Web page in which the subject conveys personal information.

One of the most useful ways to work with this information is to add fields to a sales contact management database. Even Microsoft Outlook or Netscape Navigator's address book can be used to store and retrieve these items when needed (more about organizing in Chapter Fourteen). However, a full-featured sales contact management system like Symantec's ACT! or Maximizer Technology's MultiActive Maximizer provides advanced capabilities that fully utilize collected information. For example, ACT! has programmable pop-up alarms that remind you, for example, to send a birthday card. Some of the systems are activated by telephone system Caller ID functions. If someone you know calls, all of the contact information will pop up.

Maximizer integrates with the Internet to help the user build a marketing database within the contact management system. Through **www.listwarehouse.com**, Maximizer users can download lists of selected business or consumer contacts for import directly into their contact managers. This provides an integrated approach for direct mail or telemarketing enhanced with the follow-up capabilities inherent in a contact manager.

Gathering background information

One of the most useful forms of business intelligence is the press release. It is information that seldom gets into news media in its entirety. News releases can yield names and numbers as well as esoteric industry specific information that the press usually ignores. They are excellent sources of BI, particularly in the realm of marketing because they present the face that the issuing company desires.

Many marketing people are using the Internet for press release distribution, and, from a business intelligence point of view, it pays to understand how they're doing it. When you get their information from news sources, part of it is likely to have come from PR Newswire or Business Wire. Of course, many public relations people distribute news releases directly to the media and post them on their company's Internet sites, but vast, searchable databases can be found at the Web sites of these two commercial distribution networks.

An International Press Release Tool on DigitalWork (**www. biztools.digitalwork.com**) gives users the ability to send press releases to international media. With this international service, it's easy to send a newsworthy story to media thousands of miles away because they handle translations. You can send a press release to over 100 countries. DigitalWork serves as a front end to Business Wire, the DigitalWork Press Release tool, and over 30 other DigitalWork small-business services. With more and more businesses sending news releases electronically, you can find a considerable amount of business intelligence just on the two major press release distribution sites.

Internet-accessible newspaper database searching is now commonplace. Rather than subscribe to a database reseller, you often can search the source on your own. For example, during research on the New York real estate market, items were searched for within the Crain's New York Business Web site (**www.crainsnewyork business.com**). Getting down to the level of prominent individuals (leading sales people and brokers as well as executives) required the use of fee-based access to Crain's, one of New York City's leading business periodicals. For just a few dollars, this back-issues database provided many items that were useful in that particular project. It may be several months before this database is needed again, so the pay-per-view method of paying for only what you need on a one-time basis is a good value.

Dozens of small items were turned up, and these items when pieced together gave a representative overview of new salespeople who had been promoted over the years. Each time a salesperson was promoted to positions such as senior managing director, corporate managing director, managing director, assistant director, etc., a clearer picture of the overall organization emerged. When coupled with research into where new hires came from ("formerly a vice-president at XYZ Corp.") and later news releases about deals closed, a comprehensive picture can be obtained for a variety of marketing purposes.

In researching the New York real estate market for this assignment it was easy to find lists of the top real estate firms, but it is much harder to understand the competitive dynamics and key players. No-charge trade publication sites on the Internet as well as real estate trade association sites provided information useful in selecting the biggest firms. Most of the firms had individual Web sites that also provided a great deal of information about each firm.

Developing marketing strategies

High-level market strategy can be developed in a variety of ways. Competitive gaming develops information about a company, its markets, customers, and competitors, then uses that information to simulate the results of important competitive battles. Demographics, psychographic data, market statistics, and competitor details garnered from Web sites can add to the realism of competitive gaming. Several business-oriented games as well as some types of automated business planning software might be used instead of expensive proprietary software.

Portfolio analysis in marketing deals with the proverbial stars, cash cows, question marks, and dogs approach made famous by the Boston Consulting Group. It provides a framework to assess the relative opportunities and to optimize investments in a company's portfolio of businesses. Companies use portfolio models to guide investment trade-offs among strong or weak products, brands, and business units. Numerous market measures are required to properly address the products under evaluation. Much of these data can be identified or gotten via the Internet.

Scenario Planning is a popular strategic planning tool that can be adapted to market strategy development. It avoids the dangers of single-point forecasts by allowing users to explore the implications of several alternative futures. By surfacing, challenging, and altering beliefs, managers are able to test their assumptions in a non-threatening environment. Key to this approach would be creating backgrounder documents that help the participants orient themselves to the present case so they can realistically project themselves into future scenarios. This approach also might be coupled with new product development activities.

Marketing management

The adage "you have to spend money to make money" was never more aptly applied than to marketing. It is a costly activity that can include design and production of printed materials, large-scale mailings, advertising in print and electronic media, and showing wares at exhibitions. Marketing management often means "buying things."

For example, to get an idea of what types of advertising agencies are available (beyond your local area and immediate knowledge) you can view the Web sites of these potential marketing partners. Other consulting firms with specialized expertise can be located and reviewed without even contacting their personnel. This could include Media Barter agents and buyers, video producers, direct marketing experts, event marketing specialists, fulfillment services, market researchers, telemarketing firms, and naming experts, to list just a few of the services regularly purchased by marketing departments large and small.

Then there is the need to stay abreast of marketing trends. This can be accomplished via the Internet by reviewing trade magazines and pure Internet information services. IBIS is particularly helpful for marketers selling internationally because instant information from around the world is available.

For example, the Australian publisher Yaffa Publishing (**www. yaffa.com.au**) produces trade publications such as *Ad News, Ad News Handbook, Apparel Industry, Australian Creative, Commercial Photography, Digital Photography & Design, Packaging News*, and many other trade journals. Yaffa Publishing has a long history of magazine publishing. From its inception with the flagship title *Ad News*, Yaffa has steadily built a publishing company that produces more than 30 specialty magazine titles. The visitor to the company's Web site will be able to access much of the excellent information found in Yaffa's market leading magazines and buyer's guides.

www.adtalk.com presents an outstanding variety of links. Among these are links to advertising and media news sites such as:

- Advertising Age's Daily Deadline
- Advertising Age's Interactive Daily
- Adweek
- Brandweek
- Brill's Content
- Broadcasting & Cable
- Folio

- IQ News from Adweek
- Marketing Computers
- Media News from Reuters
- Mediacentral

- Mediaweek
- Print Soup from E! Online
- PR Week
- Publishers Weekly

Links to advertising and media research sites include:

- ACNielsen
- Ad Track from USA Today
- American Association of Advertising
- Agencies
- American Demographics
- Audit Bureau of Circulations
- Advertising Age Dataplace
- Competitive Media Reporting
- Digital Marketing Services
- Folio: 500
- Forrester Research, Inc.

- IntelliQuest
- Jupiter Communications
- Magazinedata from Media Central
- Mediamark Research, Inc.
- Nielsen Media Research
- NPD Group/PC Meter
- National Association of Broadcasters
- Newspaper Association of America
- SRDS Online
- USADATA
- U.S. Census Bureau

For more than 65 years, *Advertising Age* has been the leading source of marketing, advertising, and media news, information, and analysis. Through a variety of marketing publications and new-media platforms, The Ad Age Group has expanded the magazine's scope and industry leadership with its coverage of marketing to consumers and business to business across borders and the creative world.

The Ad Age Group includes *Advertising Age, Advertising Age International, Business Marketing and Creativity,* and Ad Age's Web site, **www.AdAge.com**. Other brand products include NetMarketing, the Ad Age Daily Fax, the global Daily World Wire, conferences and seminars, events and event marketing, and custom publishing. Examples of Ad Age Web site information:

- News and Features
- Daily Deadline
- Special Reports
- Features

- Bob Garfield's Ad Review
- People & Accounts
- Marketing Conferences and Events

- SponsorQuest
- AdMarket 50
- Interactive
- Interactive Daily
- Articles & Opinions
- CyberCritiques
- Interactive Conferences and Events
- Ad Age Dataplace

- Ad Age International
- International Daily
- International Conferences and Events
- Media Kit
- Subscription Information
- Smart Marketers
- Job Bank
- interACTIONS

Many other marketing publications and associations provide a wealth of industry information for marketing management. The small-business owner or entrepreneur who wears this hat also will find this information particularly useful in making the right marketing decisions for their business.

■ **MINI CASE:** **Geographic and demographic targeting in consumer marketing**

The author of a book targeted to senior citizens wanted to identify private communities in areas with a high concentration of retirees. While certain regions, such as South Florida, immediately come to mind, finer targeting is required to enable the author to contact people on a short list of communities that might be suitable for the seminar keyed to the author's book. Using the Internet to access the U.S. Census Bureau's Web site, data was collected on counties within Florida with the highest population rates of seniors.

This was a good start toward developing the information needed. The county rankings with the largest percentage of persons 65 and older pointed us in the right direction. However, more useful are specific towns and cities with the highest concentration(s) of the target demographic within each of the counties. Once the counties were identified, reducing the total by about one-third, the towns and cities within those selected counties were examined to determine the localities with the highest populations of seniors.

Up to this point we have identified the towns and cities that would be likely to have large populations of seniors. Now our focus shifted to the use of CD-ROMs to locate private communities with golf courses, one indicator of a higher income population of seniors. By searching for golf courses within the identified towns and cities, we were able to narrow the list even further to come up with about 100 likely locations for the seminar. The telephone book CD-ROM that was used might now be replaced by Web-accessible Yellow Page listings searchable by type of business and location.

Another aspect of this marketing program involved media including cable TV and newspapers. We were searching for cable systems and weekly newspapers with subscribers in the identified communities. Contacting the paper's advertising personnel for a telephone discussion regarding their reader's demographics and whether the paper publishes obituaries was the next step because the author had determined that this section of the newspaper had high readership among seniors and was relevant to his book and seminar. Newspaper and cable TV personnel also provide interesting information about the general situation within their communities.

■ MINI CASE: Geographic targeting in business-to-business marketing

An assignment to determine the membership potential for a high-level management association started with a broad-based environmental scan. The first step in an overall market study is to define geographic boundaries. In this example the boundaries include the following sectional ZIP codes: 064-069, 100-118, 070-079, and 088-089 (SW CT, Greater NYC, and NNJ). The 1992 Economic Census for the NY Consolidated Metropolitan Statistical Area provides a breakdown of the type and number of businesses in the area. The top 10 (by gross sales) are listed in Table 4.1.

Further research using the S&P CD-ROM system in a local library showed that, within the area, there are:
- •1,549 private companies with sales > $20 million
- • 802 public companies with sales > $20 million

Assuming that there are two executives per firm, on average, who might be interested in membership, we have a pool of nearly 5,000 potential members from which to draw.

A marketing goal was to be determined based on the most likely segments of the geographically defined market. This included the top companies within the following fields:

- Wholesale and retail trade
- Business services
- Finance
- Printing, publishing, and media
- Healthcare and pharmaceuticals

A search of the S&P CD-ROM limited by geography, sales, and the above categories produced a basic list of companies that formed the target group for recruiting purposes.

Table 4.1

BUSINESS CATEGORY	SIC	SALES $000	# ESTBLS.	$000/EST.
Wholesale Trade	50-51	$453,109,164	50,179	$9,030
Retail Trade	52-59	$140,681,060	120,935	$1,163
Service Industries—Taxable	70-79	$134,365,983	166,296	$808
Depository Institutions (not all banks included)	60-67	$54,927,315	951	$57,757
Security Brokers and Dealers	621	$53,912,840	3,702	$14,563
Service Industries—Tax Exempt	70-87	$52,822,858	15,008	$3,520
Printing & Publishing	27	$29,870,500	6,774	$4,410
Real Estate	65	$27,786,520	31,134	$892
Healthcare	80	$26,115,229	40,598	$643
Engineering, Acct., Research & Mgt. Services	87	$24,165,181	22,342	$1,082

■ MINI CASE: **Defining BI process in a newly deregulated industry**

Internet Business Intelligence for utilities is a timely example of a newly deregulated industry in which existing types of marketing must change to adapt to the new environment. The competitive landscape also included unregulated businesses and new business development. Business intelligence is an important part of the change, and one industry expert was quoted as saying "Electric utilities...need to be committing enormous resources to external marketing and competitive intelligence."[2]

This speaks to the need for definition of required business intelligence and the establishment of a process that supports not only strategic decision making but also provides for rapidly obtaining required background and key facts for marketing purposes. In addition to environmental scanning to stimulate and reinforce thinking about future moves, advanced analysis techniques combined with business intelligence targeting enables marketing to really know its customers, know more about their competitors, and better understand the changing business and regulatory environment.

Sources of business intelligence for the electric utility industry had been plentiful with several commercial and nonprofit organizations compiling statistics. This began to change with the advent of competition and new regulatory environment making some statistics harder to come by. Typical industry information had to be augmented with nontraditional online services and other business-oriented online services. However, the Internet and bulletin boards began to play increasingly important roles.

The new utility company business intelligence organization needed to consider business segments. Construction of a BI matrix to chart information flows was indicated. System implementation called for using focus groups and interviews to define requirements and study existing and potential systems and resources. A summary of initial recommendations for personnel and procedures was required, along with information on sources, techniques, and methods including hardware, software, and services.

Endnotes

1. Economic Intelligence Unit, "Marketing in Europe" (*EIU*, London, June 1993:367).

2. Roger W. Gale of Washington International Energy Group, editorial, *Public Utilities Fortnightly* (April 15, 1995).

CHAPTER 5

IBIS *FOR* *FINANCE*

The traditional responsibilities of the chief financial officer, who formerly always wore the title of treasurer, were primarily those relative to the preservation of company assets. Evolution of the function ultimately encompassed duties of accounting for all business transactions, financial planning, budgets, and other responsibilities that today are conceded to be in the area administered by a controller. Large accounting functions are divided into various segments, including general or financial accounting, cost accounting, systems and procedures, information systems, internal auditing, budgeting, tax reporting, and financial analysis.[1]

From the perspective of financial management, there are two overriding goals: profitability and viability. While IBIS cannot make up for bad planning, imprudent decisions, and lack of financial planning, it can provide highly specific data for short-term decision making (less than one year) in the financial realm and long term in the strategic realm in which financial professionals must sometimes operate.

Risk and reward

Business ownership is synonymous with risk taking—at least it should be. Risk taking involves both the possibility of profit and that of loss; if the unprofitable operations exceed the profitable, closing up the enterprise is just a matter of time.[2]

The information-gathering process involved in the extension of credit is one of the earliest practical examples of business intelligence. The fascinating history of Dun & Bradstreet illuminates this aspect of using information to ameliorate the exposure of financial risk taking.

The development of the West in early 19th-century America expanded the nation, leaving behind a trail of business opportunities. Providing credit to emerging businesses in this region became a precarious venture. To help merchants substitute facts for guesswork in their decision making, Lewis Tappan began in 1841 to establish a network of correspondents that would function as a source of reliable, consistent, and objective credit information. His Mercantile Agency, located in New York City, was one of the first organizations formed for the sole purpose of providing business information to customers.

In 1849, the rival John M. Bradstreet Company was founded in Cincinnati, Ohio. Two years later, the Bradstreet organization popularized the use of credit ratings with publication of the first book of commercial ratings.

To foster expansion, in 1849 Tappan turned the Agency over to Benjamin Douglass, a former clerk. The 1850s were a time of improved transportation and communication. Douglass capitalized on this change by expanding his network of offices, essentially providing the Agency with both new customers and superb information. Working as a credit reporter was a respected position that provided strong training. Among the reporters who went on to establish names for themselves were four U.S. presidents: Abraham Lincoln, Ulysses S. Grant, Grover Cleveland, and William McKinley. In 1859, Douglass turned over the Agency to his brother-in-law, Robert Graham Dun. Under the new name, R.G. Dun & Company, Dun continued Douglass's relentless expansion.

As America entered the 1930s, the effects of rivalry and economic depression on both R.G. Dun and The Bradstreet Companies could no longer be ignored. In 1933, the arch competitors merged to form Dun & Bradstreet. The rapid development of computing and communications technology in the post-war era was central to the growth of Dun & Bradstreet. Today D&B is the leading provider of business-to-business credit, marketing, purchasing, and receivables management and decision-support services worldwide. D&B provides more than 200 products and services. Their global database covers more than 50 million businesses worldwide.[3]

Maximizing profitability

The firm wants to be profitable, and it wants to continue in business. It is possible to be profitable and yet fail to continue in business. In maximizing profits there is always a trade-off with risk. The greater the risk we must incur, the greater the anticipated profit we demand. Certainly, given two equally risky projects we would always choose to undertake the one with a greater anticipated return. More often than not, however, our situation revolves around whether the return on a specific investment is great enough to justify the risk involved. Firms have no desire to go bankrupt, so it is no surprise that one of the crucial goals of financial management is ensuring financial viability. This goal is often measured in terms of liquidity and solvency.

Liquidity is simply a measure of the amount of resources a firm has that are cash or are convertible to cash in the near term, to meet the obligations the firm has that are coming due in the near term. Thus a firm is liquid if it has enough near-term resources to meet its near-term obligations as they become due for payment. Solvency is simply the same concept from a long-term perspective. Long term simply means more than one year. A firm must plan for adequate solvency well in advance because the potentially large amounts of cash involved may take a long period of planning to generate.[4] Aside from the basic reports (balance sheet and income statement) there are many functions that require more than accurate math. These financial functions, often performed by accountants, require information for informed judgment. Table 5.1 provides a sampling of these functions and how IBIS might support informed judgment.

Where would the financial professional find all the various types of information required for these and other informed judgments? There are hundreds of Web sites that are devoted to the many facets of financial operations. Nearly every business school has at least one professor who takes great pride in maintaining an outstanding Web site in his or her area of interest. Often teams, even large groups of academics and practitioners, create and maintain large-scale sites dealing with broad areas or specialties. Then there are many commercial sites offering related products or services, and many of these sites offer much more than product descriptions. Quite often they provide much useful background information or, at the very least, eliminate a lot of legwork in product or service comparisons.

Table 5.1

FUNCTION	QUESTIONS	INTERNET INFO RESOURCE
Asset Depreciation	Methods vary depending upon the asset life, projected salvage value, and situation	IRS, state division of taxation, FASB, forums, or newsgroups for QA and to discuss
Debt Amortization	May relate to cost of capital or capital structure issues, retirement versus conversion	Competitive financing rates from lenders, debt rating comparables, monitoring market conditions
Future Value	Theoretically simple time value of money calculation but has diverse application	Application-specific sources depending on situation
Cost Center	What are industry standards for activities that generate expense?	Comparables in SEC reports, analysis of related documents containing clues, trade associations
Sales and Cost of Sales	Compensation of sales personnel and other expenses, competition's promotional programs	Various sources for input to forecast demand, human resources cost, trade, and professional sites that report on sales issues and actions of competitors
Cash Flow Forecast & Analysis	Variability of collections from sales on credit and classes of customers	Short-term economic forecasts and indices of bankruptcies filed, reports of news that may affect classes of customers

Sources of information

A quick look at Yahoo!'s Finance and Investment page reveals the breadth of this discipline and some of the Internet resources that can help the professional in this field. Listed below are examples of Yahoo!'s Web site listings. The @ sign indicates subcategories available, while the number, which constantly changes, indicates Web sites for the topic.

- Banking (176)
- Bankruptcy (4)
- Bonds (9)
- Brokerages@
- Calculators@
- Chats and Forums (22)
- Commercial Financial Services
- Commercial Investment Services@
- Conventions and Conferences (6)
- Corporate and Securities Law@

- Corporate Reports (25)
- Currency (17)
- Dividend Reinvestment Plans (DRIPs)@
- Earnings Calendars (3)
- Economic Calendars@
- Economic Indicators@
- Economics@
- Estate Planning@
- Exchanges (117)
- Financing (54)
- Futures and Options (87)
- Hard Assets (5)
- Initial Public Offerings (23)
- Insurance (53)
- Investment Models (6)
- Investment Picks (9)
- Magazines@
- Mutual Funds@
- News and Media (324)
- Organizations (22)
- Quotes@
- Real Estate@
- Reference and Guides (139)
- Retirement Planning (53)
- Small-Cap Investing (9)
- Socially Responsible Investing (7)
- Software@
- Taxes@
- Technical Analysis (15)
- Trading Games and Simulations@
- Web Directories (49)
- Youth Resources@
- FAQs@
- Usenet (9)

A financial executive who wants to learn more about the current environment for initial public offerings would have 23 resources at hand. This could range from academic papers by business school professors to Web pages that present detailed schedules for the various stages of initial public offerings.

In another example, using the Internet to find new accounting software one might click on Yahoo!'s software category, then click on commercial software in the next window that appears. The following list is an example of types of commercial software for accounting purposes:

- Accounting@
- Banking@
- Bankruptcy@
- Consulting (58)
- Consumer Services@
- Directories (3)
- Electronic Commerce@
- Estate Planning@
- Factoring@
- Financing@
- Insurance@
- Investment@
- Payroll@
- Reviews@
- Tax@

Each one of these types of software is a heading for pages with dozens, sometimes hundreds, of individual titles leading to a company's Web page. Rather than spending the afternoon on the phone seeking basic information, by using the Internet the financial professional can narrow down the choices to a handful of likely packages.

Free software

One example of spectacular software available free of charge on the Internet is Business Analyst. You can download your copy of Business Analyst 4.0 Lite from **www.redflag.com**. Accurate financial analysis is the difference between a company that enjoys financial growth and one that suffers financial distress. Lucrative decisions concerning your business are the basis for creating a thriving firm in an aggressively competitive world economy. In order to make such decisions one must look with an introspective eye at the goings on within the structure of that business. The steps leading to success start with a powerful analysis tool, and RedFlag's Business Analyst is specifically designed for just such an endeavor.

Business Analyst provides for a comprehensive analysis of your company's financial operations, interactions, obligations, assets, and liabilities, which in turn gives you a clear picture on what your company is doing right and what it's doing wrong. The reports and graphs generated by Business Analyst are a direct result of the data that makes up the input screens. RedFlag's Business Analyst is a troubleshooter that not only isolates and identifies past, current, and potential problems, it also offers solutions to those problems.

Some companies have the resources to help them utilize professional consultants to assist them with their key decisions. Others either do not understand the advantage it gives them, or do not want to invest in this kind of knowledge. Business Analyst gives you the best of both worlds. It provides you, the business owner/manager, with the tool to become your own consultant.

Business Analyst uses your existing Income Statement and Balance Sheet data together with other data to monitor the machinery that is your company. Through a series of comprehensive reports, it assists you in identifying your relative strengths and weaknesses and helps you chart a course that will amplify your strengths and substantially negate your setbacks. The reports include a series of ratios widely accepted as standard in the financial industry. With these tools you can monitor your business comparing your own historical averages, your long-term goals, and national averages. From this type of analysis you will be able to see where you should be going and develop a plan of how to get there.

There are thousands of software programs available at little or no cost under freeware and shareware distribution. Many of these are like Business Analyst—fully functional trial programs (lite versions) available at no charge to promote the sale of the more-capable versions by the developer. Several major Internet sites provide centralized access to this freeware and shareware, the latter being "try before you buy" programs.

Strategic financial management

Like the top management person who wants to save more than just time, the financial professional will want to fully utilize an Internet Business Intelligence System. That means more than balancing the books. It means taking a strategic view and using IBIS to fill in comprehensive details of the firm's long-range financial picture.

"I'm from the government, and I'm here to help you" is an oxymoron. However, government reports often provide information useful from a private enterprise financial perspective. Two examples are reports and studies prepared by the Federal Reserve and the General Accounting Office (GAO).

The Federal Reserve's duties include conducting the nation's monetary policy by influencing the money and credit conditions in the economy in pursuit of full employment and stable prices. They gauge the current and projected health of the economy as well as the all important interest rates charged on capital. The Federal Reserve Board of Governors site is indispensable.

Here's a partial listing of reports, studies, and information available at **www.federalreserve.gov**:

- Availability of Credit to Small Businesses
- Bank advisories
- Bank Regulation and Supervision
- Beige Book
- Board actions
- Community Reinvestment Act (CRA)
- Directory: Community Development Investments
- Domestic and foreign banking cases
- Domestic & International Research

- Electronic Stored-Value Products
- Enforcement actions
- Federal Open Market Committee (FOMC)
- Foreign central banks
- Humphrey-Hawkins
- Information Security and Financial Fraud
- Markets for Small Business- & Commercial Mortgage-Related Securities
- Press releases
- Reports to Congress
- Reserve Bulletin articles
- Statistics: Releases and historical data
- Supervisory staff reports
- Surveys and Reports
- Testimony and Speeches
- Working papers

Much of this is solid business intelligence for the financial professional. In addition to these current reports of a short- and medium-term nature, other government documents of interest might include GAO Reports. GAO conducts financial audits, assists Congress with public policy analysis, evaluates the effectiveness of federal programs, issues legal opinions and decisions, adjudicates bid protests filed by private companies concerning the award of federal contracts, and investigates waste, fraud, abuse, and mismanagement in government.

Here's a brief sample of GAO Reports:

Farm Service Agency: Information on Farm Loans and Losses. RCED-99-18. 11 pp. plus 2 appendices (4 pp.) November 27, 1998.

Medical Savings Accounts: Results from Surveys of Insurers. HEHS-99-34. 3 pp. plus 1 appendix (14 pp.) December 31, 1998.

Dairy Industry: Information on Prices for Fluid Milk and the Factors That Influence Them. GAO/RCED-99-4, Oct. 8 (180 pages).

Forest Service: Distribution of Timber Sales Receipts, Fiscal Years 1995 through 1997. GAO/RCED-99-24, Nov. 12 (48 pages).

*Consumer Price Index: More Frequent Updating of Market Basket Expenditure Weights Is Needed.*GGD/OCE-98-2.

Small Business Administration: Secondary Market for Guaranteed Portions of 7(a) Loans. T-GGD-98-184.

These reports cover strategically important aspects of financial issues. While many of these reports are specific to a market niche, others may be broadly applicable to most businesses. Medical savings accounts, business regulation, and product safety are applicable to a broad range of businesses while those dealing with defense contracting, dairy prices, and timber sales likely are of interest only to businesses in those markets and their suppliers. The full text of all GAO Reports is downloadable at **www.gao.gov**. Applicable reports constitute one type of input to the IBIS knowledgebase that a business would compile.

Of all the management disciplines, finance provides the most concrete metrics by which the health and performance of an organization can be judged. Such basic tools as the income statement and balance sheet are standardized methods used to measure and compare performance. Because financial people routinely interact with these and many other numerical indicators, they are in an excellent position to integrate internal accounting data combined with Internet-derived information into one or more representative management tools and techniques.[5] Included are types of external Internet-derived data (such as the Federal Reserve and GAO Reports) that might be input to the basic model.

Strategic metrics

Activity-Based Costing increases the accuracy of cost information by precisely allocating overhead and other indirect costs to products or customer segments. Possible inputs include competitor prices for similar products, inflation forecasts and economic statistics such as unit labor costs, productivity, and stage of processing producer price indices.

Balanced Scorecard defines what management means by "performance" and clarifies whether the desired results are being achieved. It translates mission and vision statements into a comprehensive set of performance measures that can be quantified and objectively appraised. Possible inputs include external comparisons of performance relating to financial, customer value, and business process or innovation aspects.

Pay-for-Performance systems tie compensation directly to specific business goals and management objectives. These systems try to improve individual accountability; align shareholder, management, and employee interests; and enhance performance throughout the organization. Possible inputs include salary information derived from resumes posted in newsgroups and positions offered, and industry-wide performance as benchmarks, as well as economic statistics such as consumer price index, employment cost, and personal income.

Shareholder Value Analysis is the process of analyzing how decisions affect the net present value of cash to shareholders. The analyst measures a company's ability to earn more than its total cost of capital. Possible inputs include economic factors surrounding the cost of capital and expected cash flows.

Economic data

A penchant for prognostication makes the business economist visible. Visibility is proportional to vulnerability. When the forecast is right, the business economist is just doing what he is paid to do, but if he's wrong he is spotlighted on center stage. Executives want more than vague projections on what course the economy will take. They want to know precisely what lies ahead.[6] The National Association of Business Economists (NABE) is a large and active group. This group and many other economics-oriented groups have substantial presences on the Internet.

Macroeconomic indicators are compiled and disseminated via a variety of sources, some of which are Internet accessible. The Federal Reserve Board's famous "Beige Book" is just one of the regular reports issued on the nation's economic health.

An increasing number of economic indicators are being reported by The Conference Board (**www.conference-board.com**), a top-management membership association based in New York City. This organization has its own staff of economists involved in an extensive Economics Program. The program provides a variety of services, publications, research, and briefings. The Board provides an excellent Economic Information Service called BoardView. See Figure 5.1.

The BoardView service includes a large existing database and frequent updates that can be downloaded via the Internet. The system includes data analysis and utility features and the ability to read commentary (written economic analyses) associated with specific indicators. Some of the more important indicators are as follows:

Consumer Confidence: The consumer confidence index is based on a monthly survey that is compiled from a representative sample of 5,000 U.S. households. It is classified as a leading indicator and measures consumer optimism and pessimism about general business conditions, jobs, and family income, and attitudes and expectations six months hence that are useful in evaluating economic trends and prospects. The index is highly volatile, plunging in the early stages of a recession, and recovering dramatically in the first year of business recovery.

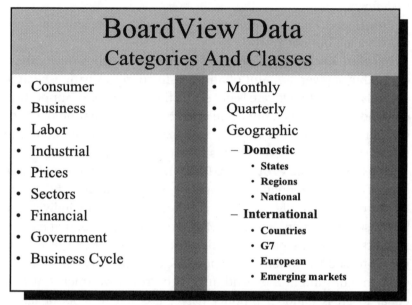

Figure 5.1

Consumer Price Index (CPI): The CPI is a measure of the average level of prices of a fixed market basket of goods and services purchased by consumers. Monthly percent changes in the index reflect the rate of change in such prices and are followed as an indicator of inflation. The CPI is available by expenditure category, and by commodity and service group for all urban consumers and for wage earners. "All urban consumers" is the more widely quoted measure since it is a more inclusive group, representing approximately 80 percent of the population.

Personal Consumption Expenditures: Personal consumption expenditures are the estimated total consumer spending for goods and services. Consumer expenditures account for about two-thirds of the Gross Domestic Product. In the national accounts, spending for durable goods, non-durable goods, and services breaks down consumer spending.

Corporate Profits After Tax: This is measured by the gross income after deducting all costs, including borrowed capital and consumption of fixed capital. Net profits after tax are minus currently accrued income tax liabilities. A portion is usually distributed to enterprise owners in the form of dividends. The residual represents retained earnings. Total funds generated by corporations are cash flow.

Employed: Persons who during survey week were either at work or with a job but not at work.

Foreign Exchange Rate: This is the rate at which one currency will buy a given amount of another. In countries with exchange controls, the exchange rate is not set by the free forces of supply and demand in the market, but more often by the intervention of either the central bank or an exchange stabilization fund to maintain the rate at some desired level. Differs from official exchange rate.

Gross Domestic Product (GDP): GDP represents the total value of the country's production during the year and consists of the purchases of domestically produced goods and services by individuals, businesses, foreigners, and units of government. The four major components of GDP are personal consumption expenditures, gross private domestic investment, net exports of goods and services, and government consumption expenditures and gross investment. GDP is equal to gross national product (GNP) less net receipts of factor income from the rest of the world.

Industrial Production Index: A measure of the physical output of U.S. manufacturing, mining, and utilities industries. The index includes a representative group of products, but excludes agriculture, construction, and services. The relative importance assigned to individual sectors is based on quantity and value data determined by government censuses.

Labor Force: The civilian labor force includes those of the civilian non-institutional population 16 years and older who are classified as employed or unemployed. Total labor force includes members of the armed forces.

Producer Price Index (PPI): PPI is a measure of the average level of prices of a fixed basket of goods received in primary markets by producers. Monthly percent changes reflect the rate of change in such prices. Changes in the PPI are followed as an indicator of commodity inflation. The stage-of-production structure of the PPI organizes products by degree of fabrication into three broad groups: finished goods; intermediate materials, supplies, and components; and crude materials for further processing. See Figure 5.2.

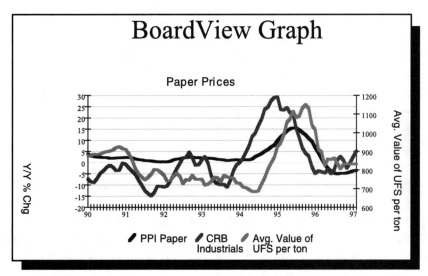

Figure 5.2

Productivity: Productivity is generally a ratio of output to input. Indexes of production, number of physical units produced, or the real value of products are among the commonly used measures of output. Labor input may be measured by the number of persons employed, or more often by the number of hours worked per person, and the capital input by the real value of the stock of tangible capital in use. According to the experts at The Conference Board, "Economic data can provide insight. It can help answer questions like:

• Is a country present- or future-oriented?

• Is a recession due? Are there signs of it?

• How volatile is a country's exchange rate?

• Are consumers optimistic and eager to spend?

"Economic data can be used to: identify business drivers and new markets; develop scenarios; make investment decisions; evaluate cost structure; perform benchmarking and compensation analysis.

"Identifying relationships between macroeconomic and industry- or firm-level statistics helps financial analysts and others to better understand how business is impacted by the economy. Determinants of demand for and supply of product also can be examined through the use of Consumer Prices, Industrial Production, Leading Economic Index, Consumer Spending, Inventories and Labor Costs.

"To identify New Markets the analyst can compare relative economic performance across countries or regions and characterize a market's short-run stability and long-run competitiveness and demographic trends. Suggested Economic Statistics for these purposes include Consumer Confidence, GDP, Consumer Spending, Balance of Payments, Trade and Personal Income.

"In the Development of Scenarios one can vary assumptions to effect different outcomes. Differing scenarios generally are developed in relation to macroeconomic change (high-growth/low-growth) and to account for innovation and Technological Development as well as external shocks (natural disasters, resource depletion). How might the operating environment be affected by emerging trends can be addressed through study of GDP, Consumer Prices, Interest Rates, Exchange Rates, Trade Statistics.

"Investment Decisions use economic analysis as backdrop by evaluating tradeoffs between risk and growth opportunities. What industries/countries are growing and what drives that growth? These decisions can be made with a higher degree of accuracy by considering financial market data, GDP, Production and Consumer Prices."

Even with a highly organized IBIS, chasing down regularly updated data from a multitude of sources can be quite time-consuming. The BoardView approach to managing and analyzing data illustrates the need for other sources of information to support or enhance the overall BI effort. BoardView is a centralized source for data and analysis with minimal effort required to maintain the database via Internet downloads from The Conference Board.

This is no small issue if you consider that BoardView has 4,000 variables from many data sets derived from state, regional, national, and international bodies, as well as proprietary Conference Board Economic Indicators such as Consumer and Business Confidence, Help-Wanted Advertising, Short-Term and Long-Term Forecasts, and Business Cycle Indicators. Conference Board commentary is a part of the system so users can read analyses of key economic variables written by Conference Board economists. Chapter Thirteen covers non-Internet sources of information more fully.

Internet and accountants

Accountants in public practice increasingly are called on to deal with the Internet in a variety of client engagements. These encounters fall into several categories including auditing of Web sites, forensic accounting, business valuation, and management advisory services. These are just some of the business activities in which the accountant must have a good working knowledge of how and where to get information as well as some technical knowledge of the Internet's workings overall.

Most accountants were early adopters of computers and spreadsheets. Many have developed a basic familiarity with the Internet and now are ready to move on to more sophisticated use of this unprecedented resource. Strictly speaking, accountants do not need external information because they deal with financial data generated within the organization. In practice, accountants do need a variety of types of information, almost on a daily basis. Higher level accountants provide management advisory services, and therefore they must be able to master the capability to quickly locate almost any required information.

Perhaps because their professional work often departs from the routine, accountants need to tie into information networks to stay abreast of changing professional practices, laws, regulations, and client needs that evolve with all of these changes. Starting with the 330,000-member American Institute of Certified Public Accountants (**www.aicpa.org**), there are hundreds of state, regional, and local specialty associations, state societies, accounting firm cooperative groups, and other related entities with which accountants need to stay in touch. Early adopters used CompuServe, but the Internet is now the preferred channel of communication.

Strategic company audits, due diligence investigations, and business valuations

We have seen how business intelligence can be integrated into the development of the organization's vision and mission statements, as well as how it supports the business planning process and also marketing and finance activities. An area of financial operations and accounting is the evaluation of a business for the purpose of merger or acquisition. This framework also can be used for periodic examination of the existing well-established organization. Common approaches usually include either some variation of due diligence investigation or business valuation process.

In the strategic audit, management takes an organizationwide perspective to:

- Evaluate performance of the business and its managers

- Scan the internal environment to determine current strengths and weaknesses

- Scan the external environment for current threats and opportunities

- Pinpoint problems

- Evaluate and select specific strategies to guide the desired actions

More practical and detail-oriented approaches that move beyond the textbook strategic audit include due diligence investigation and business valuation. Due diligence is a process by which those interested in acquiring a business examine any and all pertinent aspects of the business. Business valuation is more of a financial analysis used to determine a sale price for a business. Elements of either or both can be used to critically study a business for strategic purposes.

Let's suppose for a moment that you are a young financial professional who has been asked by the president of your company to help him evaluate a potential acquisition. You want to brush up on this topic, since your MBA diploma's frame has gathered a bit of dust since you graduated several years ago. The first stop might be a search engine, but which one? Search engine personalities are covered more in depth later in Chapter Ten. If you try Yahoo! you might find that all hits are for firms that perform due diligence. If you use AltaVista you'd find lots of hits but none really useful in reviewing a current approach to due diligence. Searching the Business Researcher's Interest site (**www.brint.com**) doesn't turn up anything but it does suggest Infoseek, which turns up a useful reference.

This reference (near the top of the list) is a well-written article about business acquisition that appeared in the *Washington Business Journal*, May 5, 1997. The Nation's Capital column by Jonathan Silver was titled, "Buying Another Business? Do Your Due Diligence."

"What is due diligence?" Silver asked rhetorically. "Due diligence is a way to assess the financial and commercial risks inherent in a potential transaction. By reviewing and verifying a company's records, you make certain you understand the real opportunity. Due diligence is nothing more—or less—than the research you should do before you put your money down. Your due diligence actually begins with your review of the company's business plan and with your first meeting with management."

Silver goes on to suggest, "Your next step is to draft a term sheet. The term sheet describes the kind of agreement you are prepared to make if your due diligence shows that the seller's representations are accurate. Drafting a term sheet early is actually useful to both parties. You don't want to undertake a time-consuming and expensive review unless a deal is likely. The seller won't want to give you access to internal data without similar guarantees."

Silver continues, "The seller accepts your terms, you draft a letter of intent and you're ready for due diligence. Now what? All due diligence answers two questions: Am I comfortable with the managers? Am I comfortable with the business? Ask all the senior executives to provide references. These should include former investors, bosses, colleagues, employees, customers, and vendors. Talk to ALL these references. It is not uncommon for professional investment firms to make twenty to thirty calls just about the management team. Increasingly, potential buyers hire investigation firms to do background checks to complement their own efforts. These companies sift through huge publicly available, but difficult to access, records, looking for litigation, name changes, criminal records and more."

Here's where IBIS begins to play a role in the due diligence process. Simply finding and contacting references may be a challenge since not all information provided may be current. Finding individuals is an art in itself, and sometimes the hardest to locate provide the best information. Also, news reports in local papers and feature articles in trade publications, some written by individuals you check, often provide substantial background verification. Other relevant data can be obtained and used, within the IBIS and PROACtive framework, to thoroughly perform due diligence. This is just the beginning of the process of looking outward to understand the company and its industry.

"To learn more about the industry, try contacting associations that focus on this sector or business schools whose faculty specialize in the field. You might also retain a consultant to do an analysis of the sector for you. Information on publicly traded companies is available by reviewing Securities and Exchange Commission filings," Silver wrote. "Most well-run companies will be able to provide you with all the data you will need to be able to make a decision. (In fact, if the information is not available, you've already learned something from the due diligence process.)"

Silver explained, "You will want financial data, including audited financial statements, copies of state and federal income tax returns, property tax bills, records of capital expenditures, equipment leases, accounts payable and accounts receivable records, a summary of commitments and contingent liabilities, and a schedule of all debt, complete with repayment detail. You will also want to verify representations about the company's assets. Include here such documents as government and general sales contracts and all trade names, patents and copyrights."

Silver suggested closely examining all external obligations, including litigation, environmental liabilities, seller obligations, joint-venture agreements, royalty or other contingent payment obligations, loan agreements, and other obligations. Some of these can be checked or expanded upon via Internet sources. Such internal obligations as payroll records, employment and consulting contracts, labor and management agreements, sales commission structures, benefits programs, and compensation policies as well as retirement plans also need to be carefully considered. All of these items must be rapidly obtained, organized, analyzed, and communicated as part of the acquisition process.

Another critical examination method that is supported by input from business intelligence is business valuation. There are three general approaches to valuation: market data approach, balance sheet analysis (comparing the standard balance sheet with market and liquidation values), and replacement cost analysis. All three approaches require external data for the analytical process.

Software is available for business valuation, deal structuring, and appraisal reporting. These programs are designed for business executives, CPAs, and others who need to determine business values. This specialized software (or spreadsheet templates) helps the user to very closely examine all financial aspects by helping him or her to gather valuation data, perform financial statement analysis, compare important financial ratios, and present different types of valuations.

In addition to specific business data gathered from investigation of an existing business or project, a variety of external information is required. For example, annual statement studies compile financial ratios and operating statistics for comparisons. Statistics on the economy as a whole and within specific types of financial instruments is another element for comparison. Reports on prices of businesses sold in the same industry provide a very valuable comparison. Other data reported on mergers and acquisitions, officers' compensation, and specific industry statistics are valuable external data.

This can be illustrated by the case of an acquisition in which a fair market value must be established. A company desires to expand its market by acquiring another company in a related business. Certain standardized questions, as required by IRS rules or Generally Accepted Accounting Principles, must be answered, and in the process the decision will become easier because business intelligence has been developed.

These topics may need to be addressed:

- History of the company and nature of the business

- General economic outlook and outlook of a particular industry

- Financial condition of the business

- Book value of the stock

- Earnings capacity of the company

- Dividend paying capacity (if applicable)

- Whether the enterprise has goodwill or other intangible value

- Sales of stock and the size of the block to be valued

- Market prices of stock of comparable companies
  traded on exchanges

While some of the above can only be derived from internal financial records, even those documents need to be checked against some type of external verification. For example, articles and government reports that deal with the local, regional, and national economy may have significance. Also, trade and professional associations and publications usually compile industry statistics. If there are comparable companies with publicly traded stock then these might be used as a comparison. Laws and regulations directly affecting the business or impacting its market may need to be researched. Much of this information can be found on the Internet.

Having used IBIS to quickly and efficiently compile a comprehensive document, those advising the decision makers provide the foundation upon which the decision will be made. In the end, personal and professional judgment is a large factor, but that judgment is based largely on the facts at hand. Internet Business Intelligence plays an important role in developing them.

The essence of business is risk. If you invest in a savings bank account you minimize your risk while earning modest returns on your investment. Put that money in a riskier investment and you may enjoy much greater return. However, the greater the potential return usually the greater the risk of losing all or part of your investment capital. Think of this on a much larger scale and you can see why business intelligence is important. Any information that helps minimize financial risk will give you a business edge.

■ MINI CASE: Shall we extend our contract with
a particular vendor?

A large manufacturing business had contracted with a software development firm to produce an enterprisewide system. There had been several setbacks, and our client wanted to better understand the software firm's inner workings and the potential for even greater future problems. The target company had a well-stocked Web site that provided a wealth of pertinent background information.

One of the first things to look for on a target company's Web site is a section for press releases. These documents are rich in detail that often does not make it into print, even if the release is issued. Stripping away the "fluff" in a press release and focusing on specific details helps the analyst gather "bits and pieces" that lead to a foundation for solid conclusions.

News releases about new products, contract awards, joint ventures, and partnerships often provide details not published elsewhere, as well as names of people who can comment on some aspect that's important to the client. Also, releases can yield interesting insights into a company's progress or lack of it, particularly when two or three years of releases are analyzed on a timeline basis.

A key executive was dealing with the client, so a careful evaluation of his capabilities was required. Information from the company's Web site biography was crosschecked against other official sources, and additional details were garnered that proved useful in the overall evaluation. We found that two brief stints in executive positions at other companies were not mentioned in his "official" bio. This mismatch between the current bio and other listings in the CorpTech reference library was significant. It provided further insight into the client's original questions about the target: management resolve; the resources to complete the task; and the internal communications within the target company.

It was generally known that the target company had been involved in contract litigation with other unsatisfied customers, but the details were unknown to my client. While it is not currently possible to access most court records via the Internet, it is likely that the federal court's Public Access to Court Electronic Records (PACER) will migrate to the Web. Many federal and state court sites are appearing on the Internet, some with actual court documents. All of these puzzle pieces were fitted together, and a summary report was prepared for the client.

Endnotes

1. Russell F. Moore, editor, *AMA Management Handbook* (American Management Association, Inc., New York, 1970: 4.1 through 4.8).

2. Sydney Prerau, editor, K. J. *Lasser's Business Management Handbook* (McGraw-Hill, New York, 1960:162).

3. **www.dnb.com/aboutdb/history/history.htm.**

4. Steven A. Finkler, *Finance and Accounting for Nonfinancial Managers* (Allegro New Media, Passaic, NJ, 1994).

5. *Management Tools and Techniques: An Executive's Guide* (Bain & Company, 1997).

6. Walter E. Hoadley, Ph.D., *Looking Behind the Crystal Ball: How to Use a Business Economist Successfully* (Vantage Press, New York, 1988).

7. Presentations by Eileen Ring, The Conference Board, October 23, 1997 and March 24, 1998, New York.

CHAPTER 6

IBIS FOR SMALL-BUSINESS OWNERS AND ENTREPRENEURS

America's 23 million small businesses employ more than 50 percent of the private workforce, generate more than half of the nation's gross domestic product, and are the principal source of new jobs in the U.S. economy.[1] However, the survival rate for small business start-ups is not encouraging. Neither is the personal bankruptcy rate.

Easy availability of charge card credit, if used judiciously, can be a great benefit to the small business. Who wouldn't be tempted by a significantly below market six-month interest rate that coincides with a buying period just before the business's peak sales months? More risky but not uncommon is the rolling of several thousand dollars of business expense from card to card and paying the very low introductory rates during a slow year. These tactics are not too risky for an established business that can predict cash flow. Financing inventory, additional personnel, and expansion expense is a constant hurdle for the growing business, but it is by no means the only challenge faced by the small-business owner.

The small-business owner or entrepreneur usually wears many hats, serving as CEO, CFO, marketing director, and more. They must create and market the product, finance the operation, and deliver the goods or services to the customer, as depicted in Figure 6.1. This is compounded when the small business is a professional practice. Small-business people must perform an information juggling act, keeping on top of all aspects of their own business, knowing what's happening in the marketplace, and keeping a wary eye out for potential problems.

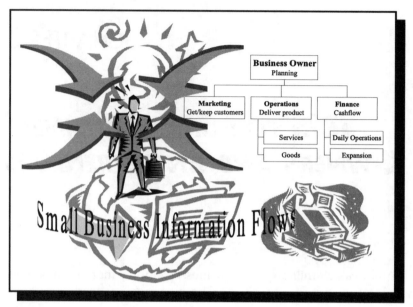

Figure 6.1

What business are we in? That's a common question that must be frequently addressed by many small-business owners. High energy, enthusiasm, and resources can be wasted if the business lacks a focus and appropriate strategy. Corporate strategy, discussed in Chapter Two, begins with vision and mission. While vision describes a succinct image of what the company is and how it fits into its marketplace, corporate mission sets forth the goals, in a very broad sense. All too often the dynamic and fast-growing small business gets off track while aggressively striving to capitalize on tempting opportunities. Any size business should strive for the optimum position within its marketplace. Gaining a better understanding of the market and aligning short- and long-term strategy also can be efficiently accomplished with IBIS.

Retaining existing customers and finding new ones is another major project for all but the mom and pop corner store, which, like it or not, is disappearing. Nearly all small business owners would kill for the "gold list," one that produces even five percent response in a direct mail campaign. Some businesses pay list brokers $1 per name or more for lists that often don't work. By taking advantage of the collection and communication aspects of IBIS, one can quickly, perhaps at little or no expense, compile something close to a personalized gold list.

Financing the small business, determining which markets to exploit, and developing customers are three major interests of small-business owners.

Small-business financing

Actually, many businesses do use credit card financing in their early phases of growth. The difficulty in arranging a commercial line of credit during the first year or two versus the quick and easy availability of charge card credit (sometimes as much as $25,000 or more) makes the latter very attractive. When you consider that there are some ridiculously low rates (as low as 2.9 percent for the first few months) for balance transfers, you get the picture.

Going to **www.excite.com** and clicking on Money and Investing takes us to **quicken.excite.com** and presents a finance-oriented Web page with lots of choices. Click Banking and Credit and you find another subtopic, Credit Cards, under banking topics. This screen presents information about credit cards, including "Searching for a credit card?" which takes you to the **www.bankrate.com** card selector page. Making some selections from pull-down menus presents card company choices with various rates and features. Bankrate. com even has a rate alert service to keep you informed about changes in the personal finance industry.

This is just one example of the many ways you can determine which cards might be most useful for your particular situation. If you travel frequently, it might make more sense to find a card that quickly accumulates points toward free travel or one that offers a time-saving concierge service to free you up from travel planning tasks. Using the Internet for business intelligence means developing a system for competitive advantage. Certainly, the fastest, lowest-cost competitor always has an advantage in the marketplace, and this next example shows how you can do it too.

As a small business establishes itself, it develops a credit history upon which banks look favorably. Finding the right bank can be accomplished using IBIS sources and methods. But what happens when you're involved in a business where a fairly large amount of upfront capital is required? If you have $200,000 equity in your home and are willing to secure the loan with it, then a similarly valued loan would be no problem. If you're not, you may want to take a look at the various small-business financing programs supported by the United States Government (USG).

SBA financing programs

The U.S. Small Business Administration (SBA), established in 1953, provides financial, technical, and management assistance to help Americans start, run, and grow their businesses. With a portfolio of business loans, loan guarantees, and disaster loans worth more than $45 billion, SBA is the nation's largest single financial backer of small businesses. America's 24 million small businesses employ more than 50 percent of the private workforce, generate more than half of the nation's gross domestic product, and are the principal source of new jobs in the U.S. economy.

A quick glance at **www.sba.gov** shows you that when the subject is small business, the topic often is financing. There is a great deal of information to be discovered via the Small Business Administration. Rather than playing telephone roulette and wasting two or three weeks in the process, the Web site will give you the exact information you need and the forms to fill out too. Loan and surety bond programs, lending studies, loan statistics, and even software to calculate costs and other information directed toward financing for small business can be found at the site.

One of the SBA's major financing programs is the Small Business Investment Company (SBIC). A news release from **www.sba.gov/news/** details the SBA Venture Capital Program and how it produced a payoff for U.S. taxpayers. A venture capital fund licensed and funded by the SBA paid the agency $5.3 million, the largest shared profit to that date in the agency's revamped SBIC.

The payment to SBA from MidMark Capital of Chatham, New Jersey, represents taxpayers' share of the profits realized from investments made with funds backed by SBA. One company that benefited in its early stages from SBA-backed SBIC investments, Intel, paid more in taxes last year than the SBA's entire budget for 1998, according to the SBA. Apple, Compaq, Federal Express, Outback Steakhouse, and thousands of other companies obtained SBIC funding in their early stages. SBA-backed SBICs made more than $2 billion in investments in small businesses in FY 1997. Since September 1994, the SBA has licensed almost 70 new SBICs in the participating securities program with private capital of $1.2 billion. To date, SBA has provided those licensees with SBA-backed leverage amounting to almost $1 billion. Those licensees have invested $1.2 billion in much-needed equity capital in 1,500 small-growth companies.

Financial staging

While SBA is a significant financial facilitator, there are many other organizations and individuals that provide a wide range of funding for growing businesses. There are at least eleven distinct stages of business development that require an inflow of resources:

- **Seed**—Developing the idea, market research, and study of concept feasibility

- **Research and Development**—Development of a new technology or product

- **Start-up**—Planning and preparation for a new business

- **First-Stage**—Initial expansion and development of an existing, profitable business

- **Second-Stage**—Second significant funding effort

- **Recapitalization**—Refinancing or consolidating debt

- **Mezzanine** (Expansion)—Third significant funding

- **Acquisition**—The purchase of another company or facility

- **Bridge**—Financing between stages of significant funding

- **Leveraged Buyout**—Using the assets of the acquired company to fund acquisition by another business interest

- **Management Buyout**—A business is purchased by its management

Each stage requires access to external information. Seed, R&D, and start-up cover a broad path that includes not only finance but also research into potential joint venture, partnership, licensing, or franchising activities. The birth of the business could be the proverbial light bulb suddenly turned on, idea scratched out on a napkin in the restaurant, or garage tinkerer fulfilled. Today's marketplace demands swift execution of new or developing technology and rapid exploitation before the next generation surfaces. Fortunately, there are many places one can turn to for idea development. Government labs, academia, and large corporations all are involved in this type of work and most eagerly seek partners of one sort or another.

A business requires a different mixture of resources as it evolves from one growth stage into the next, and every business has a distinct resource requirement distinguishing it from other businesses. Manufacturing operations, for instance, require a lot of start-up money up front. The bulk of the cash that goes to high-tech businesses is in the form of seed money. Service businesses may have a desperate need for financing at the mezzanine level. Some entrepreneurs never reach the later stages of development, and are content with that. Your particular business and the direction you want to take it are additional factors determining the amount of financing.[2]

Venture capital

Finding venture capital (VC) via the Internet is simple, but getting the VCs to invest is quite another story. Let's tackle finding first.

Using the newsgroup search engine **www.deja.com**, type the phrase "venture capital" into the query box. You can search for messages (772-plus when queried) or forums (39-plus when queried). Although we'll go into more detail about newsgroups and mailing lists in Chapter Eleven, it's important to note here that person-to-person connections are important in packaging and submitting a VC proposal. By connecting to individuals through newsgroups, you'll get personal assistance, learn a lot, and possibly get the all-important referral or connection that results in getting the financing you need. For example, among the 39-plus forums are alt.business, alt.business.consulting, alt.business. misc, alt.invest, misc.entrepreneurs, misc.invest, misc.invest. canada, and misc.invest.stocks among many others, including several non-U.S. newsgroups. You'll also find references to Web sites like **www.capital-connection.com** and for further information.

Whether you go to credit card or capital market to finance your business, all venues can be researched quickly and easily using IBIS.

Research and planning

There are numerous Internet sites where small business start-up or expansion is the main focus. For example, **smallbusiness. yahoo.com** presents to the visitor a complete Web page with topics such as starting a business, finance, office supplies, technology, communications, e-commerce, legal, taxes, sales and marketing, human resources, and international business and trade. There are featured articles, selected news items, conference and seminar listings for many different fields (though not very complete at the time we checked), a similar conventions and trade shows listing, various tools and services and, of course, things to buy. Overall this page is an excellent grouping of resources for someone who is starting a small business.

Follow **www.altavista.com**'s top-level choice of Business and Finance and you will get a subcategory for Small Business among other business-related topics. Click on Small Business and you get several subcategories including Advice and Guides, Credit and Financing, Education for Women, Franchising and Opportunities, Government and Law, Home Business, News and Magazines, Organizations, Products and Services, State and Local, and Venture Capital. Clicking on news and magazines provides a very comprehensive list of sites for small business. Clicking on Venture Capital results in a similarly extensive list of useful Web sites.

www.lycos.com presents a variety of Web guides including one for business. The selection result presents Industries (follow your field), Issues (hot topics), and Small Business (ideas and advice). Click on Small Business and you get 28-plus choices. Business Opportunities presents many good sites offering an enormous amount of useful information. Free software for business brings you to the ZDNet software library, which presents hundreds of general purpose and specific industry shareware, freeware, and demo programs. One interesting program was StockVue2000 by AlphaConnect.

This is a good example of the kind of software of particular interest to businesspeople who can't rely on a corporate computer department to supply them with standard (though expensive and sometimes insufficient) name brand software. Entrepreneurs aren't bashful about trying something new, and they like to get a bargain in the process. Shareware (and increasingly available freeware) is a perfect way to find and try specialized software.

For example, StockVue2000 is a free 32-bit tool that uses the Internet to get valuable information about major companies, making it perfect as a core tool in IBIS. Tell it which businesses you want it to track and which Web pages to watch, and it automatically monitors them. It can alert you when the competition is in the news, when a vendor updates its pricing Web page, and more. It stores all the information you might want about each company on your hard drive for instant access.

It uses the Web to retrieve CEO and CFO names, company address, and phone numbers. Stock quotes and recent stock history can be displayed. You can even get a street map to company headquarters. The program also helps track all of your contacts at each company. You can enter free form, date-indexed notes detailing any additional information, along with company-specific information.

StockVue2000 keeps you up-to-date on general economic news by retrieving the online, public edition of *Investor's Business Daily* every day. Sample data is included to let you see how StockVue2000 stores and updates information, without having to enter anything yourself. Although the program is free (actually, advertiser-supported), you'll need to complete a brief survey before you can use it. StockVue2000 is a great way to keep tabs on both your competitors and your customers.

Finding customers

Small-business customer development, supported by IBIS, might begin with an overview of the market. There are two basic types of business: retail and business to business. The first type requires a storefront or some means of presenting your product or service to the public. This can be walk-ins who are just passing by or people who are responding to your marketing, say by bringing in a discount coupon. Most of the principles of IBIS apply to retail operations, and there are many resources listed in the appendix that will be very useful. For the purpose of this discussion about finding customers, we'll assume a scenario that involves a business-to-business operation that, at least initially, can be home-based.

Let's assume that we have decided to establish a business selling laboratory supplies. We know the business, having worked in the field, and, due to circumstances related to a corporate restructuring, we have the opportunity to leave our current employer, a manufacturer of specialized laboratory equipment, with a generous severance package. The next step is to go into business selling related but noncompeting products and services to the same market. We even have the blessings of our former employer and promises to supply their specialized products for resale in a geographic area traditionally underserved by the company.

Of course, the promise does not extend to sharing customer lists, so that's the first thing we need to do. Being a forward-thinking entrepreneur, we will set up an Internet Business Intelligence System as a first priority. The first step involves planning our marketing program, which will rely heavily on the promotion of personalized service with direct customer contact. We want to search out and find a highly select group of unique technologies that can be offered along with our laboratory supplies line. One possible approach is to find U.S. government-developed technology that can be commercialized. Check **iridium.nttc.com** for a wealth of tech-transfer information.

Focusing in on individual people is another way to market laboratory equipment and supplies. One of the first steps should be to telephone friends and colleagues and find the correct people to talk to in their organizations. Depending on the size of your circle of acquaintances, this can be very fruitful. However, most people will run out of leads after a relatively short time. The next step might be to draw upon the information resources of professional associations and societies in your field. Most of them publish a membership directory, and many are included on Internet. Also, you'll find that there are Internet mailing lists for members and others who are interested in the field.

Managing these contacts brings us to the heart of IBIS—organizing. This topic will be covered in depth in Chapter Fourteen, but we need to address the issue now to illustrate what to do with a growing list of personal contacts. A basic contact management system is a must. This can be performed with software ranging from a spreadsheet (each contact record is a row, columns are common fields) to a sophisticated contact manager or database system networked for multiple users. Most people will use ACT!, Goldmine, or Maximizer, which are specifically designed for contact management. An alternative is to use Microsoft Outlook, which is designed to keep individuals and small groups operating efficiently with a calendar, schedule, and address book. If you do most of your correspondence by e-mail, you might consider using Netscape Messenger's address book, which is surprisingly versatile.

Marketing organization for small business

Actually planning and conducting a marketing program is beyond the scope of this book. However, once the potential buyers start contacting you by returning bingo cards, calling on the telephone, or responding to your marketing efforts in some other way, you'll need to track them and build business intelligence files on the most likely prospects. Of course, the size of the sale will dictate the amount of effort that should go into this part of a small business IBIS. Obviously, if your average sale is a few hundred dollars you'll probably only maintain the bare-bones minimum of name, address, telephone number, etc.

On the other hand, many business-to-business situations, including our laboratory systems and supplies scenario, could yield thousands of dollars in sales over a one-year period. The largest clients often have the longest gestation periods, meaning that you'll have to court them for a year or two before getting a contract. IBIS can help enormously. For example, if you have met someone at a professional society event and they seem like a potential customer, you may need to maintain regular contact over a long period to finally "close the deal." First you might send a note saying "It was a pleasure meeting you." Then you might follow up with a friendly call to say hello and "touch base." Beyond that, you'll have to dream up something unless both of you really enjoy talking with each other. For busy professionals, it usually takes more than that.

IBIS can help by giving you a reason to maintain contact and the means to do so. If you follow the PROACtive process and install some form of IBIS, you'll be tracking the individual, his company, and the niche within his industry. From this you'll be able to derive the ability to stay in regular contact. You can congratulate the person on his promotion or the big order his company just landed. Sometimes you'll surprise him with news he should have known and you'll be respected for that.

Getting the message across, communicating in the PROACtive process, can be accomplished in many ways. A simple letter or faxed note, an e-mail, or a telephone call might be appropriate at certain times. Keeping track of all the contacts is important so you don't overdo it or underrepresent yourself. Most of the better contact-management systems will keep a record of every action taken from within the system. It logs phone calls each time one is placed. It logs each letter sent or document created. This way, you can decide how often or over how long a period you want to contact that person.

When a visit is in order, you can use the contact management system to tell you who your contacts are in a certain ZIP code area. Then you can decide which ones to call on for a personal visit. You might want to consider supplementing your personal contacts with some from a database. This is particularly effective if you are starting out and only have a few potential clients in a particular area.

You can utilize several Internet resources or library CD-ROMs to look up potential clients and export them to a file that can be imported to your contact management system. Let's continue with the laboratory salesperson scenario. Go to **www.companiesonline. com** and you'll find Dun & Bradstreet's site that let's you search for companies by size, location, and industry. To go beyond the basics you'll need to register. Once you register, you can specify the industry category, desired size, range, and location. Your hits will give you the name and address of the company, the DUNS number, phone number, type of location (branch or headquarters), immediate and ultimate corporate parents, contact name and title, annual sales and employee size, trade names, industry description, Web address and e-mail, and ownership structure.

Other sources of similar information are the Yellow Pages directories on various Web sites. A good example is **www.infospace.com**, which has a powerful Yellow Pages capability. You can enter business type and click to get a list of business categories. Let's assume you want to find all of the testing laboratories in Atlanta. If you click on that specialty, you get a list of those businesses. The basic list gives name, address, and telephone number information.

You can generate a street map showing the exact location or generate driving instructions. These can be handy if you like to "drop by" to introduce yourself. Detailed information and a basic credit rating are available at a cost of $5 per listing, which is pretty steep considering you can get most of the same information free at D&B's site. A nice feature of Infospace.com Yellow Pages is the ability to expand the list of companies generated by going outward in ten-mile increments. At the bottom of the list you can click on "expand search area" to continuously increase the size of your dragnet.

You can print this out and use it, or copy and paste it into your word processor. One procedure is to print the listing then have an assistant call to determine who is the right person to contact and to check the information and perhaps ask for additional information. This person then can enter the information into your contact manager.

To import the data into your contact manager you'll need to rearrange the data and make it into a comma delimited file by searching for carriage returns and replacing them with a comma (assuming each piece of information is on a separate line). After you have copied and pasted listings and translated them into a file that can be imported, you can begin to populate your contacts database so that when you visit a city, you can call to introduce yourself and suggest a brief introductory meeting if appropriate.

■ MINI CASE: Entrepreneur-investor's study of temporary staffing industry

A report was commissioned to orient venture capital investors who were considering the future growth prospects in the temporary staffing industry. The report provided an overview of the field and explored industry leaders' growth strategies. This group felt that investment in the staffing industry had strong potential and a high rate of return on investment. The industry was growing rapidly but was complicated by fragmented niche services. The report also provided the foundation for a well-defined business plan that could capitalize on the specific sectors that had the best potential for growth.

First stop in the research was the U.S. Bureau of Labor Statistics Web site. Data for the Help Supply Services category and Personnel Supply Services, falling into the Standard Industrial Classification (SIC) code were downloaded. These data showed significant growth. Employment growth in SIC 736 went from just under 1.4 million workers in 1989 to nearly 2.4 million in January 1995. Briefly quantified, this translates into a projected $41.2 billion market in 1995, predicted by another industry source found via the Internet. Estimated revenues during the period were (in billions) $21.5 for 1991, $24.6 for 1992, $28.9 for 1993, and $35.7 for 1994 with $41.2 forecasted for 1995. Industry segments that were the largest percent gainers during the five year period were professional/specialty and technical/computer, which includes accounting and technology.

Using a telephone directory CD-ROM for gross counts, it was determined that the total number of office locations within this industry included 23,469 placement agencies, 2,243 employment registries, 857 employment agencies, 11,146 labor resource services, and 5,195 help supply services. A breakdown of office locations by geographic area was possible by exporting the records to a spreadsheet and sorting them by ZIP code then using database analysis functions in Excel (more about this in Chapter Fifteen).

More and more professional occupations are joining the ranks of the temporary workforce—doctors, lawyers, engineers, system analysts, and chief executive officers to name a few. This demand has given rise to local or regional specialty niche staffing companies that have built substantial businesses focused on providing particular industries or locales with the needed professionals. Finding relevant associations via the Web led to the National Association of Temporary Services and their annual "Profile of the Temporary Workforce."

Comments from a variety of industry experts were located electronically either on the Internet or CD-ROM. For example, an Andersen Consulting managing partner based in New York City was quoted in an article on outsourcing published in the *Florida Times Union*. A relevant article about temporary workers in the accounting field was found in *The Wall Street Journal*. The Gartner Group, an industry research firm with a significant Web presence, estimated the worldwide commercial and governmental information technology services market.

Using a library CD-ROM the top 25 companies were determined. This provided the targets for further research.

1. CDI Corp.	$1,097.6 M
2. Adia Services, Inc.	$918.5 M
3. Robert Half International, Inc.	$446.3 M
4. Butler International, Inc.	$393.3 M
5. Watsco, Inc.	$283.7 M
6. Management Recruiters International, Inc.	$209.0 M
7. RemedyTemp, Inc.	$187.0 M
8. Accountants On Call Div.	$130.0 M
9. Hospital Staffing Services, Inc.	$120.6 M
10. Alternative Resources Corp.	$94.5 M

11. Source Services Corp. (Dallas, Texas)	$91.0 M
12. Nurses' House Call	$85.9 M
13. Technical Aid Corp	$78.0 M
14. Heidrick and Struggles, Inc.	$77.0 M
15. Interim Healthcare, Inc.	$65.0 M
16. Lee Hecht Harrison, Inc.	$50.0 M
17. Fairfax Opportunities Unlimited, Inc.	$46.0 M
18. Russell Reynolds Associates, Inc.	$46.0 M
19. Travcorps Corp.	$45.0 M
20. Romac and Associates	$40.0 M
21. Spencer Stuart and Associates, Inc.	$40.0 M
22. Digital Solutions, Inc.	$38.0 M
23. Arlin Personnel Services	$36.0 M
24. MSI International, Inc.	$35.0 M
25. Boyden World Corp.	$30.0 M

The top companies are publicly owned and therefore required to provide regular reports to the Securities and Exchange Commission (**www.sec.gov**) for inclusion in the Electronic Data Gathering And Reporting (EDGAR) database. Any material development that could significantly affect the decision to buy or sell shares must be distributed in a timely manner and usually is transmitted via a press release. The majority of these press releases are transmitted via Business Wire and PR Newswire. SEC filings include a management discussion section in which corporate strategy is outlined. The following representative information was compiled primarily from SEC documents:

Adia Services, Inc. is a provider of temporary and permanent employees. The parent company is Adia S.A. Adia Services employs 2,500 people and has an operating revenue of $918.5 million (FY ending December 31, 1993). Revenues have increased steadily from $185 million in 1984, although the increase was reversed during the period from 1990 to 1991, most likely tracking the recession of that period. According to Staffing Industry Report, August 28, 1995, Adia's North America operations increased by 20 percent and operating profits increased 21 percent in the second quarter of 1995. However, it was reported that "the company warned that there are signs for a slowing of growth in our main markets." Ranked by the Report in terms of second quarter 1995 revenue, Adia was fourth, behind Manpower, Olsten, and Kelly.

Adia Services operated through 523 offices under multiple brand names as of January 2, 1994. The company services over 20,000 business, professional, and governmental organizations in the U.S. The personnel provided by the company have a wide range of skills, including secretarial, clerical, accounting, healthcare, light industrial, marketing, data processing, and word processing, according to S&P. During 1993 the company employed about 250,000 temporary employees, including the temporary personnel employed at franchised offices.

The company operates under the names Adia throughout the U.S., Thomas Temporaries in California, TempWorld mainly in the Southeastern U.S., FirstWorld Temporaries in Dallas, Texas, Abar Personnel in San Francisco, West Temporaries in Chicago, Staffinders in Houston, Texas, and Temp Connection in the greater NYC area, and several other brand names.

Accountants On Call specializes in providing temporary and permanent accounting personnel from entry-level positions, such as bookkeepers and payroll clerks, to professional positions such as staff accountants and controllers. Accountants On Call had an estimated revenue of $130 million (FY ended December 31, 1994). Nursefinders specializes in providing relief staffing to hospitals and nursing homes and personnel for home healthcare. Adia Information Technologies specializes in providing data-processing professionals to business and industry. Lee Hecht & Harrison provides outplacement counseling.

Computer Horizons, a diversified provider of information technology services and solutions, is representative of publicly traded companies whose fortunes are tracked by investment company analysts. The opinions of these analysts sometimes are available via finance-oriented Internet sites, which may be hyperlinked from the company's own site. Also library CD-ROMs, particularly the InfoTrac General Business

File, sometimes have industry analyst reports. This information was distilled from such a report:

Computer Horizons Corp. coverage in a company report by R. F. Reed of Janney Montgomery Scott, Inc., Nov. 14, 1994, stated that "A richer mix of service offerings, combined with better focus on managing direct and indirect costs at both the corporate and branch levels, has resulted in ongoing margin expansion. Operating margins are expected to increase to 7.4% in 1994, up from 6.2% and 5.2% respectively in 1993 and 1992...The company is benefiting from both strong market demand for computer programming personnel as well as management's successful development and marketing of higher value-added services in the areas of mainframe applications reengineering, client/server applications development, and outsourcing. We believe that the secular trend toward converting fixed costs to variable costs among large corporations will be a key driver to the industry's and Computer Horizons' growth over the next several years."

A company report by K. A. Stulo of Robert W. Baird & Co., Inc. dated October 19, 1994, stated that a "New Emphasis on Profitability Is Proving Successful. After a past mistake of emphasizing topline growth to the detriment of profits, Computer Horizons' management has spent the past several years eliminating the worst performing branch offices, replacing several branch level managers, tying compensation levels to profit goals, and generally preaching the importance of profitability to all employees. The improvement in operating margin from a low of 2.6% in 1989 to 7.3% in the most recent quarter provides proof that management's efforts are succeeding...We believe the strength of Computer Horizon's business reflects the growing trend toward MIS outsourcing and flexible staffing, as well as rapid changes in technology which drive end-users to seek outside expertise to solve data processing problems. Computer Horizon's pipeline of potential outsourcing business for both large and small deals continues to look promising."

The report commissioned by the venture capital investors illuminated various facts and points of view that pointed toward a potentially lucrative investment.

Endnotes

1. U.S. SBA statistics, **www.sba.gov.**

2. "Vankirk's Venture Capital Directory," vol. 1, from Entrepreneur's Guide to Raising Money, CD-ROM program (Online Publishing, Inc., Arlington, VA, 1994).

3. Information U.S.A., CD-ROM program (InfoBusiness, Inc. and Matthew Lesko, 1995).

CHAPTER 7

A FRAMEWORK
FOR INTERNET
BUSINESS INTELLIGENCE

Now that the reader knows more about the current and potential characteristics of the Internet that relate to its use for a business intelligence system, we need to examine a framework for business intelligence (BI) process. Anyone in business will benefit from a structured approach to the acquisition and use of information. The focus here is on creating valuable business intelligence from electronic information.

Many people suffer from varying degrees of anxiety due to information overload. During the early 1990s, executives began to feel overwhelmed as new forms of computer communication began to pile on to the already growing heap of print and electronic information they had to deal with. They began to look for various means to harness technology and manage information overload. See Figure 7.1.

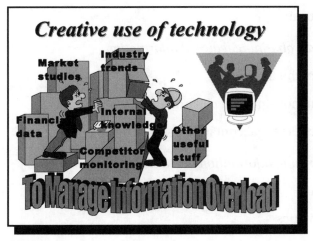

Figure 7.1

Various types of Executive Information Systems and Decision Support Systems were tried and largely rejected. During the second half of the 1990s the dominant trend was development of systems to facilitate communication with everyone in the organization who had access to a computer. The standard bearer for this was Lotus Notes, and later became Microsoft with its Exchange platform. Netscape to some degree became a player when it began to integrate conferencing features into its software.

The PROACtive methodology

To enhance any of these technological facilities, one needs to adopt a methodology that guides its use. This is particularly important in the Internet Business Intelligence System (IBIS). Let's look at the basic steps that are required for a formal IBIS program. Understanding the overall process will set the stage for putting together the right tools. These tools must be selected on an individual basis and sometimes even on a project-by-project basis.

The PROACtive process (Figure 7.2) includes the following steps:

Planning the intelligence cycle

- For a particular research project

- For an entire system

- Strategic

- Tactical

Rapidly obtaining required information

- From the Internet

- From non-Internet electronic sources

- From personal contacts

Organizing information and data

- Text

- Numerics

- Multimedia

Analyzing collected information and/or data using appropriate methods

Communicating intelligence to decision makers

- Translating, interpreting, verifying, evaluating

- Creating and enhancing mobility, if required

Figure 7.2

Software is more than a means to accomplish a task on a computer. *Often the software itself provides a framework for accomplishing the task.* It is in effect a methodology. In a way, software transfers knowledge from the developer to the end-user. Years of schooling and apprenticeship are no longer needed for basic competency in a variety of intellectual endeavors. Sophisticated knowledge and even wisdom can be packaged into software and easily digested by the end-user.

Scoping out the system

As shown in Figure 7.3, the overall goal of IBIS is to combine information from the Internet, supplemented with information from other sources (CD-ROMs and purchased data files as well as internal documents and human intelligence), and organize, analyze, and communicate so it becomes valuable business intelligence aligned with business goals. Various intelligence products are derived from one or more IBIS databases, with appropriate analytical tools employed when required.

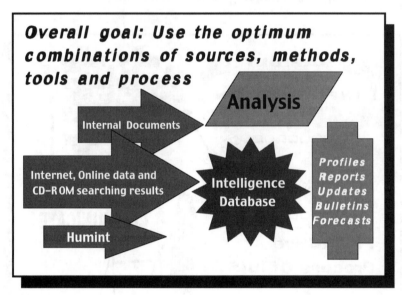

Figure 7.3

Why do you need such a system? That's a fair question, especially considering the amount of "team" activity in business today. But, despite management's orientation to facilitating this somewhat collective approach, there often are people who don't fit the "team" mold. Then there are small-business people or solo professionals. It's important to note that an IBIS can be established for one person, or it can be expanded to accommodate a large team.

This latter situation can be viewed in a hunter/gatherer context. Entrepreneurs, business owners, and salespeople tend to be street fighter types (hunters), while the categorization of information-intensive knowledge workers (bespectacled and sporting pocket protectors?) might coincide more with the agrarian notion of gatherers. These laughable and gross generalizations are nonetheless useful to understanding why an IBIS system is necessary while taking into account different personality types. Simply put, the gatherers need to provide the hunters with information as depicted in Figure 7.4.

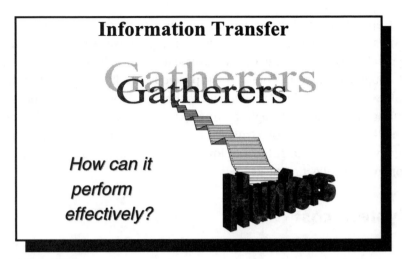

Figure 7.4

Before one launches into any endeavor, some type of assessment is called for. It's natural to do market research before developing and marketing a product. Similarly it's wise to perform a needs assessment when more than a handful of people will be utilizing an IBIS. The first goal of any business intelligence function in a large organization should be: "How can we help you to do your job better?" See Figure 7.5.

Figure 7.5

Depending upon the situation, a focus group needs to discuss the issues, examine current resources, and propose an action plan. Typically, there are one or two advocates who drive the process, although it's quite possible that a top executive will charge a subordinate with the task. In a small business there may be a similar process, but needs assessment might be thought out and written down by the small-business owner or a trusted employee. The implementation can involve one or two talented employees who can take on the more time-consuming collection tasks.

System cost

Once assessment is accomplished, planning begins for the system. This book presumes that the Internet will serve as the core of the system. However, as previously shown in Figure 7.3, other sources will supplement the Internet. These sources are covered in Chapter Thirteen. Building outward from that requires planning as a first step. Strategic planning skills need to be brought to bear for decision making that will shape your IBIS. Choices are made among business issues, objectives are determined, and action strategies are developed. See Figure 7.6.

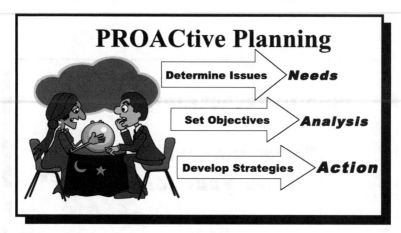

Figure 7.6

An analogy is called for here. For those who purchase printing, you can get three things from a printer, but you can only have two at one time. Those things are good quality, fast turnaround, and low price. You can get fast turnaround and high quality but you sacrifice low price. Alternatively, you can get high quality and low price but you'll have to wait longer for your order to be completed. Similarly, knowledge has a cost.

The dimensions of BI are usefulness and timeliness. In an ideal world we would have the best possible business intelligence instantly. In reality, cost gets in the way of a perfect solution.

BI has value because it develops information that can be used to enhance business decisions that result in more profitable activity. But determining the value and usefulness in relation to the cost is an important consideration when establishing an IBIS. For example, putting a part-time lower-level person in charge of developing business intelligence may result in a valuable end product at the cost of speed. It might take weeks to do what a few higher-skilled people can accomplish in a day or two with the right tools.

The cost function of BI is nonlinear because usefulness peaks at some point in time and levels off or even declines thereafter. At the same time, a push to rapidly develop important BI in a short time means that initially the cost curve might be steeper.

BI often is an iterative process of discovery and knowledge building. If the usefulness of an IBIS is measured by the degree to which comprehensive and relevant end products are developed in the shortest possible time at the lowest possible cost, a curve is suggested as represented in Figure 7.7. Finding the optimum point on the cost curve is the goal. Cost variables are human resources, sophistication of tools, and expense of information sources. Human resources employed generally are controlled exclusively by management choice.

Categorizing tools

IBIS can be implemented with software ranging from that already residing on most business computers to sophisticated, costly software with a steep learning curve that provides extraordinary capabilities. Major functions (organizing, analyzing, and communicating) will be covered in later chapters. At this point in the development of an IBIS we should group the types of software into three categories, depicted in Figure 7.8, roughly correlated to cost. Let's examine three broad categories of software for IBIS functions that can be compacted into basic, intermediate, and advanced levels.

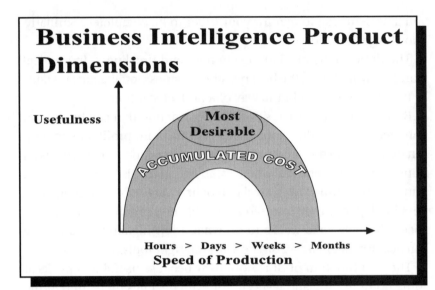

Figure 7.7

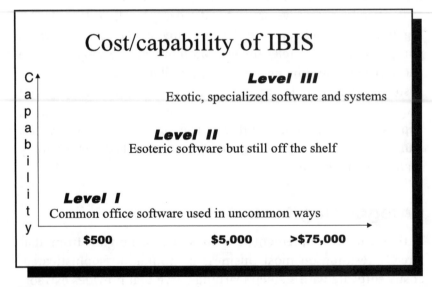

Figure 7.8

Level I—Basic IBIS

Business intelligence production can be accomplished using common office software to its maximum capability. This level could be characterized as a personal business intelligence system because it overlays the PROACtive methodology onto everyday software found on most business computers. One can employ the PROACtive process using Level I tools to perform basic business intelligence functions:

- **Plan**—Spreadsheet, word processor

- **Rapid Retrieval**—Internet browser

- **Organize**—Windows Explorer

- **Analyze**—Spreadsheet, word processor

- **Commmunicate**—Presentation, word processor, and browser's HTML publishing capability

Organizing with common office software can mean storing and managing text (even complex documents with embedded multimedia) using a word processor (Microsoft's Works, Office, or even Notepad) by creating directories for certain categories of information. Find File functions of Windows with text search features (part of the word processor software) can be used to locate one or more desired files containing text appropriate to the task at hand.

Analysis can be accomplished by compiling data and analyzing it in spreadsheet software. For example, Microsoft Excel is capable of performing quite sophisticated analysis functions. The user can import or enter statistics, analyze them in various ways, graph these data, and export them to other software.

For those folks who want to be independent of Microsoft (or are die-hard WordPerfect fans) or are just plain loyal Canadians, Corel Corporation's WordPerfect Office (WPO) Professional is an excellent alternative to Microsoft Office. In addition to the great word processor, WPO has spreadsheet, database, and presentation modules as well as CorelCENTRAL.

Corel's suite is a cost-effective Level I approach. It's a good choice for those who want to implement IBIS on a strict budget.

All WPO functions are applicable to the production of business intelligence in IBIS. This package goes beyond the capabilities of Microsoft Office because of its strengths in communication. The CorelCENTRAL and Netscape integration as well as the Web site builder and portable document creator all weigh in Corel's favor over Microsoft. Corel (which in the mid-1980s was best known for its graphics programs and clip art) has great strength in communication with other features that enable it to provide a strong foundation for IBIS.

Level II—Intermediate IBIS

Acquiring software other than that commonly found on the business desktop (word processor, spreadsheet, etc.) thrusts us into level II. This software can range in price from under $100 to a few thousand dollars. This software is function specific, designed to move the user to a much higher level of sophistication than can be accomplished with common office software.

You can store and find text in Microsoft Word, but a low-cost software package called "askSam" provides greater magnitude capability for managing textual information and creating reports from it. The software from askSam Systems (**www.asksam.com**) provides a range of solutions, but their basic package permits entry or import of information using free-text or template formats as required. This software is considered to be a free-form database, and it has many advanced searching capabilities as well as a variety of other functions that greatly increase the efficiency of working with unstructured information.

Covered more thoroughly in Chapter Fourteen, askSam illustrates a point on the cost curve where a modest investment in specialized software can add disproportionate value. Dealing with 200 or 300 text items can be easily accomplished with common office software. When an IBIS gathers that many items in a week, the situation soon demands a more powerful solution. At this point there is a need to consider acquiring a specialized package like askSam. It should be pointed out that the planning of your IBIS should anticipate the level of need prior to implementing the system.

Another illustration of a Level II type of software is DI-Diver, an analytical "front end" for business intelligence development. DI-Diver, a product of Dimensional Insight (**www.dimensional insight.com**) helps users perform ad-hoc reporting and analysis without SQL or a complex report writer. Dimensional Insight pioneered multidimensional data visualization, analysis, and reporting solutions, enabling flexible, easy, fast access to large amounts of corporate data, whether in data warehouses, relational or ODBC-compliant databases, or flat text files.

All reports and graphs are live objects. This means users can click on any data to display the underlying detail in very large databases. The advantage of this software is that users can perform a variety of sophisticated analyses from multiple large-scale existing databases without programming knowledge. DI-Diver can process data from any ODBC-compliant data source, or it can read ASCII files on the desktop or file server.

DI-Diver transforms data into a multidimensional model that nontechnical managers can navigate quickly and easily, following a natural thought process. It allows users to obtain successively more detailed levels of information by delving deeper and deeper into the multidimensional model.

When creating a report, the user chooses a category from the DI-Diver console. The initial dive retrieves summary data for this category. The user then chooses a second category from the console. In the second dive, DI-Diver will only search through the data retrieved from the first dive and then display the data that relates to the category for the second dive. The third dive goes deeper still into the data retrieved by the second dive. Once the report is generated, it can be refreshed when new data is available and shared with others. If the report generates additional questions, the user can go back to the multidimensional model directly from the report to answer them.

Once the model has been created, DI-Diver allows users to view their data in many formats, including CrossTab, MultiTab, bar charts, pie charts, and scatter plots. The user can switch between them instantaneously. All graphical elements are live, giving immediate access to underlying detail. DI-Diver makes it easy to rank, group, and compare data. The user can define new calculations to use in displaying data. DI-Diver also calculates statistics and supports alert agents.

The software includes a mapping function and automated report generation. All of these features allow the user to perform ad-hoc analysis quickly and easily without predetermined assumptions about what trends or factors the user was looking for. For example, DI-Diver is able to automatically compute year-to-date vs. last year-to-date summaries of data along any dimension. DI-Diver's time series wizard allows the user to compare this year-to-date and last year-to-date, this period and last period, or rolling totals using any available date, month, quarter, or alternate calendar scheme. DI-Diver includes three-dimensional graphical views for presentations.

Level III—Advanced IBIS

Various programs, heavy-duty software systems costing in excess of $10,000, can be part of an advanced IBIS platform for serious business intelligence operations. Two examples of this category of software are Pathfinder and DB2 by IBM.

Pathfinder Intelligence Software development was sponsored by the U.S. Army's National Ground Intelligence Center. It is heavy-duty software that operates on SunOS 4.1.3 or Solaris 2.x operating systems in either a networked or in a stand-alone environment under UNIX using TCP/IP.

Pathfinder provides computer tools and methods to analyze and gain intelligence from large amounts of textual information. Its software tools allow relationships of people, facilities, or other user-defined entities to be easily seen and used as a guide for more detailed investigation. The software automates the process of loading electronic media into a database, organizing the data for analysis, and identifying relationships, which allows one to visualize information and draw conclusions.

The windowing capability of the Pathfinder environment allows the use of multiple tools, simultaneously increasing speed and efficiency of its users. It also provides administrative tools to manipulate, edit, delete, and share databases. This environment encourages teamwork, the sharing of relevant data among team members, the rapid assimilation of new information, and the quick identification of data relevant to a problem.

The Pathfinder system was designed to automate the labor-intensive steps in gathering intelligence from large amounts of information. It allows the user to sort, arrange, assemble, compare, group, match, search, graph, and build matrices and clusters. Data can be used from virtually any information source as long as it is textual data in ASCII format. Pathfinder uses commercial software tools to reach its full capability. This software includes intelligent full-text search and retrieval, word and phrase counts, and the means to display links and relationships between important elements in the data. All of these tools have been conceptualized and developed over the past five years by government intelligence analysts.

Business decision makers have vastly different levels of expertise and different needs for data analysis, ranging from tailored reports delivered over the company intranet to interactive mining to identify clusters, associations, and trends present but often hidden in the mass of unwashed data. IBM offers a wide range of approaches and tools to meet varied needs. Applications provide tailored user interfaces to address specific problems.

IBM's DB2 Universal Database is a relational database management system that is fully Web-enabled, scalable from single processors to symmetric multiprocessors and to massively parallel clusters, and features multimedia capabilities with image, audio, video, text, and other advanced object relational support. Various components can be combined to suit requirements.

DecisionEdge is IBM's complete, end-to-end business intelligence solution. This includes database, database servers, data mining, text mining, data analysis, industry data models, consulting, implementation services, and training. DecisionEdge is a solution for customer-relationship management, containing a number of standard and customized product and service options.

The IBM Intelligent Miner family helps you identify and extract high-value business intelligence from your data assets. Through a process of "knowledge discovery," your organization can leverage hidden information in its data, uncovering associations, patterns, and trends that can lead to competitive advantage.

Intelligent Miner for Data enables users to mine structured data stored in conventional databases or flat files. Its mining algorithms have been successfully used to address business problems in areas such as customer-relationship marketing and fraud and abuse detection. It allows users to increasingly leverage the data warehouse and more quickly derive business value from that investment.

Intelligent Miner for Text harvests information from text sources such as customer correspondence, online news services, e-mail, and Web pages. It has the ability to extract patterns from text, organize documents by subject, find predominant themes in a collection of documents, and search for relevant documents using powerful and flexible queries.

The basic PROACtive framework for IBIS can be used in any size business. However, there are additional factors that must be considered when establishing a process in a larger corporation. Development of objectives, understanding current processes and capabilities, alternatives, resource requirements, and the willingness of management to make a commitment are some of the factors that must be considered. The entire process could be a multi-year undertaking or can be implemented in about six months, following the timetable given later in this chapter. The first step in any case is planning.

Planning—What do we want to know?

One of the most interesting books I have ever seen is the *Businessman's Checklist for Success* by W. C. Shaw and G. J. Day,[1] published in 1979 by Coles Publishing Company, Ltd. in Toronto. This book, with its politically incorrect title, is a wonderful collection of checklists for every conceivable type of business problem. Corporate planning, management, marketing and selling, manufacture, distribution and storage, personnel, and finance and accounting fields are covered. The book shows how nearly all business situations can be boiled down to several steps or areas of concern.

This is the beauty of templates: They excise verbiage to highlight the essential elements of information. These elements can serve as a guide for information gathering, or they can become fields in a database record. Addressing the basic principles of company planning, *Checklist* asks "What do you need to know to plan ahead for the company?" Its answer:

Producing a plan
- What is necessary
- What is possible
- How it can be done

Results of plan
- Application of plan
- Management needed
- Controls
- Systems
- Organization

Essential elements of information

The correct definition of the essential elements of information (EEI) category leads to the most efficient use of limited resources, particularly in the case of competitor analysis. Certain key pieces of the information puzzle will help you more than an entire library of information, and it saves time and money.

One of the biggest challenges in developing a business intelligence system to enhance corporate knowledge is deciding what to include in the collection, in total, and how much information is enough. With nearly all information generated today by computer processes, it is easy to store just about everything, from critical accounting data to letters and memos, in a searchable database of one sort or another. One international consumer health products company considered doing that using a data-warehousing concept. Business-savvy executives prevailed over the techies who were advocating what one of the executives called their "shovelware" plan. The organization is proceeding down a more intelligent path with a well-thought-out system that provides enough information to solve business problems but not too much so that users do not become overwhelmed.

Stages can be used to determine the depth and breadth of research. The first stage of research could include a scoping study to determine all of the competitors and obtain basic information. Second-stage reporting might include additional information about each competitor and basic analyses of its strengths, weaknesses, and the potential threats. Finally, three or four key competitors might be targeted for in-depth research and comprehensive analysis.

Stages two and three might require development of primary and secondary data. One way to approach this is to construct a survey form and obtain input (by mail, telephone, or in-person) from a variety of in-house and external personnel. Fellow employees are usually motivated to cooperate, but those not employed by your company usually have little to gain and might even be suspicious of your efforts. One way to overcome this obstacle is to promise and provide a report containing the information provided by all of the respondents. In addition to the survey, from which you will create the public report distributed to study participants, you may want to follow up with specific questions that may or may not be a part of the public report.

Information quality

When setting up an IBIS it's important to consider the quality of your sources of information. Those who had been wined and dined by the salespeople for the expensive online database services often dismissed early Internet adopters. It was common to hear the condescending warning "if you got it off the Internet you can't trust it!" Little by little these naysayers came around. As more and more people and organizations put data onto the Internet, the decision as to what is reliable data became a bigger issue. All of us consider the source when we hear certain points bandied about. Is it mere opinion or solid fact? Long before there was an Internet we had to evaluate the sources of our information.

The Internet can put us in touch with people who are studying the issue of data quality. There are people who are rigorously pursuing the various ways of evaluating information. One such group is the American Library Association, which publishes a basic checklist[2] for use as a guide in evaluating information in its many forms. They state, "In this data-rich environment, information consumers must learn to cope with information anxiety and to sift through the information for sensible decision making."

The checklist includes more than 40 questions relating to evaluating information. They are grouped into four categories: identifying your information needs; evaluating the source of the information; determining if the information source is suitable for your need; and evaluating the information content. Some of the questions, pertinent to our need to evaluate information to be analyzed for business intelligence purposes, are:

- What type of source is it (scholarly, popular, governmental, or private)?

- What are the author's or producer's qualifications?

- When was the information published?

- What is the reputation of the publisher, producer, or distributor?

- Was the material reviewed or edited for publication?

- Are a bibliography or other forms of documentation included?

In the category of evaluating the information content, questions include:

- What is the author's thesis or purpose?

- What facts and opinions are presented?

- Is this a report of primary research: surveys, experiments, observations?

• Are various points of view presented?

• Is this information verified in other sources in the discipline?

• Do experts in the field agree on the findings?

Finding business and competitor intelligence is the first step in a process that involves the equally important steps of analysis and dissemination. Integrating BI into strategic planning is a circular process. All of this information is retained, and as the collection grows it becomes corporate knowledge.

These and other pieces of external information keep an organization's decision makers informed. When combined with groupware, appropriate people within the organization assimilate the external information. Reactions to it become important parts of corporate knowledge as the information is used on a strategic and tactical basis. An archive of external information relevant to the organization rounds out corporate knowledge.

BI Focus

Any strategic management process requires some degree of competitor analysis. There are at least three approaches that can be used to focus competitor analysis activities:

Template example: Target organization focus

• Mission and objectives

• Current position and future outlook

• Management and ownership

• Uniqueness and differentiation

• Financials and capabilities

• Marketing and distribution strategies

• Production/service delivery capabilities

• Forecasts and predictions

Template example: Key business issues focus

• Broader view of a group of key competitors

- Pricing dynamics within the industry

- Investments and expansion strategies

- New lines of business, M&A, divestiture, joint ventures

- Economic conditions that affect the industry

- Labor union activity

- New technologies

- Governmental policy/regulations

- International issues

Template example: Customer focus

- Who are the key actors and what are their profiles?

- Assess risk of dropping you as a supplier

- Discover new product, service, and pricing opportunities

- Know their plans and SWOT

- What else do they need?

These methodologies are examples of how an organization can focus its business intelligence collection effort. Each organization will have a unique approach based on its vision and mission and the resources and constraints outlined in their own business plan.

The basic question about what broadly constitutes business intelligence can be answered by examining a business plan template. All businesses require a wide array of information to function. The template can serve as a checklist for what you want or need to know about a competitor or types of information about your own business, competitors, or non-competitors, to include in IBIS. An abbreviated view of information inherent in most business plans includes these elements:

Business plan template

- Present situation

- Objectives

- Critical success factors

- Product/service description

- Technologies

- R&D, patents

- Market analysis
- Customers
- Competition
- Regulatory impact(s)
- Marketing strategy
- Pricing & profitability
- Selling tactics, channels
- Adv., PR, and promotions
- Manufacturing (if applicable)
- Facilities and inventory

- Personnel
- Logistics and distribution
- Operations (for service business)
- Financial plan
- Present financial condition
- Requirements and funding
- Projected capabilities
- Management team
- Executives and directors
- Employees and HR issues

Another approach to scoping out the information required in your IBIS is contained in the template relating to new product development. It too is generic, but in this state of being it provides a topical road map for information collection. Forget its specific orientation to computer hardware for a moment. Consider that it could be a list of fields that make up one record in a database of competitors.

New product plan data requirements template (Sony Corporation—Workstation Division)[3]

Product Concepts and Main
   Features

Competitor's Products

Sales and Distribution
   Channel

Target Market Segments

Target Price Points
   List
   FOB

Competitors' Prices

Cost of Material

Production Cost

Maintenance Information
   Technical
   Warrantee Length

Special Services (Periodic
   Maintenance, etc.)

Applicable Safety Regulations
   (UL, CSA, FCC, etc.)

Other Regulations (EMI,
   EBU, etc.)

Manufacturing Plants to Be
   Used

Product Lifecycle

Estimated Sales
   Monthly
   By Geographic Region
   Market Share

System Concept
   Monitor

Computer	Design Leader
How to connect the peripherals, network, etc.	Design Manager
Accessories (Power Cords, etc.)	Senior Manager
Anticipated Product Line Evolution	Accounting Manager
Approvals	Department Manager
Planner	
Plant Manager	General Manager

If you've filled in all the fields in all the records, you can print some dynamite reports for your senior executives to use when developing strategy. Just imagine how pleased they'll be when you hand them a neat, concise page with the major points from selected fields in an attractive table with columns representing subjects (selected fields appropriate to the task at hand) and competitors arranged in rows of the table. This matrix can be printed on paper or, if you are part of the meeting and you have a good quality projection system, the database can be configured on the fly to show required subjects and targeted competitors as the need arises (real time) during the meeting.

Competitive analysis template

Often BI efforts are not tasked to assemble a complete dossier such as filling in all of the blanks of a complete business plan or product plan on a competitor company or acquisition target. Some executives task their BI people with key business issues to be closely investigated. On the other hand, those who want a picture that includes more than just a few key issues but less scope than a full business plan may want to consider using a narrower focus template to define and standardize their BI process. One such template is found in Lotus Freelance Graphics. Designed for use as a guide to creating a presentation, it also provides topic guidance that includes the following:

- Background

- Business definition

- Market share

- Key products or services

- Recent financial performance

- Current strategies in R&D, HR, Ops, Financial, Distribution, Marketing

- Strategic evaluation of strengths, weaknesses, opportunities, and threats

- Ability to adapt

- Anticipated moves

- Expected future strategies

- Probable moves

The general survey outline

McKinsey & Company is a leading global management consulting firm founded in the United States in 1926. Its approach to consulting was different from the management "engineers" and "time and motion" experts of the day. McKinsey was built around two ideas: serving senior management on problems important to them and their enterprises, and maintaining the knowledge and skills necessary to serve clients.

Speaking about client service at McKinsey, John Neucomb, former McKinsey partner and professor emeritus, Columbia University, said, "James O. McKinsey always looked at where the firm was and what its outlook was before we began to talk about what you did in terms of the particular problem that needed your attention. It was certainly different than what most consulting firms were doing. Competitors at that time talked about coordination, but mostly that was a coordination of systems. They weren't talking about coordinating the activities of the business toward some basic economic thrust."[4]

An early (1936) diagnostic tool developed by McKinsey is the General Survey Outline (GSO).[5] Although about 30 pages long, it can be summarized in the following categories:

- Cause and nature of present problems
- Outlook for the company
- Policies
- Administrative organization

- Executive personnel
- Facilities
- Controls and procedures
- Financial condition
- Financial requirements

More comprehensive than the most detailed business plan format, the GSO is a diagnostic tool, but it does provide a comprehensive framework that can be used to structure information gathering for IBIS.

Organizing a BI team

Large corporations often operate with a "team" concept. This approach might even be useful for the entrepreneur with no full-time employees. Team meetings with personnel from various disciplines work on a major project and meet periodically to report and coordinate actions. Representatives from various departments or organizations within the corporation can form a business intelligence team. Their task may be to focus on a specific project or to develop an overall business intelligence program relevant to the entire company, including numerous product lines selling in various markets.

Developing objectives for the BI team is the first step. Objectives might be narrowly focused (understanding key competitors and their strategies) or complex and broadly focused (entire range of threats and opportunities, several levels deep). Objectives can include understanding competitors, markets, customers, areas of technology, or any other aspect that may affect the corporation. Because the large corporation spans a wide range of activities, there are many opportunities for input from various sources as well as potential "customers" within the corporation who may benefit from the business intelligence product. Finally, to be worthwhile, the intelligence product must have impact. That is to say, it must have some tangible value for the corporation, providing sufficient information from which good decisions can be made.

Depending on the size of the organization and its current or previous efforts, understanding current processes and capabilities also is important. In the larger organization, personnel from several functions (marketing/sales, R&D/operations, finance, etc.) may be involved. The specialized expertise of the specific disciplines brings unique insights and resources to the effort.

The larger corporation has many people in the field who can report rumors or small bits and pieces of information that, when organized and analyzed, may yield insight into an important matter. Executives and managers of larger corporations can draw upon the opinions and observations of a wide variety of knowledgeable people, from industry analysts to board members. All can provide factual input or qualitative judgment. Further, the larger corporation can afford to maintain its own library and to subscribe to costly information services. All of this demands a system to avoid inefficiencies and redundancies.

Best practices of competitive intelligence project teams for one large company[6] are as such:

- Multifunctional team (Operations, R&D, Engineering, Distribution, Finance, Marketing)

- Prioritize/focus target areas

- Define level of analysis, timing, resource availability

- Define role of consultant vs. internal team

- Competitively bid consultant work to choose best consultant

- Ongoing weekly team meetings with consultant

- Determine business implications

Management often recognizes the need to enhance an existing system that already produces a less organized form of business intelligence. An initial definition of business intelligence (a starting point for agreement of purpose) could be the use of open source information to anticipate threats and discover or clarify business opportunities. However, a process of internally defining business intelligence facilitates consensus among producers and consumers. There are numerous (and often redundant) information resources, print and electronic as well as human, now being used by many organizations. Sometimes, in the largest organizations, consultants are paid to do studies for one division that could be used by another division but go unknown to all but those who originally commissioned the study. Fortunately, corporate intranets are making that situation a rarity.

Cataloging, systematizing, and sharing of resources often is helpful in the process directed toward development and successful use of actionable intelligence. Generally, two categories of sources are designated: primary (original research) or secondary (published information). Sources can be very expensive with custom studies carrying price tags in excess of $100,000. Matching resources available (money spent) to defined needs may very well depend upon top management's commitment to business intelligence and how well the effort has performed. Expense might be proposed based on the level of need with predefined categories established. For example:

Stage I—Basic, ongoing situational awareness, routine monitoring

Stage II—Heightened awareness with focused response or research project assignment

Stage III—Full mobilization for new product introduction, acquisition, etc.

Business intelligence program implementation

Overall, a roadmap to initiate the program must be created. A typical six-month program to create an IBIS for a large organization can include the following steps:

Awareness (phase one, weeks 1 to 3)

- Conduct two or three group meetings to define characteristics of "business intelligence"

- Write a summary of these meetings with comments and submit summary for comment

- Compile comments, conduct follow-up interviews, and prepare a document that defines business intelligence

Inventory (phase two, weeks 4 to 6)

- Schedule interviews with designated individuals to determine their "blue sky" needs and existing information resources

- Compile information and develop draft and final presentation

- Present and discuss findings

- Obtain input and write gap analysis

Systems (phase three, weeks 7 to 12)

- Develop proposed templates for desired intelligence products

- Conduct interviews with information technology personnel to determine existing and planned capabilities

- Research potential system refinements and available system elements to achieve a higher level of efficiency in developing business intelligence

- Compile information and develop draft and final presentation

- Present and discuss findings

- Obtain input and write proposed implementation plan

- Refine implementation plan based on further input

Implementation (phase four, weeks 13 to 26)

- Assist the organization in acquiring and developing actionable intelligence capability and capacity

- Work with key players to facilitate the process

- Plan and conduct seminars

This process will help an organization acquire and develop capability and capacity to produce business intelligence. The process can be stated simply as using tools applied to tasks designed to produce business intelligence. The overall goal is to deliver a system that provides information in the form of briefings, analyses, and competitor profiles and product evaluations/comparisons to multiple users.

System features

These information products could include on-screen summaries with hypertext links to sources from which the summaries are derived. Significant searching and report generation capabilities to facilitate saving more information also are important. The optimum system would allow end-users to easily locate specific items from stored information. Purge features that allow removal of information dated before a specified date also are required.

Additional system features make it easier for end-users to do some of their own research on the Internet. Research topics might include areas such as product, strategy, pricing, and other information relating to competitors or the industry in question. Sources, methods, and tools to facilitate creation of analytical information products from diverse source material also are desirable, especially in the larger organization. Further, this system would, ideally, facilitate identification of pockets of knowledge (individuals' knowledge and expertise as well as existing documents, etc.) within the company. It would provide a platform for sharing of that and other information via the system usually referred to as an "intranet."

The operating environment for this system normally would be a Wide Area Network (WAN) utilizing TCP/IP. Dial-up, ISDN with 128 Kbps, frame relay, or T1 connections can be selected depending on level of need. The central business intelligence database would reside at the corporate headquarters. Going back to our initial planning we might have determined that within two years this database could include files totaling about ten gigabytes.

One feature that could cause the database to rapidly expand would be large-scale scanning capabilities. Raw material for business intelligence consists of numerous printed materials acquired from mailings, trade shows, and other common methods of literature distribution. Scanned items usually are contained in Tagged Image File Format (TIFF). This is a bitmapped graphic format used for images like facsimiles transmitted to you by a fax machine.

A fax image is like a picture—you can view it, export it as a graphic image file, and alter its appearance with the viewing and annotation tools. However, you cannot alter text as you would in a word processor, changing fonts, adding or deleting text, and so on. If you want to edit a fax or another scanned document as if it were an original text file, you can convert it with Optical Character Recognition (OCR) software. OCR scans the text electronically and converts it to a file that you can open, edit, and use with other programs, meaning that you can search on the text that it contains after it is stored in a searchable database.

Knowledge building

In-house expertise of specific individuals is always useful to the rest of the members of the organization who are concerned with business intelligence. This can be shared via production of applicable information products.

For example, the production of a series of videotapes, for use by employees at home or in a local training area, could include several instructional modules, starting with the intelligence cycle. Monthly meetings could reinforce these instructional modules. Meeting activities could include instruction and presentations. An in-house expert or an outside resource could deliver instruction. Presentations could take a problem-solving case study approach. The goal would be to raise awareness of the importance of a robust and ongoing business intelligence program and to transfer knowledge from those who know more to those who know less on particular topics of value.

An internal computer communication channel could be set up so that each BI organization member has the capability of broadcasting inquiries or information alerts/updates to all members of the network. There are several approaches that would likely garner wider participation more quickly because of simplicity. Multiple channels could develop as a result of the natural formation of subgroups or special-interest groups. A reward system could be established to encourage productive use of this computer communication network.

There is usually a desire to disseminate information by means of some type of newsletter, although the intranet Web page is rapidly replacing paper. Such information as trends and customer intelligence could be included, and editorial content also could be included with direction from higher management. An electronic version would be easier and less costly than a print version, and use of it would be complementary to the other information-exchange mechanisms. It is hard to predict how information might fit together or to whom it might be most important at any given time, so internal communications should be available to all concerned. These internal communications could feed data extraction, analysis, and reporting through a characterization process.

Network message traffic could be transmitted in a specific format so it can easily be categorized and then archived weekly in a searchable historical database. A relational database format might include check boxes to indicate importance to various groups within the organization. Each network member could easily scan a constant flow of perhaps 10 to 15 messages per day on all topics. Some 20 to 30 percent of the members might post, reply, or query daily.

The database would allow for grouping by category to facilitate retrieval and analysis. A second dimension could be added in a matrix-like manner that would also include functional divisions within the organization. Additional checkboxes might also be included to indicate importance to such departments as information systems, corporate public affairs, legal, finance, and corporate planning. Over time a matrix representation of message characterization would reveal important insights.

Database characterization of ongoing electronic discussion could guide and support a critical issues roundtable or BI council. This group could meet monthly or as needed to help set direction for the BI. Acting as a "steering committee," the goal would be to meld current activities with past information to discover unique, possibly hidden, solutions to problems and to produce actionable intelligence that can be communicated to higher management.

Developing business intelligence is a major step toward making better business decisions. Achieving this objective should be oriented toward the larger goal of using the business intelligence network to maximize existing business and discover and develop new business.

High-level strategy seminars put on at various conferences and trade shows often feature speakers who talk about where their organizations are headed in general. Personal coverage of carefully selected sessions may be fruitful. An internal mechanism that provides business intelligence gathered from these seminars and conferences can be supplemented with information garnered from various nontraditional channels.

Much of this information has been disseminated via e-mail transmission of reports, voice mail broadcast of alerts, and other information-exchange mechanisms. However, a gap analysis might reveal some weaknesses in the traditional sources and methods. An Internet-centric approach to creating a faster, better, lower cost, and more comprehensive BI system could include the following:

- Advanced analysis software and training to make better use of information gathered

- Automated system to receive large-scale input (e.g., 2,000 to 3,000 items per week from three to five services) and route specific items (five to ten per week) to individuals (500-plus)

- Better exploitation of the Internet through more in-depth sourcing and investigation of unconventional information pathways

- Enhanced communication among users and producers by offering users multiple cost-effective message vehicle and storage options

- Ongoing internal training to maximize employee BI skills efficiency

- Various alternatives for surge capability to meet high-priority one-time requirements

Premium online sources of business information cost thousands of dollars per month. Until recently, a corporation had little choice but to subscribe to a few of the "majors" to get the information needed to effectively scan the external environment. This has changed dramatically with the growth of the Internet and concurrent devaluation of information. Some of what once was properly categorized as "premium" business information now can be readily obtained at no charge.

Ease of dissemination and a highly competitive environment (on the Internet) have contributed to this dramatic "commoditization" of business information. As millions of people go online, those attempting to attract this upscale demographic are providing "feeds" of information ranging from daily newspapers to scientific journals. Additionally, significant business communications are being conducted outside the mainstream of traditional publishing via newsgroups and mailing lists. There are now nearly 200,000 newsgroups and mailing lists, many covering professional subjects.

Organizing IBIS in a larger organization might include a single consultant (internal or external) project that reviews and analyzes current subscriptions to premium online services and low- or no-cost Internet alternatives. This would be accomplished with the following steps:

- Meet with users to understand present and future information requirements

- Review invoices for online services purchased by your organization

- Search for Internet alternatives

- Create summaries of Internet-accessible substitutions and suggested additional resources

- Recommend and detail software utilities to facilitate Internet information gathering

- Develop custom desktop hotlinks to new information resources

- Document potential savings, provide monthly Internet URL updates and other additions

As the Internet becomes an even more dominant means of communication, access to relevant professional information will, to some degree, move from the traditional publishing venues to the Internet. Therefore, another benefit of this work will be to provide a new window on the external environment.

IBIS is the goal, the PROACtive process is the framework, and other guides along the way can help you structure an activity that can serve an individual entrepreneur or the largest of global business. Go-getters can wage guerilla warfare with little more than their wits. Put a few basic tools in their hands, and they become an unbeatable force. IBIS can be as simple or as complex as you want to make it. There's no substitute for hard work, persistence, and attention to detail. With the Internet, IBIS is really only limited by your imagination.

Endnotes

1. W. C. Shaw and G. J. Day, *Businessman's Checklist for Success* (Coles Publishing Company Ltd., Toronto, Canada, 1979).

2. *Evaluating Information: A Basic Checklist* (American Library Association, Chicago, 1990).

3. David B. Yoffie, *Strategic Management in Information Technology* (Prentice-Hall, Inc., Englewood Cliffs, NJ, 1994: 258).

4. **www.mckinsey.com.**

5. William B. Wolf, *Management & Consulting: An Introduction to James O. McKinsey* (ILR Publications Division, New York State School of Industrial and Labor Relations, Cornell University, Ithaca, NY, 1977).

6. "Competitive Intelligence Evolution at Pillsbury," presentation at SCIP Minnesota Chapter seminar, October 2, 1998.

CHAPTER 8

ACCESS

With a thorough grounding in what you want to do with an Internet Business Intelligence System (IBIS), it's time to consider how you will access the Internet. Most businesspeople already have some type of access, but this chapter will help you better understand your options.

Historical background

The Internet is a large network made up of smaller networks composed of academic, commercial, government, and military networks. Using a packet-switching diffused networking concept originally developed for the military, the Internet became widely used for academic and commercial research during the late 1970s and 1980s. There was a notable spurt of growth during the mid-1980s when the nation invested in regional supercomputers for the academic community.

As the major online services (CompuServe, America Online, etc.) connected to Internet for e-mail exchange, the Internet began to function as a central hub for e-mail outside of the Internet community. Academic users briefly struggled with the notion that the Internet might be opened up to the "unwashed masses." And come they did, by the millions, explorers and immigrants to the new world of cyberspace.

Enabling the Web

In addition to the common connection for exchange of e-mail, the Internet's second major growth factor was the incorporation of World Wide Web links providing an incredible array of information-exchange capability. Made possible largely through the efforts of the National Center for Supercomputer Applications, the Mosaic browser software worked with HTML coding developed at the European Center for Nuclear Research (CERN) in Geneva from a proposal by Tim Berners-Lee in 1989. Originally the Web was created to share research information on nuclear physics. In 1993, there were about 50 Web servers, and CERN introduced its Macintosh browser, while the National Center for Supercomputing Applications (NCSA) in Chicago introduced the X Window version of Mosaic. Marc Andreesen developed Mosaic at the National Center for Supercomputing Applications and left to form Netscape.

The Web is made possible by coding text document in HyperText Markup Language (HTML). These codes are ASCII characters that can be created with any text editor or word processor. Most word processors can export normal pages saved in the HTML format. Netscape Composer also has a full range of HTML page composition functions.

Analogy illustrates how Internet technology has matured while it has subtly woven itself into our lives. Until the mid-1970s photography was clearly delineated between amateur (Kodak Instamatic) and professional (Nikon 35mm). Prior to that time anyone who wanted to take pictures chose between equipment that was designed for users in one of the two categories. Figuratively speaking you had an Instamatic or a Nikon and there was little in between.

As space program-inspired microelectronics began to find their way into cameras, amateur photographers had many more options available to them, including autofocus and autoflash as well as sophisticated zoom lenses. The same is true today of video cameras. Near-broadcast-quality video cameras cost today what amateur units cost when they first came on the scene in the late 1970s. Today's amateur video cameras have more functionality than most people will ever use.

The nearly imperceptible but constant maturation of these technological tools is not unlike the growing sophistication of capabilities given to us with the Internet. The information-gathering capabilities of the Internet (mostly access to databases of text) predate the widespread adoption of the Internet and the World Wide Web. The cost of accessing databases was very high. A handful of resellers provided single-point access to aggregated data. Since they had the only game in town, you had to pay the dictated price and dial their telephone number to connect to their proprietary service.

Now anyone can publish information electronically via the Internet, so there's unlimited choice for little or no dollars. And publish they do. Overnight anyone can publish breathtaking graphical pages using new Web site creation software. The best Web sites have a wealth of information.

Most users interact with the Internet via their Web browsers, such as Netscape's Navigator and Microsoft's Internet Explorer, which display graphical Web pages from HTML files. Older UNIX utilities provided separate File Transfer Protocol (FTP) functions to download information or files to the user's hard drive. This now is an integral part of the Web browser. Such stand-alone Internet functions as Telnet (a terminal emulation program to run programs via Internet), gopher (a utility to access hierarchical menus of text files), and Veronica (searches of gopher sites) can still be found but are rarely used today.

Technicalities

The Internet consists of high-speed communications links between local "points of presence." These points of presence (POPs) provide users with a local telephone number with which they can log onto their online services. The U.S. National Science Foundation maintained the backbone, called the NSFNET, but later privatized most of the telecommunications services. Today, Internet Service Providers (ISPs) hook into the backbone through Network Access Points (NAP) providing the points of presence that represent the local telephone numbers online service subscribers dial to connect to the Internet.

Internet computers use the TCP/IP communications protocol. Millions of host computers connect to the Internet using the Internet Protocol worldwide via gateways that convert TCP/IP into other protocols. Information on TCP/IP networks is contained in packets, and this flow is switched via routers. Most people connect to the Internet via a modem that connects the computer to a telephone line. Computers on networks in larger organizations that have tens, hundreds, or thousands of Internet users utilize other types of connections.

The Internet Protocol (IP) is the method by which data is sent from one computer to another on the Internet. Each computer (known as a host) on the Internet has at least one address that uniquely identifies it from all other computers. When you send or receive data (for example, an e-mail note or a Web page), the message gets divided into little chunks called packets. Each of these packets contains both the sender's Internet address and the receiver's address. Any packet is sent first to a gateway computer that understands a small part of the Internet. The gateway computer reads the destination address and forwards the packet to an adjacent gateway that in turn reads the destination address, and so forth across the Internet until one gateway recognizes the packet as belonging to a computer within its immediate neighborhood or domain. That gateway then forwards the packet directly to the computer where the address is specified.

A packet is the unit of data that is routed between an origin and a destination on the Internet or any other packet-switched network. When any file (e-mail message, HTML file, GIF file, URL request, and so forth) is sent from one place to another on the Internet, the Transmission Control Protocol (TCP) layer of TCP/IP divides the file into "chunks" of an efficient size for routing. Each of these packets is separately numbered and includes the Internet address of the destination. The individual packets for a given file may travel different routes through the Internet. When they have all arrived, they are reassembled into the original file (by the TCP layer at the receiving end).[1]

Traffic routing

To fully understand the Internet one should have some idea of how traffic flows through it. According to the National Science Foundation (NSF), "In 1985, the NSF decided to support Internetworking for research and education. By 1995, the Internet had become a worldwide system of more than 100,000 networks; and NSF retired the NSFNET backbone network service, transferring the provision of commodity Internet services to the emerging Internet industry."

Also in 1995, NSF authorized the creation of the vBNS, a next-generation network for research and education, with initial connections to the NSF-supported supercomputing centers and Network

Access Point (NAP). In 1996, NSF updated its Connections to the Internet Program, including a high-performance connection option for research and education institutions with significant successful Internet experience, which have new application requirements that cannot be met on the current generation commercialized Internet.

In 1993 the National Science Foundation awarded WorldCom the status of NAP to the NSFNet backbone in Washington, DC. Prior to the awarding of this NAP status, WorldCom and a small group of ISPs helped create an exchange "point" that eventually grew into what they currently call a MAE (the origin of this acronym is murky, but some think it stands for Metropolitan Area Ethernet), or an Internet networks traffic-exchange facility. Since then, WorldCom has set up seven MAE sites nationwide where Internet Service Providers can establish peering relationships for the exchange of IP traffic.

Today, WorldCom operates two of the major interconnect points for the Internet in the United States: MAE EAST and MAE WEST. In fact, a major portion of the traffic that flows between ISP networks passes through WorldCom MAE facilities. MAE EAST is located in the Washington, DC metropolitan area and connects all of the major ISPs as well as European providers. MAE WEST is located in California's Silicon Valley providing a second interconnection point linking major ISPs in that area. Many are connected at WorldCom in San Jose, while a smaller number (but individually larger in size) are connected at NASA Ames Research Center, home of the western Federal Internet Exchange (FIX West). The two sites are linked together with multiple 155-Mbps circuits.

A MAE is the WorldCom facility where ISPs connect to each other to exchange Internet traffic—an Internet networks traffic-exchange facility. The easiest way to think of it is as a local area network (LAN) switch where all the "pieces" of the Internet connect together to exchange traffic at high speeds. The MAE forms part of the "Inter" in Internet. WorldCom owns and operates the switching platforms used to interconnect the various ISPs. The switching platform is a combination of an Ethernet Switch, a Fiber Distributed Data Interface (FDDI) Concentrator, and in the case of MAE EAST and MAE WEST, an FDDI Switch. These devices enable a range of speeds and connection types. They are all linked using FDDI and serve to give customers a variety of connection options.

In addition to the Internet Society and its task forces, there are other coordinating groups that play important roles in the continuing operations of the Internet.

The North American Network Operator's Group[2] (NANOG) is an educational and operational forum for coordination of network operations in North America. Membership is open, and conference participants typically include senior engineering staff from tier 1 and tier 2 ISPs.

The Cooperative Association for Internet Data Analysis[3] (CAIDA) is a collaborative undertaking to promote greater cooperation in the engineering and maintenance of a robust, scalable, global Internet infrastructure. CAIDA provides a neutral framework to support these cooperative endeavors.

At the National Science Foundation, the Division of Advanced Computational Infrastructure and Research[4] (ACIR) provides access to and support of high-end computing infrastructure and research for the national scientific community through the Partnerships for Advanced Computational Infrastructure (PACI) program, and through the Advanced Computational Research program. The Directorate for Computer and Information Science and Engineering has three goals:

- To enable the U.S. to uphold a position of world leadership in computing, communications, and information science and engineering

- To promote understanding of the principles and uses of advanced computing, communications, and information systems in service to society

- To contribute to universal, transparent and affordable participation in an information-based society

The National Laboratory for Applied Network Research[5] (NLANR) has as its primary goal to provide technical, engineering, and traffic analysis support of NSF High Performance Connections sites and HPNSPs (high-performance network service providers) such as the NSF/MCI very high performance Backbone Network Service (vBNS).

Internet Service Providers

For many people a consumer online service (usually America Online) may provide a solid foundation for access to Internet. The

Internet can be accessed through an online service that adds proprietary content as part of the service. For example, certain forums
and discussion groups, as well as other value-added services, may
only be available on the service's computer, and you need a subscription to access the computer, usually through a local telephone
number dialed by your modem.

Internet Service Providers (ISPs) sell direct connections to the
Internet. ISP costs range from less than the online services for the most
basic packages to much more for advanced services. ISPs become
more cost effective than the online services if you use the Internet for
more than about 10 to 15 hours per month or if you need higher speed
access for several employees. Many power users have high-speed
Internet access in their offices and maintain an online service account
too. For many casual users and those who travel frequently, such services as America Online provide inexpensive access to the Internet with
the all-important local telephone number connection.

There are thousands of Internet Service Providers throughout the
U.S., and many have become more like online services, although
they still basically provide little more than access to the Internet.
There may be subscriber-accessible custom features such as a
news-clipping service or premium database. Local or regional ISPs
may not have access numbers or "points of presence" in many cities
outside their service areas. Some of the larger ISPs do provide global connectivity. If you travel nationally or internationally, this can be
an important feature. In addition to ISPs that provide dial-up service on local telephone numbers, other more sophisticated ISPs may
be more desirable, especially for an advanced IBIS, if they provide
ISDN or cable modem access or digital subscriber lines.

ISDN

Most business Internet users have a need for speed. Graphics-
heavy Web pages often take many minutes to fully download. The
first big step up in speed from a 33.6- or 56-Kbps standard modem
is an Integrated Services Digital Network (ISDN) from the local telephone company.

Much like TCP/IP, ISDN is an international standard for transmitting voice, video, and data over digital lines at 64 Kbps. ISDN uses
64-Kbps circuit-switched channels, called B channels, or "bearer"
channels, to carry voice and data. It uses a separate D channel, or
"delta" channel, for control signals. The D channel is used to signal

the telephone company computer to make calls, put them on hold, and activate features such as conference calling and call forwarding. It also receives information about incoming calls, such as the identity of the caller. Data users can bond two channels to achieve 128-Kbps service.

ISDN is the least cost-practical entry point for Internet service on a local area network (LAN). Basic service from the phone company costs as little as $25 per month for metered service, but this provides two telephone numbers. These numbers will still work even if there is traffic on the system, making ISDN a good investment for the home or small office. ISDN can provide 128-Kbps digital connection to an ISP, but the ISP must have an ISDN port for you to dial into. Some ISDN terminal adapters support Ethernet connectivity to as many as ten computers on a LAN. Basic terminal adapters start at about $150, and these provide at least a serial port connection to your computer and two RJ-type phone jacks for simultaneous use of such telephone equipment as fax machines and telephone answering devices.

"Cable modem" service

Despite half-hearted efforts by Regional Bell Operating Companies to achieve significant market share with ISDN Internet Access Service, cable television companies have been steadily moving forward with high-speed access into homes and offices. Motorola, Inc.'s shipments of cable modems have been accelerating, and this is attributed to pent-up demand from users who want a faster way to access the Internet.[6]

Multiple system owners like Comcast, Cox Communications, TCI, and Time-Warner have worked to set Data Over Cable Service Interface Specifications (DOCSIS). This standard reportedly enables consumers to buy lower cost modems in retail stores.

Cable TV providers are marching forward into this battleground. Since August 1997, I have had high-speed Internet access provided by Comcast@Home in my home office in New Jersey. When the conditions are right, this service is the equivalent of having a T1 line with the ability to download a 10-megabyte file in less than a minute. Coverage at the time I signed up is depicted in Figure 8.1.

Unfortunately for the majority of would-be subscribers, cable modem access is limited to a relatively small segment of the millions of neighborhoods across the country. Home office or business users must have cable connections and the appropriate systems installed to service their area. If not, no service.

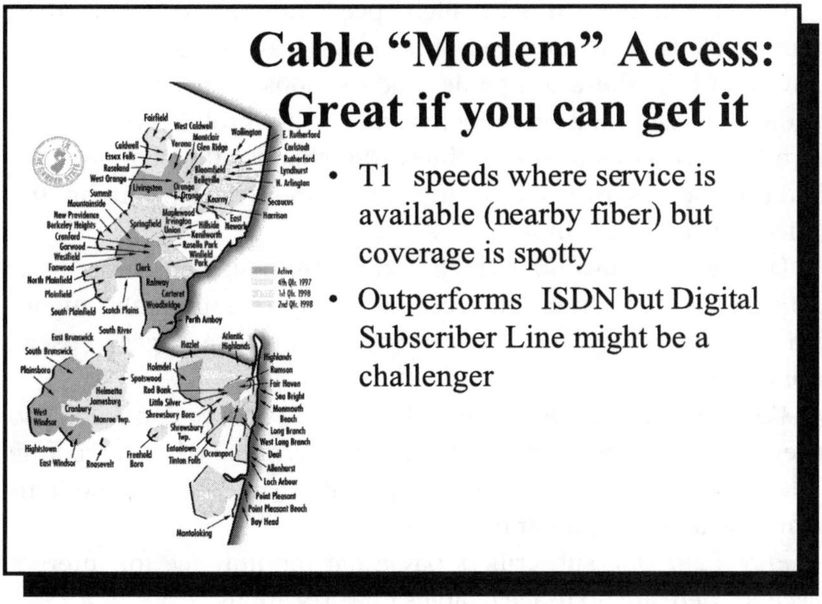

Cable "Modem" Access: Great if you can get it

- T1 speeds where service is available (nearby fiber) but coverage is spotty
- Outperforms ISDN but Digital Subscriber Line might be a challenger

Figure 8.1

Digital Subscriber Line

Digital Subscriber Line (DSL) technology uses existing copper telephone wiring to deliver high-speed data services to businesses and homes. In its various forms—including ADSL, HDSL, IDSL, R-ADSL, SDSL, and VDSL—DSL offers users a choice of speeds ranging from 32 Kbps to, in laboratory settings, more than 50 Mbps. These digital services will ultimately be used to deliver bandwidth-intensive applications like video on demand and distance learning. More immediately, today DSL is for the first time putting high-speed Internet access within the reach of small and medium-size businesses.

DSL takes existing voice cables that connect the customer premises to the phone company's central office (CO) and turns them into a high-speed digital link. Over any given link, the maximum DSL speed is determined by the distance between the customer site and the CO. At the customer premises, a DSL modem connects the phone line to either a stand-alone computer or a local area network (LAN). This DSL equipment differs from other Internet access devices in two key respects: It requires no end-user configuration, and it is not a dial-up solution. Once installed, the DSL modem provides the customer site with continuous connection to the Internet.

DSL technologies provide high-speed Internet access at prices that small and medium-size businesses can afford. Before the advent of DSL, these companies had to choose between cheap but agonizingly slow dial-up modems and fast but prohibitively expensive ISDN services or leased lines. DSL changes the economics of Internet access by establishing an entirely new point on the price/performance curve.

DSL services also offer small and medium-size businesses significantly higher Internet access for only incrementally higher prices. This conveys a number of compelling advantages to users. For example:

Continuous Connection: DSL users are always connected, so they get immediate Internet access. ISDN terminal adapters require 5 to 10 seconds to establish a connection, while dial-up modems can take nearly half a minute.

Flat Fee: DSL subscribers pay a flat monthly fee for Internet access. There are no usage charges to worry about.

Dedicated Bandwidth: DSL line speeds are constant and provide the same speed (hence the "Symmetric" moniker) in both directions.

Unlike cable modems, DSL equipment is not accessing a shared infrastructure that throttles down individual connection speeds when traffic gets heavy. Bell Atlantic's version of DSL is diagrammed in Figure 8.2.

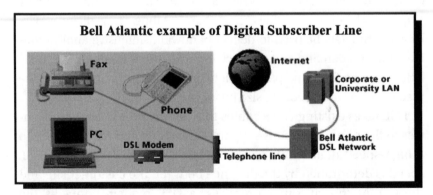

Figure 8.2

Digital satellite service

Hughes Network Systems several years ago launched a service that can be described as "slow trigger, fast download." The speed of

DirecPC (**www.direcpc.com**) is the result of using advanced satellite technology (see Figure 8.3) to supplement dial-up Internet connection and download the bandwidth-intensive part of Internet surfing. DirecPC downloads content from the Internet directly from the server to their satellite network and straight into your PC. When you launch cached Web sites using DirecPC, the request (mouse click) is sent to a cache management PC via a telephone line. From there, content (the bandwidth-intensive part) is acquired between the Internet and the DirecPC Network Operations Center. Selected content is routed to the satellite, which delivers the content to the satellite antenna at the end-user's location. From the antenna, the information is delivered, full circle, to your PC. DirecPC receives a regularly scheduled Usenet Newsgroup feed from the Internet, which allows Turbo Newscast to automatically broadcast thousands of newsgroups over the DirecPC satellite system.

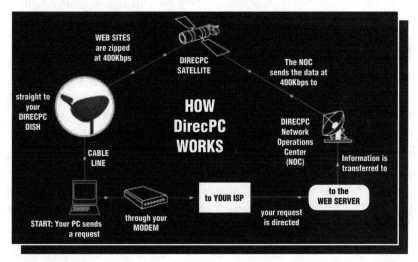

Figure 8.3

DirecPC Personal Edition provides all the hardware and software for service, including a 21-inch elliptical Satellite Dish, DirecPC Internal Satellite Modem (32-bit PCI card), DirecPC Personal Edition software, and Universal Mount for the disk. Additional hardware is required for use on network servers. DirecPC services are listed below:

• **Turbo Internet**—Fully interactive access to the Internet at speeds up to 400 Kbps

- **Turbo Webcast**—Broadcast delivery of the most popular Web sites to your PC's hard drive

- **Turbo Newscast**—Broadcast delivery of up to 30,000 Usenet Newsgroups to your PC's hard drive

- **ISP service**—Dial-up access to the Internet and WWW

Prices start at about $30 per month, plus hardware costs.

Biggest and oldest ISPs

America Online was incorporated in 1985. Headquartered in Dulles, Virginia, AOL has more than 20 million members and is by far the world's largest online service.

AOL's mission, through its three product groups—AOL Interactive Services, CompuServe Interactive Services and AOL Studios, and AOL International—is to build a global medium as central to people's lives as the telephone or television. To accomplish this mission, AOL is implementing a multiple brand strategy supported by a common infrastructure to build programming and other content and services as a foundation for growth in subscribers and revenues. The announcement in January 2000 that AOL would become AOL Time Warner Inc. through a merger with media giant Time Warner—best known for its television and publishing properties—shouldn't have shocked anyone familiar with AOL's mission.

AOL Interactive Services operates AOL's flagship service and manages the Instant Messenger service and the AOL.com and AOL NetFind products, as well as content properties, such as Entertainment Asylum. The AOL.com Web site offers features including MyNews, a personalized news service, as well as the Instant Messenger service and other features and programming. AOL NetMail, which will allow members to send and receive electronic mail on the Web, is in beta testing.

AOL acquired the online services business of CompuServe Corporation in January 1998. That business now comprises AOL's CompuServe Interactive Services product group ("CompuServe"). CompuServe targets the busy, adult audience that relies on its service as a resource to provide needed information and services quickly and efficiently. In 1999 CompuServe 2000 was launched, providing several enhancements.

CompuServe began operations in the late 1970s. It grew steadily and has always offered a wide variety of professional forums as well as access to research databases. These features are becoming less important as the Internet grows in popularity. However, CompuServe does offer some benefit for IBIS, which will be covered later in this chapter.

Figure 8.4

AOL's many facets

AOL Studios builds new businesses and brands, targeting specific interactive audiences for the AOL and CompuServe services and the Internet. Under AOL Studios are Digital City, Inc. (owned approximately 80 percent by AOL and 20 percent by the Tribune Company), a local content and community guide delivering local news and information in 50 U.S. markets, and ICQ, an Internet-based trial instant communications and chat technology AOL acquired in June 1998 that appeals to young, Web-savvy adults worldwide.

AOL International manages the AOL and CompuServe services outside the United States. AOL offers its AOL and CompuServe branded services in Canada through a wholly owned subsidiary, in Europe through joint ventures with Bertelsmann AG, and in Japan through a joint venture with Mitsui & Co., Ltd. and Nihon Keizai Shimbun, Inc. (Nikkei), and through a local distributor, and offers access to these services in over 100 countries. See "International Expansion."

AOL employs a diversified portfolio approach in designing and implementing its network services. The AOLnet is a data communications network, which AOL expanded during fiscal year 1998 to approximately 800,000 modems, resulting in increased network capacity, higher speed access, and reduced per-hour data communication costs. The portfolio of AOL networks is available in approximately 1,500 cities in more than 100 countries worldwide.

AOL's networked neighborhood

AOL provides subscribers with a global, interactive community offering a wide variety of content, features, and tools. The AOL service also includes simple access to the Internet with search functionality through AOL NetFind. The range of content, features, and tools offered on the AOL service includes the following:

Online Community

America Online promotes interactive community through electronic mail services; public bulletin boards; the Buddy List feature, for members to keep an up-to-the moment account of whether fellow members are online, subject to a blocking feature; the AOL Instant Messenger service, which allows members to communicate online instantaneously without having to access an electronic mailbox; an online community center; public or private "meeting rooms"; and interactive conversations (chat). Guest interviews, with participation by members, take place at live "auditorium" events.

Channel Line-Up

Content on the AOL service is organized into channels, allowing members to navigate the service easily to find areas of interest. The following are some examples of informational content and commerce and community opportunities: AOL Today, News, Sports, Influence, Travel, International, Personal Finance, WorkPlace, Entertainment, Games, Interests, Shopping, Health, Families, Kids Only, and Local. Some of the content providers on the AOL service include ABC News, CBS SportsLine, *The New York Times*, and *Business Week*.

Personalization and Control Features

Members can personalize their experiences on the AOL service through a number of features and tools, including a reminder service that sends e-mail in advance of important events; stock portfolios that automatically update market prices; Mail Controls, which allow members to limit who may send them e-mail and to block certain types of e-mail; Favorite Places, which allows members to mark particular Web sites or AOL areas; and Portfolio Direct and News Profiles, which send stories of particular interest to members.

AOL launched its Web site, AOL.com (**http://www.aol.com**), in October 1995, which offers Internet users (who may not be AOL members) content, features, and tools, including AOLNetFind, an Internet search and rating tool, and the AOL Instant Messenger service, which allows Internet users to communicate in real-time with their friends and family. AOL.com also offers AOL members the opportunity to exchange e-mail on the Internet, without signing onto the service, and My News, a personalized news service. Content provided on the AOL.com site includes news, shopping, Web search services, classified advertisements, and White and Yellow Pages directories. AOL plans to continue to expand content and services available through the AOL.com Web site.[7]

IBIS features of AOL

One of the most useful of America Online's business features is its no-extra-cost news clipping service. An easy to use wizard interface is provided to create profiles that target the news items wanted by users. Simplified syntax for creating these clipping profiles make the process more intuitive. After setting up news clipping profiles, users can schedule FlashSessions to go online (immediately or at designated times) to send and retrieve e-mail, and send and retrieve newsgroup messages. Because news clips arrived as electronic mail, FlashSessions can handle them. Additionally, files collected in a download manager enable users to retrieve multiple files or programs and write them to their hard drives without having to request each file.

All of these downloaded items arrive in the AOL Personal Filing Cabinet. This helps users organize various items retrieved online in FlashSessions. Each AOL screen name has its own Personal Filing Cabinet, but you can use the Personal Filing Cabinet feature within

America Online to access the information. Inexperienced users have Member Services for online help.

AOL's databases (live news feeds, some magazine article searching, limited company profiles, etc.) are not surcharged. An important difference between AOL and CompuServe is that the latter permits simplified access to hundreds of important business databases (including business credit reports) and newswires, but many of them are surcharged with fees ranging from about $1 to $35 per use.

You can search an entire database of information about AOL's content areas and forums. To search this database, click the Find button on the toolbar. Type the subject of interest in the box where you see the blinking cursor, and click the Search button. A list will appear of areas on AOL that match the subject you entered, and you can double click on the name of an area for a description. If it looks interesting, click the Go There button at the bottom of the description and you'll be taken there.

Like bookmarks in a browser, AOL's Favorite Places is a customized list of online areas or Web sites that you like to visit. Click the heart in the top-right corner of that area's window and the area will be added to your Favorite Places list. To return to a Favorite Place, click the Favorite Places icon on your toolbar. It's the one that looks like an open folder with a heart on it (to the left of the red question mark). Once your Favorite Places list is open, double click on one of the areas you have saved, and you'll be whisked right to that spot!

For the smaller IBIS, perhaps operated by a solo professional, entrepreneur, or small-business owner, information management features in AOL's software are useful. It helps you organize your e-mail, downloaded files, and Favorite Places in a Personal Filing Cabinet. You even can set AOL to automatically download and save your mail in your Personal Filing Cabinet so you can read it off-line. To access your Personal Filing Cabinet, click the file cabinet button on the toolbar. It's right next to the Favorite Places button.

AOL's News Profiles

News Profiles searches news sources for articles that match your interests and sends them to you as mail. Instead of making you search for the news yourself, News Profiles puts it all in one place for you as soon as you sign on or download articles automatically using

Flash Mail. With News Profiles you can search up to 12 news sources covering general news, business, sports, and entertainment, both national and worldwide. News Profiles is a powerful tool that gives you faster and easier access to the wealth of information on America Online. There is no additional charge for the News Profiles service.

Each profile is a separate automated search of America Online's news sources for a set of search words. For example, if you wanted to find out the latest news about aerospace activities, you could set up a profile to search news and business wires for all articles containing "NASA," "satellite," or "shuttle." Once you create a profile, it searches the news for you throughout the day and sends you the articles as mail. You can have up to five profiles per screen name. Each profile can deliver up to 50 articles a day to your mailbox.

When you create a profile for the first time, you have to enter which words to look for and which words to ignore. For example, if you wanted to set up a profile to look for news about the Middle East, "Jordan" is a word you want to look for. The word "Jordan," however, is also significant in sports news, so you also tell your Middle East profile to ignore articles with the word "Michael." Once you create your word list, you pick which of America Online's many news sources you want your profile to search, set the maximum number of articles you want News Profiles to send you each day, and name the profile.

When you create a news profile, there are three types of search criteria you define that help you narrow your search to select only those articles you want to read. You first enter a list of words you want to appear somewhere in the article. These words are entered in the "Find articles containing any..." box. These words can be thought of as general subject search criteria. All of the words you list at this point are not required—only one must be in an article for it to be selected.

Second, you list required words that must appear in an article. These words are entered in the "Require that all..." box. Each word you specify at this point must be in an article for it to be selected. Required words let you considerably narrow your search and help ensure that you only get articles that meet your profile criteria. Finally, you complete your search criteria by listing words that you want News Profiles to ignore even though an article satisfies the previously specified "any" and "required" criteria. These words are entered in the "Ignore the Article if..." box.

Once you create a profile, you can modify it at any time or delete it. Also, you can temporarily turn off profiles without deleting them. For example, if you are going on a two-week vacation, you probably don't want old news filling up your mailbox. Simply turn your profile off while you are gone, and turn it on when you come back.

In addition to searching for words, the News Profiles system can also search for partial words using wild cards or symbols that represent characters. You can use partial words with wild cards in any of the boxes on the Search Words screen.

Fine-tuning News Profiles

The wild cards are listed here:

Asterisk (*): The asterisk represents a string of zero or more characters, whether they are letters or numbers. You can use it at any place in the word. For example, typing "chin*" in the Find Articles box finds articles containing any of the following words: chin, china, chinese, chinook, chinquiapin, chintz, etc.

At Sign (@): The "at" sign represents a single letter. You can use it at any place in the word. For example, typing "gra@e" in the "Ignore" box ignores articles containing the words "grape" and "grate."

Plus Sign (+): The plus sign represents a single number. You can use it at any place in the word. For example, typing "902+0" in the Find Articles box finds all articles containing the ZIP code "90210."

Question Mark (?): The question mark represents a single letter or number. (In other words, it combines the functions of @ and +.) You can use it at any place in the word.

Pound Sign (#): The pound sign represents any single word. For example, typing the phrase "washington # area" in the Find Articles box finds the following phrases: Washington Metropolitan Area, Washington Metro Area, Washington Baltimore Area, Washington-Baltimore Area. (Note that it will NOT find Washington Area.)

To use any other special characters in a search (such as an ampersand "&"), precede the character with an equal sign (=) and surround the word/phrase with single quotes (' ').

Context restriction:

Dash (-): The dash identifies phrases to ignore that contain your search word. For example, typing 'news - news reel - news clip - evening news' in the Find Articles box finds all occurrences of news except news reel, news clip, and evening news. Keep in mind various search word contexts. For example, to identify "e-mail" as a search word, exclude commonly occurring phrases containing "e-mail," such as when people include their e-mail address within articles, correspondence, etc. Typing 'e-mail - e-mail address - e-mail: - send e-mail to' solves the problem in this example.

You can use News Profiles in combination with America Online FlashSessions. With FlashSessions you can have America Online download your news articles (and other mail) while you are away from your computer.

This listing is a general description of the types of news articles:

Reuters News Report: Reuters primary U.S. newswire, containing all the general news items collected from Reuters; 23 North American news bureaus, as well as the top stories from the rest of the world.

Reuters World Service: Includes six news wires produced by Reuters in North America, South America, Europe, Asia, Africa, and the Middle East.

Reuters Business Report: Contains Reuters' U.S. business news stories, as well as the top business stories from the rest of the world. Also includes the following weekly columns: Computing (Sunday); Workplace (Monday); Home Technology (Tuesday); Products, Finance, and International Features (Wednesday): Travel, Auto, and Funds (Thursday); and Stocks Week (Friday).

Knight Ridder/Tribune Business News: Business news coverage from more than 60 newspapers, supplemented by national and international news updates from the Knight Ridder Financial News service. Also includes articles from *The Journal of Commerce, Adweek, Traffic World,* and *AirCommerce* magazines.

Business Wire and PR Newswire: Press releases and announcements from corporations and organizations.

Reuters European Business Report: Contains all European, African, and Middle Eastern business stories from Reuters.

Reuters Asia/Pacific Business Report: Reuters' business news coverage from Asia and the Pacific Rim.

Reuters European Community Report: Includes Reuters' European Community legislative news, transcripts, and press releases from the EC Commission, selected European business and general news, and the definitive daybook/diary, offering a full listing of upcoming events, as well as news from all over the world that would impact the EC.

Reuters/Variety Entertainment Report: Contains the top stories from Daily Variety, as well as Reuters' own coverage of the entertainment industry.

CompuServe

AOL's CompuServe Interactive Services product group manages the CompuServe service in the U.S. and Canada, which is available in over 500 cities worldwide. The CompuServe online service targets an audience of busy adults, who look to their Internet online service as a way to answer questions and solve problems. Like the AOL service, CompuServe organizes its content into channels, including News & Weather, Personal Finance, Business, Research, Sports & Recreation, Arts & Entertainment, Home & Hobbies, Lifestyles, Computing Support, International, Local, Travel, Health, Car Club, Shopping, Games, Sight & Sound, Forum Center, Member Center, and Communications Center.

CompuServe is the oldest online service, providing an electronic bridge to many business and professional databases long before the Internet was popular. Starting in the late 1970s as an effort to utilize H&R Block's off-hours computer capacity, the tax preparation company was closely followed by General Electric, which attempted the same with their vast computer network. Largely unused night and weekend computer power was offered to the general public as microcomputers became more affordable.

From the outset, CompuServe provided good news monitoring services (at a premium during the early years) with a news clipping service. Also available via this dial-up service was business news, feature stories, sports scores, public and aviation weather, and even Hollywood gossip. Access to electronic versions of magazines and newsletters, as well as electronic forums, provided unprecedented capabilities for end-users.

Professional forums dating back to the early 1980s first enabled professionals to exchange ideas and information with others in the same field. People interested in the law, medicine, business management, and other fields will find a forum to suit their professional interests. Like today's Internet sites devoted to the same subject, finance resources provided users with quotes on stock prices, information about companies, and other aspects of investing.

Although a slow starter in providing full access to Internet, CompuServe provided Newsgroups, Gophers, File Transfer Protocol (FTP), and various Internet-related forums. Other major sections of the service included travel, shopping, home/leisure, and games.

Long before Newsgroups and mail lists on the Internet became popular, CompuServe's forums offered members the opportunity to meet others who shared their special interests. Forum members exchanged information, expounded opinions and ideas, and participated in general conversation (keyboard chat). Forums have message boards, data libraries, and conference rooms where special meetings and seminars take place.

It remains to be seen just how CompuServe will fare given the explosion of Internet content and information resources. One of the biggest features of CompuServe was the ability to access many professional databases without subscribing to them individually. This has largely been supplanted by direct Internet access to those databases with simplified navigation and often inexpensive pay-per-view access. Additionally, much of what was part of "proprietary" content has been replaced by no-charge Internet- accessible resources.

When compared to early CompuServe, today's CompuServe is different in some ways and similar in others. While AOL has almost always been directed to novice users, CompuServe users need extra skills (and lots more patience) to master the service. Everything from software configuration and sign on, to navigating the service seems to be more difficult than AOL. CompuServe users can easily use their Internet Explorer or Netscape browsers.

The unplugged future of Internet access

Wireless communication technologies are poised to bring dramatic changes to the nation's telecommunications and information infrastructure, reshaping how people communicate, access information, and are entertained. These technologies, which use radio waves instead of wires to transmit information, already play an important part in the daily lives of almost all Americans. For more than 70 years, radio and television broadcasters have entertained and informed millions of people each day. Satellites connect the

countries of the world, allowing people to converse, share information, and transact business. Recently, cellular telephones have
extended the reach of the public telephone system to people who
are on the move or beyond the reach of traditional telephones.

Over the next several years, use of wireless technologies is
expected to grow dramatically as a wide range of new radio-based
communication, information, and entertainment services and
applications is introduced, and the prices of both equipment and
services fall. Some of the wireless systems now being developed
include a wide range of data communications systems that expand
the reaches of computer and information services. These emerging
wireless technologies, along with existing wireless services, will
become an integral part of the nation's evolving telecommunications and information infrastructure—formally known as the
National Information Infrastructure (NII).

Meeting various needs

Wireless data services use a mix of terrestrial and satellite-based
technologies to meet a wide variety of local (in-building or campus
settings), metropolitan, regional, national, and international communication needs. Most often, wireless data systems are designed to
serve user needs for mobility or portability—mobile data is a widely
used term—but many mobile systems and applications can also
serve the data communication needs of users who do not move
about. A number of wireless data applications, in fact, are being
designed with fixed users in mind. Traditionally, wireless data applications and services have been concentrated primarily in a few narrowly defined, vertical, business markets.

Today, however, the kinds of people and companies that use
wireless data products are changing and expanding. As the United
States has moved into a more competitive international environment and a more service- and information-based economy, the
use of computers in the workplace has increased. In addition,
more workers are getting out of the office—but even within the
office or factory setting, the value of being mobile (but in touch) is
being recognized.

These changes are beginning to affect the consumer mass market
and the more general, horizontal business market for wireless data
products and services. Some general applications have been identified, including computer network extension, Internet access, wireline

replacement (point-of-sale terminals and alarm monitoring), personal services (computer services, online services, and other information services), and other data applications.[8]

Satellite technology has been part of the communication system since the middle 1960s. Satellite communication is an integral part of the international telephone network. Today, when high-speed optical fiber capable of carrying immense volumes of communication to Europe or the Far East fails, satellite communication links stand ready to carry the redirected traffic. Most of the early satellite systems were matched to the commercial need of wholesale communications, i.e., from one service carrier's switch to another carrier's switch, hence to wire lines. New satellite systems on the drawing board or in early phases of implementation will link directly with the user.

Various methods of operation

Some propose to operate much like cellular or personal communication systems (PCS), linking the user and his or her handset directly to the space-based satellite system. Two classes of satellite-based communication services are being considered: GEOS— Geosynchronous Earth Orbiting Satellites; and LEOS—Low Earth Orbiting Satellites.

GEOS systems will be placed in a geosynchronous orbit at the prescribed distance of 22,300 miles above the equator. These satellite systems will use a higher transmitting power level than will the LEOS because of the difference in distance to the earth. GEOS can be deployed either in a constellation (several satellites), or as a single satellite, depending on the nature of the service that they will deliver. Deployment of a constellation of GEOS in several different orbit locations can provide global communication. Intersatellite communications to manage the switching and administration would link the system satellites.

Interconnection with the Public Switched Telephone Network (PSTN) can be provided, and subscribers can manage their own communications through personal ground stations. A single GEOS satellite can be equipped to aim spot beams to achieve regional communication coverage. Such systems operate much like a cellular system (each beam representing a space-deployed cell site), with switching systems analogous to the Mobile Cellular Switches (MCSs) of a ground-based cellular system.

LEOS are placed in lower orbital positions (500 to 1,400 kilometers [310 to 870 miles]) than are GEOS. The lower orbital paths allow them to be operated with less power and reduce the time delays that plague communications using GEOS (time delays limit the usefulness of GEOS communications for some time-sensitive applications), which orbit at distance up to 60 times greater than LEOS.

Big and Little LEOS

There are two classes of LEOS: Little LEOS—those using many small satellites (36 or more for global communications); and Big LEOS. The Federal Communication Commission (FCC) created the distinction between Big and Little LEOS based on the allocation of frequencies to be used (Little LEOS below one Gigahertz; Big LEOS above one Gigahertz) and on the services they are authorized to provide. Little LEOS handle data traffic only, e.g., messaging, tracking, and monitoring; Big LEOS can provide global mobile telephone service (similar to cellular and PCS) as well as data services, facsimile, paging, geographic positioning, and other services tailored to users needs.

The services offered by Little LEOS will primarily operate in non-real time, i.e., store and forward messaging and data. Little LEOS were deployed between 1996 and 2000. Little LEOS systems will be between 25 and 50 satellites orbiting at about 621 miles above the earth. One or more earth stations will serve as a gateway to the space-deployed system.

Big LEOS systems are in the development stage and have not yet been assigned international frequency allocations, although the FCC has recently granted licenses to three of the five potential service providers.

Big LEOS can provide a wide range of voice and data services, including all of the services provided by Little LEOS, plus cellular— or PCS—like telephone service. Communications can be from mobile or fixed Earth stations. These satellite-linked services are considered to be possible alternatives to expensive land-based wire systems in the remote areas of developing countries. The cost, however, will be high and international country-by-country regulatory questions may slow global deployment. Big LEOS, operating at frequencies above one Gigahertz, will orbit at distances of 310 to 870 miles above the earth.

The Iridium system uses 66 LEOS orbiting in 11 different planes of six satellites each. This provides worldwide telephone and data communication linked to 15 to 20 Earth stations connected to terrestrial wire-line networks. Satellite-to-satellite cross links would be capable of data rates up to 25 Mbps. Several other companies are proposing similar systems, e.g., Globalstar (Loral and Qualcomm, Inc.), Odyssey (TRW, Inc. and Teleglobe), Ellipso (Mobile Communications Holding, Inc.), and ECCO (Equitorial Constellation Communications—Constellation Communications, Inc., Bell Atlantic Enterprises International, and Telecommuniccacoes Brasileiras S.A.).[9]

Telecom deregulation

The deregulation of the local telephone business during the 1990s opened up new vistas for all types of telecom services. For example, prior to the turn of the century only the largest companies could get massive amounts of communications power. The folks at Teligent (**www.teligent.com**) thought otherwise. The company provides local and long-distance phone service, high-speed Internet access, and many other services all on one bill. Teligent is a communications company that has dedicated itself to serving small and mid-sized businesses with its own national facilities-based network based in Vienna, Virginia.

Teligent gives companies a 12-inch digital microwave antenna on the roof. The antenna sends voice, data, and video signals to and from a nearby Teligent base station via microwave (bandwidth provides data transmission speed of 1.544 Mbps). With Teligent's bandwidth, applications that would otherwise be too slow over copper wire, such as multiple Internet connections, videoconferencing, and transmitting large files over the Internet, now are possible.

The company's digital wireless technology can be "scaled" so service meets customer bandwidth needs. And as you add more phones, more lines, and more data-intensive applications like the Internet and videoconferencing, the service can increase your bandwidth to accommodate them. For business customers requiring high-speed Internet access, Teligent offers high-quality, highly reliable bandwidth options ranging from 56K to a full T1. Teligent's Dedicated Access service provides competitively priced connectivity options, all of which are easily upgraded. This is supported by continuous network management and monitoring. TeligentHost service provides several Web hosting solutions, making use of the economies of scale offered in a shared server environment. Its server farm and nationwide ATM backbone make this possible.

This, and emerging direct-to-satellite services, will supplant in-the-ground wired connections at some point in the future. Wireless, digital telecommunications services will provide enormous flexibility and, hopefully, much lower prices for services that haven't even been invented yet.

The biblical words, "the race is not to the swift or the battle to the strong...wisdom is better than weapons of war" might be contemplated when considering your next phone bill. People made fortunes on Internet stocks in the 1990s. The new millennium may see new fortunes made in telecommunications services. That high-performance PC in your teenager's bedroom was considered a super-computer when he was born. This constantly evolving technology will continue to dramatically change the ways we live and work. Telecommunications services will become much more important. Choose wisely because your business may depend upon it.

Endnotes

1. **www.whatis.com/IP.htm**.

2. **www.nanog.org/**.

3. **www.caida.org/**.

4. **www.cise.nsf.gov/**.

5. **www.nlanr.net/**.

6. "Cable-Modem Sales Going Strong," *Cable Foreman* (October 1998:4).

7. AOL, 10-K via www.sec.gov (September 1998).

8. U.S. Congress, Office of Technology Assessment, "Wireless Technologies and the National Information Infrastructure," OTA-ITC-622 (Washington, DC: U.S. Government Printing Office, September 1995).

9. U.S. Congress, Office of Technology Assessment, "Electronic Surveillance in a Digital Age," pages 59-60, OTA-BP-ITC-149 (Washington, DC: U.S. Government Printing Office, July, 1995).

CHAPTER 9

COLLECTION TOOLS TO RAPIDLY OBTAIN REQUIRED INFORMATION

Motivation for the collection of information and data for business intelligence purposes can range from answering a single question to developing input for a comprehensive organizationwide strategic plan. Using the PROACtive process and framework covered in Chapter Four to help us plan what we need to collect, it's time for more detail as to how this actually is accomplished at the operational level.

Since the Internet is our primary source of information, it follows that the browser is our primary collection tool. Netscape's Navigator browser has been installed on millions of corporate desktops. Experience, albeit subjective, shows that Navigator is the better browser when compared to Microsoft's Internet Explorer (IE). Smoother operation and much more inherent capability in Netscape itself (as opposed to IE's use in the Microsoft Office context) brings me to that conclusion.

I prefer Microsoft Internet Explorer for only one purpose—printing Web pages so that the URL prints in nice big letters in the upper right hand corner of the page. Both Navigator and IE allow you to print various items of information in all four corners of a printed-out Web page, but only IE does it automatically in 12-point Times Roman. IE's functions are similar to Navigator's and the toolbar icons are nicer, but Navigator works faster and more efficiently, and it's installed on more corporate desktops than IE. If you are a heavy user of Microsoft Exchange and Outlook on a corporate network, there may be a benefit to using IE as part of a tightly integrated desktop. Having said that, it still seems that most corporate users have Netscape Navigator for their browser, not to mention the fact that it does seem to work better than IE, especially for IBIS.

Netscape Communicator suite

Netscape provides a suite of tools called Communicator. This software tool set enables the user to collect business intelligence and efficiently harness the power of the Internet. Yes, there are other browsers (just take a look at Yahoo!'s browser page under Computers and Internet) but Netscape Communicator seems to have the best functionality (in my opinion) and crash-free characteristics for use in an Internet Business Intelligence System (IBIS).

Communicator consists of four major components. Viewed from the Communicator drop down menu in the main menu bar of the program, they are (with the control key activation code) as follows:

- **Navigator**—The well-known Web browser (Ctrl+1)

- **Messenger**—To receive, send and manage multimedia electronic messages (Ctrl+2)

- **Composer**—To create HTML pages and post them to a server(Ctrl+4)

- **Address Book**—To store information about individuals and to create mailing lists (Ctrl+Shift+2)

Taken together these tools help users create a business intelligence system using the PROACtive method introduced earlier.

Netscape's Communicator suite of tools includes the well-known Navigator browser. Navigator can be your doorway to Internet. It is a graphical user interface of sorts, somewhat akin to America Online's front-end software. Communicator will play an important role in creating the Internet Business Intelligence System. Building on the first U.S. government-sponsored Web browser called Mosaic, Netscape has continuously innovated in the realm of Internet software. A discussion of just how Internet Web sites work might be helpful.

Browser mechanics

According to Netscape, "To understand how a single page is kept distinct in a world of electronic pages, you should recognize its URL, short for Uniform Resource Locator. Every page has a unique URL. Not only does each page have a unique URL, but also each image and frame on a page. You can access a page, an image, or an individual frame by supplying its URL. A URL is text used for identifying and addressing an item in a computer network. In short, a URL provides location information and Navigator displays a URL in the location field. Most often you don't need to know a page's URL because the location information is included as part of a highlighted link; Navigator already knows the URL when you click highlighted text, click a toolbar button, or select a menu item.

"Communicator uses the URL text to find a particular item, such as a page, among all the computers connected to the Internet. Within the URL text are components that specify the protocol, server, and pathname of an item. Notice in the URL **http://home.netscape.com/index.html** that the protocol is followed by a colon (http:), the server is preceded by two slashes (//home.netscape.com), and each segment of the pathname (only one here) is preceded by a single slash (/index.html). The first component, the protocol, identifies a manner for interpreting computer information. Many Internet pages use HTTP (short for HyperText Transfer Protocol).

"Other common protocols you might come across include file (also known as ftp, which is short for File Transfer Protocol), news (the protocol used by Usenet discussion groups), and gopher (an alternative transfer protocol). The second component, the server, identifies the computer system that stores the information you seek (such as home.netscape.com). Each server on the Internet has a unique name that identifies the location of the server. The last component, the pathname, identifies the location of an item on the server. For example, a pathname usually specifies the name of the file identifying the page (such as /welcome.html), possibly preceded by one or more directory/folder names that contain the file (such as /home/welcome.html)."

Bookmarks

The most common way to store the links you want to revisit is to create bookmarks. Netscape states, "Bookmarks offer a convenient means of page retrieval. You store your bookmarks in a list. Once you add a bookmark to your list, the item stays until you remove it or change lists. The permanence and accessibility of bookmarks make them invaluable for personalizing your Internet access.

"Navigator offers many options for creating a bookmark list. Basic options let you add and access a page through a pop-up menu on the location toolbar or through the Communicator menu of the main menu bar. The simplest way to obtain direct access to a favorite page is to open the Bookmarks menu and choose Add Bookmarks. This adds the current page as an item in the Bookmarks menu.

"More advanced options, available from the Bookmarks window, let you create hierarchical menus, partial menu displays, multiple and shared bookmark files, list descriptions, and list searches. The Bookmarks window lists your bookmarks and offers a set of menu items to help you organize your list. In addition, many drag-and-drop options are available for creating and filing your bookmarks."

Bookmarks are a must, but there's an even simpler way to access international news or any other Web site that you want to get to quickly. The drag-and-drop features of object linking and embedding allow you to create an icon on the desktop that will launch the browser and bring you to the desired site. If you don't have a network connection to the Internet you may have to log onto your Internet Service Provider first.

Drag and drop

With Netscape, as indicated on their Help page, you can drag and drop icons, text, and images from place to place in Communicator. In addition, Communicator's mail, discussion group, and page-composing components offer similar drag-and-drop capabilities.

You can drag the following:

- From the Navigator window, drag the page proxy icon
- From the Bookmarks and History windows, drag page icons
- From the content area of the Navigator window, drag linked text or linked images

You can drop icons and links on the following targets:

- Personal toolbar (to create a toolbar button)
- Another Navigator window (to open the page)

- Bookmark pop-up menu or Bookmarks window
  (to create or reposition a bookmark)

- Desktop (to create an Internet shortcut)

Netscape power tips

Collecting information via the Internet using Netscape Navigator can be greatly facilitated with several "power tips." The following are useful techniques for speeding up the collection process:

Set start-up home page (Edit, Preferences, Use current page) to that which is most useful for your needs. This may change from project to project, or you may prefer to leave it set for your most often used search engine.

Find text string in a long page (Ctrl+F) when your browser has loaded a page found via a search engine. This is especially useful when you search for a specific keyword and then review pages presented by the search engine. When the page has loaded you can go directly to the keyword on the page using this technique.

Save page as plain text (File, Save as, *.txt) in a specific directory. This goes to the heart of the matter of collection. When a page is loaded you have three basic options for saving it. If you save as text you filter all but the words and save it in a file. If you save as HTML you will retain the formatting but not the graphics. If you right-click on a graphic you can save the specific graphic. This is especially important for retaining charts and graphs.

Manage your contacts with the address book. When you are reading an e-mail in the Messenger module you can click on the sender's e-mail address (in the "from" field while you are reading the e-mail) and a New Card dialog box pops up with the first four fields filled in from the information in the e-mail's sender address field. There are 17 fields for each "card" in Communicator's address book function, including a generous size box for notes, name search functions, view by, and sort options.

Set info printing in page corners (file, page setup, dialog box, help for codes for items to print) is a handy way to imprint information for manual filing. If you file printouts in manila folders or three-ring binders, you'll have the information on when and where you got the information printed on the page.

Copy and paste from Web page to word processor document is a key technique for selectively saving Internet information. By highlighting the desired text (drag the cursor across it with left mouse button pressed) and then pressing Ctrl+C to copy and Ctrl+V to paste into the word processor's document (use Alt+Tab to switch applications), you can quickly build a new document with selected information from many Web pages.

Save images as graphic file to retain and file important charts, graphs, or photos that will not be saved if you use File, Save as, HTML. To save a graphic, position the cursor on object, click the right mouse button, Save as, specify storage directory, and save the item.

There are many other time-saving techniques that can be performed in Netscape Communicator. For example, the Messenger module toolbar buttons permit rapid review, filing or deletion of messages. Clicking on the Subject, Sender, Date, Priority, Status, or Other header above the messages displayed in the Inbox will sort all the messages in ascending or descending order (click once or twice). Creating new folders to store different types of messages will help you speed up the collection process.

Automatically download, store, and locally search Web pages

Part of IBIS can be an Internet-Derived Intelligence System (IDIS) module. This can provide a large quantity (500 MB to 2 GB) of information (text, photos, audio, video, graphics) automatically derived from a variety of Internet sources (automated with the least amount of human intervention) in a highly portable, self-contained format, such as a CD-ROM or DVD. This CD-ROM- or DVD-based system then could be used anywhere, without an Internet connection, on a laptop computer.

- Needs assessment provides a framework for targeting of required information (see Chapter Seven)

- Internet sites worldwide are located that will provide the information (see Chapter Ten)

- Netscape Netcaster is programmed to automatically download the information on a regular basis to maintain up-to-date information

- The information is written to directly to a CD-ROM or DVD using Netcaster

- The CD-ROM or DVD includes software that enables the user to quickly retrieve and work with specific items of information

- After initial operation, refinements and/or enhancements are made

This combination of process and tools enables IBIS to better utilize Internet-derived information for business intelligence purposes. The CD-ROM or DVD format ensures a reliable means of accessing the information rather than via a direct connection to an Internet site that can be unreliable. Internet information on CD-ROM or DVD has other benefits. For example, viewing a video clip downloaded in real time takes up an extraordinary amount of bandwidth and requires a high data-rate connection. The CD-ROM or DVD allows the same information to be flawlessly accessed without the need for an Internet connection. Although not real time, the update frequency for production of CD-ROMs or DVDs can be adjusted to take into account circumstances that demand more frequent updates.

While human intervention is required to target the precise information needed, Netcaster software can be utilized to automate most of the additional steps necessary to download the pages and produce the CD-ROM or DVD. Essentially, this is a simple concept that utilizes simple software. However, the system's actual usefulness is very much determined by optimization of the concept and components needed to make it a reality. One such component is the Netcaster module within Netscape's Communicator package. Netscape Netcaster delivers information to you automatically, and it will write it to the CD-ROM writer. The CD-ROM writer is simply specified as the drive to which the information should be written.

According to Netscape documentation, "Channels are Web sites that are automatically delivered to your desktop. Using Netcaster, you can subscribe to just the channels you want and get just the information you need. This way, you don't have to search the Web on your own and look through irrelevant information. Netcaster can also update your channels automatically so you can always see current information. You can make any channel into a full-screen Webtop. In

Windows, a Webtop always remains on your screen underneath other windows that you're working in. With a Webtop, you can easily see late-breaking information on the channel while you complete other tasks. With offline browsing, you can download any Web site and view it when you're offline (disconnected from the Internet).

"With Netcaster, you can collect both channels and Web sites. Channels are like Web sites; they are built with the same tools, such as HTML and JavaScript. However, instead of navigating to the site where you want information, you subscribe to a channel by adding it to Netcaster. Then the desired information is delivered automatically to Netcaster at predefined intervals. In essence, a channel is a Web site delivered automatically to your computer. By default, Netcaster is set to automatically update sites once a day. However, you can change this update schedule to almost anything you want—for example, every hour between 5:00 a.m. and 5:00 p.m., or every week at 8:00 a.m. on Thursday.

"When Netcaster updates a channel or site, it downloads the site's content and stores it on your computer. By default, Netcaster downloads two levels of a site—that is, it goes two links deep into a site. Levels represent the page structure of a Web site. The main page of a site is the first level; links on that page go to other pages, or the second level; each second-level page has links to yet more pages, or the third level, and so on. When Netcaster updates a channel or site, it downloads the site's contents and stores it on your computer in its own cache. Each site's cache takes up room on your hard disk, measured in kilobytes (KB). You simply tell it to write to the CD-ROM drive.

"With offline browsing, you can browse or view a Netcaster channel while you're offline (disconnected from the Internet). Offline browsing gives you the following advantages:

- View a site when it's inconvenient to connect to the Internet, such as while traveling

- If you're charged for connection time, viewing a site offline can reduce the cost of your Internet connection

- Because Netcaster stores a site locally (on your hard disk), you can quickly navigate the site without the delays caused by a slow connection

"Offline browsing works because Netcaster downloads the contents of a site and stores it on your computer in a cache. Because the site is stored on your computer, you can view it even when you're offline. Writing information to a CD-ROM and performing offline browsing is a very effective use of resources."

Data sculpting

Almost all information that isn't part of an executable program or a graphic file is transmitted as ASCII (American Standard Code for Information Interchange) text. This means that almost all of what you can save as a file and store in folders can be easily manipulated and reformatted to suit your specific need. This could range from selected portions of a text document to delimited strings of text that can be used to populate a database.

The most basic form of data sculpting is the common practice of trimming off portions of a Uniform Resource Locator (URL) to back your way into a Web site. For example, you search for a particular item and get some hits. You click on a promising link only to get some type of error message. If you type or copy and paste the URL into the location box in the browser and trim off characters starting from the right end of the string, you can work your way section by section up to the top or domain name.

Data sculpting often is required to correct deficiencies in the format of a downloaded text file. If the file you are working with includes too many paragraph marks, you can remove them in the following manner: By selecting your word processor's search-and-replace function, find and replace with an odd character the paragraph marks delineating each paragraph. Frequently this will involve a series of three paragraph marks, so the first round of search and replace should specify this number.

In Microsoft Word this is accomplished by first selecting More in the search and replace dialog box, then selecting Special to reveal a list of searchable characters. Select paragraph mark three times for the Find What field and use an odd character in the Replace With field. The second search and replace pass might find all occurrences of two paragraph marks replacing them with one space. The third pass replaces the odd character with two paragraph marks to recreate the paragraph breaks with just two rather than the three found in the original file.

Control key combinations are very useful in the process of data sculpting. To illustrate a common set of control key combinations, let's say that you are working on a project that involves a very large company that has an extensive Web presence. There are thousands of pages of information spread over multiple Web sites around the world. You need to create a brief from this massive material. To do this, you'll need to collect snippets of relevant information from dozens of Web pages mounted by the company.

In the IBM-compatible world a separate key usually marked "Ctrl" (control key, or Apple key on Macintosh computers) is pressed and held while another key is depressed to invoke a specific function. If you have a Web page displayed in your browser and you want to copy one paragraph to a summary on which you are working, you would highlight the desired paragraph using your cursor and mouse button. After you highlight the text you press the combination control and C keys at the same time. This copies the text into the computer's buffer. An "Alt" and "Tab" key combination is simultaneously pressed and this will take you to your word processor document, assuming you loaded the word processor software. Once you are in the document window, press "Ctrl" and V keys simultaneously and the highlighted text will be pasted into the document from the buffer. See Table 9.1 for a comprehensive list of useful control key combinations.

Table 9.1

SUMMARY OF CONTROL KEY COMBINATIONS		
	Microsoft Word 97	**Netscape Navigator & Composer**
Copy	Control + C	Same
Paste	Control + V	Same
Cut	Control + X	Same
Undo	Control + Z	Same
Repeat	Control + Y	Not available
Select all	Control + A	Same
Insert hyperlink	Control + K	Control + Shift + L
Find	Control + F	Same
Find again	Not available	Control + G
Go to	Control + G	Not available
New	Control + N	Same
Open	Control + O	Same
History	Not available	Control + H
Print	Control + P	Same

From text to database

Text files often can be turned into databases through the use of a basic variation of search and replace. This type of data sculpting is useful for "cleaning up" Web page lists to create fielded data that can be imported into a database. First, highlight the text of the list and then copy it into your word processor. When you examine the list's text you may find that each element of information in the record (person's name, company name, address, etc.) is delimited with one paragraph mark while the end of the record is delimited with two paragraph marks.

The double paragraph marks after each set of name and address blocks must be replaced first. You can search and replace these with an odd character that is not found elsewhere in the text. This serves as your record delimiter. Next, search and replace the remaining single paragraph marks so that they are replaced with commas. This process creates a comma-delimited file. This file can be imported into spreadsheet and database programs with fielded data. Fielded data can be sorted and used for various reporting purposes, just like a regular database. Once a file has been cleaned up and imported into a spreadsheet or database program, more than likely it can be exported into a variety of other format files for other uses later on.

Additionally, many types of CD-ROM systems allow you to output a file, but it seldom is in the format you need for your database. Unless you are using a free-form database system like askSam (described further in other chapters), you need to match certain fields from the source file to the destination database. Data sculpting enables you to create a suitable file. This can be combined with Excel's ability to manipulate text data. After you've created a suitable comma-delimited file as detailed above, you can import the result into Excel. This software presents the records in rows and the fields in columns. If you need to delete columns or change their order it is a simple matter. Presto! You have a useful database.

All of this may sound very complicated but it's not hard to do. It is simple but essential because you can easily become overwhelmed with thousands of bits and pieces of information, so you need to collect them in a format that will make organization, analysis, and communication easy. In fact, rather than limit you to some manageable amount of information without process and tools, IBIS gives you the ability to save even more information than you might have without a system. IBIS enables you to not only collect more information, but to make better use of the larger quantity you collected.

CHAPTER 10

SEARCHING THE INTERNET FOR BUSINESS INTELLIGENCE

There are various methods of search and discovery. The often-used journalistic formula helps us frame the problem: Who? What? When? Where? Why? How?

Then there is the problem-solving approach where we specify the problem, analyze the problem, formulate a hypothesis, and test the hypothesis.

"Fill-in-the-blank" approaches presuppose that we have a template—a set of predetermined questions—or have organized the categories of required information into a matrix.

While it is easy to turn to your favorite search engine and type a few words to get an answer, that informal approach may not be the best within the framework of a business intelligence function.

When it comes to the Internet, the important question is: How do you find the good stuff without wasting hours of fruitless surfing? Thankfully, as the Internet has grown and expanded (there are probably at least 40 million regular U.S. users now, up from just a few thousand prior to 1990), so too have the means to pinpoint desired information. Let's consider information that might be required for strategic planning.

The ability to rapidly locate and acquire data and information is a cornerstone of the Internet Business Intelligence System (IBIS). The ability to rapidly obtain needed information is at the core of the system, and we examined the mechanics of collection in the previous chapter. But, as the amount of information available via the Internet increases dramatically, so must your capability to locate the desired item(s) of information. Search engines fulfill this need. In fact, they increasingly are multipurpose portals to the Internet that provide a variety of free services as well as sophisticated searching capabilities.

Search engines become mini online services

The traditional search engines turned mini online services are the first places to look for grist for the business intelligence mill. Over the years search engines have evolved into full-featured Internet entities that provide many sophisticated services previously available only through expensive subscription services. News clipping by keyword or phrase and topic alerts e-mailed to the user are just two of the services that are helping search engines compete with online services for "face time" in cyberspace. Sophisticated content focus is another major trend.

Some search engines turned "portals" have pulled together a combination of commercial and free Web-based information. They format these elements to create Web pages that present, for instance, a large amount of relevant and timely information about public companies. This includes current stock price, trading range with graphs, brokers recommendations and analyst reports, industry groupings (major players in the company's line of business), some financial details, and one-button access to SEC data, as well as current news articles. Yahoo! Finance, shown in Figure 10.1, is a good example.

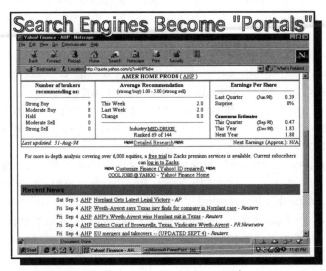

Figure 10.1

The better search engines include additional features like links to commercial databases that will provide a capsule of information about the company one click away from the telephone listing. One click takes you to the information provider's sites, and up pops the company you previously searched for in the telephone directory. Now you have several items of basic information that can include lines of business, estimated sales or employee head counts, number of locations, and perhaps even officer's names. If you want more detail, you generally can purchase it at these secondary sites.

Some of the better-known search engines have the corporate resources to mount a large-scale effort to develop Web-derived content in specific categories. This is particularly true with financial information. More and more detailed and aggregated information on public companies is being presented at no charge. You now have the ability to type in a ticker symbol and automatically get current stock prices as quotes and in historical charts covering user selected periods, broker recommendations, financial details, and a list of current news items relating to the company. All of this is available in one place and at no charge.

While there are only about 15,000 publicly traded companies, they do tend to dominate their markets and often serve as trendsetters. This makes the information valuable as it relates to private companies in the same industry.

Another area of focus for major search engines is news. They've long ago gone beyond basic offerings of a few "top stories." As search engines have transformed into portals and have begun to challenge online service packagers of content, more sophisticated news search, topic tracking, and news clipping has become available, frequently at no charge to the user. Excite seems to have a dominant position in the news arena providing several search capabilities to find specific items or to monitor news. Figures 10.2 and 10.3 highlight Excite's powerful news service capabilities.

Search engine personalities

Search engines have developed personalities. The key to rapidly obtaining the required information is in understanding the different personalities. For example, some search engines are oriented to finding people, places, and things. While they may have a variety of other strengths, their distinctive competency may be an excellent link to residential and business telephone directories with automatic mapping capabilities. Often this is the first step in compiling information on a private company. The correct name (at least the way it is listed in the telephone book) and the exact street address, as well as other telephone numbers they may be using (and possibly the other businesses at the address), all are important bits of information. A good example is **www.info space.com** (Figure 10.4), with its telephone directories and reverse search capability.

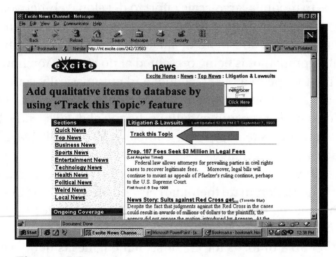

Figure 10.2

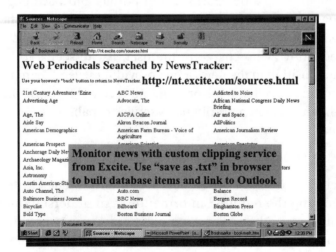

Figure 10.3

Another type of search engine might emphasize news and provide various means of delivery, including custom news clipping. Still another personality type is the specialty search engine, which, for example, might help you locate subject-specific search engines. Still others are strong on hierarchical or keyword searching.

Figure 10.4

Hierarchical

The Argus Clearinghouse (**www.clearinghouse.net**) provides a central access point for topical guides that identify, describe, and evaluate Internet-based information. The service states that its focus is narrow and is operated on the belief that human effort must be combined with searching and browsing technologies. It applies intellectual labor for qualitative assessment of Internet's information.

Argus' hierarchical categories include: Arts & Humanities; Business & Employment; Communication; Computers & Information Technology; Education; Engineering; Government & Law; Health & Medicine; Places & People; Recreation; Science & Mathematics; and Social Sciences & Social Issues. These top-level categories are explained in a concise paragraph and then subdivided into disciplines within each category. A brief explanation of each discipline is given alongside a clickable link.

The Argus Clearinghouse features searching and browsing capabilities. You can search the full text of information pages for each of the guides including titles, the names of authors, their institutions, and descriptive keywords. Limited Boolean operators are available as well as truncation.

An additional category is the Internet Searching Center. This centralizes other resources (other search engines, directories, and related information) to help you find information external to Argus Clearinghouse.

Yahoo! (**www.yahoo.com**) is another good example of a hierarchically structured search engine where the categories seem to prove more useful than the search capability. The main menu for Yahoo! is intelligently laid out with logical categories. In fact, it appears that many other newer search engines have adopted Yahoo!'s approach in recent years. In addition to such major categories as arts and humanities, business and economy, government, news and media, reference, etc., there is a growing list of countries that have separate Yahoo! search engines. Several U.S. cities also have specific search sites listed on the main page.

Yahoo! is a directory of sites rather than a true Web search engine. Yahoo! searches generate category and site matches from the Yahoo! directory. If no matches exist in Yahoo!, the search defaults to a Web-wide search powered by AltaVista. Yahoo!'s organized and fairly extensive directory provides an excellent search starting point. A search for freeware and shareware useful for an Internet Business Intelligence System is illustrative.

From Yahoo!'s main menu, choose Software under the main heading of Computers. This brings you to a list of software topics including Freeware. Click on that and you'll find two more categories, GNU Software (22-plus sites) and Operating Systems (seven-plus sites), and two Web sites for freeware. Choosing one of these two Web sites brings us to **www.moochers.com** where we find several categories of freeware in a frame at left and several featured programs in the frame at right. Clicking on the Internet Search Tools category, we get a look at one-paragraph descriptions of 16 search tool programs ranging in size from 55 Kb to 2 Mb.

You'll note that the Moochers.com site does have a keyword search function, but we've used the hierarchical approach here too. Going back to the main menu and clicking on the Business category takes us to a screen with three business subcategories: Finance, Organizers/Reminders, and Word Processors/Text Editors. Clicking on Organizers/Reminders presents a variety of simple programs that could be very useful in the organizing of Internet Business Intelligence. One of the programs looks promising, so clicking on the home page for its developer brings us to another fork in the road.

Freeware and shareware generally are smaller programs and utilities. However, despite their size, they may serve the user extremely well in providing a solution to a seemingly insurmountable problem. Browsing these programs on various sites provides an education relating to what's possible and what's new and different. Viewing these possibilities may provide a unique, personalized approach to building an Internet Business Intelligence System. You may find something that you'd never come across if you depended solely upon a keyword search.

After taking a quick look at this program we decide to use another site for further investigation. There are several sites on the developer's home page that deal with freeware and shareware, presumably all of which feature that developer's program. But it gives us several other appropriate sites to review. Now we're surfing more than we're searching (hierarchical or otherwise), but you get the picture. Sometimes this approach is more useful than narrowly defined keywords.

Keyword search

AltaVista was an early Internet creation of Digital Equipment Corporation's research unit. It was designed to make Internet search capabilities easy to use. A major refinement was the "Specify Your Language" capability to get search results in 25 languages and receive search results that include only pages published in the specified language. Other features that were added included "Customize AltaVista" for results in a particular format and level of detail. Another useful feature was a capability to refine results to narrow earlier search results. But the real power of AltaVista was its Natural Language Search and sophisticated Boolean query capability using keywords. A LiveTopics feature uses a graphical interface to help users narrow a general query to generate relevant results.

Perhaps the best way to find something when you know specifically what you are searching for is to perform phrase searching. You would type "keywords within quote marks" to search for the exact string within the quotation marks. This is one of the best ways to quickly find exactly what you are looking for in a search. Putting a specific string of keywords in a specific order within quote marks often will return exactly what you need.

AltaVista's advanced search capability enables you to perform Boolean searching using operators. Many other major search engines also have similar capabilities. For example, you can specify that you want to find bread AND NOT butter.

AND

Finds only documents containing all of the specified words or phrases.

OR

Finds documents containing at least one of the specified words or phrases.

NOT

Excludes documents containing the specified word or phrase.

NEAR

Finds documents containing both specified words or phrases within 10 words of each other.

To include multiple operators within a search query, group the operators with the search words using parentheses. For example, "(Mary NEAR lamb) AND NOT contrary" tells AltaVista to search for documents with Mary and lamb, then to sort through those documents and root out ones with contrary in them. Unless you specify the order with parentheses, AltaVista interprets NEAR, then NOT, then AND, then OR, moving from left to right through the query.

AltaVista provides many specialty search capabilities. You can search by host name, find pages on host, and search for titles, images, links, anchors, domains, and objects as well as search within date range. You can set advanced search as the default. (The simple search page normally appears first when you visit AltaVista.) AltaVista offers one of the widest ranges of power search functions, and it is noted for its full and varied advanced-search syntax. AltaVista serves the sophisticated searcher especially well. One of the first search engines to do so, AltaVista Translations enables you to translate from one language to another.

Other major search engines

It seems that everyone has a favorite search engine, probably because each search engine has a distinct personality, and most have certain unique capabilities. While entire books have been written about this subject, you only need the highlights here. The following is a capsule statement about some of the more prominent search engines and why they might be used in IBIS.

Excite uses statistics and artificial intelligence to find synonyms for your queries, searching for sites relevant to a concept rather than an exact keyword. As such, it's a great choice for general searches. Once you find a particularly well-suited site, use the More Like This function to search for other sites that are similar in content. Excite has some of the best news search and news article management capabilities on the Internet in its NewsTracker (**www.nt.excite.com**).

HotBot (**www.hotbot.com**) search features a flashy interface, a speedy engine, and a comprehensive and fresh index. HotBot provides drop-down boxes for Boolean beginners and boasts power search options for more advanced searches. A very handy feature in More Search Options beyond the main page is the ability to check boxes to search on very specific criteria using the "pages must include" function. You also can limit your search to specific locations and domains.

Infoseek's (**infoseek.go.com**) specialty is its ability to process plain English questions, providing a friendly alternative to Boolean syntax. Infoseek also suggests related topic areas for a combination browsing/searching experience. Like HotBot's advanced search, there are easy-to-use drop-down selector boxes, but their search-by-location selector has more. The Express desktop software is available free of charge. Now a Disney company, Infoseek offers intranet software to make their service available on your network.

Lycos (**www.lycos.com**) has a network of sites with different functions and search engines for various countries. Lycos Pro Search lets you use a natural language query or several "look for" specifiers. A frequency of words relevancy control provides for additional search refinement. Complete Boolean operators round out the capabilities of this powerful service.

Table 10.1 compares the features and syntax of several major search engines.

Table 10.1

	BASIC BOOLEAN	OTHER OPERATORS
AltaVista **www.altavista.digital.com** Power searches specify language, one-time setting for customization, refine-by-topic selection, natural language queries, search by host, domain, title, find anchors, images, links, and objects	AND& Finds only documents containing all of the specified words or phrases. ORI Finds documents containing at least one of the specified words or phrases. NOT! Excludes documents containing the specified word or phrase. NEAR Finds documents containing specified words or phrases within 10 words of each other. NOTE: Use operator word only or symbol if operator word is part of search.	*(wild card), +(to require words), -(to exclude words), NOTE: + and - work only in Simple Search mode, "phrase" (searches for phrase or when the operator word is a search word, also can use () to denote phrase), case sensitivity.
Deja News **www.dejanews.com** Advanced newsgroup searching and such information functions as author profile and posting as well as sorting by date, newsgroup, author. Combined with relevancy also can browse groups from top-level hierarchy downward	Same as above but symbol for near is ^ and &! for AND NOT	Same as above but adds {} braces to include variations of a word. Deja News adds search filter form with context operators a to require specific author name, s for specific subject, g for specific newsgroup, and dc for creation date in 12/31/97 format. Deja News allows you to search through subject headers of individual messages posted to the Usenet newsgroup bulletin boards.
Excite **www.excite.com** Presents various options on home page including broad subject areas called "channels" for decision tree approach. News Channel option searches current news articles from over 300 Web-based publications.	Same as above but also features Intelligent Concept Extraction that learns how words are related to other words. Uses statistics and artificial intelligence to find synonyms for queries, searching for sites relevant to a concept rather than an exact keyword. Use the More Like This function to search for other sites that are similar in content.	Use the "+" (plus) sign for words that your results MUST contain. Or use the "-" (minus) sign in your query to tell the search engine that your results should NOT contain a certain word. When using these options, do not leave any space between the sign and the word.

HotBot **www.hotbot.com** Interface allows novice users to execute complex queries. Links to this URL permit searching for all of the people who are linking to any page on the Web.	By default, HotBot only displays documents containing "all of the words" that you specify. (This is the equivalent of a Boolean "AND" search.) By setting the main search pop-up box to "any of the words," you'll find documents that contain as few as one of your requested words. (This is a Boolean "OR" search).	Select "the exact phrase" from the search pull-down menu, or simply enclose your phrase terms in double quotes (" "). Selecting "the person" tells HotBot to look for near matches to your search pattern. Date menu options allow narrowing search to documents created or modified within a specific date range.

Content ratings

Magellan (**magellan.excite.com**) is famous for its five-star rating system and extensive collection of reviewed sites. Users can search the Web or search within reviewed sites only. A search of Green Light sites generates only G-rated results, a feature of particular interest to parents.

Magellan adds some additional features including ideas closely linked to the words in your query. This feature broadens your search. This search engine determines relationships between words and concepts. Magellan searches all the Web sites in their database, which includes reviewed sites and sites they have rated as Green Light sites. If you choose the Reviewed Sites Only option you get a high-quality, targeted search of the more than 60,000 Web sites chosen and reviewed by Magellan's experts. Choose the Green Light Sites Only option for a high-quality, targeted search of reviewed sites that, at the time of review, contained no content intended for mature audiences.

Magellan uses Intelligent Concept Extraction (ICE) to find relationships that exist between words and ideas, so the results of a search will contain words related to the concepts for which you're searching. Boolean operators tell Magellan's concept-based search mechanism to switch to keyword searching. This allows you to search for documents that contain exactly the words you are looking for. Boolean operators include AND, AND NOT, OR, and parentheses.

Magellan's search results are sorted by relevance. Magellan lists 10 search results at a time in decreasing order of relevance. The percentage sign to the right of each result is the relevance rating. The closer the rating is to 100 percent, the more confident Magellan is that the document will fit your needs. The relevance ratings are automatically generated by the search engine, which compares the information in the site against the information in your query.

Metasearch resources

In a way, metasearch resources can be as simple as one page that presents many search engine alternatives. This is the case with several major search engines that provide choices to search their own database but also present buttons to take you to other search engines. However, a true metasearch resource is a search engine that works on multiple search engines at one time. This distinction can be blurred however, and each type of search you require may be best performed in a different type of metasearch resource. There is no "one size fits all."

Yahoo!'s All-In-One Search Page (under Computers and Internet) lists dozens of search engines that either present multiple search engines on one page or submit your query to multiple search engines at one time. You can use a search engine to find specialized search engines. A good example is Search.com, which provides searchers easy access to more than 300 search engines and databases. A fair number of these are specific to particular subject areas.

Checking Yahoo!'s Internet category (Computers and Internet > Internet > World Wide Web > Searching the Web > All-in-One Search Pages) reveals a long list of metasearch sites. Here is a selection:

- **123 Search**—Search over 75-plus search engines by queries, descriptions, reviews, and forms

- **1Blink**—Search with all major search engines from one place

- **All-in-One Search Page**—Search over 120 of the Internet's best engines, databases, and indexes

- **ANeedle.com**—Offers directory of search engines and sites

- **Beaucoup Search Engines**—More than 350 search engines in categorized tables. Also in 6 languages

- **CUSI**—A unified interface for several search engines that perform resource discovery

- **Dogpile**—Multi-engine semi-parallel search interface. Searches logically through several search engines until 10 matches are found. Allows use of Boolean and proximity operators

- **Dr. Webster's Big Page of Search Engines**

- **EZ-Find**—Utility that lets you enter keywords to search for on the Net, and then submit them in turn to several search engines without having to retype them for each engine

- **Find-It!**—A complete Internet search tool for finding Web/www documents, people, software, and Usenet news-groups from one page

- **FormSeek**—Provides an index of search engines' forms by category

- **Internet Navigator**—A unified interface for over 77 search engines all on one page

- **Internet Sleuth, The**—Collection of over 1,500 searchable databases covering a wide variety of topics. Parallel searching allows the simultaneous search of up to 10 databases within categories

- **Mechanical Bull**—JavaScript "remote control" system for searching multiple search engines at the same time

- **MetaCrawler**—Allows you to search through multiple search engines at once. Part of the Go2Net Network

- **Metafind**—Searches through all the large search engines and collates results

- **Metasearch**—Enter your search terms and choose advanced features like Boolean operators just once, then search multiple engines

- **Personal Compass**—Search any (up to four at a time) major Web databases

- **Powersearch**—Search two topics at once, triple & quad engine searches

- **Proseek**—Searches a selection of engines worldwide, by region or by topic

- **SavvySearch**—Sends your query in parallel to many search engines. The results are displayed in a homogeneous format

- **Search Satellite, The**—Pop-up window that accesses 20 Internet search engines from one convenient input field

- **Search.com**—Online forms for most major and minor search engines from CNET

• **SuperSeek**—Search up to four engines simultaneously, side by side

• **SuperSeek Web Search**—Search your choice of eight engines at the same time, as well as newsgroups and more

• **Surfer, The**—Compilation of links to search engines, and a thematically organized Web site directory

• **U.K. Search Master**—Searches all the well-known and not so well-known engines and directories to display the results

• **Websight**—A client-side Web-search utility written in JavaScript that uses the same syntax for searching the nine major search engines. Downloads to reside in your PC

Search engine features

An often-overlooked method of finding information using "traditional" search engines involves specialized syntax. Using such prefixes as domain, host, or url can provide dozens of relevant pages that might not have otherwise surfaced in a regular keyword search. To find these specialized capabilities, carefully review the help information on some of the major search engines. AltaVista can be used in this way to search for "hidden" documents that you might not find through a keyword search in the search engine. Here are some of the special commands that can be used in conjunction with your keyword search:

anchor: text

Finds pages that contain the specified word or phrase in the text of a hyperlink anchor: "Click here to visit AltaVista" would find pages with "Click here to visit AltaVista" as a link.

applet: class

Finds pages that contain a specified Java applet. Use applet: morph to find pages using applets called morph.

domain: domainname

Finds pages within the specified domain. Use domain:de to find pages from Germany, or use domain:org to find pages from organizations.

host: name

Finds pages on a specific computer. The search host: dilbert.united media.com would find pages on the computer called dilbert at united media.com.

image: filename

Finds pages with images having a specific file name. Use image:elvis to find pages with images called Elvis.

link: URLtext

Finds pages with a link to a page with the specified URL text. Use link:altavista.digital.com to find all pages linking to AltaVista.

text: text

Finds pages that contain the specified text in any part of the page other than an image tag, link, or URL. The search text:cow9 would find all pages with the term cow9 in them.

title: text

Finds pages that contain the specified word or phrase in the page title, which appears in the title bar of most browsers. The search title:Elvis would find pages with Elvis in the title.

url: text

Finds pages with a specific word or phrase in the URL. Use url:altavista to find all pages on all servers that have the word altavista in the host name, path, or filename—the complete URL, in other words.

Relevance ranking

Search engines return results of searches in a list of documents. Each search engine has a unique way of presenting the results.

AltaVista uses a ranking algorithm to determine the order in which matching documents are returned on the results page. Each document gets a grade based on how many of the search terms it contains, where the words are in the document, and how close to each other they are. Repeating a word over and over in a Web page, known as "spamming," has a negative effect on a site's ranking. As soon as it is discovered by software programmed specifically to detect spamming, the offending site is prevented from appearing in the AltaVista index.

Similarly with Excite, the search-results page displays the relevance rating as a percentage that appears to the left of each site's title. The higher the percentage, the more confident they are that the site listed matches the search query that was entered. The rating is generated by an algorithmic equation that measures the site against the concept described in the query.

However, when you search using Lycos, their software compares the words you enter in the search box with the words found on the millions of pages across the Web. They then show you the results of these comparisons in the form of a list—and they put the Web pages that best match your search expression at the top of that list. This is different from an algorithm that ranks the results and displays best-to-worst matches.

Lycos gathers the list of Web pages that match your search expression, adds everything they know about resources related to your search, and organizes all that information on your Search Results page. Displayed prominently in the center of your Search Results page is a list of the Web pages with contents that best match your search expression. The results are grouped by Web site, and the "root" URL —the address likely to take you to the site's home page— is displayed under the Web address.

Navigation links are located at the top and bottom of the list of Web pages to help you move through multiple pages of results. The Previous Page and Next Page links allow you to browse through the results one page at a time.

Similar Pages is a way to fine-tune your Lycos queries. It uses the search results themselves to identify the kind of information you seek. Another enhancement that goes beyond relevance ranking is Matching Categories.

At the top of your Search Results page is a collection of Lycos resources the software suggests are likely related to your search topic. Finally, Search These Results can whittle down an overwhelming number of suggested links. You can refine your search and ask Lycos to search the same set of documents for another word or phrase. In effect, you can create a subset of your original results, this time including only documents that also match your second query.

Searching your search results is as easy as entering your new words in the search box and clicking the Search These Results radio button.

Yahoo!'s relevancy ranking works differently and takes advantage of their strength in categorizing information. After you've typed a keyword (or keywords) into the query box and clicked on the Search button, Yahoo! searches for matches in five areas of the database. Yahoo! looks for matches with category names, Web site titles and comments (as they appear in the Yahoo! directory), content from individual Web pages (a service provided by Inktomi), Yahoo! News stories, and Yahoo! Net Events.

Matches are presented on the Search Results page in this same order: Yahoo! categories first, then Web sites, then individual Web pages scanned by Inktomi, followed by news stories, and Net Events. Keyword matches are also organized by "relevancy" depending on such factors as these:

- **Multiple Keyword Matches**—Sites, categories, or documents with more keyword matches are ranked higher than those with fewer keyword matches.

- **Document Section Weighting**—Sites and categories with keyword matches found in the title are ranked higher than those found in the comment, body, or URL.

- **Generality of Category**—Matching categories that are listed higher up in the Yahoo! hierarchy are ranked higher than specific categories listed deeper within the hierarchy.

These relevancy rankings influence the order in which various matches appear on any given Search Results page.

Other types of searches

Search engines geared to finding multimedia sites increasingly are important, as more multimedia content becomes available on the Internet. More and more real-time and archived audio-only and audiovisual content is available, some of it relevant to business interests. Most major broadcast news organizations have some type of search feature on their site that leads the user to pertinent clips. This is particularly true with international information and consumer-oriented information. RealAudio's Web page provides more than 150 broadcast stations with audio available via the Internet. Many of these are of interest to business users seeking information from a specific market.

Another type of multimedia search engine is provided on conferencing sites. You can locate specific categories of users of Microsoft NetMeeting and as time goes on there will be more and more specialized niche conferences on the Internet using NetMeeting-like conferencing packages. Microsoft NetMeeting provides a complete conferencing solution for the Internet and for corporate intranets. It lets you communicate with both audio and video, collaborate on virtually any

Windows-based application, exchange graphics on an electronic "whiteboard," transfer files, and use text-based chat. You'll find more about this in Chapter Sixteen, "Communicating Business Intelligence."

There are many ways to search for things on the Internet. Even simple search engines on specific corporate Web sites can be of value to the analyst concerned with competitive intelligence. Consider that most major companies have dealers or representatives and often they provide a search engine to find them. By methodically capturing all of the dealers listed (do a search for dealers in each state) and copying and pasting the information into a word processor, one can quickly compile a database that can be used for various analyses.

Browser search features

A feature instituted by Netscape effectively put an efficient search engine on every Web page you visit by providing a "What's Related" button in the upper right corner of the screen. This feature, made available in Communicator in 1998, is surprisingly good. By clicking on the button, a drop-down list of several sites related to the one you are viewing is revealed. Clicking on one of the provided links rapidly transfers you to other potentially relevant information. Smart Browsing intelligently recommends other Web sites and information that are related to the site you are viewing. See Figure 10.5.

Smart Browsing also understands regular words typed into the location field to guide you to the correct information. This feature, called Internet Keywords, enables you to type the name of a product, service, company, or other keyword into the browser's URL location field. Communicator uses the power of Netcenter, Netscape's Internet portal, to automatically find and send you to the Web site that best matches what you typed.

Don't forget the basic text-search features built into your browser. One of the handiest is the text-search function that enables you to do a search of the page loaded into the browser. This is a real timesaver when you have a large amount of text to scroll through to determine if the page is even relevant. There are search capabilities built into the e-mail functions of the browsers. These provide various capabilities that are useful in locating specific messages from the hundreds or thousands you may have acquired from newsgroups and mailing lists.

Figure 10.5

Link sites

Many specialty sites are maintained by trade and professional associations. There are tens of thousands of such associations in the U.S. representing people in just about any field of business activity. Many associations have Web pages that include links to related sites and sometimes to members' home pages. This makes it easy to rapidly find a good deal of industry-specific information.

One area of particular interest in business intelligence is the various associations of government officials. A notable site is maintained by the National Association of State Information Resource Executives (**www.nasire.org**) providing links to thousands of individual sites within the 50 states, categorized by government department. This is a good jumping-off point for public records and government documents that may be helpful in looking at a private company. The organization's site provides thousands of links to state sites in the following categories:

- Auditors
- Criminal Justice
- Economic Development
- Education
- Employment Services
- Energy/Environment

- Executive Branch
- Finance and Admin
- Governor's Offices
- Health/Human Services/Welfare
- Information Resource Management
- Judicial
- Libraries/Records Management
- Lieutenant Governors
- Procurement
- Regs and Licensing
- Revenue
- State Homepages
- State Legislatures
- Tourism
- Transportation
- Treasurers
- Y2K Problem Information

At the state level, such departments as the secretary of state and various sub-units and agencies maintain a mountain of public records. These governmental unit Web sites often provide search facilities for the user who wants to locate such specific information as a corporation record or a specific workers' compensation case (or series of cases for a particular company). Not all of the states have elaborate Internet offerings, but many do and it's likely more will do so as time goes on.

For companies doing business internationally there is increasing availability of newspapers, magazines, and other sources of similar information from a growing list of countries. Many organizations, ranging from trade associations to universities, have devoted time to searching out high-quality news sources in other countries. They create very useful links pages that can help the researcher, analyst, or strategist find the right sources in the desired subject area or region of the world.

There are many sites on the Internet that attempt to link to as many international newspapers, magazines, and news services as possible. These can be as simple as business school-maintained pages with 30 or 40 links or as comprehensive as pages with metasearch engines that will simultaneously query dozens of news sources. There may be several hundred good-quality mainstream news outlets available from all of the world's major cities and many of the smaller ones too.

Viewing the two columns of search results enables you to see a list of Newsgroups where people are discussing the topic for which you searched. You also get a list of the messages that matched your search. You can sort your results by how well each one matches your search criteria, by date, by author, etc.

A standard view (Figure 11.2) shows results in columns including Date, Score, Subject, Forum, and Author. Simply by clicking on the header you can sort by any of these.

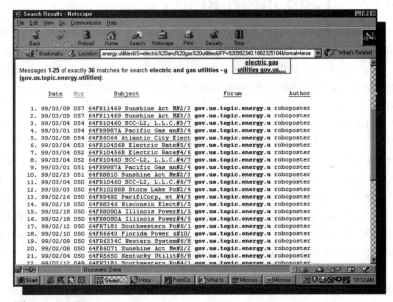

Figure 11.2

The Search Results page presents the most important information about each message in a concise, one-line display. This format allows you to see as many messages as possible on a page and helps you to quickly scan your search results for the message(s) you want.

The Forums toolbar provides you the opportunity to switch from a search results system that lists all of the individual messages to a list of all the forums that came up in your search. You can search on a particular date (instead of the message's text) by using a context operator.

The Score column shows how confident the Deja.com search software is that the forum on the right is the best match for your search words. Higher is obviously better. You can search for message subjects by using a context operator. You can search on a particular forum name (instead of the message's text) by using a context operator. You can search for messages written by a particular author by using a context operator.

Other features allow you to move from one message to the next, view related discussions (called threads), mail the posting to someone else, or subscribe/unsubscribe to the Newsgroup. After registering with Deja.com (free), you will automatically get all updated postings from the Newsgroup(s) to which you've subscribed.

Newsgroup information

Yahoo!'s Newsgroup page (found in the Internet subsection of their Computers section) has information in the following categories: About FAQs; Abuse; Archives; Humor; Information and Documentation; Newsgroup Listings; NNTP; Public Access Usenet Sites; Searching and Filtering; Software; Usenet Servers; Web Directories; FAQs; and Usenet. It's a good starting point for thoroughly exploring the ins and outs of Newsgroups. There are other pages devoted to the topic elsewhere, and various shareware and freeware packages enable you to maximize your use of Newsgroups.

The Web site **www.newsreaders.com** is about Newsgroups and software related to them. This site provides a wealth of basic and advanced information about the subject. For example, the following excerpt from the site explains online and off-line newsreaders:

"Online newsreaders assume you maintain an Internet connection during the time the program is running. When you run the newsreader, it polls the server to see how many new messages there are in the groups to which you are subscribed. You can then enter a group, and the newsreader downloads just the message headers, and you see what looks like a mailbox. The messages themselves, however, are not on your machine. As you access a particular message, the newsreader gets it from the server. When you are done reading a message, it is not stored on your machine, unless you save it specifically.

"Offline newsreaders, on the other hand, connect to the server, download all new messages for the Newsgroups to which you are subscribed, upload any posts you wrote since the last time you connected to the server, and then disconnect. You can then read the messages as you wish, composing replies and new posts to be uploaded next time you choose to connect."

The Liszt Newsgroup Search Page provides a tool to search for Newsgroups by keyword in the name of the group.

Free Agent

Free Agent is freeware, available in both 16-bit and 32-bit versions. You can configure Free Agent for online or off-line operation. In off-line mode, it briefly connects to the server to retrieve article headers, lets you browse them off-line and mark the interesting ones, and then goes online for another quick session to retrieve the marked articles. In online mode, you can browse Newsgroups at will, dipping into threads as they interest you. You can still mark long articles to be downloaded later, or you can download one article while browsing others.

Free Agent does internal multitasking, allowing you to do many online tasks at once. For example, you can browse articles in one Newsgroup while retrieving headers for another or download long articles while continuing to browse. You can post and receive articles with binary attachments, with automatic splitting and combining to span multiple messages. If the attachment is viewable (like an image or a sound) you can view it from within the newsreader. It maintains an intelligent database of headers and articles, and allows you to control its pruning strategy. You can have it keep only the new headers, keep headers for as long as they remain valid on your news server, or several other options.

Free Agent does multilevel article threading, using both the subject and the article ID, so you always know exactly what an article is a response to. It also offers watch and ignore commands for threads and rapid navigation within and among threads. When combined with the intelligent pruning described above, this gives you a coherent view of threads. Free Agent is able to thread new articles in with old ones, recreating all the relationships between the articles. This means that if somebody posts a response that just says "Don't try that—it wipes out your hard disk!" you'll know what article they're responding to and what they're talking about. Free Agent makes it easy for you to quickly sample threads and Newsgroups. You don't have to subscribe to a Newsgroup to see what's happening.

News Rover

News Rover software is a tool for extracting information from Usenet Newsgroups. News Rover automates the process of searching for messages, downloading them, decoding file attachments, and reconstructing files that are split across multiple messages. News Rover does all of this automatically while you are at work, sleeping, or browsing the Net. When you are ready to read messages and look at the pictures it has collected, they are ready for instant access on your computer. News Rover does the work, so you don't have to waste time waiting for messages to be downloaded and decoded.

News Rover allows you to specifically include or exclude expressions that control which messages are collected. These expressions can be elaborate and can include "AND," "OR," "NOT," and "NEAR" operators and parentheses. By using an exclude expression, you can easily exclude many spam messages. In addition, you can exclude messages that are cross-posted to more than a specified number of Newsgroups.

Mail lists

A mailing list is a list of people's names and e-mail addresses that is used to send certain messages or announcements to many people at once, who are usually expected to share a common interest in the contents of the message. Electronic mailing lists are more like clubs or magazines than a "real-world" mailing list.

Although commonly referred to as a Listserv, LISTSERV is a registered trademark licensed to L-Soft International, Inc. (**www.lsoft. com**). LISTSERV is a system that makes it possible to create, manage, and control electronic mailing lists on a corporate network or on the Internet. Since its inception in 1986 for IBM mainframes on the BITNET academic network, LISTSERV has been continually improved and expanded. The first version was written in 1986 by Eric Thomas, now L-Soft's manager of technical services.

Today, there are thousands of public mailing lists covering virtually any imaginable topic. Think of it as a virtual encyclopedia that is always up to date: No matter what you need to know, or at what time of the day, the chances of finding a list from which you can get an answer (usually in a matter of hours, or just minutes if you are familiar with the database functions) are very good. The more specialized a question, the higher the chances of success. Not all lists are question-and-answer forums. In fact most lists are more like virtual coffee house, where people you haven't met are comfortably discussing topics you enjoy conversing about and will be happy to have you contribute experiences.

Mailing list basics with LISTSERV

A mailing list is managed by a list owner (or sometimes several owners for large lists). The list owner is the person with formal responsibility for the operation of the list. The list owner defines the list's charter and policy, i.e., what the list is about and what are the general rules all subscribers must accept in order to be allowed to join the list. The list owner is also responsible for all administrative matters and for answering questions from the subscribers.

The messages sent (or posted) to a mailing may be saved in files known as list archives for future reference. These archive files are owned by the list owner who sets the policy for their use. Other expressions you may encounter are list notebooks and list logs. These archives are usually organized in log files. A log file is a disk file containing everything that was said on the list on a given month (or week). There are two ways to access these list archives. You can ask LISTSERV to send you, say, the log file for March 1993. Alternatively, you can use the database functions to search the archives for messages related to a particular topic, or sent by a certain person, and have LISTSERV return a copy of the messages that matched a search criterion.

Given a reliable and reasonably fast network, mailing lists are highly interactive. When you send a message to a mailing list, LIST-SERV will distribute it immediately and you can expect most subscribers to receive their copies within one to 20 minutes, depending on location and mail system. While this is great if you are looking for the answer to a problem a boss just reminded you needed to be solved yesterday, in some cases it can be annoying because you would rather not be interrupted while you are working.

When you are not in a hurry, it can often be more convenient to read all these messages during a break or at any other time where you are not too busy. LISTSERV provides digest subscriptions for this purpose (also called "list digests" or "subscriptions in digest format"). A digest is simply a larger file with everything that was said on the list in a particular day (or week for low-volume lists). Unlike their real-world counterparts, LISTSERV digests are not edited and you get exactly the same information as with a normal subscription, just in a single message that is usually sent during the night when the lines and computers are less busy.

Sometimes even digests take up too much time to be worth the effort—or maybe you have a limited amount of disk space to store mail, and the large digest files occasionally fill up a disk or quota. If interest in the list is only peripheral, you may want to get an index subscription, which is similar to a digest but much smaller, as it only contains a directory of all the messages posted in the last day. That is, sends you a list of all the messages, in chronological order, with the name and address of the author of the message, the message subject, and its size (in lines). It only takes a few seconds to identify the messages you are interested in, and you can then order a copy of just these messages from LISTSERV. And if there was nothing interesting that day, all you have to do is throw the index away.

Public vs. private

A public list is a totally open list—anyone can join or leave, ask questions, see who is on the list, search archived messages, and so on. Public lists usually attract a lot of subscribers and tend to generate quite a lot of traffic. Conversely, a private list is a list exercising some measure of access control. Usually, you need to apply for membership to the list owner, and only people who are subscribed to the list may send messages and access archived postings, but there are many other possibilities. Private lists are usually smaller, more focused, and more "professional."

Some lists do require you to apply for membership but are still called "public." Usually this is because the list owner really lets anyone join the list, but has to ask a few questions before letting you through, for instance, because the list is funded by a grant that requires all subscribers to state where they work.

With a normal list, messages submitted to the list by users are either accepted or rejected. If the message is accepted, the original text is published in its entirety, and the other subscribers can know that nothing was censored. A moderated list is similar to a real-world newspaper: When you send mail to the list, it is opened by a human being, called the editor or the moderator, who then decides what to do with a message. Usually the editor "cleans up" a message, shortens it if it was too long, and includes it in the next "issue." (This is called a "moderated digest," because the editor sends a new issue at regular intervals with selected contributions from the readership.) Sometimes the editor just acts as a filter, deciding whether or not to accept articles.

Locate lists

There are several other subscription mailing-list search resources. The Liszt Directory of E-Mail Discussion Groups (**www.liszt.com**) lets you use keywords to search for an e-mail discussion circle that you can subscribe to. The Index of Publicly Accessible Mailing Lists (**www.neosoft.com/internet/paml**) lets you browse alphabetized indices of mailing lists that you can subscribe to. Tile.Net (**www.tile.net/lists**) enables you to search or browse lists and other databases.

One individual who has devoted a Web site to mail lists is Vivian Neou (**www.catalog.com/vivian**). She maintains a very comprehensive Web site dealing with Internet mail lists. For example, she has a detailed, searchable directory of lists. Here are two examples:

GLOBAL INTELLIGENCE UPDATE
Subscription Address: info@stratfor.com
List Owner: Strategic Forecasting, L.L.C. <info@stratfor.com>
Last Update: 11/04/97
Description: The Global Intelligence Update (GIU) provides real-time intelligence reports daily, with quarterly summaries of events relevant to a particular business or region. Updated almost daily by staff who constantly monitor the world, the Global Intelligence Update will try to give you next month's headlines today. We focus on the geopolitical issues: political and military events that can affect your immediate economic interests.

I-BARTER
Subscription Address: subscribe-I-Barter@I-Barter.com
List Owner: Michael S. DeVries <I-Barter@I-Barter.com>
Last Update: 03/15/98
Description: I-Barter is a moderated list for business people who want to trade ideas on getting more business through trade/barter. It is e-mailed in digest format. Subjects that would be typical for the list would be: how to negotiate trades; how to tell a good trade from a bad one; barter as a complement to business networking; using barter to get profits from excess inventory; how to barter for advertising; barter resources; using barter to boost your online business;

trade/barter exchanges. To subscribe to I-Barter, send any e-mail to mailto: subscribe-I-Barter@I-Barter.com. See the I-Barter Home Page at: **http://www.I-Barter.com**.

In addition, Vivian's resources include E-Mail List Management Software, which is a list of e-mail list management software packages. Some of these packages have mailing lists that provide support. You may also find helpful information in the mailing list management software frequently asked questions (FAQ) section. Another useful resource is Mailing List Manager Commands by James Milles at the Saint Louis University Law Library.

Increasingly, various services that provide facilities for free mail list creation are popping up on the Internet. It remains to be seen whether these will be as completely indexed as more traditional lists, but for those who want to start a semi-private mail list, these resources are a good way to do it.

How to join and leave a mailing list

All LISTSERV commands are sent to the server by e-mail. This means that you must create a new mail message using whatever command this requires for a mail client (click on New Message or its equivalent for most mail clients) addressed to the LISTSERV address. Let's say for the sake of argument that the list you want to subscribe to (or are currently subscribed to) is running on a server called LISTSERV.mycorp.com. So you would create a new message and address it to LISTSERV@LISTSERV.mycorp.com if you wanted to send a command to that server.

Given the list name, joining the list is very easy. The command that needs to be sent is: subscribe listname. LISTSERV will then automatically insert the name you supplied in the headers of messages you send out to the list. When other people read the messages you post, they will see a name in addition to an e-mail address.

When you join a list, you are sent a little pamphlet that looks very boring and does not seem to have anything interesting to say about the list itself. Do not discard it! Treat it like a warranty card—no immediate value, but you never know when you might need it. You should make a new folder in a mail program for these little pamphlets and search it whenever you have an administrative question about a mailing list. The pamphlets are customized to the individual lists and do not contain the same information. Saving them in a dedicated mail folder makes it very easy for you to know what mailing lists you are subscribed to and when you joined.

You can leave the list at any time by sending a SIGNOFF command to the host server. LISTSERV does not need a name for a sign off command, so there is no need to type it. Do not hesitate to subscribe to a list to see what it is really about, and then sign off a couple days later if it turns out not to be what you expected.

How to send mail to a list

Now that you are subscribed to the list, all you need to do is ask a question or participate in the current discussion and wait for someone to answer. To post a new message to the list, you send mail to the list address using the same procedure as when you send mail to other people. Your mail program does not need to know that you are sending to a list. The list address is the name of the list, followed by the name of the machine where it is hosted. Depending on how the list is set up, LISTSERV may or may not send you a copy of the messages you post.

Once you become familiar with LISTSERV and mailing lists, you will probably want to respond to a posting you have read. The best way to respond is by using the Reply function of a mail program. This way the message subject is preserved and the other subscribers can see that a message is a reply to the original question. You can of course post a new message, but you will then have to retype the subject, and if you enter something slightly different people may not realize it is a reply to a previous post. There is no universally correct place to send a reply.

In general, if a reply is short there is little harm in sending it to everyone: It does not take much time to discard a message that is not interesting. On the other hand, if a reply is a 2,000-line paper you wrote on the subject, it might not be a good idea to send it to the list unless you are sure everyone is interested. The best thing to do in that case is to send a short message to the list saying you wrote this paper and that people who are interested can contact you for a copy.

Most lists are organized as "forums" where public discussion is actively encouraged, and many of them are set up so that hitting the Reply key or button will automatically direct replies back to the list.

Unfortunately, this can sometimes be embarrassing if you end up inadvertently sending a private comment to the whole list.

How to see who is on the list

To see who is subscribed to the list, send the REVIEW command to LISTSERV. If the list owner allows this option, LISTSERV will return a copy of the "list header" and a list of all the subscribers. The list header contains the title of the list, various configuration parameters, and a short description of what the list is about. There are also some statistics about the list, after the name and address of the last subscriber, and there may be a mention of "concealed" subscribers.

Options that may be set

Mail/NOMail: Setting this option to Mail indicates that you will receive mail from the list. NOMail is the complementary command that stops mail but leaves you subscribed to the list. (NOMail is often a good compromise for users who are leaving the office for vacation or on extended business trips, and who don't want a full mailbox on their return.)

DIGest/NODIGest: This causes the subscriber to receive one posting per digest cycle (typically daily) rather than individual messages as they are processed by LISTSERV. The MAIL/NOMAIL option controls whether messages should be delivered, and the DIGEST/INDEX/NODIGEST/NOINDEX option controls the format in which messages should be delivered. Thus, switching to NOMAIL and back to MAIL does not destroy the digest/index/normal delivery setting; it simply determines whether or not LISTSERV should send any list mail to you.

INDex/NOINDex: This causes the user to receive one posting per digest cycle containing only an index of subject topics for all messages during that cycle. Instructions on how to retrieve the individual postings are included with the index. See the section on DIGEST (above) for further information.

ACK/NOACK/MSGack: These three command words control the level of acknowledgment you receive when posting to the list. ACK causes LISTSERV to send a short confirmation message to the sender of the postings when the post has been received and distributed. NOACK disables the confirmation feature for the sender.

MSGack is essentially obsolete; if you do not have BITNET/NJE connectivity to the LISTSERV host in question, setting a list to MSGack is equivalent to NOACK.

CONCEAL/NOCONCEAL: Occasionally, a subscriber may not want his presence to be known to someone else making a casual review of the list. You may choose to "hide" a subscription from the review command by using the CONCEAL command. Conversely, a subscriber may choose to remove this restriction by issuing the NOCONCEAL command. Note that the list owner can always obtain a list of all subscribers.

REPro/NOREPro: This option controls whether or not you will get a copy of a posts back from the list after they are processed. Generally, if a mail program is configured to file copies of outgoing mail, or if you have one of the acknowledgment options (ACK/MSGack) enabled, this option should be set to NOREPro. If, on the other hand, you are set to NOACK and it doesn't keep a copy of outgoing mail, this option should probably be set to REPro.

MIME/NOMIME: This toggles MIME functions on and off. Currently this is only useful if the user has a mail client that supports MIME digests. Note that users who send their SUBSCRIBE command using a MIME-compliant agent will have this option set automatically unless "Default-Options= NOMIME" is specified for the list.

Topics

List topics provide powerful "sub-list" capabilities to a list. Not all list owners use them, but when properly set up and used, topics give subscribers the ability to receive list postings in a selective manner, based on the beginning of the "Subject:" line of the mail header. If list topics are enabled, this option allows you to specify which topics you will receive. The syntax of a SET TOPICS statement is significantly different from that of the other options. It is: SET listname TOPICS: xxx yyy zzz where xxx, yyy, and zzz, is a list of all the topics the subscriber wishes to receive. In that case these topics replace any other topics the subscriber may have subscribed to before.

Other LISTSERV software uses

In addition to mailing lists, LISTSERV also acts as a file server—a program that manages collections of files and makes them available to users upon request. Among these files are the list archives we have already mentioned, but LISTSERV can store just about any kind of file: papers put up for discussion, agendas and minutes of upcoming meetings, survey results, programs, electronic magazine issues, etc. These files are organized in file lists (VM version) or catalogs (other versions), which are very much like directories on a PC. Each file list or catalog contains a list of files, along with some descriptive text and two file access codes (or FACs) that define who is allowed to order a copy of the file and who is the person in charge of updating it (the file owner).

Knowledge development

Knowing how to use Newsgroups and mail lists provides the technical foundation for user-derived knowledge development within these "cyberplaces" or Internet environments. Just as young people gather in malls to socialize and families attend school functions and church socials, many people are meeting and conversing electronically via the Internet. Many professionals congregate and share ideas as well as ask questions, using Newsgroups and mail lists. To develop business intelligence of value to both parties requires a deeper commitment than simply exchanging a few messages over a period of weeks or months.

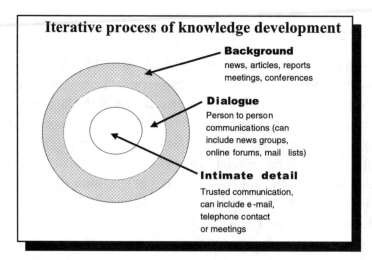

Figure 11.3

Trusted communications, at the center of Figure 11.3, result from mutual respect and a sense of shared purpose. Indulge my armchair psychology for a moment: You'll see that for intentional business intelligence purposes, intimate detail must be derived. After understanding a subject enough to begin a dialogue, the person-to-person communication must develop in a way that builds mutual trust. Only after this is achieved, and frequently reinforced with personal contact via telephone or by meeting, can meaningful sharing of important information take place.

Endnote

1. http://wsrv.clas.virginia.edu/~klb6q/infopaper/ECPA.html.

CHAPTER 12

WHAT ELSE IS AVAILABLE VIA THE INTERNET?

The Internet is the basis of a fundamental shift in our lives. Information never before accessible to the general public now is at our fingertips. Because the market for information is expanding dramatically the price being charged is dropping rapidly. For example, the growing availability of Internet access to public records and government archives makes them truly public. Publishers don't need a middleman to distribute information, and the cost to do so has been reduced almost to zero.

Subscription services (free and commercial) via the Internet

One of the most significant developments on the Internet in recent years is the growth of various types of registration/subscription services that provide everything from news clipping to forum creation. This trend is due largely to the drive to "stake out" a spot in cyberspace and build traffic. Offering various free services often costs these businesses little, if anything, more than putting up a site. The added service, very likely to build traffic, is an inconsequential incremental cost.

These free services level the playing field for small businesses that must compete with larger corporations. Many small-business owners cannot afford thousands of dollars each month in expenses for premium database services. Although not nearly as comprehensive as the costly premium services, free Internet services are respectable competitors. When you combine these free services with databases in public libraries (discussed in Chapter Thirteen), you can rival and in many cases outperform the big-budget information user.

So, like the TV commercial that questions the value of high-priced hotels, you might ask yourself, is that mint on the pillow in your hotel room really worth the extra $50?

Free and low-cost communications

The next type of free subscription service to come along was the portal-based e-mail account. Nearly every major search engine portal now offers free e-mail to registrants. These are particularly handy for people who travel, especially those without a computer. They simply register at a site, give out their e-mail address, and use a borrowed computer with Internet access to log on and check their e-mail. Nearly all libraries now have Internet-connected public-use computers, and there are even a few at such public locations as highway rest areas and hotels.

Closely related is the "private pod" available through Tripod, a division of Lycos. This Web site building and hosting service (first 11 megabytes of space free) provides private online communities that feature chat and message boards. Premium services that include automated Web site creation and other support for "home page" users also are available.

The HotOffice (**www.hotoffice.com**) Web-based intranet service is of particular interest for its value in an IBIS. Secure document sharing, private bulletin boards, online chat, e-mail, and access to a personal calendar is available for $12.95 per month per user. While it costs tens or hundreds of thousands of dollars per year to set up and maintain a Lotus Notes intranet operation, HotOffice provides very much the same thing for a tiny fraction of the cost. It is especially valuable for small- to medium-sized operations.

These communications services are a good example of how Internet technology is providing significant competitive advantage for small business. Even the solo professional can afford to set up and maintain a sophisticated communications system for the benefit of business operations. These operations could include client and subcontractor or vendor communications, coordination, and file sharing.

News now

The first free service of specific use in the Internet Business Intelligence System (IBIS) was the PointCast Network (**www.point cast.com**), which provided a unique screen saver combined with news ticker. The service rapidly added content that featured prestigious national business news sources. Shortly after their debut, PointCast began providing a limited customization feature that enabled the user to specify types of information and to update frequency. This later specification is greatly enhanced by a continuous network connection to the Internet. Today, PointCast (Figure 12.1) is a premiere push provider (you subscribe and information is automatically sent to you) with good customization features, but it has been acquired by Launchpad Technologies—a consumer-oriented service.

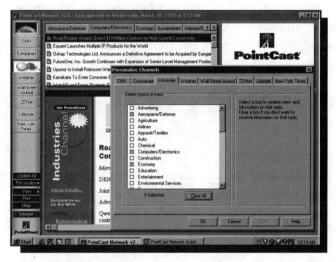

Figure 12.1

Another very significant development for business intelligence purposes is the wider availability of news clipping services. For example, Excite News Tracker (**www.nt.excite.com**), covered in depth in Chapter Ten, provides an excellent news clipping service. My Yahoo! (**www.my.yahoo.com**) offers a similar capability. As electronic commerce grows, it becomes more important to establish a relationship with visitors to a particular site. For this reason, lots of value-added features will be provided at no charge to those who provide basic identification information, sometimes no more than simply providing their names and e-mail addresses.

A good example of this is the Dun & Bradstreet site (**www.companies online.com**) where you can look up basic information on many public and private companies. Register and you can get even more detail on each company, as well as more sophisticated selection features. For example, after registering you can use additional selectors of company size (revenue or number of employees) and then get company information that includes contact names. This site also provides e-mail and Web site addresses for these companies, if available.

During the late 1990s, Netscape created a portal called Netcenter. Customizable news pages at that site are representative of a genre. By registering, you can create a custom news page. This is an advantage for those concerned with business intelligence (BI) because it can serve as a home base for the individual charged with operating the IBIS. Netcenter can be set as your browser's default home page (in Browser Options or Preferences) so when you start your browser it will appear automatically. See Figure 12.2 for a view of a custom page and 12.3 for the selector panel to choose content for the custom page.

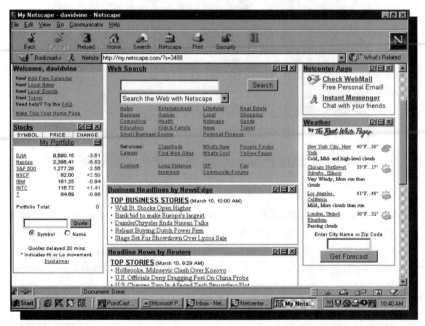

Figure 12.2

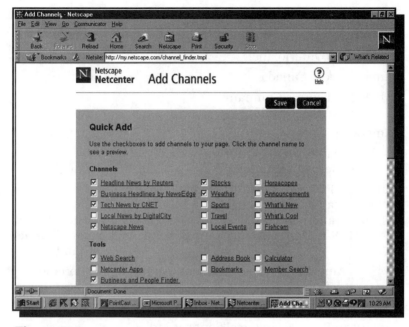

Figure 12.3

Public company information

All you ever wanted to know about publicly traded companies can be found on the Internet. A good example of this is Securities and Exchange Commission (SEC) public documents, which only a few years ago cost many dollars for basic reports from commercial middlemen. Today, the records our tax dollars already have paid for are accessible to us via the Internet. For example, while it might be easy enough to scope out the main competitors in a particular industry, the larger players usually have a number of subsidiaries that might bear on your specific market. Although the American Express Company is incorporated in New York, there are many, many subsidiaries. An SEC filing found at **www.sec.gov** detailed them. Here is a small portion of the voluminous listing of hundreds of subsidiary companies:

Name of Subsidiary	State of Incorporation
I. American Express Travel Related Services Company, Inc. and its Subsidiaries	
American Express Travel Related Services Company, Inc.	New York

Amex Canada, Inc.	Canada
1001674 Ontario, Inc.	Canada
1001675 Ontario, Inc.	Canada
Amex Bank of Canada	Canada
American Express Company (Mexico) S.A. de C.V.	Mexico
American Express Centurion Bank	Utah
American Express Centurion Services Corporation	Delaware
American Express Credit Corporation Delaware American Express Overseas Credit Jersey, Corporation Limited	Channel Islands
AEOCC Management Company, Ltd.	Jersey, Channel Islands
American Express Overseas Credit Corporation N.V.	Netherlands Antilles
Credco Receivables Corp.	Delaware
American Express Financial Services Ltd. (50% owned)	England & Wales
American Express Receivables Financing Corp.	Delaware
American Express Receivables Financing Corp. II	Delaware
American Express do Brasil Tempo & Cia, Inc.	Delaware
Amex do Brazil Empreedimentos e Participacoes Ltda.	Brazil
Banco American Express S.A. Brazil	
American Express do Brasil Servicos Internacionais, Ltda. (90% owned)	Brazil
American Express do Brazil Tempo & Cia	Brazil
American Express do Brasil S.A. Turismo	Brazil
American Express Limited	Delaware
American Express Argentina, S.A.	Argentina
American Express (Malaysia) Sdn. Bhd.	Malaysia
American Express (Thai) Co. Ltd.	Thailand
TRS Card International Inc. (75% owned)	Delaware
American Express de Espana, S.A.	Spain
American Express Viajes, S.A.	Spain
Amex Asesores de Seguros, S.A.	Spain
American Express International (B) SDN.BHD.	Brunei

South Pacific Credit Card, Ltd.	New Zealand
Centurion Finance, Ltd.New Zealand	
American Express International, Inc.	Delaware
American Express Hungary KFT	Hungary
American Express Company A/S	Norway
American Express Reisebyra A/S	Norway
AMEX Services, Inc.	Delaware
American Express Company, S.p.A.	Italy
American Express Locazioni	Italy
Finanziarie, S.r.l.	
Amex Broker Assicurativo S.r.l. Italy	
American Express Int'l A.E. (Greece)	Greece
American Express Int'l (Taiwan), Inc.	Taiwan
American Express of Egypt, Ltd.	Delaware
American Express Carte France, S.A.	France
AllCard Service GmbH Germany	
Schenker Rhenus Reisen	Germany
American Express Bureau de Change S.A.	Greece
Amex (Middle East) E.C. (50% owned)	Bahrain
American Express Exposure	
Management, Ltd.	Jersey,
	Channel Islands
American Express Travel Poland Sp.Zo.O	Poland
American Express Czechoslovakia,	
SPOL.SRO.	Czech Republic
American Express Company A/B	Sweden
American Express Resebyra A/B	Sweden
Amex Services Sweden A/B	Sweden
American Express Finland OY	Finland
Sociedad Internacional de Servicios	Panama
de Panama, S.A.	
American Express Voyages Tourisme France	
Havas Voyages American Express	
(20% owned)	France
Amex Sumigin Service Company, Ltd.	
(40% owned)	Japan
American Express International	
Services Limited	Russia
Amex Marketing Japan, Ltd.	Delaware
American Express (India) Pvt., Ltd.	India
P.T. American Express Travel Indonesia	Indonesia
(80% owned)	
BTO Ticket Delivery Office (80% owned)	Belgium
American Express Holdings AB	Sweden
Nyman & Schultz Resebyraer AB	Sweden
Nyman & Schultz AB	Sweden

Nyman & Schultz Grupp och Konferens AB	Sweden
Resespecialisterna Syd AB	Sweden
Resespecialisterna Helsingborg AB (84% owned)	Sweden
Nyman & Schultz Group AB	Sweden
Book Hotel AB	Sweden
Forsakringsaktiebolaget Viator	Sweden
First Card AB	Sweden
Profil Rejser A/S (50% owned)	Denmark
Resespecialisterna Enkoping AB (26% owned)	Sweden
Scandinavian Express AB	Sweden
Oy Scandinavian Express Finland AB	Finland
Central Hotel AB	Sweden
Nyman & Shultz Forretningsreiser A/S	Norway
American Express Insurance Marketing, Inc.	Taiwan
American Express Publishing Corp.	New York
Southwest Media Corporation	Texas
Societe Francaise du Cheque de Voyage, S.A. (34% owned)	France
Travellers Cheque Associates, Ltd. (54% owned)	England & Wales
American Express Service Corporation	Delaware
Bansamex S.A. (50% owned)	Spain
American Express Europe Limited	Delaware
Travel Places (City), Ltd.	England & Wales
Travel Places (Incentives), Ltd.	England & Wales

This is only a partial listing. Material has been deleted from the original list.

The American Express example shows the extent of global activity and is particularly important when your company needs to track competitors internationally.

SEC regulations mandate that public companies (whose equity shares are publicly traded) must file information that nonpublic companies almost never release to the general public. Here's a fraction of the more strategically important elements of just one business segment from a 1997 SEC filing by Allied Signal for Engineered Materials, just one of its many business units:

Engineered Materials operations are mainly located in the U.S., France and Germany. Polymers and Specialty Chemicals manufacturing facilities are also located in the Netherlands; Electronic Materials maintains facilities in Southeast Asia, including Taiwan, Singapore, Thailand and South Korea. Engineered Materials also has significant exports worldwide.

The Engineered Materials segment also includes the following other businesses: carbon materials, environmental catalysts and specialty films. The carbon materials business produces binder pitch for electrodes for the aluminum and carbon industries, creosote oils as preservatives for the wood products and carbon black markets, refined naphthalene as a chemical intermediate, and driveway sealer tar and roofing pitch for the construction industry.

The environmental catalysts business is a major worldwide supplier of catalysts used in catalytic converters for automobiles. In November 1994, the Company and General Motors Corporation formed a joint venture to produce coated automotive catalytic converter substrates. Major products in the specialty films business include cast nylon (Capran®), biaxially oriented nylon film (Capran Emblem®) and fluoropolymer film (Aclar®). Specialty film markets include food, pharmaceutical, and other packaging and industrial applications.

The Company has 339 locations consisting of plants, research laboratories, sales offices and other facilities. The plants are generally located to serve large marketing areas and to provide accessibility to raw materials and labor pools. The properties are generally maintained in good operating condition. Utilization of these plants may vary with government spending and other business conditions; however, no major operating facility is significantly idle. The facilities, together with planned expansions, are expected to meet the Company's needs for the foreseeable future.

The Company owns or leases warehouses, railroad cars, barges, automobiles, trucks, airplanes, and materials handling and data processing equipment. It also leases space for administrative and sales staffs. The Company's headquarters and administrative complex are located at Morris Township, New Jersey.

International news

Throughout the Internet you'll find many individuals and organizations that have carefully tended their patches of cyberspace. These folks want to "give back" to the community of Internet users. This is a tradition that, hopefully, will endure. There are a variety of Web sites on the Internet that aggregate links to newspapers, and some of these sites are devoted exclusively to sources of international business news such as:

- Ambito Financiero (Argentina)

- Anzeiger Online (Switzerland)

- Australian Financial Review

- Baltic Business Weekly (subscription required)

- Bilanz (Switzerland)

- BOERSE.DE (Germany)

- Brazil Financial Wire (registration required)

- Bulgarian Economic Review (biweekly)

- Business Day (South Africa)

- Business Day (Thailand)

- Business Day from the Evening Standard (United Kingdom)

- Business Journals of Central Europe
  (Hungary, Poland, Czech Republic)

- Business Line: Internet Edition (India)

- Business Times (Singapore)

- BusinessWorld (Philippines)

- Cape Business News (South Africa)

- Chinese Commercial News (Philippines)

- CNBC Asia Business News

- Crónicas Económicas (Uruguay: weekly)

- Dagens Industri (Sweden)

- Daily Commercial News (Australia: subscription required)

- De Financieel-Economische Tijd (Belgium)

- Dinero: Semanario de Análisis Económico (Spain)

- Economic & Business Review Indonesia
  (weekly: registration required)

- Economic Review (Kenya)

- Económicas de El Colombiano (Colombia)

- Eesti Ekspress Online (Estonia: weekly)

- El Comercio (Ecuador)

- El Comercio (Peru)

- El Cronista (Argentina)

- El Economista (Mexico)

- El Financiero International Edition (Mexico)

- Far Eastern Economic Review
  (Asia: weekly; registration required)

- Financial Mail Interactive (South Africa: weekly)

- Financial Times (United Kingdom: registration reguired)

- Finanstidningen (Sweden)

- Gazeta Bankowa OnLine (Poland: weekly)

- Gazeta Mercantil Online (Brazil)

- Globes Business Arena (Israel)

- Indobiz News (Indonesia)

- Indonesian Observer (registration required)

- Indústria Interactive Investor (United Kingdom)

- Intereconomía (Spain)

- Iran Weekly Press Digest

- Jahan Eghtesad (Iran: weekly)

- JapanBizTech

- Korea Economic Daily (includes Korea Economic Weekly)

- Le Revenu en ligne (France)

- Marketing Week Online (United Kingdom)

- Milano Finanza (Italy)

- Minsk Economic News (Belarus: registration required)

- myindia Business Watch

- NAFTA Information Center database
  (from Texas A&M International University)

- News Brief Weekly (Taiwan)
- Nikkei Net (Japan)
- PARI Daily (Bulgaria)
- Polonia News (Poland)
- Russian Economic News
- Russian Insurance (monthly)
- Scandinavia Now
- Singapore Business Times Online
- South China Morning Post (Hong Kong)
- Su Dinero (Spain)
- Sunday Times (South Africa)
- The Economic Times (India)
- The New Australian (weekly)
- The St. Petersburg Times (Russia)
- Trade Daily (India)
- Trend: Economy and Business Weekly (Slovakia)
- Veckans Affärer (Sweden)
- Vietnam Business News
- Virgin Islands Business Journal (weekly)
- WirtschaftsWoche (Austria)

Listen in live

If you are too busy to read the news, the Internet affords an opportunity to listen to it. RealAudio program samples and feeds, including some in video, are available from a variety of sites worldwide. A pioneer in the field of sophisticated Internet multimedia, RealAudio software is free for the download and the list of radio stations using that format is growing. Below is a sampling of the hundreds of outlets available:

95.8 Capital FM—Popular music and news from London

ANA Radio—Arabic station in Washington, DC

BBC World Service—World's most successful and trusted network

Bahrain TV—Live news feed from Bahrain, in RealVideo

CBN 90.5 FM—News and talk in Portuguese from Rio de Janeiro

CBN Anhanguera—News from Brazil

CFRB 1010 AM—News/talk from Toronto, Canada

CNN—Live audio of CNN's cable station, from CNN Audioselect

Catalunya Informacio—Live news from Barcelona, Spain

Court TV—Covers all the high-profile court cases

Deutsche Welle—Live programming from Germany

Extra 103.9 FM—News and talk in Portuguese from Brazil

FOX News Channel—Live RealAudio and RealVideo

Globo 1140 AM—News from Sao Paulo, Brazil

Globo 1220 AM—News from Rio de Janeiro, Brazil

INBC—International News in Farsi and English, from NV

IRNA TV—Islamic Republic News Agency from Iran

InfoBerlin—Brandenburg-Live news in German

Intl. Community Taiwan—English in Taipei

Jornal de Brasilia FM—News from Brasilia, Brazil

KFI 640 AM—Talk from Los Angeles, CA

KHJJ 1380 AM—News/talk from Los Angeles

KIRO 710 AM—News from Seattle,WA

KJOJ 880 AM—Supertalk from Houston, TX

KLIF 570 AM—Talk from Dallas, TX

KLVI 560 AM—News and information for Beaumont, TX

KMJ 580 AM—News/talk from Fresno, CA

KOGO 600 AM—News/talk from San Diego, CA

KPRC 950 AM—SuperTalk from Houston, TX

KQV 1410 AM—All news station from Pittsburgh, PA

KSDO 1130 AM—News/talk from San Diego, CA

KSEV 700 AM—SuperTalk from Houston, TX

KSYG 103.7 FM—Talk from Little Rock, AR

KXL 750 AM—News/talk from Portland, OR

KXLY 920 AM—News/talk in Spokane, WA

MBC AM—News/talk in Korean from Seoul, Korea

NRK Alltid Nyheter—Non-stop news live from Norway

Northwest Cable News—All news from Portland, OR

Oman Radio—The Sultanate of Oman broadcast

Omega Network—Talk national satellite broadcast

RCN Radio—Live news broadcasts from Bogota, Colombia

America—24-hour conservative talk network

B92—News and music from Belgrade, Serbia

Comercial—A Portuguese station, live 24 hours a day

Galega-Radio—Television Company of Galicia, Spain

NZ—News/talk from Wellington, New Zealand

Programas De Peru—News/sports from Lima, Peru

Tunis—Live news, sports, and music in Arabic and French

Radio FM 104.5—Live talk programming in Italian from Rome

Red AM 1110—News and more from Mexico

Sarimanok News Network—TV from the Philippines

Sun Sounds Radio—News and magazines to print-disabled

TNL Radio—English language from Sri Lanka

TSF Noticias—News/talk from Lisbon, Portugal

TVW—Washington State's legislature

WBAL 1090 AM—News, political talk from Baltimore, MD

WSYR 570 AM—News from Syracuse, NY

WTKS 104.1 FM—Talk from Orlando, FL

WVON 1450 AM— African American talk, Chicago, IL

WZNZ 1460 AM—News from Jacksonville, FL

ZDTV—Devoted to high technology and the Internet

Industry-specific resources

The proliferation of "industrial parks" and "shopping malls" of all sorts on Internet can make your life easier when it comes time to track down resources for a particular industry. Let's take a look at two examples, one in construction and the other in life sciences.

"The World's Most Popular…" is a moniker that doesn't come easily or often, and is always well earned. Within a relatively short span of time, the Internet and the World Wide Web have changed the product categories and the metrics for such a boast. AEC (architect, engineer, construction) InfoCenter (**www.aecinfo.com**) makes the claim: "The World's Most Popular AEC Business Center," based on 1.25 million hits and 85,000 visits per month to the company's Web site. As a point of clarification, a "hit" is a file request, while a "visit" is a user session during which a user can make multiple file requests. Therefore, "hits" result from "visits."

In business since 1994, AEC has been built around a Web site that provides a broad range of information services to the AEC market. The range of information available includes: Building Services; Support Services; Software/Hardware; Governmental Authorities; and Spec-Center. This last category provides architects, engineers, specifiers, and others with specifications courtesy of contributing manufacturers free of charge. Other AEC InfoCenter Web site features include:

- AEC Interactive, which is comprised of discussion forums, AEC InForm, a free monthly e-mail newsletter, and an opportunity for users to submit their views in a section called "Speak Your Mind News," which contains top stories, feature articles, a classified section, projects, and events.

- AEC FreeWeb is a Build Your Own Web Site for Free feature. This is popular among the smaller participants in the AEC market, as AECInfo provides a tutorial, making it very easy for anyone to get on the Net.

In another field, BioMedNet (**www.biomednet.com**) is an Internet community for biological and medical researchers with more than 300,000 members. BioMedNet's facilities include a library of more than 100 full-text journals and searchable biological data-bases, a job exchange containing hundreds of jobs offered and jobs wanted, a daily scientific Webzine, a shopping mall, and more. Membership to BioMedNet is free, and members can search all of BioMedNet without charge. However, viewing full-text articles from publishers often requires payment or a subscription.

BioMedNet is supported by sponsorships. Sponsors include: BioMedNet's sister site, ChemWeb (provides information and collab-oration facilities for the chemistry research community); Electronic Press, Ltd. (develops the free-text retrieval and Web site software that is used to run sites such as BioMedNet and ChemWeb); NCBI (National Center for Biotechnology Information); and other advertis-ers and sponsors. BioMedNet, Ltd. is part of Elsevier Science, and is a member of the Reed Elsevier plc group of companies.

HMS Beagle is the award-winning BioMedNet electronic maga-zine that provides up-to-date news and in-depth analysis of the most important issues in biology and medicine.

Corporation-provided information

Many corporations and other organizations actively marketing via the Internet make high-quality information available via their Web sites. Dataware Technologies, Inc. (**www.dataware.com**), a leading provider of software for enterprise information access and professional electronic publishing, is one such company. Dataware's software products integrate information from a wide variety of sources and allow for access and publishing via intranets and the Internet, enterprise networks, CD-ROM, commercial online servic-es, print-on-demand, and combinations of these media.

The company has a vested interest in promoting the concept of Knowledge Management, so they provide access to several educa-tional white papers on the subject. The Dataware Technologies' e-mail newsletter was created to deliver timely news on technology solutions for information access and professional electronic pub-lishing needs. Potential subscribers are asked to complete a form to get on the mailing list.

Dataware's corporate executive briefing on "Seven Steps to Implementing Knowledge Management in Your Organization" pro-vides 32 pages of information about the subject. Sophisticated corpo-rations like Dataware know that if they can present factual, relatively unbiased information, they can position themselves as experts in a particular market. This particular briefing is quite good and presents an excellent overview. As a source of information about Knowledge Management, the Dataware Web site can be used by individuals who need to quickly and cost-effectively learn about that subject. It's a good example of a site that provides a subscription newsletter as well as in-depth background information.

Another way to approach this is through services that provide a selection of freeware and shareware. Let's say you are interested in several areas of technology and subscribe to a newsletter from **www.download.com** that is mailed to you each week. Upon receiving the newsletter you quickly scan the highlights of each program and find one that is in the computer security category that you've been researching. You click on the link in the newsletter and go to a page that briefly describes a new shareware offering. You can download the program from this page or you can click on the name of the company to go to their Web site. You do the latter and find that the site has in-depth product literature that can help educate you on the subject while providing background on the company's product.

Harbor Telco's Web site at **www.lockdown2000.com** provides product news and information as well as several other editorial features that would be useful to someone who wants to learn more about the subject of computer security. The site has a form for subscribing one or more individuals to a mailing list as well as a newsletter. In addition, a hacker demo and hacked page archives are available. A special section on the latest computer security problem describes the problem in detail and states that the company's program would fix it. This section also provides a list of commonly used hacker plug-ins.

Government documents (federal, state, county, and local)

The U.S. federal government took the early lead in placing government documents online and providing sophisticated search tools to find them. The General Accounting Office (**www.gao.gov**) provides many reports that could have strategic implications for businesses in many fields. Also, the Government Printing Office (**www.gpo.gov**) provides a wealth of information via a robust search engine. And everyone uses the EDGAR search feature at **www.sec.gov** to unearth public company filings.

For well-written overviews of specific industries impacted by the federal government, General Accounting Office reports can't be beat. These types of government documents are usually available in various appropriate formats (HTML, ASCII, PDF, spreadsheets, etc.). They illustrate the strides that many jurisdictions have made in making it easier for taxpayers to get their money's worth from the bureaucracy. Here's a list of the subjects covered in GAO Reports:

- Agriculture and Food
- Budget and Spending
- Business/Industry
- Consumers
- Civil Rights
- Economic Development
- Education
- Employment
- Energy
- Environmental Protection
- Financial Institutions
- Financial Management
- Government Operations
- Health
- Housing
- Income Security
- Information Mgt.
- International Affairs
- International Relations
- Justice/Law Enforcement
- National Defense
- Natural Resources
- Science/Space/Technology
- Social Services
- Special Publications
- Tax Policy and Admin.
- Transportation
- Veterans Affairs

Downloadable software

Small-business owners and others are challenged to squeeze more from their budgets. Shareware is a smart way to try out various types of software for a particular function to see if it meets your needs before purchasing it. Finding the right tool for the job is particularly important in business intelligence. That's because parts of the process, particularly organizing and analyzing information, are personal, sometimes specialized, but often a repetitive function that is dependent on the requirements of each situation. You can save big dollars and still find just the right software for each function. Shareware and freeware often can fit the function and perhaps expose you to software that you might never have seen in stores or catalogs because it is not "mainstream."

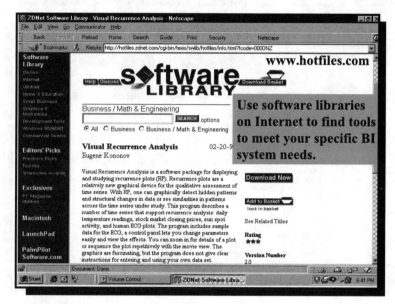

Figure 12.4

We live in a fragmented and specialized world where those who are interested in visual recurrence analysis software (Figure 12.4) or those interested in Brazilian financial news (Figure 12.5) are on equal footing. Both (or in a rare case the single interested party) are just a few clicks away from fulfillment. We've covered specialized news, so now let's look at specialized software that can facilitate Internet Business Intelligence.

The ZDNet Software Library (**www.zdnet.com/downloads**) lets you download freeware and shareware. Although you might not be too interested in the Budweiser Lizards screensaver, a free package like WebFerret provides a handy and efficient way to use Web search engines to find information. It adds an entry to the Find option of your Windows 95/98 Start button, which gives users the option to find Web pages in addition to the standard files and folders.

Enter your search terms, click on Match All Keywords or Match Any Keywords, and WebFerret will use your Internet connection to check several of the more popular search engines such as Lycos, AltaVista, Excite, Infoseek, Yahoo!, Search.com, AOL Netfind, Euroseek, and LookSmart. You can also conduct more advanced searches, limiting the number of matches in total or by engine.

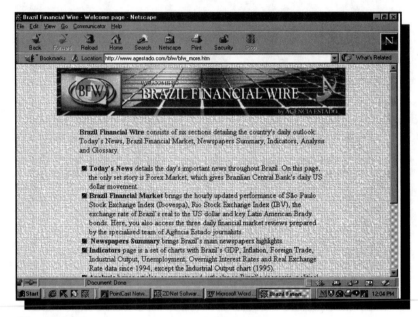

Figure 12.5

Once the results are returned, "tooltips" give you a little more information about a site. Just double click to bring up your browser and launch the page. WebFerret is fast, easy to use, and best of all—free!

In case you're wondering "what's the catch?" you'll be interested to know that there is a full commercial version of WebFerretPRO, which includes exact phrases and Boolean searches. (Use AND, OR, and AND NOT to construct complex Boolean searches. An example would be car AND trucks AND NOT convertibles). WebFerretPRO also has twice as many search engines to increase search coverage (including over 20 major search sites).

Freeware and shareware categories

ZDNet categories of interest to those building an IBIS include these:

- Internet (tools, browsers, e-mail and newsreaders, chat, Netscape plugins, reference tutorials, general communications, networks)

- Utilities (file, hardware, printer, security, system, desktop accessories)

- Small business (finance, inventory, employee management, general, project management, vertical markets, databases, math and engineering, personal information managers, spreadsheets, word processing, other applications)

A closer look at some of these categories follows.

Personal information managers

A full-featured desktop organizer or sales and prospect management package provides an excellent way to stay in touch with current, former, and prospective contacts. There are many types of address-manager and telephone-organizer software. Telephone calls and e-mail help you stay in touch with important people who can provide business intelligence. Regular contact over the long run is an excellent collection method. Specific features of desktop-organizer software can include the ability to code your contacts and will help you sort contacts into very specific categories. A friendly but brief phone call to say hello and stay in touch usually is much appreciated. The feature of a built-in telephone dialer can help you zip through a long call list. My experience is that the best time for calls is Tuesday or Wednesday, before 9 A.M. and after 4 P.M. EST. Use a "last contacted on" date field to sort a list of current contacts you haven't talked to within the past month or so.

A sophisticated and always appreciated touch is the birthday card or note on a special occasion. Birthdays and anniversaries are most frequently noted, but special circumstances, like news about the individual, should prompt you to send a note. Desktop organizers facilitate this process with alarms to alert you to programmed dates for personal calls or business follow-up calls.

Primary research

If you are developing BI through primary research (developing new information based on a sampling of questionnaire respondents) you can find shareware. This software can help you generate survey forms and tabulate results. Questions that avoid bias, random selection of respondents, and a variety of other technical factors are required for truly professional surveys. Used in combination with a contact-management system, this type of software can be particularly effective. However, generating predictable data with high confidence levels requires a random sampling of the surveyed population. Nonetheless, the survey technique can yield valuable results with a small, non-random sample.

Quotes, bids, and estimating

For those who work in the business arena where quotes and proposals are a necessary part of the landscape, specialized packages might be useful. Consider that you may have to "reverse engineer" a competitor's bid, and this type of software might prove to be especially useful. Bids based on time and materials may be your required format, but some packages also handle financial analysis capability that is useful in analyzing bids. Planning and graphing features of certain types of estimating software can help you analyze large or complicated proposals.

Online courses

The U.S. Small Business Administration (SBA) provides online education resources for training current and aspiring entrepreneurs. The SBA Small Business Classroom provides interactive, easily accessible business courses on the topics most in demand by small-business clients. The SBA Small Business Classroom's online courses are short (seven to 30 minutes) and self-paced, and learning modules are formatted into easy-to-follow learning templates. The content of each course is enhanced with graphics, audio, and numerous links to other smal-business learning resources. Certain courses are offered in both Spanish and English. Current class offerings are listed here:

- **The Business Plan**—Comprehensive course on how to prepare an effective business plan; profiles each component in detail and includes additional resources

- **How to Raise Capital for a Small Business**—Provides instruction on how to prepare a loan proposal, how banks review financial requests, and information on SBA's financial assistance programs.

The SBA also plans to include more courses on financial assistance, marketing, and how to do business with the federal government in the near future. Additional components of the SBA Small Business Classroom include online counseling with SCORE volunteers, a library, and a Course Evaluation & Comments Forum. The SBA Small Business Classroom is accessible through the agency's Web site at **www.sba.gov**.

CHAPTER 13

OTHER INFORMATION SOURCES TO SUPPLEMENT THE INTERNET

The common perception is that all information on the Internet is available free of charge. That is largely true. However, publishers and other information creators must earn money so they can pay their employees and stay in business. While there is an incredible wealth of no-charge information, some of it is provided by publishers who "give away" a small portion of their product as an introductory sample. This new marketing paradigm can help you to zero in on what you need by finding it on the Internet, then, if required, purchase more complete or detailed versions of the same basic information you found on the Net. In this chapter we'll provide a broad-brush overview.

CD-ROM databases

Bela Hatvany, a co-founder of the SilverPlatter company, recognized the promise of optical disc technology. In 1983 he began developing a way to store and read data on compact disc. With a team of engineers, he created a technology that would allow users to precisely locate specific information amidst millions of bytes of data. As progress was made, relationships were created with owners of important and authenticated information sources. The American Psychological Association (APA) and *Sociological Abstracts* were among the first to realize the opportunities that this new publishing media presented. Both became SilverPlatter's first publishing partners.

In June of 1985 the first prototypes of SilverPlatter reference databases were unveiled at the American Library Association

Conference. The library community immediately recognized how this new technology could enhance the services that it provided. The CD-ROM industry was born. SilverPlatter now specializes in CD-ROM distribution of scientific information.

CD-ROMs (Compact Disc, Read Only Memory) are today standard on any full-featured notebook or desktop computer. The CD-ROM player permits use of very large amounts of information, more than 600 megabytes, on an inexpensive disk. A good example is the telephone book CD-ROM disk, containing every business listed in all of the nation's Yellow Page directories. It can be purchased for under $20. This type of CD-ROM information product enables you to search and find almost any listed telephone number and obtain the subscriber's name (person's name for residential CD-ROMs and business name for CD-ROMs containing commercial listings) and address. Furthermore, the business type also is listed, and an enhanced CD-ROM product by American Business Information also provides limited sales and credit information.

Each year players are faster and cost less. CD-ROM users may want to consider a tower that permits loading of several discs for faster access. Lower-end towers cost under $1,000. Notebooks not equipped with a CD-ROM drive can be outfitted with a unit that plugs into the computer via the parallel port or through a PCMCIA slot.

Low- to medium-cost CD-ROMs

Perhaps the most useful product in this category is telephone directory CD-ROMs. Prices range from $25 to $150. The more expensive versions have powerful reverse search business category look-up, as well as abilities to "walk up and down the street" to find the names and numbers of persons or businesses next door or across the street from the target. Some of these capabilities have been incorporated into Internet search engine features.

Telephone book CD-ROMs also can be used for business intelligence (BI) and especially in marketing. For example, you could look up all the lawyers in a particular ZIP code and produce a telemarketing campaign. Listings can be printed on labels for mailings or exported to a database for generation of sales letters and follow-up phone calls.

Other publishers have taken various types of information and created low-cost CD-ROM products. Surprisingly, some of this information is very business specific and voluminous. It's a gold mine for the right user who needs the specific information. A good example of this type of low-cost (under $20) product is the "Government Giveaways for Entrepreneurs" CD-ROM published by InfoBusiness. Among many other interesting categories of information applicable to small businesses was a two-year archive of government contract data. A search for "Lockheed" produced the following:

Search: Lockheed

Hits: 3955/3955

Air Force Department Of The (Headquarte—Lockheed D
Corporation—8972

Air Force Department Of The (Headquarte—General Dynamics
Corporation—8985

Air Force Department Of The (Headquarte—Lockheed D
Technical Services Co—9367

Air Force Department Of The (Headquarte—General Dynamics
Corporation—9483

Air Force Department Of The (Headquarte—General Dynamics
Corporation—9491

Air Force Department Of The (Headquarte—General Dynamics
Corporation—9492

Air Force Department Of The (Headquarte—General Dynamics
Corporation—9506

Air Force Department Of The (Headquarte—General Dynamics
Corporation—9509

Air Force Department Of The (Headquarte—Lockheed D
Western Export Co—9518

Air Force Department Of The (Headquarte—General Dynamics
Corporation—9521

Air Force Department Of The (Headquarte—General Dynamics
Corporation—9539

Air Force Department Of The (Headquarte—General Dynamics
Corporation—9540

Air Force Department Of The (Headquarte—General Dynamics
Corporation—9574

Air Force Department Of The (Headquarte—General Dynamics
Corporation—9594

Dollars: $636,000

Action Date: 9210

Reporting Agency: 5700

Number: F3360093C0031

Completed Date: 9309

Agency Name: AIR FORCE, DEPARTMENT OF THE (HEADQUARTE
Office Name: DOD/DEPARTMENT OF THE AIR FORCE
Address #1: 4400 CONS/CC
Address #2: BLDG 647, 3RD FLOOR
City: Langley AFB State: VA Zip: 236655558
SIC Description: ENGINEERING SERVICES SIC: 8711
Contractor Name: LOCKHEED CORPORATION
Woman Owned: N
Parents Name:
2nd Contractor Name: LOCKHEED CORPORATION
Address: 1011 LOCKHEED WAY
City: PALMDALE State: CA Zip: 93599-0001
Place Name: SUNLAND
County Code: 037
Country: US
Contractor Type: Other than Full and Open Competition
Contract Type: Large Business
Subcontracting Plan: Not Required
Service Code Description: PROF SVCS/ENGINEERING TECHNICAL
Kind of Contract: Modification
Solicitation: Firm Fixed-Price
Preference Program: No Preference Program or Not Listed

This is a very low-cost source for the researcher developing BI in a particular field encompassing this type of information. It is extensive and can be used to create a specialized database that can be used for a variety of purposes. By exporting selected records, or just by copying and pasting into a document, these data can be manipulated to create comma-delimited files that can be imported into a database, saving a lot of research and typing time.

The U.S. government is a big producer of CD-ROMs that fit into this price category. For example, complete transcripts of testimony before and comments from Food and Drug Administration pharmaceutical and medical devices advisory committees can be purchased for about $15. Video of the meetings also is available at about $300 per day for CD-ROM format. Generally the transcript text CD-ROMs are produced and sold by the FDA, while the video is produced and sold by contractors. Webcasting of live video and audio is available via **www.fdalive.com**, also produced by a contractor.

A blend of Internet and CD-ROM is offered in government-compiled statistics. Energy InfoDisc is touted with the phrase "It's not just a CD-ROM…" The National Energy Information Center, Energy Information Administration (EIA) of the U.S. Department of Energy (**www.eia. doe.gov**) provides a quarterly CD-ROM "brimming with more than 600 megabytes of information produced by the EIA. It is easy to use, yet robust enough for serious number crunching and analysis."

In addition to information from more than 200 of EIA's periodicals, reports, forecasts, models, and databases like the State Energy Data System, U.S. Emissions of Greenhouse Gases and World Energy, the CD-ROM contains hundreds of hypertext links. These links to the EIA Web site provide direct access to the latest information. The CD-ROM also contains software for advanced search of the disc as well as Netscape Navigator and Adobe Acrobat Reader with search and Web-link plug-ins, as well as supporting Windows database engines. A single issue costs $45 and the quarterly subscription is $100.

Another example of your tax dollars at work is the bargain-priced five-CD-ROM set titled The OTA Legacy: 1972-1995. This set of CD-ROMs contains all of the published reports and many of the background papers and other textual material produced by the Office of Technology Assessment (OTA) during its 23 years of service to the Congress and people of the United States. In all, this archive contains over 700 OTA documents and 110,000 pages of the best available analyses of the scientific and technical policy issues of the past two decades.

The reports are stored as Adobe's Portable Document Format (PDF) files that maintain the original layout and graphic design of the published documents. This format allows users to search, copy, display, and print the reports on a variety of computer platforms using the Adobe Acrobat software found on Disk 1. Hypertext "bookmarks" indicating chapters and other major sections have been added to the reports along with thumbnail images of the pages to facilitate rapid navigation through the documents. This reference work, excerpts of which are used in this book, costs under $30.

High-cost library CD-ROMs

Today, nearly every library has at least one publicly accessible personal computer in addition to an Internet connection. If you enroll in an inexpensive computer course at a local community college, you have the authority to access computer labs and library services at these institutions. If you are an alum and your alma mater is nearby, count those resources in too. These are just some of the many other opportunities to access the unprecedented world of knowledge and experience available via the Internet as well as the more pricey databases on CD-ROM.

Much more sophisticated (more detail, better search capabilities, and multiple sort and output options) business database CD-ROMs are available at prices up to $15,000 for an annual subscription. Many of these expensive CD-ROMs are available at public libraries as listed in Figure 13.1.

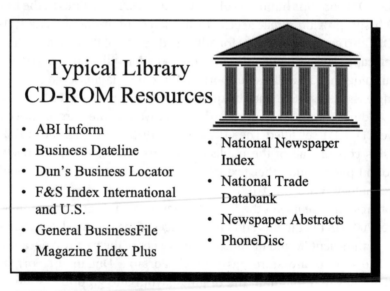

Typical Library CD-ROM Resources

- ABI Inform
- Business Dateline
- Dun's Business Locator
- F&S Index International and U.S.
- General BusinessFile
- Magazine Index Plus
- National Newspaper Index
- National Trade Databank
- Newspaper Abstracts
- PhoneDisc

Figure 13.1

Larger public and academic libraries have many different CD-ROM databases while the smaller libraries may have just one or two. These systems usually permit downloading of data from the CD-ROM to floppy disk, so you can create a personal-use database from the information. An example of a basic business directory database follows:

Companies International 3.1
A.B. Young Cos.
P.O. Box 90287
Indianapolis, IN 46290-0287
Telephone Number(s): (317) 844-7001
Fax Number: (317) 848-2606

Officers:

Bruce H. Young—President

Mike Smith—Sales Mgr

SIC Code(s):

5074—Plumbing & Hydronic Heating Supplies

5075—Warm Air Heating & Air Conditioning

Description:

Wholesale Heating and cooling equipment

Revenue: 1994 Sales 6,500,000 U.S. Dollars

Fiscal Year End: 12/31

Number of Employees: 30

Company Type: Private

Year Established: 1952

Local libraries often have the very useful Standard & Poor's Corporations CD-ROM. It contains three separate databases: one on 12,000 public companies with up to several hundred pages of text and financial data on each company; a second database of about two pages of information on each of 45,000 private companies; and a third database of 70,000 executives associated with the companies. The following is a partial record (the full listing contains much more information, mostly SEC disclosure reports) from the S&P CD-ROM Public Companies database:

Bank of Boston Corp.

100 Federal St.

Boston, MA 02110 USA

TELEPHONE: 6174342200

TYPE OF COMPANY: Bank Holding

CUSIP: 060716

THIS IS AN SP 500 COMPANY.

PRIMARY SIC CODE: 6712 Bank holding companies

SECONDARY SIC CODE (S):

6021   National commercial banks

6091   Nondeposit trust facilities

6099   Functions related to depository banking, not elsewhere classified

6141   Personal credit institutions

6153   Short-term business credit institutions, except agriculture

6159   Miscellaneous business credit institutions

6162   Mortgage bankers and loan correspondents

OFFICERS

C. K. Gifford, Chairman, Chief Exec Officer & Pres
E. A. O'Neal, Vice Chrm
W. J. Shea, Vice Chrm, Chief Fin Officer & Treas

CORPORATE BACKGROUND

BUSINESS DESCRIPTION

Company, through subsidiaries, conducts a general banking business, offering a broad range of individual, corporate and global banking services, through 500 offices across the U.S. and more than 100 offices in 23 countries in Latin America, Europe and Asia.

Company's principal subsidiary is The First National Bank of Boston, wholly owned, a national banking association with its headquarters in Mass. Co.'s other major banking subsidiaries include Bank of Boston Connecticut and Rhode Island Hospital Trust National Bank (Hospital Trust), both of which are wholly owned. Financial services provided by Co.'s subsidiaries include domestic corporate and investment banking, leasing, mortgage origination and servicing, international banking, retail banking, private banking, trust, correspondent banking, securities and payments processing, and commercial real estate lending.

Domestic operations provide customers with services that range from lending to an array of fee-based investment and merchant banking products; and offer merchant banking, acquisition finance, private placements, merger and acquisition advisory services, and syndications. Co.'s national bank subsidiaries are members of the Federal Reserve System and their deposits are insured by the FDIC. Hospital Trust is also a member of the Federal Home Loan

Bank of Boston. Co.'s state-chartered bank subsidiary is subject to the supervision of the FDIC as well as by its state bank regulator.

International operations offer a wide variety of banking and financial services, including trade finance and credit services to large multinational corporations; local currency lending; treasury operations; retail banking; correspondent banking; commercial banking; corporate and institutional trust services; global custody; and services to insurance companies and mutual funds.

PARTNERSHIP Boston EquiServe, L.P., owned equally by Co. and Boston Financial Data Services, which is a joint venture owned by State Street Bank and DST, Inc.

EMPLOYEES Dec. 31, 1995, 17,881.

MEMBER BANKS First National Bank of Boston
  Bank of Boston Connecticut
  Rhode Island Hospital Trust National Bank
  Bank of Boston Maine, N.A.
  Bank of Boston International
  Bank of Boston Florida, N.A.

OTHER SUBSIDIARIES wholly owned
  Boston Overseas Financial Corp.
  Boston World Holding Corp.
  Boston Overseas Holding Corp.
  Fidelity Acceptance Corp.
  FSC Corp.
  Colonial Bancorp, Inc.
  Ganis Credit Corp.
  1784 Investor Services, Inc.
  Thor Credit Corp.
  Bullfinch Indemnity, Ltd.
  Boston International Holdings Corp.
  Multibank Financial Corp.
  RIHT Life Insurance Co.

The company also has several other subsidiaries with the names Bank of Boston or BancBoston in their titles.

Kompass (**www.kompass.com**) has served business and industry for over 50 years. It originated in Switzerland and is now present in close to 70 countries on all continents. The Kompass Group employs over 2,500 people. National CD-ROMs are available for the following countries: Australia, Austria, Belgium, Bulgaria, China, Czech Republic, Egypt, France, Germany, Hungry, Ireland, Israel, Italy, Korea, Lebanon, Luxembourg, Netherlands, New Zealand, Poland, Portugal, Russia, Singapore, Slovakia, Slovenia, South Africa, Spain, Switzerland, Thailand, UAE, United Kingdom, Yugoslavia. Multi-country CD-ROMs also are available.

Kompass' free search engine contains the Kompass Worldwide Database, which covers 1.5 million companies worldwide; 50,000 product and service codes; 23 million product and service references; 2.7 million executives' names; 400,000 trademarks; and brand names from nearly 70 countries.

The Gale Group, which includes the former Information Access Company (IAC), provides information-based products in CD-ROM, microfilm, print, and online formats. The company adds value to the articles, reports, scientific and educational information, and business and financial research it collects from more than 6,500 sources worldwide by applying advanced indexing, coding, and abstracting. Among its best-known products are InfoTrac, ComputerSelect, PROMT, and Trade and Industry Database. In addition to its headquarters in Farmington Hills, Michigan, the Gale Group has offices in Foster City, California; IAC has offices in Cambridge, Massachusetts; London, England; New York, N.Y.; and Melbourne, Australia. The Gale Group was formed in 1998 by the merger of IAC, Gale Research, and Primary Source Media. Gale's Web site is **www.galegroup.com**

CD-ROM indexes to magazine articles can be used to find leads for Internet searches. For example, the InfoTrac CD-ROM Magazine Index Plus contains citations and abstracts for about 400 periodicals. While searching for background information about uninterruptible power supplies, a number of articles were provided. Note that in the abstract for each article there are one or more terms (underlined here) that can be searched via the Internet to broaden the research effort to collect more relevant material:

Database: Magazine Index Plus

Subject: uninterruptible power supply

Library: plainsboro

Power outages spark a drive for back-up. (wafer fabrication facilities in five western states hit by massive power outage) (Technology Information)

Electronic News (1991), August 19, 1996 v42 n2130 p1(2).

Author: Peter Brown

Abstract: A massive five-state power outage in the western US has focused emphasis on the need for uninterruptible power supplies (UPS) for semiconductor facilities. The <u>Western Systems Coordinating Council</u> (WSCC) states that it is impossible to prevent future power outages, but the organization is taking steps to make the system as reliable as possible. <u>American Power Conversion's</u> (APC) UPSs are already protecting some major semiconductor facilities, including National Semiconductor, LSI Logic and Applied Materials. Intel and Motorola suffered wafer losses and equipment damage because neither company has formulated contingency plans or purchased backup power generators. Fujitsu's Portland, OR, suffered minor losses, but the company feels that the possibility of more blackouts in that state are so minimal they do not warrant preventive measures.

Subjects: Uninterruptible power supply—Usage

Semiconductor industry—Equipment and supplies

Mag. Collection: 85B6230

Bus. Collection: 95X4549

AN: 18611492

Database: Magazine Index Plus

Subject: uninterruptible power supply

Library: plainsboro

A belt and suspenders? (products that allay the fears of network-managers) (Multiple Access) (Product Information)(Column)

PC Magazine, June 11, 1996 v15 n11 pN26(1).

Author: Steve Buehler

Abstract: Network managers know it pays to be extra careful, and they appreciate products that provide them with added security. HT Communications offers the LineSaver, which monitors a data line and automatically dials up a standby ISDN line when traffic fails. The device costs $595 per side, which puts it out of the reach of many network managers, but it does give them a little more peace of mind. American Power Conversion's PowerShield UPS is useful for ISDN lines, which need external power, unlike the plain old telephone system. LinkPro's $89 PowerSync 3.0 32-bit PC-to-PC file synchronizer allows file synchronization to be scheduled for times or events, such as Windows startup; it also lets quick-pick lists of directories and files be set up, which is useful when having to start from the same configuration repeatedly.

Subjects: Uninterruptible power supply—Usage

Communications equipment—Management

Disk tape file utilities—Usage

Computer networks—Management

Companies: American Power Conversion Corp.—Products

HT Communications Inc.—Products

Linkpro Inc.—Products

Products: American Power Conversion PowerShield ISDN (UPS)—Usage

HT Communications LineSaver (Telephone management device)—Usage

PowerSync 3.0 (File synchronization software)—Usage

Mag. Collection: 86G2767
Bus. Collection: 97V2909
AN: 18313731

This CD-ROM provides good background information along with access to the original article with illustrations if the subscribing library has the corresponding Magazine or Business Collection microfilm cartridges. The code numbers at the end of the record correspond to the specific cartridge and film location of the article. These cartridges are viewed using a machine that usually allows the user to print a photocopy of the article being viewed.

From time to time a particular writer will show up as frequently covering a specific subject. This information may be very valuable if that person is willing to talk to you about the subject you are researching. If you can trade information you'll be more likely to get some valuable insight of fact from the writer. On the other hand, if you are compiling an industrywide report and need to interview several personalities cited in the articles, you may get the brushoff unless you offer something in return for that person's comments. This obstacle can be overcome by providing to the interviewee a copy of all or part of the completed report.

All of these CD-ROM databases can be used to establish the core of your own internal database. By exporting selected records from the CD-ROM and then importing them into your database, you can save considerable time and resources. Remember that use of this information must meet Copyright Fair Use provisions, which generally means that a small selection exclusively for your personal use is acceptable, but if in doubt, consult an attorney.

To use the CD-ROM's export capability, select a group of records and download them to a floppy disk. The disk file can be imported to your database augmenting or creating records for your own use. The software that provides the search and utility functions may have a dialog box to set the number of records that can be downloaded in one operation. If you find that you can only select and download 20 or 50 records at a time, check with the library's database expert to have the limit increased.

You may find the library's floppy drive locked with a small insert that fits into the drive, most likely for protection against viruses. In most cases you can have the librarian remove the insert for your legitimate use. However, some libraries lease the database with download restrictions or they may be concerned about potential copyright violations. If you intend to use the records for other than personal reference, you may want to consult a legal authority on their use.

Premium databases

Although mostly supplanted by Internet-accessible versions, these services provide access via modem to proprietary information content in various types of databases. Although overall prices have been dropping during the past few years, several of these services still charge hefty prices for premium data that is controlled by the publisher (e.g., Dow Jones and *The Wall Street Journal*) or is highly processed and formatted (e.g., Questel/Orbit patent data). Given the long history of some of the providers, one could assume that the Information Age is still in its infancy.

In 1972 Dialog Information Services, Inc. became the world's first commercial online service. Today there are a handful of huge information conglomerates and a proliferation of many small competitors, most fueled by ease of entry to the Internet. The Dialog Corporation is illustrative of the merger and acquisition path of growth that some of these companies have taken. Nearly a decade after its inception, Dialog became a subsidiary of Lockheed, the aerospace company. After owning Dialog for about seven years, Lockheed sold Dialog in 1988 to newspaper publisher Knight-Ridder, Inc. for $353 million. In 1997 Knight-Ridder Information, Inc. (a unit of Knight-Ridder, Inc. that had acquired or invested in other information services) was acquired by the British firm M.A.I.D plc for $420 million.

The Thomson Corporation owns dozens of individual companies in fields of legal and regulatory, financial services, reference, scientific and business information, educational, and healthcare. They also publish more than 250 newspapers and magazines in North America. Among the significant online databases related to IBIS are Derwent Information, Gale Research, Information Access Company, Medical Economics, Information America, and KnowX.com.

Reed Elsevier plc, a joint venture of Reed International and Elsevier, publishes trade, scientific, and professional journals and magazines totaling about 1,200, including *The Lancet*. Two of their online services are LEXIS-NEXIS and the Congressional Information Service. In terms of market capitalization, Reed Elsvier is the largest publicly traded publisher and information provider at more than

$18 billion. They lead Wolters Kluwer, Reuters, Thomson, Pearsons, McGraw-Hill, and Dun & Bradstreet.

Bertelsmann AG is the third largest media company in the world. The company has interests in book, magazine, and newspaper publishing; music; television; online; film; and radio. With more than 600 individual companies, Bertelsmann currently employs nearly 60,000 people in 53 countries. A fundamental component to the success of Bertelsmann companies is its highly decentralized corporate organization. Online activities are mostly outside the U.S., but they span science/economics, medicine, transportation, construction/environment, direct marketing, entertainment, and patent fields.

Dow Jones & Company was founded in 1882 by three young reporters: Charles Dow, Edward Jones, and Charles Bergstresser. In their basement office near the New York Stock Exchange they produced handwritten newsletters called "flimsies" that were delivered by messenger to subscribers in the Wall Street area. Business boomed, and by 1889 the staff numbered 50. The company decided to turn its small "Customers' Afternoon Letter" into a newspaper that would be called *The Wall Street Journal*. The first issue, which appeared on July 8, 1889, was four pages and sold for two cents.

The Journal prospered, but Messrs Dow, Jones, and Bergstresser saw the need for a faster way to deliver the news. To that end, the company began delivery of its Dow Jones News Service via telegraph. About a century later, Dow Jones Interactive provides a customizable enterprise-wide business news and research solution. This Web-based product integrates a wide range of business content—from current news from the top national newspapers and Dow Jones Newswires to in-depth background information from Market Research and Investment Analyst Reports to sources in the Publications Library. Information from Dow Jones Interactive can be incorporated into a company's intranet or formatted for any computing environment, including Windows, Macintosh, and Lotus Notes.

Knight-Ridder is the nation's second-largest newspaper publisher, with products in print and online. The company publishes 31 daily newspapers in 28 U.S. markets, with a readership of 9 million daily and 12.6 million Sunday, and maintains 34 associated Web sites under the name Knight Ridder Real Cities. The mission of the

Real Cities Network is to be the best, most authoritative, most complete source of news, information, and Internet services in each market they serve. Integrated into Real Cities, NewsHound is a customized online news search and retrieval service that delivers personalized information to subscribers by continuously scanning newspapers and domestic and international wire services.

Dun & Bradstreet (D&B) is best known for its basic coverage of private companies. Their information is based upon self-reported data provided by the companies on which they do their reports. D&B has a fascinating history and probably is the first example of organized business intelligence in the U.S, as previously described in Chapter Five.

Premium online databases at libraries

Some libraries have subscriptions to online services that help you look up citations of newspaper, magazine, and journal articles relevant to your project. One such search at the Philadelphia Public Library yielded the following results that were e-mailed to the requester. The search was performed at the library, but the results only could be e-mailed to the researcher's own e-mail address. Here's what was found in a project for a corporate security director:

Subject: 'Documents Requested from EBSCOhost'

Date: Tue, 17 Feb 1998 14:53:31—0500

From: ehost@epnet.com (EBSCOhost Mailer)

To: bizintel@home.com

Subject: CORPORATIONS—Corrupt practices—Japan; EXTORTION—Japan

Title: The jig is up.

Source: Barron's, 12/01/97, Vol. 77 Issue 48, p13, 1/4p, 1bw

Author: Martin, Neil A.

Abstract: Looks at how the Japanese handle companies that pay off corporate blackmailers. The efforts of the Ministry of Finance to get tougher on the 'sokaiya'; The move by the Japanese parliament to strengthen an anticrime bill banning payment to sokaiya; The stiffer penalties on the gangsters demanding money and the executives who pay them; The executives of firms indicted or implicated in making payments.

AN: 9712056167

ISSN: 1077-8039

Note: This title is held locally.

Subject: ARNOTTS Ltd.—Finance; EXTORTION—Australia

Title: Arnotts emerges from its blackest hour with a new will to win.

Source: Business Review Weekly, 09/22/97, Vol. 19 Issue 36, p84, 5p, 6c

Author: Shoebridge, Neil

Abstract: Deals with how the Australian biscuit company, Arnotts, emerged from an extortion crisis and won new market shares. The $8-10 million loss; The timing of the crisis; How rival biscuit companies picked up consumers; Arnotts loss of production time; The change in the advertising approach of the company; New flavors added to the line; Comments of Peter Bush, general manager of Arnotts.

INSETS: Extortion bid forced some fine-tuning; How not to use a celebrity in ads.

AN: 9710035849

ISSN: 0727-758X

Note: This title is not held locally

Subject: TERRORISM—Venezuela; GUERRILLAS—Venezuela

Title: Cross-border terror.

Source: Economist, 05/24/97, Vol. 343 Issue 8018, p34, 2/5p, 1 map

Abstract: Discusses problems in Venezuela caused by guerilla groups from Colombia. The involvement of guerilla groups like the Revolutionary Armed Forces of Colombia (FARC) and the Army of National Liberation (ELN) in terrorism, kidnapping, and extortion; The groups' links to drug-trafficking and money-laundering; The inability of Venezuelan armed forces to stop the guerillas; The devastation of the economy where the guerilla incursions take place.

AN: 9706031394

ISSN: 0013-0613

Note: This title is held locally.

** Full text is available **

As you can see, some of the citations indicate that full text was available or that the publication was held by the library. There may be cases where you need an article and must pay for a single copy on a one-time basis. There are many services that provide document delivery via fax or e-mail with payment by credit card.

Smaller online business information providers

The Bureau of National Affairs, Inc. (BNA) was founded in 1929. BNA is a leading publisher of print and electronic news and information, reporting on developments in healthcare, business, labor relations, law, economics, taxation, environmental protection, safety, and other public policy and regulatory issues. Today, BNA produces more than 200 news and information services, including five daily publications.

EBSCO Information Services provides integrated information management worldwide through subscription services, reference database development and production, and online multi-database access. The EBSCO Information Services group consists of EBSCO Subscription Services and EBSCO Publishing. EBSCO's Corporate ResourceNet delivers business journals, company data, and Web links to the desktop in one convenient tool. Corporate ResourceNet offers content including 1,700 full-text periodicals, 3,500 searchable sources, and profiles on over 150,000 companies.

Knowledge Express Data Systems (KE) has been in business since 1991. A subsidiary of Telescan, Inc., KE was started to provide an online solution for the tech transfer and business development field. The company successfully completed a two-year DOE-sponsored program providing access to small corporations, and university and government laboratories. Since then, KE transitioned to a business-to-business, flat-fee-based pricing strategy. Its plans are to remain a major player in the niche business development and competitive intelligence fields.

NewsBank resources contain information from newspapers, newswires, business journals, and periodicals, as well as historical and scholarly documents. Their information is delivered to schools and libraries via the latest Internet technology, CD-ROM, and microfiche. Known as the world's largest publisher of newspapers on CD-ROM, NewsBank also offers its newspaper and periodical collections online via NewsBank InfoWeb. NewsBank InfoWeb contains information from over 2,000 regional, national, and international sources.

Questel•Orbit is a subsidiary of France Telecom Multimedia and a leading provider of intellectual property online information services specializing in the online provision of patent, trademark, scientific, technical, chemical, and business information. Intellectual Property Gold is Questel•Orbit's offering for customers who have identified intellectual property information as a real strategic asset for their businesses. With Intellectual Property Gold, Questel•Orbit is developing a comprehensive and complete offering that will allow users to search their entire catalog of databases. The new service reinforces Questel•Orbit's product lines and will complement their QPAT•US Internet service.

Directory publishers

There's a relatively small group of publishers that produce very specialized business information directories. For the purposes of developing and maintaining an Internet Business Intelligence System, we can divide these publishers into two categories. The first is the electronic business information directory, and the second category is the local and regional index of businesses.

An outstanding source is the *Gale Directory of Databases 1999* (ISBN: 0-7876-2296-6) published by Gale Research. This massive four-part print product sells for $390. It profiles more than 13,000 databases available in a variety of computer-readable formats. It provides descriptions and contact information for approximately 6,500 online databases made publicly available through the producer or an online service, and more than 6,000 database products offered in "portable" form (CD-ROM, diskette, magnetic tape, hand-held, and batch access). All varieties of databases are listed: bibliographic, numeric, bulletin board, directory, full-text, dictionary, audio, time series, image, statistical, properties, video, software, and transactional.

Gale Research produces databases covering a range of subjects, from literature and biographies to science and technology, as well as general reference—primarily for the public, school, and academic library markets. They began in 1954 with the Encyclopedia of Associations. In 1998 Gale Research merged with IAC and Primary Source Media to form the Gale Group.

Information Today, Inc. (corporate parent of CyberAge Books, publisher of *Internet Business Intelligence*) provides several directories that help users find electronic information. Also, they publish periodicals that cover the electronic information industry and run conferences that serve to educate the participants and create an efficient marketplace for person-to-person exchanges at the associated trade shows held concurrently.

The *Fulltext Sources Online* directory is published by Information Today, Inc. each January and July with a complete new edition. Listing over 13,000 newspapers, journals, magazines, newsletters, and newswires found online in full text, this directory saves time and money for the user. *FSO* also lists journals that have free Internet archives and provides subscribers with access to the Private Zone for up-to-date listings of titles with free archives via the Internet. While this directory covers full-text sources primarily supplied by major aggregators and content providers, other Information Today directories provide a more targeted approach to helping the end-user find electronic information.

The *Online Manual* is a unique reference tool for searching international business information online. The easy-to-use sections guide you through the mass of databases, helping you to locate where the journal you need is available online; discover which databases cover your subject; find the host that covers a database; and answer specific queries, e.g., which database gives sales for German companies.

Books that serve as directories

Finding Statistics Online:
How to Locate the Elusive Numbers You Need
By Paula Berinstein
Edited by Susanne Bjørner

Need statistics? Find them more quickly and easily than ever—online! Finding good statistics is a challenge for even the most experienced researcher. Today, it's likely the statistics you need are available online—but where? This book explains how to effectively use Internet and professional online systems to find the statistics you need to succeed.

1998/320 pp/softbound
ISBN 0-910965-25-0
$29.95

Internet Blue Pages: The Guide to Federal Government Web Sites
By Laurie Andriot

With over 900 Web addresses, this guide is designed to help you find any agency easily. Arranged in accordance with the *U.S. Government Manual*, each entry includes the name of the agency, the Web address (URL), a brief description of the agency, and links to the agency or subagency's home page. For helpful cross-referencing, an alphabetical agency listing, and a comprehensive index for subject searching are also included. Regularly updated information and links are provided on the author's Web site.

1999/368 pp/softbound
ISBN 0-910965-29-3
$34.95

Magazines to help you find information

The most widely read publication in the information industry, *Information Today* is the only monthly tabloid newspaper designed to meet the needs of the information professional. *Information Today* delivers total coverage of late-breaking news and long-term trends in the information industry. Accurate, timely news articles inform the reader of the people, products, services, and events that impact the industry, while hard-hitting, topical articles explain significant developments in the field.

Another helpful periodical is *Searcher: The Magazine for Database Professionals*. It explores and deliberates on a comprehensive range of issues important to the professional database searcher. The magazine is targeted to experienced, knowledgeable searchers and combines evaluations of data content with discussions of delivery media. Searcher includes evaluated online news, searching tips and techniques, reviews of search aid software and database documentation, revealing interviews with leaders and entrepreneurs of the industry, and trenchant editorials. Whatever the experienced database searcher needs to know to get the job done is covered in *Searcher*.

Information Today, Inc.'s editorial products as well as their databases and conferences are highlighted at their Web site, **www.infotoday.com**.

Business directories

Generally, specialized local and regional business directories are much more accurate than those published by those published by national publishers. This is because local publishers can obtain more detailed or up-to-date information from local businesses. Other publishers of specialized industry-specific directories can invest the time and resources necessary to compile their special interest directories because they have a built-in market in the people or companies they survey. Further, many of these publishers sell "slices" of these data on floppy disk or CD-ROM so the purchaser can simply load some or all of the data into his or her own system. Information about many of these directories can be found on the Internet, and in some cases a searchable version with limited capability is available. These directories generally fall into the following categories:

Representative directories:
Company information

Colorado Business Directory

Dallas County Business Directory

Dallas Ft. Worth Metro Business Directory

Dalton's Philadelphia Metro Directory of Business & Industry

Directory of American Firms Operating Foreign Countries
(3 vols.)

Directory of Foreign Firms Operating in the United States

Florida Business Directory

Georgia Business Directory

Hillsborough County Business Directory

Houston Business Directory

KOMPASS Register of Business & Industry Catalog

Minnesota Business Almanac-Minnesota's Guide to Business

Portland Metro Business Directory

Southern California Business Directory

Ward's Business Directory & Supplement (5 vols.)

Representative directories:
Specialized

Business & Economic Research Directory

Business Organizations, Agencies & Publications Directory

Corporate Guide to International Telecommunications &
Information Technology Organizations

Directory of Business Information Resources

Directory of Buyout Financing Sources

Directory of M&A Intermediaries

Encyclopedia of Business Information Sources

Franchise Annual Directory

Major Mass Market Merchandise

Market Scope—The Desktop Guide to Supermarket Share & Category Sales

McFadden Golden States Financial Directory

Plunkett's Entertainment & Media Industry

Plunkett's Health Care Industry

Polk Financial Institutions Directory, North American Edition

Retail Tenant Directory

Independent Specialty Stores

Shopping Center Directory & Top Contacts (5 vols.)

Sporting Goods Buyers

American Wholesalers & Distributors Directory

Stern's SourceFinder—Master Directory to Human Resource & Business Management

The Directory of Convenience Stores—The Book of C-store Market Facts

Thomson National Directory of Mortgage Brokers

Thomson Risk Management Directory

Thomson's Bluebook—The Banker's Guide to Product & Service Providers

U.S. Sourcebook of R & D Spenders

Who's Who among Top Executives

Who's Who of Institutions & Mutual Funds

A summary of these publishers cross-referenced by subject category is contained in Table 13.1.

Sources of exotic BI

The Internet can be used to find data that must be acquired via other channels. There are tens of thousands of large-scale data sets available from a wide variety of public and private sources. The nature of the Internet makes it an excellent medium in which those who offer data for sale can do so at little cost, making the information accessible worldwide. Often governments have an interest in promulgating such data for political, economic, or social reasons.

For example, NASA's Global Change Master Directory (GCMD) at **http://gcmd.gsfc.nasa.gov/** is a comprehensive directory of descriptions of data sets of relevance to global change research. The GCMD database includes descriptions of data sets (DIFs) covering climate change, the biosphere, hydrosphere and oceans, geology, geography, and human dimensions of global change.

Table 13.1

Publisher Category	Local Companies	Intl. Companies	Personnel	Distribution	Info Sources	Specialty	Financial
American Bus. Directories	X						
C.J.S., Inc.	X						
Carson Group			X				
Dalton	X						
Europa					X		
Gale Research	X	X			X	X	
Info Press						X	
Kaleo Publications, Limited					X		
Michael Daniels Publishers					X		
National Research Bureau				X			
Plunkett Research						X	
Schonfeld						X	
Thomson						X	X
Trade Dimensions				X			
U.S. Council-Intl. Business							X
Uniworld		X					
Venture Economics							X

Through search interfaces, the public may freely search the GCMD database as shown in Figure 13.2. The resulting metadata records provide information on the nature of the data (e.g., parameters measured, geographic location, time range) and where the data are stored.

Some of the features of the GCMD include:

Announcements: Important news regarding the status and operation of the GCMD are presented here. Announcements of changes in the GCMD are also posted here. In addition, these announcements are posted to the Interoperability Forum (see below).

Data Set Registration via the WWW: GCMD's DIFWeb tool provides a quick way to include a description of your data in the database. Describing your data in the GCMD is free and provides international recognition.

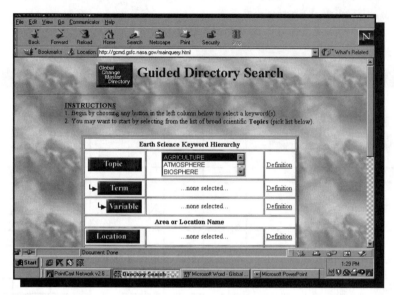

Figure 13.2

Search the GCMD Database: The GCMD database contains descriptions of thousands of data sets held by the U.S. government, universities, foreign agencies, research institutions, companies, and private individuals. Data descriptions in the GCMD provide a brief overview of data sets and information on how they can be obtained. Its search interfaces are simple and free to use.

Global Change Conference Calendar: The GCDIS Conference Calendar is maintained by the GCMD and is a comprehensive listing of conferences, meetings, symposia, and workshops having relevance to global change. Links are provided to other calendars as well.

Software and Documentation: GCMD's software and documentation includes freeware of its popular metadata writing, editing, and indexing tools. Also, for those writing descriptions, the GCMD provides an online writers guide with definitions and guidelines for writing metadata.

Interoperability Forum: The Interoperability Forum is a moderated discussion list where users and staff can interact to share views on the operation and directions of the GCMD. Proposed changes in the GCMD system are discussed and voted upon here.

Links to Other Earth Science WWW Sites: The GCMD maintains a large and up-to-date selection of links to Web sites that may be of interest to its users. In addition, GCMD highlights several interesting Web sites each month.

Projects & Outreach: The GCMD collaborates with several other NASA projects (EOSDIS, DAAC, etc.) as well as with USGCRP, other government agencies, and university data projects, and is the American Coordinating Node of the CEOS IDN.

Metadata Standards: In addition to the GCMD's Directory Interchange Format (DIF), a number of other groups have developed metadata formats for various purposes. The GCMD is involved with these groups in promoting metadata use and working toward a uniform metadata standard.

GCMD and Global Change FAQs: Have a question about the GCMD? Want an overview of a global change issue? Check out its frequently asked questions.

While these data have the common theme of "global change," the directory's actual scope is quite broad. For example, in the category of EARTH SCIENCE > AGRICULTURE > are the following subcategories:

Agricultural Aquatic Sciences > Aquaculture
Agricultural Aquatic Sciences > Fisheries
Agricultural Chemicals > Fertilizers
Agricultural Chemicals > Pesticides
Agricultural Engineering > Agricultural Equipment
Agricultural Plant Science > Crop/Plant Yields
Agricultural Plant Science > Cropping Systems
Agricultural Plant Science > Irrigation
Agricultural Plant Science > Plant Breeding and Genetics
Animal Commodities > Dairy Products
Animal Commodities > Livestock Products
Animal Commodities > Poultry Products
Animal Science > Animal Breeding and Genetics
Animal Science > Animal Management Systems
Animal Science > Animal Nutrition
Animal Science > Animal Physiology and Biochemistry
Animal Science > Animal Waste
Animal Science > Animal Yields

MATERIAL DELETED

A representative partial list of the more than 1,000 sources in the GCMD database includes the following:

AARC > Arctic & Antarctic Research Center

ACC > Alaska Climate Center

ACCA21 > Administrative Center for China's Agenda 21

AES > Agricultural Experiment Station, Texas

AES/EC > Atmospheric Environment Service, EC

AETL > Army Engineers Topographic Laboratories

AFI > Aquarius Flight Inc.

AGNET > Agriculture and Aquatic Sciences Network

AGU > Aoyama Gakuin University

AIRS > Aerometric Information Retrieval System, EPA

ALF > National Agricultural Library Forum, USDA

AMES > Ames Research Center, NASA

AMES/GRAPES > NASA Ames Research Center GRAPES Project

AMPTE/APL > CCE Science Data Center, APL

AMRC > Antarctic Meteorology Research Center

AODC > Australian Oceanographic Data Centre

APHIS > Animal and Plant Health Inspection Service

APRF > Atmospheric Profiler Research Facility/Army Research Laboratory

APSRS > Aerial Photography Summary Record System

ARSI > Atmospheric Research Systems Inc.

ASF DAAC > ASF Distributed Active Archive Center

ATSDR > Agency for Toxic Substances and Disease Registry

AWIS > Agricultural Weather Information Service, Inc.

AXYS > AXYS Environmental Consulting Ltd.

AZGS > Arizona Geological Survey

MATERIAL DELETED

A portion of one record about GlobeSAR2/RADARSAT includes this:

GlobeSAR2 is a three-year geomatics technology transfer program focussed on the use of RADARSAT for improved natural resource management in Latin America as well as the establishment of cooperative linkages between Canadian and Latin American government organisations and universities, and exposure for Canadian geomatic companies. Participating Latin America countries are:

Argentina, Bolivia, Brazil, Chile, Colombia, Costa Rica, Honduras, Panama, Peru, Uruguay and Venezuela.

Projects identified for use of RADARSAT data in Bolivia includes: identification of farming areas and crop types, monitoring of soil humidity, geology, and mapping.

Data Center Name: RSI > RADARSAT International

Data Center URL: http://www.rsi.ca

Dataset ID: GlobeSar2 data for Bolivia

Data Center Contact: ORDER DESK

Phone: +01-604-244-0400

Phone: +01-604-244-0404 FAX

E-mail: pconnor@rsi.ca

Address:

RADARSAT International Inc. (RSI)

Building D, Suite 200

3851 Shell Road

Richmond, British Columbia

V6X 2W2

Canada

Satellite imagery is much discussed but little used in business intelligence. This is partly due to cost and availability, but this is changing with the advent of Internet services that sell these products.

Small private firms have provided processing and analytic data services since the beginning of satellite communications and remote sensing. These so-called value-added companies take raw remotely sensed data and add other geospatial data to them to generate information of value to a wide selection of governmental and private customers. State and local governments have made significant use of the information provided by these firms, generally in the form of maps used for monitoring and planning. This small but rapidly growing sector of the U.S. economy has helped fuel the development and use of geographic information systems (GIS) and imaging-processing software. The United States leads the world in the development of the remote sensing value-added industry.

The French space agency, CNES (Centre National d'Études Spatiales), has the largest national remote sensing program in Europe. CNES was the first European agency to develop and deploy a remote sensing system, the commercially operated SPOT (Systeme Pour l'Observation de la Terre) system[1] (**www.spot.com**).

Interpreting clouds from satellite pictures was the first application of remotely sensed data from environmental satellites in the early 1960s. Satellite image interpretation is still critical today for monitoring weather patterns, severe storms, snow and ice fields, flood coverage, biomass burning, volcanic ash dispersion, and numerous other applications. High- and low-resolution satellite imagery are received by users worldwide in real time through local ground receivers and by central processing facilities where the image data are further processed into quantitative products. Three operational satellite systems provide continuous views of Earth— the Geostationary Operational Environmental Satellite (GOES) and the polar-orbiting National Oceanic and Atmospheric Administration (NOAA) satellites, both operated by NOAA; and the Defense Meteorological Satellite Program (DMSP), operated by the Department of Defense (DOD).

Data produced by remote sensing have intrinsic value because they carry information that can be displayed pictorially for the worlds of science, resource management, and commerce. When properly interpreted, "pictures" produced by remote sensing, whether from satellites, aerial photography, ground-based radar, or other sources, can show the location of a hidden bunker, a caravan route used a thousand years ago, ancient stream beds, or the relative health of agriculturally significant crops. Remote sensing can also be combined with other techniques to produce additional kinds of information for decision-makers. GIS and the global positioning system (GPS) are two technologies often used to add value to remotely sensed data. Remotely sensed data are increasingly accessible to users. Potential data users can also purchase a wide array of geographic information systems of varying levels of sophistication that run on inexpensive desktop computer platforms to process and interpret those data. Similar advances in GPS technologies have assisted in making remotely sensed data much easier to use and more affordable.[2]

Check out **www.terraserver.com**, **www.spin-2.com**, **www.orb image.com**, **www.terrasatgeo.com**, and similar sites for up-to-date product information.

Picking your source(s)

Obviously, Internet-derived sources of business intelligence are the main focus of this book. However, there are many other complementary sources and even a few that are not available via the Internet. Considering the variety of sources, one must take into account depth of coverage (or simply applicability), ease of use, and overall cost. Proprietary content on such online services as America Online sometimes cannot be found elsewhere. Premium online databases usually require hefty subscription prices, and sometimes you can find 80 percent of that pricey information available free on the Internet. Purchasing data files from various compilers of data often is a cost-effective option, and public libraries will probably always be the best overall bargain. General considerations for choosing sources of business intelligence are given in Figure 13.3.

Source Considerations

	Depth of Coverage	Ease of Use	Overall Cost
AOL	Fair	Excellent	Low
Internet	Good	Fair	Low
Premium Online	Excellent	Good	High
Purchased Datafiles	Good	Good	Low
CD-ROM Subs.	Excellent	Excellent	Medium
Public Library	Good	Excellent	Low

Figure 13.3

Endnotes

1. U.S. Congress, Office of Technology Assessment, *Civilian Satellite Remote Sensing: A Strategic Approach*, OTA-ISS-607 (Washington, DC: U.S. Government Printing Office, September 1994).

2. U.S. Congress, Office of Technology Assessment, *Remotely Sensed Data: Technology, Management, and Markets*, OTA-ISS-604 (Washington, DC: U.S. Government Printing Office, September 1994).

CHAPTER 14

ORGANIZING INFORMATION TO PRODUCE INTELLIGENCE

The *Encyclopaedia Britannica* is a massive work in many volumes. Organizing the voluminous collection of mankind's knowledge is a daunting challenge, but the experts have, for many years, risen to the task. They created an "Outline of Knowledge." It is a very orderly and logical outline consisting of major parts and subdivisions of the parts. Understanding their organizational concept can be beneficial for those who would design an Internet Business Intelligence System (IBIS). The Outline of Knowledge closely parallels the organizational chart and the directory and subdirectory structure of file storage.

For example, part five of the encyclopedia is titled "Human Society" and the six divisions include: Social Groups; Social Organization and Social Change; The Production, Distribution and Utilization of Wealth; Politics and Government; Law; and Education.

In division three, The Production, Distribution and Utilization of Wealth, there are six subdivisions: Economic Concepts, Issues and Systems; The Consumer and the Market; The Organization of Production and Distribution; The Distribution of Income and Wealth; Macroeconomics; and Economic Growth and Planning. Of course, there are further subdivisions and finally individual articles on specific topics within. Cross-references, that could easily be hyperlinked in an electronic version, take you to related material.

Like the orderly hierarchical arrangement of knowledge found in the *Encyclopaedia Britannica*, the organization of diverse information from various sources in an IBIS can be viewed as proceeding from the general to the specific. From a micro view, storing a couple of hundred text files on a single computer's hard drive and being able to retrieve them is a very modest challenge. Organizing tens of thousands, perhaps millions of files from hundreds of individuals and dozens of major sources demands a well-thought-out macro method of management. This later approach to organization is an integral part of information architecture (IA). We are concerned with an IA that encompasses the entire process of developing and using Internet Business Intelligence as shown in Figure 14.1.

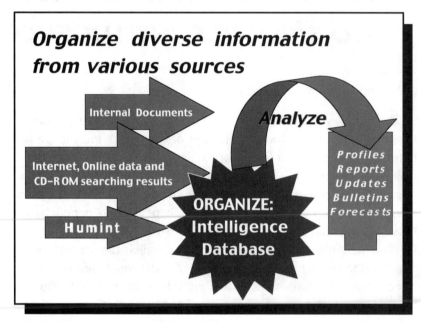

Figure 14.1

Information architecture

Describing IA, the noted author and consultant John Diebold said, "Its aim is to make information into a readily accessible, indispensable tool for senior management. It will expedite and enhance decision making, facilitate planning, make possible improved output and productivity measurement, transform compliance management—in short, increase corporate adaptability to changing circumstances."

Speaking about the development of a strategy for IA he said, "A corporate information policy attempts to shape a unified outlook for dealing with the acquisition, standardization, classification, inventory, dissemination and use of information of every kind. It should be holistic and forward-looking, and it is intended to encourage the sharing of information between departments, among other organizational units, and among different levels of the corporate hierarchy to achieve synchronized action. When successful, a corporate information policy can help orchestrate the uses and users of information of every kind into a workable system to aid management in targeting and fulfilling corporate goals."[1]

A variety of methods and tools can be used to organize the diverse formats and types of data and information that will be collected in an IBIS. This chapter covers a broad range from simple, low- or no-cost methods and tools to the very sophisticated and very expensive. The latter will be addressed to make the reader aware of what is possible. Technological advances and other factors have worked to make some of the high-end technology available to the general public. For example, a filtering and routing system originally developed for the U.S. Intelligence Community (Logicon's Message Dissemination System) serves America Online subscribers who use the service's News Profiles capability.

Micromanagement methods

Storing and managing a personal collection of files on one's own computer is a simple matter of file management. According to Microsoft Windows documentation, "In Windows, you store your work in folders, just like you would in your office or at home. You can look at your files and folders by clicking My Computer. Inside My Computer, you can see a list of all of the disk drives on your computer. Just double-click any icon to see what's inside. When you open a disk drive, you can see the files and folders that it contains. Folders can contain files, programs, and other folders."

The easiest way to organize information is to create folders and subfolders, naming them for the subject categories in which you will store information. For example, you may have a markets folder and several subfolders, one for each market you are monitoring. Likewise, a competitor's folder might have several subfolders with one for each competitor. Theoretically, you could create additional subfolders to sectionalize information with additional subcategories. In the markets example, you might have subdirectories for regions of the world and additional subfolders under subfolders for countries within each region. This could be subdivided further by cities within each of the foreign countries.

To create a new folder in My Computer or Windows Explorer, on the File menu, point to New, and then click Folder. The new folder appears with a temporary name. Type a name for the new folder, and then press ENTER. You change the way files are displayed using commands on the View menu. Also, if the file is on someone else's computer, double click the Network Neighborhood icon instead of My Computer.

When you are browsing the Web and want to save information you can pull down file and select Save As to save the information as an HTML page or plain text. Similarly you can save a document to a subfolder in which you have other similar documents. Once your collection of documents becomes voluminous you'll need a way to search for documents meeting specific criteria.

The most basic way to do this is to select Find from the Windows Task bar Start Menu then select files or folders. This presents a dialog box containing fields for search criteria. You can search by file name or text contained within the file. Other search criteria include finding files created, modified, or last accessed during specific time periods. Also, file type and size search criteria are available. You can toggle case sensitivity and specify the format for viewing search results. A Quick View function is accessible from the file menu. A handy Save Results button will place on your desktop an icon representing the search results or search criteria. Figure 14.2 summarizes the basic methods.

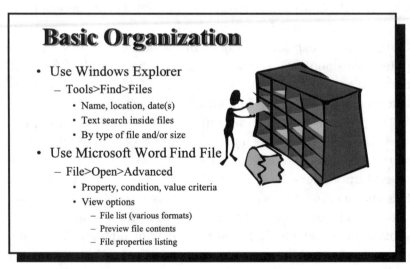

Basic Organization

- Use Windows Explorer
  - Tools>Find>Files
    - Name, location, date(s)
    - Text search inside files
    - By type of file and/or size
- Use Microsoft Word Find File
  - File>Open>Advanced
    - Property, condition, value criteria
    - View options
      - File list (various formats)
      - Preview file contents
      - File properties listing

Figure 14.2

Find Fast

Find File works well when you are searching for a simple text string in one subdirectory that contains a relatively small number of files, say less than 100. It is very slow if you are searching many megabytes across a number of directories and subdirectories.

Find Fast (usually located in Control Panel) builds indexes to speed up finding documents from the "open" dialog box in Microsoft Office programs and from Microsoft Outlook. When Find Fast is installed with Office, it automatically creates an index on each local drive of your computer for all of your Office documents. Find Fast indexes are not created for documents on removable drives or read-only mediums, such as CD-ROM. Once created, an index is automatically updated so you don't need to do anything to take advantage of faster searching. This is a processing-intensive function so you may want to be judicious in using it, particularly with older model PCs and large volumes of files.

Find Fast technology also allows full-text searching of both HTML and Office documents on a company network. The user initiates a search by clicking the Search button on the Web toolbar or in a browser. After filling in the search criteria such as title, author, or other standard Office properties, the user clicks Search. The results are returned in an HTML page with hyperlinks to each of the found documents. Find Fast technology supports several search types and indexing characteristics:

- **Full-text searching**—The full text of every document is indexed and searchable.

- **Phrase searching**—Find Fast looks for phrases such as "business plan" or "John Doe."

- **Proximity searching**—Find Fast looks for words that occur within a certain distance; for example, the search text "Plan NEAR Catalog" finds "Proposed Plan for Online Catalog."

- **Property searching**—Properties, such as author and title, are indexed and searchable.

- **Multiple volume indexing**—Documents can reside on multiple file servers, so a user does not have to move documents to index them.

- **Relevancy ranking**—Results are returned sorted by relevance; in other words, documents that most likely pertain to the query are listed first.

- **Centralized index**—The index is stored centrally for greater simplicity and better performance.

Contact management with Netscape Communicator

Personal contacts are the sources of human intelligence, referred to by intelligence professionals as "humint." With IBIS, you'll be developing a preponderance of humint sources via e-mail. You can use Netscape Communicator's Address Book window to create, store, and edit address book entries. An address book entry (called a card) stores names, postal addresses, e-mail addresses, phone numbers, and other information about an individual. You can also use an address book to associate a number of e-mail addresses with a single nickname, which becomes a mailing list.

Netscape Address Book Message Folders permit you to organize information by filing messages from your Inbox to another folder, or from one folder to another. When you open a message folder, the folder's message list is displayed in a Message List window. You can move messages from one folder to another by dragging messages from the message list and dropping them into a folder in the folder list. Once you accumulate many items in various folders you can search folders or discussions for a specific message. Address Book's search dialogue allows you to provide keywords for which to search, specify which parts of messages you want to search, specify a folder in which to search, launch the search, and select from a list of matches.

Organizing e-mail into categories

Next to files created on the PC, the next most common item (and maybe the most voluminous) that should be organized for IBIS is e-mail. Everyone gets e-mail, but how they deal with it makes a big difference. Some click and toss while others methodically save each piece. Lots of little pieces can add up to a whole over time, especially in business intelligence. If you are regularly receiving e-mail messages from people you consider good sources of information, save them in their own folder for future use.

When you open your inbox to view the list of e-mail messages you can pull down File, then create a new folder. In Netscape Communicator the New Folder dialog box lets you name it and make it a subfolder of any other folder. If you create a subfolder of Local Mail, it will be easier to find and use when saving e-mail to its proper folder. You can also drag and drop folders to move them around to better organize your growing collection of business intelligence (BI) source material.

By clicking on the serrated bar on the sides of the list of messages, you'll open or close other windows that help you manage e-mail. Clicking on the bottom portion of the e-mail list window opens a window to display the message. Clicking on the left side of the e-mail list window opens the list of folders. With both the list of folders and list of e-mail showing in two windows you simply drag and drop one or more messages into the appropriate folder.

Going back to the Inbox, you can sort the e-mail by clicking on the header bar just above the message list. For example, if you want to sort all of the messages by author, you just click on the portion of that bar to sort in ascending or descending alphabetical order. Clicking twice reverses the order. With the messages sorted you can deal with them more effectively, highlighting several at one time for filing or deletion. By pulling down View and highlighting Sort you'll get a list that allows you to sort by several different criteria.

After you've accumulated messages, you will want to search through them at some point to answer a question or research a particular topic. Pull down Edit then highlight Search Messages (Ctrl + Shift + F) to use the search messages dialog. This feature is described in more detail later in this chapter. Search options allow you to search subfolders you may have created within main folders. This allows you to pull up the subset of e-mails relevant to your immediate need. A portion of Address Book's input fields are shown in Figure 14.3, while the drag-and-drop filing feature is depicted in Figure 14.4. The powerful search capabilities of Netscape Messenger are illustrated in Figure 14.5.

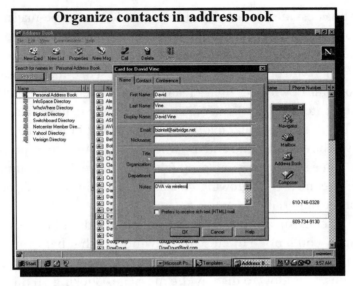

Figure 14.3

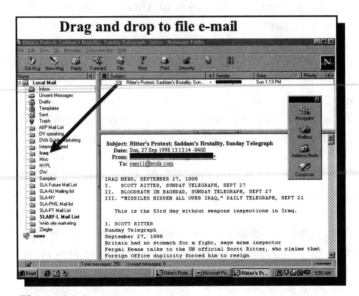

Figure 14.4

Using Netscape's e-mail features to organize Web pages

Since IBIS is about the Web, you'll collect a great deal of Web pages. People often say it is better to bookmark a page and to return to it later if you need the BI that resides there. But, consider the changing nature of the Internet's myriad content and you'll quickly agree that you run a risk of not finding that information when you return even the next day, let alone a week or a month later.

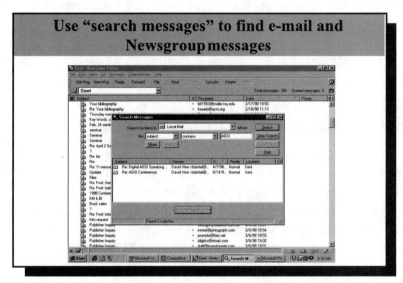

Figure 14.5

By clicking the mailbox icon on the Navigator desktop, you'll go to the workspace for mail. In the master toolbar, the Communicator pull-down menu selections include Tools. Clicking Tools brings another drop-down menu, and if you click Message Center you'll get a list of all the folders in your Message Center. You can create additional folders (via File, New, Folder Selection) under Local Mail or subfolders below folders and sub-subfolders as well. These folders create convenient storage places for a variety of information, including Web pages.

Let's consider storing Web pages in folders. By pulling down the File menu and clicking Send Page, a send mail form pops up. If you type your own e-mail address and click Send it will e-mail to you the link and a copy of the page. By filing the message in one of the folders you retain the information. After you've saved the information you can find it by browsing the list of folders in Message Center or using Messenger's search function.

Pull down Edit and select Search Messages. A Search Messages dialog box appears. It provides drop-down menus to select various search criteria. For example, you can search the message body for words contained in it. A More button allows you to add search strings and radio buttons permit you to specify Match Any or Match All criteria. Once a list of found files pops up, you can sort by clicking on the headers for subject, sender, etc. Additional buttons let you go to the message folder in which a search message was found, file the message in another folder, or delete the message.

By clicking the Subscribe button in the Message Center toolbar, you get a window that displays newsgroups. You can follow the same general procedures to file and retrieve newsgroup messages.

Filter and file e-mail messages

To automatically handle incoming e-mail messages that match criteria you set, Netscape Communicator's Messenger allows you to filter your mail. To bring up the Mail Filters dialog, from the Edit menu choose Mail Filters. Use the Filter Rules dialog to edit or define an action you want a filter to perform and the type of messages to which you want to apply the action. This software function provides conditions for matching messages and assigning actions, such as automatically filing messages to a folder and automatically setting message priority. You can change the order in which filters are applied, which is called filter precedence.

Manage information with Microsoft Outlook

You'll recall the treatment of Maximizer, the contact management software, in Chapter Three. There we looked at sales contact management from a marketing viewpoint. Considering the widespread adoption of Microsoft Office (which contains Outlook) this also is a good place to go when considering your approach to managing personal contacts in an IBIS. Its added benefit is the tight integration with the other components of Office, primarily Word, Excel, and PowerPoint.

According to Microsoft, "Outlook is a desktop information management program that helps you organize and share information on your desktop and communicate with others. You can use Outlook to manage personal and business information such as your e-mail messages, appointments, contacts, tasks, and files as well as track activities. You can share information with a group by using e-mail, group scheduling, public folders, and more.

"Also, share information with other Microsoft Office programs, and browse and find Office files from within Outlook. Other capabilities allow you to connect to and share information across the World Wide Web. If you are a developer, use programming options to customize Outlook."

As you can see in Figure 14.6, there are many features and functions in Outlook. Some people have found this to be a bit overwhelming or intimidating. Others have said that it is too highly structured but not in a way that suits their needs.

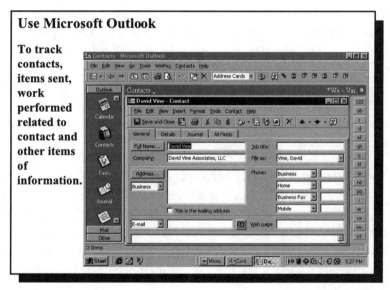

Figure 14.6

Organizing information in CorelCENTRAL

We've examined various features of Corel's WordPerfect Suite 8 Professional in previous chapters. As a direct competitor to Microsoft Office, it provides all the features of Office plus many other goodies to compete with America's software monolith. Like Outlook, CorelCENTRAL helps the user to organize time, tasks, and information using the Calendar, Address Book, Card File, and Activity Log views. You can also send and receive e-mail messages in the Mailbox view, and instantly access the Corel Web site in the Help Desk view. But there's much more capability inherent in the software, particularly in the realm of organizing information.

Calendar features powerful calendar and scheduling features. Display schedules in a Day, Week, Month, or Year view. Create personal events (such as meetings) and tasks (To Do items). Use the Internet to schedule others for events or To Do items. Add multi-day events and special occasions. Print your schedule in a Day, Week, Month, Year, or List format.

Address Book lets you access shared contact lists or build your own custom list. Link data fields to Card File entries and Web sites on the Internet. And the Address Book is available to the other applications in the Corel Suite, making it easy to maintain and keep your contacts at your fingertips.

The Activity Log conveniently lists all your events, To Do items, notes from the Calendar, and Phone Dialer call information in separate card lists. The card lists are similar to those available in the Address Book or Card file.

The Mailbox is your center for managing your e-mail and discussion groups. You can also launch the Netscape Communicator tools from the Mailbox.

Card File in CorelCENTRAL

Card File helps you organize and centralize your critical information. Create a separate card file for each kind of information you need to keep. Link to other cards in the same card file, other card files, files, applications, and Web sites on the Internet. Even store your Web site addresses (URLs) and launch Netscape Navigator with a single click.

Deceptively simple sounding, CorelCENTRAL's Card File helps you keep track of any type of information. You can have as many card files as you want and you can organize a card file into groups of cards for easy access to particular types of items. Each card in a card file is divided into fields of information. You can create local fields for the current card only, or you can create global fields that appear in each card (or group of cards) in a card file.

Fields in a card file can be assigned links that let you jump from card to card, or between the Card File and Address Book. You can even create links for calling with the Phone Dialer, sending e-mail messages, displaying Web sites, opening documents and folders, and starting applications.

When you add a field to an address book or card file, the field type is normally alphanumeric, which means you can type general information (text and numbers). The field can remain blank and you can add any number of characters and lines in the field. To select another field type (such as currency, date/time, or telephone) or change the settings for the field, use the Field Properties dialog box. You can change field properties for all fields in the Card File.

Using check boxes or radio buttons in a field makes it easy to indicate information for the field without typing it. For example, you could list titles (such as Mr., Ms., and Mrs.) as radio buttons in a Title field, then click the appropriate title for the individual.

To sort the cards in the card list, click a Field Name button at the top of a column in the card list. The cards are sorted on that field. Click the same Field Name button again to toggle between ascending (A-Z, 0-9) and descending (Z-A, 9-0) sort order.

Although you can keep addresses in a card file, the Address Book is specifically designed to help you organize your personal and business contacts. Card files can be shared over a network.

Linking information

You can link between cards inside the Address Book or Card File, or from the Address Book to the Card File (and the opposite direction). When you add a link to a card, a back link is created automatically that allows you jump from the destination card back to the original card.

Phone Dialer links phone numbers for you. Links to Web sites automatically launch Netscape Navigator. Links to files and applications give you a variety of options, such as retrieving your current projects, playing movies and sound files, and organizing and starting other software. Links to folders display the folder in a window, and links to e-mail messages display the Message dialog box with the e-mail address inserted for you.

CorelCENTRAL automatically adds Phone Dialer, E-mail, and Web Site links to global fields in the Address Book that are defined as phone number, e-mail, or Web site fields. This feature does not apply to custom global fields. In addition, you can only add links to local and custom global fields in the Address Book.

Organizing bookmarks

Bookmarks offer a convenient means to retrieve pages with locations (URLs) you've saved. You store your bookmarks in a list that's saved on your hard disk. Once you add a bookmark to your list, the item stays until you remove it or change lists.

There are many ways to return to Web pages you've previously viewed. Organizing your links to Web pages for easier access in Internet Explorer is similar to the technique in Netscape Navigator where they are referred to with the more generic term Bookmark.

Internet Explorer

To add a page to your collection of Favorite Pages in Internet Explorer (not to be confused with Favorite Places in America Online's graphical user interface software), go to the page that you want to add to your collection of favorite pages, and on the Favorites menu click Add to Favorites. Type a new name for the page if you want to. To open one of your Favorite Pages, click the Favorites button on the toolbar, and then click the page you want to open.

To keep track of your Favorite Pages, you can organize them into folders. Click the Create In button in the Add to Favorites dialog box. To organize your favorite pages into folders, on the Favorites menu, click Organize Favorites. Click the Create New Folder icon, type a name for the folder, and then press ENTER. Drag the shortcuts in the list to the appropriate folders. You might want to organize your pages by topic. For example, you could create a folder named Art for storing information about art exhibits and reviews. If the number of shortcuts or folders makes dragging impractical, you can use the Move button instead.

Just above the viewing area in Internet Explorer, you'll find toolbars that can be turned on and off by selecting them in the View toolbars menu. Once the Links bar is displayed you can add Favorites to it for fast access. To add a page to your Links bar, drag the icon for the page from your Address bar to your Links bar. To drag a link to the Links folder in your Favorites list, you can either drag it directly to the Favorites menu and then into the Links folder or you can drag it to the Links folder when displaying your Favorites in the Explorer bar. You also can organize your links by dragging them to a different location on the Links bar.

For fast access even before starting your browser, you can create a desktop shortcut to the current page. Right click in the page, and then click Create Shortcut. If the Internet Explorer window is not maximized, you can also create a shortcut by dragging a link from the Internet Explorer window to the location you want, such as your desktop or a folder.

Netscape Navigator

Navigator offers many options for creating a Bookmark list. Basic options let you add and access a page through a pop-up menu on the location toolbar or through the Communicator menu of the main menu bar. The simplest way to obtain direct access to a favorite page is to open the Bookmarks menu and choose Add Bookmarks. This adds the current page as an item in the Bookmarks menu.

More advanced options, available from the Bookmarks window, let you create hierarchical menus, partial menu displays, multiple and shared bookmark files, list descriptions, and list searches. The Bookmarks window lists your Bookmarks and offers a set of menu items to help you organize your list. In addition, many drag-and-drop options are available for creating and filing your Bookmarks.

A Bookmark file on your hard disk represents the Bookmark list you create. Each item in the list contains the title of the page (which you can choose in a menu), the associated URL (which lets Navigator retrieve the page), and some additional date information.

The same Bookmarks menu is displayed by either the pop-up menu in the location toolbar or the Communicator menu of the main menu bar. To display the Bookmarks menu using the pop-up menu, position the mouse cursor over the Bookmarks button in the location toolbar, and press the mouse button. To display the Bookmarks menu using the main menu bar, open the Communicator menu then choose Bookmarks. The Bookmarks item displays a submenu.

To add and file bookmarks using the Bookmarks menu choose one of the following items:

Add Bookmark: Adds the title of the currently displayed page as the last item in the Bookmark list. The Bookmarks menu grows as you add Bookmarks. File Bookmark: The pull-right File Bookmark menu item lets you add the current Navigator page to a selected Bookmark folder. The items in this menu are bookmark folders.

To edit or delete bookmarks using the Bookmarks menu, choose Edit Bookmarks to open the Bookmarks window. You can drag and drop Bookmark icons or use the window's menu items to arrange the display of your Bookmarks and Bookmark folders. To delete a Bookmark, select the Bookmark icon in the Bookmarks window, then press the Delete key (or choose Delete from the Edit menu).

To quickly add and file a bookmark for the current page, place the cursor over the Page Proxy icon in the location toolbar. The cursor and icon changes when the cursor is over the icon. Drag the Page Proxy icon (an icon image follows cursor) to the Bookmarks icon, which is at the left side of the location toolbar. If you release the Page Proxy icon over the Bookmarks icon, a bookmark for the current page is added to the bottom of the bookmark list. If you hold the Page Proxy icon over the Bookmarks icon, the Bookmarks menu is displayed, allowing you to further drag the Page Proxy icon to a particular position in your bookmark list. When you release the mouse button, the bookmark is filed at the menu position you have selected.

You can drag and drop the Page Proxy icon anywhere in the list, including nested Bookmark folders (displayed as pull-right menu items). As you drag the icon over your current list of Bookmark names, a horizontal line appears between menu items to indicate where the new Bookmark will be placed when you release the mouse button. The Bookmarks window offers the full set of Bookmark capabilities. You can double click Bookmarks to access pages, drag and drop icons to arrange your Bookmarks, and use the window's menu bar to create new Bookmark items and manipulate Bookmark lists.

To find out if a Bookmark's page has been modified since your last viewing, from the Bookmarks window's View menu, choose Update Bookmarks. The What's New dialog box appears. Choose a radio button to specify whether you want to look for changes in all Bookmarks or selected Bookmarks. Click the Start Checking button. Navigator checks the specified Bookmarks for changes, while displaying progress and results in a dialog. If a page has changed, Navigator lists it alongside a distinct, accentuated icon. If the page's modifications have not been verified, Navigator lists it alongside a question mark in the icon.

Navigator lets you import HTML files (or hotlists) as Bookmarks. You can read any HTML file containing links and convert the links into Bookmarks. The links are placed in a folder atop the Bookmark list. To import a hotlist into Navigator, you should first convert your hotlist to HTML. Several downloadable utilities perform this conversion. You can also use another browser's mail command to transmit a hotlist in HTML format. From the Communicator menu, choose Bookmarks to open the Bookmarks window. In the Bookmarks window, open the File menu and choose Import. Select the file you wish to import in the Import Bookmarks File dialog. Click the Open button.

To find a Bookmark, from the Edit menu in the Bookmarks window, choose Find in Bookmarks. In the resulting dialog, type the text you want to locate among your bookmarks. Select one or more of the Look In check boxes to specify whether you want to search for text contained in the Bookmark name, location (URL), or description (stored with Bookmark properties). Select the Match Case check box if you want capital letters in the search to match exactly. For example, with Match Case selected, the search text "internet" will not find "Internet." Select the Whole Word check box if you want to search for only whole words that match your search text. For example, with Whole Word selected, the search text "Net" will not find "Netscape."

Bookmarks and delegation

Heavy users of the Internet may accumulate hundreds of Bookmarks in their browsers. While the capability to organize by folder and subfolders is helpful, another method may be more suitable in certain situations. For example, a direct report may actually perform the hunt for required information, but this person might need direction from a supervisor. In this case, a checklist of sites to search can be helpful.

This grid format is useful as a printout the supervisor can review to select specific Web sites for use in the research project to be undertaken by the direct report. An electronic version in HTML also can be used with live links created for each listing. The check boxes to the left of the resource title can be filled with an X for each site the supervisor recommends. To use the live links, the subordinate would open the file in a browser and simply click on the name that corresponds to each check mark.

Auxiliary software to manage bookmarks

Freeware and shareware were discussed at length in Chapter Twelve. Here's another example of the functionality of this type of software in building an IBIS. There are many low-cost or free utility programs to help you organize and manage your Bookmarks. For example, The shareware/freeware site **www.jumbo.com** boasts of having 300,000 programs available. Here's a selection of programs to manage bookmarks:

- **Bookmark Importer Lite Version 2.0**—The Bookmark Importer product line allows you to exchange bookmarks between your favorite browsers.

- **ViaConference Version 3.0**—Includes a complete chat client that lets you make use of color and fonts, a full-featured e-mail client, a great FTP client, and the new SurfSilly Bookmark bar for automatically creating and organizing WWW bookmark lists using your browser.

- **1st There Version 1.1**—A Desktop Bookmark assistant. It allows the user at the click of a button to browse through any of their bookmarks and then navigate to a selected Web page.

- **Bookmark Converter Version 2.0**—Converts your bookmarks/favorites between the Netscape and Internet Explorer formats in both directions. Very easy to understand and very effective.

- **Bookmark Importer Version 1.0**—A 32-bit application that converts Internet Explorer Favorites to Netscape Navigators Bookmarks. Version 2.00 supports Internet Explorer 4.0 and Netscape Communicator.

- **Compass Version 2.0**—This is a powerful Bookmark and Favorites manager that works with Netscape Navigator and Internet Explorer. Compass imports your Bookmarks or Favorites and allows you to easily organize them into categories.

- **Link Sweeper Version 1.0**—A utility to automatically clean up your Internet Bookmarks/Favorites. It systematically tests each bookmark, and removes, moves or updates every link that doesn't work, is not found, or has moved, depending on how you configure it.

- **Linkman Version 2.51**—LinkMan is a very versatile book-mark tool that will bring in bookmarks from most browsers, links from any page you have saved, and any other URLs you want to add.

• **WebTabs Version 1.0**—WebTabs is a sophisticated bookmark manager and Web watcher that helps you to manage your use of the World Wide Web.

Organizing information with hyperlinks

Probably the simplest way to organize information required for business intelligence is to use a matrix. The neat and tidy rows and columns of the matrix (called a table in word processing or a spreadsheet in that type of software) lend themselves to two-dimensional categorization of closely related information. When constructed in software, matrix elements (the cells that intersect the rows and columns of the table or spreadsheet) can be hyperlinked to another document, graphic or other software "object." This is how Web pages are created.

The following matrix was used to summarize some of the complex information needs of a client involved globally in multiple product lines. After meetings and interviews to draft and refine the information requirements the following organizational matrix was developed. Excerpts are shown in Table 14.1.

Using this method to organize information about companies, a master document containing a list of all the competitors in the left column, arranged in alphabetical order, was correlated to the three categories of information (See Table 14.2). A click on a hyperlink calls up a potentially ever-expanding collection of documents (some even dynamically linked to Web pages external to the company) and other software objects embedded in the HTML pages. The beauty of this type of arrangement is that the cells can contain text or numerics that can be sorted in ascending or descending order.

Creating HTML-linked documents

Most word processors and many other programs including Netscape Communicator's Composer module can be used to create a page that is embedded with HyperText Markup Language (HTML). Corel's Suite 8, Microsoft Word, or Netscape Communicator can be used to create a "main page" and to link other pages to it. These additional pages could be downloaded in plain ASCII text, complicated HTML pages, or even spreadsheets, presentations, or any other computer-readable information.

For example, if you want to set up a basic system to monitor 10 competitors, your main page would have the 10 business names highlighted as clickable items. By opening the main page in a browser and clicking on the name of one of the competitors, an HTML link would open another page that might contain a summary of the competitor.

Table 14.1

MARKETING INFORMATION MASTER GUIDE			
	Market Assessment	Companies in the Market	New Product Development
POLYMERS			
Nylon carpet fiber/ residential, commercial, and specialty	hyperlink to text or other type of file		hyperlink
Nylon and polyester fiber/industrial	hyperlink	hyperlink	hyperlink
Engineering plastics (thermoplastics, nylon resin, alloys, blends, recycled PET, and nylon resins)	hyperlink	hyperlink	hyperlink
Text or other type of file Nylon	hyperlink	hyperlink	hyperlink
Performance materials (polyethylene, aramid, and composites)	hyperlink	hyperlink	hyperlink
SPECIALITY CHEMICALS	hyperlink	hyperlink	hyperlink
Fluorine specialties	hyperlink	hyperlink	hyperlink
Fluorocarbons	hyperlink	hyperlink	hyperlink
Pigments and dyes	hyperlink	hyperlink	hyperlink
Electronic chemicals	hyperlink	hyperlink	hyperlink
Laboratory chemicals	hyperlink	hyperlink	hyperlink
Hydrofluoric acid	hyperlink	hyperlink	hyperlink
Low molecular weight polyethylene	hyperlink	hyperlink	hyperlink
Polymer additives	hyperlink	hyperlink	hyperlink
Hydrofluoric acid	hyperlink	hyperlink	hyperlink
Petroleum, petrochemical, gas processing plants, and equipment	hyperlink	hyperlink	hyperlink
Adsorbents	hyperlink	hyperlink	hyperlink
Molecular sieves	hyperlink	hyperlink	hyperlink

Within that competitor summary (really an executive-level brief), you might have several words highlighted indicating further links that lead to more detail. For example, you might have a list of states in which the competitor does business. By clicking on the word New York you might get a list of all of the competitor's dealers in that state or perhaps the top-20 largest known customers. In this manner, a user can step down through succeeding layers of documents to browse information that may answer a specific question or shed light on a particular aspect under consideration. Figure 14.7 shows how this HTML linkage occurs.

These document creation capabilities can be used for editing and publishing online documents. The Composer portion of the Communicator suite of enables the user to create dynamic online documents and publish them to local file systems and remote servers.

Table 14.2

	COMPANY PROFILES	TECHNOLOGY ASSESMENT	COMPETITIVE ANALYSIS
ABB Lummus	hyperlink	hyperlink	hyperlink
Air Products	hyperlink	hyperlink	hyperlink
Akzo	hyperlink	hyperlink	hyperlink
AlliedSignal	hyperlink	hyperlink	hyperlink
Asahi Glass	hyperlink	hyperlink	hyperlink
Atochem	hyperlink	hyperlink	hyperlink
Ausimont	hyperlink	hyperlink	hyperlink
BASF	hyperlink	hyperlink	hyperlink
Beaulieu	hyperlink	hyperlink	hyperlink
Cameco (Canada)	hyperlink	hyperlink	hyperlink
DSM	hyperlink	hyperlink	hyperlink
Du Pont	hyperlink	hyperlink	hyperlink
Eastman Chemical	hyperlink	hyperlink	hyperlink
Enichem	hyperlink	hyperlink	hyperlink
FCFC	hyperlink	hyperlink	hyperlink
Toshiba	hyperlink	hyperlink	hyperlink
Ube	hyperlink	hyperlink	hyperlink
Vacuum Smelze	hyperlink	hyperlink	hyperlink
Zeochem	hyperlink	hyperlink	hyperlink

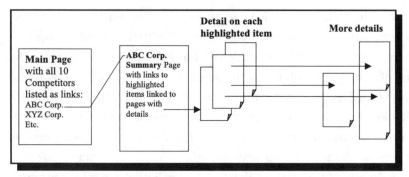

Figure 14.7

Using Netscape to create HTML documents

Netscape Composer (a module within Netscape Communicator) is a powerful and easy-to-use Web-based word processor. It can be used to author most documents, with the added benefit that it is optimized for use on the Internet or an intranet. Composer gives you the flexibility to create richly formatted text, tables, and graphics while also providing you the benefits of HTML—a universally readable, compact, open-document standard.

Composer provides one-button publishing of Web documents to a server. It supports rich formatting, including fonts, styles, paragraph alignment, and bulleted and numbered lists, and create and edit tables, and it includes a built-in spell checker. You can drag and drop images, links, and Java applets.

With tools familiar to anyone who uses a word processor, you can quickly and easily create professional-looking electronic documents and make them accessible to other users on intranets or the Internet. You even can publish them to diskette or CD-ROM for secure distribution.

Netscape Composer is well integrated with the other components of Netscape Communicator to facilitate document creation, editing, and publishing. Netscape Messenger uses Composer as its editor, making it possible to create messages with all the richness of the Web.

Composer's composition toolbar is used to create, open, and save Web pages; publish (upload) files to a remote server; view your Web page in the browser; perform standard editing tasks; create links and targets; insert images, horizontal lines, and tables; and check spelling. The Formatting Toolbar is used to apply paragraph formatting; specify fonts, font sizes, and font styles; apply text color; and control text alignment. You can hide or display these toolbars by clicking the tab to the left of each toolbar. You can also hide or display these toolbars by choosing their respective menu items from the View menu.

Using Microsoft Word to create HTML documents

Word offers two easy ways for you to create HTML pages. You can start a new page by using a wizard or template, or you can convert an existing Word document to HTML, the format used for Web pages. When you create a Web page with either of these methods, Word customizes some toolbars, menu commands, and options to provide the Web page authoring features.

Using the Web page authoring features to create your Web page will usually produce the best results. You can use the Web Page Wizard to start with sample content. If you prefer, you can start with a blank page. Use the HTML conversion method when you have existing Word content that you want to quickly convert to a Web page. With Word's HTML features you can make the pages look more interesting by adding bullets and numbering, horizontal lines, background colors and textures, tables, pictures, videos, scrolling text, and forms. You add most of these items in much the same way as you do in a Word document.

When you save a Word document as an HTML page (File—Save As HTML), Word closes the document and then reopens it in HTML format. Word displays the page similar to the way it will appear in a Web browser. Formatting and other items that aren't supported by HTML or the Web page authoring environment are removed from the file.

Building the IBIS database

We've examined simple methods to find files and other information using existing software. The next step up in sophistication is to create a BI database with more functionality than simple file search features. Let's consider a scenario in which an individual is responsible for creating and managing an IBIS.

You've gotten top management to believe in your surfing skills. Your reports have been well received and you're a respected information "hunter." Your boss and fellow employees understand that you can get, via the Internet, a lot of the information your organization needs for a variety of management decisions. You've done it hundreds of times for marketing, finance, business strategy, and competitive intelligence projects.

In the process, you've downloaded more than a thousand HTML, text, spreadsheet, and graphic files covering dozens of important business topics during the past year alone. Some of it is only needed once, and some items go out of date shortly after they're used. But, several times in the past few weeks, you have experienced the frustrating problem of having to find two or three pieces of critical information at a moment's notice. Or, worse yet, a brush fire pops up suddenly and the boss needs "everything you've got on XYZ Corp." right after lunch! Looking at the big picture, you could say "we're awash in data but information poor." But that won't get you a raise. What will is talking in terms of corporate knowledge through business intelligence.

To continue to amaze your boss with the comprehensive material you can put together in a short time, you need to manage this growing database of information. You'll want to take the material you've been collecting and create a business intelligence database so that, in seconds, you'll be able to retrieve the handful of documents covering important aspects of the topic at hand. The key is organization—the first step toward knowledge management whether you are working on a quick competitor analysis or a five-year strategic plan.

Free-text databases with askSam

A database like askSam, by askSam Systems (**www.asksam.com**), helps you archive a higher level of sophistication in storing, retrieving, and working with a variety of electronic information including e-mail and Newsgroup messages and downloaded HTML documents. You can even create new HTML documents from all types of existing material. An HTML import filter allows you to take any useful information you find on any Web page, and import it into askSam. You can download information from the Internet, import it into askSam, and search for any word or phrase using Boolean and proximity searches to pinpoint exactly the information you're looking for.

According to the company's product literature, askSam helps the user organize information to create knowledge: "Somewhere hidden in the raw data is valuable knowledge—but you must know how to distill the important news from the unrefined bulk. With askSam you spend less time searching for information and more time putting it to use. askSam increases the value of information by allowing you to present it in a manner appropriate to your specific needs.

"askSam is a tool to organize the information that crosses your desk. It doesn't matter whether you deal with sticky notes, memos, phone messages, faxes, resumes, depositions, newspaper articles, or e-mail. All contain information that you need to track. With askSam we provide a solution.

"Download, type, scan, or import your information into askSam. Straight away you can search and retrieve any word or phrase in the text. Finding your information is easy. askSam offers the widest variety of searches found in any database program. These searches include full-text, fuzzy, wildcard, Boolean, proximity, date and numeric.

"If your information is structured (like names and addresses), you can take advantage of askSam's freeform database capabilities. Create an Entry Form for your data. Every time you add a document to your database, call up the Entry Form and fill in the fields. Unlike traditional databases, askSam does not require pre-defined field lengths or field types. Fields expand as you enter information, so you never need to worry about running out of room.

"askSam is as flexible as your information. For example, if you're tracking magazine articles you may want some fields (like magazine name, date, etc.). You may also want the complete text of the article. askSam's unique combination of database and text retrieval features allows you to do just that. You can find an article by doing a full-text search and use the fields to create overview reports. For example, you can search for all articles containing "database" and "flexible" and get a sorted list of magazine names, article titles, and dates. askSam allows you to add fields to free-form text and turn it a full-text searchable database." Figure 14.8 illustrates a few of the many functions available in askSam.

askSam's automatic field recognition enables you to download information, such as simple text, and turn it into an instant database. For example, a downloaded message often contains words like "To:", "From:", "Date:", and "Subject:". askSam lets you automatically use these words as fields. You can search, sort, and even create reports using these newly created fields. This feature also makes it easy to import various types of database records from other sources like CD-ROMs and purchased data files so you can do field searching and create reports from specific fields. One of the many special import filters handles CompuServe information you've saved in the CompuServe file cabinet. askSam prices start around $140 with network versions available.

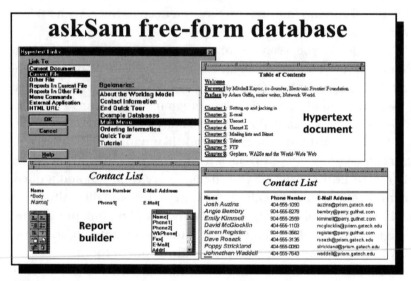

Figure 14.8

Scanning and storing documents

A package similar to askSam is dtSearch from DT Software (**www.dtsearch.com**).

DT Software develops, manufactures, and sells the award-winning dtSearch line of text search-and-retrieval products. The company started research and development in the text retrieval area in 1988. dtSearch products instantly search through gigabytes of text. Current dtSearch products include dtSearch, the dtSearch Text Retrieval Engine, dtSearch Web, and the dtSearch Electronic Publisher's Toolkit.

Proprietary indexing and searching algorithms allow for fast indexing and searching performance even over extremely large databases and other diverse collections of documents. dtSearch has over two dozen text search options. After a search, dtSearch offers multiple options for display of retrieved documents with search terms highlighted.

Text search options include such capabilities as fuzzy searching adjustable from 1 to 10, multiple-level concept searching, natural language with precision relevancy ranking, variable-term weighting, and more. dtSearch's searching algorithms allow it to handle many levels of complexity. A single search request can contain multiple Boolean, proximity, numeric range, phonic, fuzzy, synonym, etc. elements.

Built-in file viewers display popular file formats such as word processing documents, databases, spreadsheets, and Zip files with highlighted hits. dtSearch also integrates with other popular display mediums, such as popular Web browsers for HTML files and the Adobe reader for PDF files. For documents in these formats, dtSearch displays them with the hits graphically marked and with all existing hypertext links and embedded images intact. dtSearch also includes a built-in image viewer.

Alphabet customization options make dtSearch adaptable to most non-English languages, accounting for its strong international presence. dtSearch also supports heterogeneous language environments for international organizations and other mixed-language users.

DT Software, Inc. and Xerox Corporation released a 32-bit bundle combining DT Software's dtSearch text retrieval software and Xerox's TextBridge Pro OCR software. The purpose of the bundle is to bring together scanning, OCR, and searching capabilities, giving the user all three in one integrated solution. After a search, users can view files either as text or as graphic images.

The partnership provides an integrated solution for users who need to expand their search and retrieval capabilities with TextBridge Pro. TextBridge Pro permits scanning, recognizing, and editing paper-based information bound for the Web. The bundle lets users turn stacks of papers into instantly dtSearchable, automatically formatted word processor and HTML documents including "live" hypertext links. When a user clicks Launch, dtSearch will automatically locate the user's Web browser and retrieve the HTML document in that browser (connecting to the Internet, if necessary). TextBridge Pro can OCR pages directly into the HTML file format. One of askSam's import files handles RTF (rich text files) that contain ASCII text as well as some of the original document formatting.

dtSearch automatically recognizes most popular file types including databases (through ODBC), HTML, and Zip files. dtSearch builds an index of the words in a user's documents, then uses the index to perform very fast text searches. While indexing speed can vary depending on the type of computer and documents, dtSearch 4.1 can index up to 13 megabytes per minute of word processing documents. Indexed searches usually take less than a second. Additional search capabilities also exist within the package.

After a search, dtSearch offers multiple ways to browse retrieved documents. Search reports show each "hit," along with as much context as the user requests. Hypertext links let the user jump from viewing a search report to viewing a retrieved document. A built-in graphics viewer displays images. Other capabilities include cut, paste, print, copy, delete, and launch.

Capture and manage all required information

These techniques can be used to store and retrieve many types of information in a variety of file formats. Skeptics might suggest that this is not sufficient. For example, they might point to conferences, seminars, and professional society meetings and say that much of what is heard there is of great value. How can you capture, store, and manage this valuable business intelligence?

The solution to this problem is simple and getting easier to implement. Many voice recognition software packages are sold today. Nearly all can input audio files, process them, and output ASCII text. Some even work in conjunction with word processor software. As higher speed Internet connections become more common, more and more providers of audiotapes and other digital audio products are selling them on the Web. Audible, Inc. (**www.audible.com**) sells more than 10,000 selections from business conference providers, educational and cultural institutions, and audiobook publishers.

Although not entirely perfected, it is technically possible to purchase an audio file, use voice recognition software, and create an ASCII file that can be imported to askSam or dtSearch for use as stated above. Similarly, the use of newer audio recorders designed with features to turn voice into text can be used to add spoken information to a BI database.

Another approach to this type of input might include the CrossPad and other pen-based handwriting recognition devices that (more or less) turn handwriting into word processing files. If you're concerned about capturing televised information, you may want to consider a computer video card that enables you to watch television on a computer. Some of these have circuits and software that decode the closed captioning text broadcast on many news programs.

Lotus Notes groupware

Groupware helps people share information. Through sharing information, executives expect their businesses to benefit through reduced product-development time, enhanced relationships with customers, and better interdepartmental cooperation. Lotus Development Corporation (now a unit of IBM) debuted Lotus Notes in 1989. Notes makes the process of communicating, collaborating, and coordinating easier and more productive. Notes combines a replicated document database, an enterprise-scalable messaging infrastructure, and a cross-platform client/server application development environment.

By 1996 Notes was fully integrated with the Internet, having native support for HTTP, HTML, and Java technology. For example, Notes users surfing the Web will be able to click on an object, download Java applets from the Web, and integrate the applets with Notes applications. This Internet functionality is made possible through the InterNotes family of modules. These include a Web publisher, news server, client navigator, and Web retriever. Additionally, third parties offer connectivity solutions for those who want to implement a Notes system for mobile users without making large infrastructure expenditures.[2]

Large organizations are using groupware to leverage intellectual capital within the corporate framework. Lotus Notes is the leading groupware product with Netscape groupware being the main competitor. Notes provides an environment where several members of a department or project team can use Internet-derived business intelligence among themselves or with others on an intranet or externally via the Internet. Use of a collaborative platform is one aspect of knowledge management and an approach to generating greater return on intellectual capital through a sort of corporate "group think."

Information fed into a Lotus Notes system can be presented in several "views." For example, they might be categorized by author of report, company featured, publication date, source, title, or other profile established by an end-user. Collapsing views (similar to an outline format) can be activated to show just subject categories or all items within the subject categories (similar to most Usenet Newsgroup readers). Search functions also are readily available, and comment or reply-to capabilities are built into the basic system.

Once groupware is in place, it can be expanded to encompass and manage Internet information. For example, InterNotes Web Navigator is used for team surfing and collaboration. InterNotes Web Navigator allows companies to integrate Internet resources directly into their core business process, retrieving and converting Internet content into Notes documents. Note's programmability and agent technology in Navigator allows users to automate and customize information management. Agents can be built to perform such tasks as scanning customers' or competitors' Web sites for new or modified pages and sending daily summaries to a user's e-mail file every morning with doclinks to the complete articles. Verity, a highly respected developer of search engines, provides the capability for InterNotes Web Navigator.

InterNotes News helps users access and manage Newsgroups. A potentially market-expanding component is Lotus Notes: Newsstand, which creates a complete environment for publishers of all types of information. InterNotes Web Publisher provides the tools to create and publish to the Web while NotesNIC is used to connect with Notes users outside of the organization. Many third-party vendors provide a variety of news and information "feeds" for Lotus Notes users.

Notes R4 introduces a multi-pane user interface that allows users to "surf" through folders and lists of documents. Users can conduct full-text searches with a point-and-click query builder. Notes R4 users can search on attachments and OLE objects in addition to fielded text. Access to data in relational data stored in legacy systems and other large-scale computing platforms also is possible. All information to be published to the Web or captured from the Web is stored on a local Notes database. Notes prices range from several hundred dollars for a small network setup to many thousands of dollars for a large organization with hundreds of users.

Managing the fire hose flow

Experts have compared the amount of information flow via the Internet to a big, high-pressure fire hose. Controlling that flow, harnessing its power, is what IBIS is all about. Matching the appropriate level of computer solution to a given situation will yield a system that adds to organizational knowledge management by capitalizing on the information flow. This means more data can be saved, retrieved, and used in a much more efficient manner.

To create a "big company system on a small company budget," it is helpful to understand what the big companies do. Logicon is one of many software engineering firms that provides products and services to the intelligence community. Logicon's Message Dissemination System (LMDS) provides automatic filtering of incoming documents based on their content, prompt delivery of the documents to users for review or action, and rapid indexing of the documents for subsequent retrieval from a stored database.

A variety of corporate clients and government departments, including intelligence agencies, use LMDS to rapidly screen information pouring into watch-and-alert centers around the clock. LMDS is ideally suited to support continuous efforts to monitor incoming data and immediately identify information matching interest profiles. Various optional features make it possible to put together a comprehensive, sophisticated text-management system tailored to individual needs. A World Wide Web interface makes LMDS available via the Internet or to users linked within an intranet.

Understanding the scope and sophistication of the application will enable you to better understand the direction you may want to take in building your Internet Business Intelligence System.

Screening with LMDS

The LMDS process starts with the screening of incoming documents in real time, based on profiles defining users' current interests. LMDS routes each document to the appropriate people in a fraction of a second, even when profiles number in the thousands. Documents that match a user's profiles may be sent to that user's workstation or delivered via fax, e-mail, or any other available medium.

The core LMDS product is a fast, sophisticated filter of text content. When it is combined with other components of the LMDS product suite, the result is a comprehensive text-management system for handling the large amounts of electronic information—including sensitive information—that normally flow into, within, and out of an organization. Information is screened automatically to assure that the right information gets to the right people, that sensitive material is not routed to unauthorized recipients, and that databases for retrospective searching are built rapidly and efficiently.

LMDS determines the recipient of each incoming document by comparing the document with all of an organization's user-interest profiles. LMDS profiles contain terms consisting of words or phrases, linked in logical relationships. Profiles may be very simple, consisting of only one or two terms, or highly complex encompassing up to 1,000 terms. Profiles can be quickly added, modified, or deleted online without interrupting dissemination. The process of matching document terms with profile terms is exceptionally fast.

Profiles may be grouped in libraries, each containing as many as 100,000 profiles. Comparing multiple 100,000-profile libraries with each incoming document in effect removes any limits on the number of profiles an organization can handle—a capability of high interest to organizations that serve hundreds of thousands of users. Not all LMDS applications require this extraordinary capacity. LMDS is flexibly designed to accommodate a wide range of environments, large and small.

LMDS profiling is distinguished by a sophisticated ability to divide documents into subsections, or zones, and to target profile terms to particular zones. This feature greatly enhances the precision with which user needs can be defined. It is ideally suited to screen multiple news services—AP, DowVision, Reuters, for example—as well as information available on the Internet or from online data providers in real time. LMDS can accommodate an unlimited number of news sources, an unlimited number of text formats, and an unlimited number of user profiles. LMDS is the power behind America Online's News Profile service, described in an earlier chapter.

Matching the incoming information against user profiles, LMDS identifies the recipient(s) of each incoming news story in a fraction of a second. This high-speed dissemination capability can serve an organization wishing to automatically sort and disseminate current information to staff members. It enables the organization to offer its customers Selective Dissemination of Information (SDI), current-awareness services, or clipping services from multiple sources.

Organizing and retrieving information

LMDS can categorize documents and build databases automatically. Profiles can be written to tag incoming documents for inclusion in index categories or in particular databases. Bibliographic citations can be created automatically, and an automatic records creation tool, ARC, can automate the otherwise time-consuming, labor-intensive process of reformatting documents for entry into a structured database. An organization can thus update its databases at the same time that incoming documents are routed in their original form to individual users or user groups for immediate alerting and review.

A customized version of LMDS, called LMDS for Lotus Notes, adds a real-time, content-based dissemination capability to the Lotus Notes groupware product. Any electronic documents—newswire stories, business reports, financial information, or electronic mail—may be disseminated to Notes databases in accordance with LMDS profiles. A fully integrated interface enables users to utilize Notes "forms" and "views," to which they are already accustomed, to formulate and manage their profiles, and to view the results.

A Message Delivery and Review (LMDS MDR) module may be combined with LMDS Message Storage and Retrieval (LMDS MSR) in a comprehensive system that routes documents in real time to interested users and concurrently indexes the documents for immediate entry into a database. MDR allows users to receive LMDS-profiled documents instantly in personal electronic "folders" and to browse rapidly through their folders, displaying and disposing of documents as they wish. Users may have an unlimited number of folders. MDR allows users to:

- Display the number of messages in a folder
  and the number not reviewed

- Display message folder contents in a list of summary lines

- Display the text of any message, with the key
  terms highlighted

- Print, save, send, or delete any message

- Receive instant alert notification—audible and visual

The user can fine-tune the system to meet individual needs. Profiles may be written to define multiple message folders and may be added, modified, or deleted online. The Alert criteria may be changed at any time.

There are many solutions to the problem of organizing information from the Internet and other sources. Generally speaking, need and budgetary resources will dictate the sophistication of the solution. However, it should be clear that creative use of simple tools often could create an IBIS that would rival the performance of systems costing much more.

Endnotes

1. John Diebold, *Managing Information: The Challenge and the Opportunity* (AMA-COM, New York,1985:30,45).

2. Dahl, Andrew, *Lotus Notes 4 Administrator's Survival Guide* (Sams Publising, Indianapolis,1996).

CHAPTER 15

ANALYZING DATA AND INFORMATION TO CREATE INTELLIGENCE

Business decisions lead to actions that can make or lose money. The stream of choices in business decision making can seem frustratingly or frighteningly swift and endless. Ultimately, goals need to be established and decisions made regarding how to reach those goals. Applying the Internet Business Intelligence System (IBIS) to these goals might relate to a task at hand or strategic planning for long-term profitability.

Rational decisions must be based on some type of analysis. This analysis might be qualitative or quantitative, but it usually follows the input/output model. We are stimulated to make a decision, we take in information, process it, and output the result, which, in business, we hope will lead to a profit maximization in some way.

Analysis is directly related to problem solving. If we are confronted by a problem to be solved, we consider how to go about solving the problem. Solving a problem means finding an appropriate way to cross a gap. When there is little uncertainty one can utilize optimizing methods. Dominance relations among alternatives, specification of the order of importance of alternatives, and additive weighting given to more important properties are optimizing methods. A non-optimizing method called "satisficing" includes finding the first satisfactory alternative.

Making business decisions in a complex world includes risk, uncertainty, and conflict. Risky decisions sometimes are made by choosing the alternative with the greatest expected value, often involving probability calculations while decisions under uncertainty use judgmental probabilities. Decisions under conflict might involve such techniques as zero-sum gaming and payoff matrices. Cost-benefit analysis is called for in some situations.

The fully functional IBIS yields raw material to be forged on the anvil of analysis. To create a thing of beauty, the dross of data must be carefully refined with appropriate technique. Much the same as a sculptor transforms a lump of clay into a thing of beauty, the business intelligence (BI) specialist must create something of value in the business world. With IBIS, this means subjecting data to analysis and extracting meaning, adding value to otherwise lifeless information. This can take a variety of forms:

- Organization charts

- Matrix in spreadsheet with weighted scoring

- Link analysis and visualization of complex relationships

- Sorted reports from databases

- Content analysis of textual information

- Graphing and statistical functions in spreadsheets

In earlier chapters we focused on decisions pertinent to specific management disciplines. In this chapter, before we proceed to specific analytical techniques common to many business problems, we'll take a look at where we'd like analysis to take us.

In general there are two types of analyses—quantitative and qualitative. Quantitative analysis is numerical and often statistical in nature. Qualitative analysis usually seeks to reduce some amount of nonnumerical data to a digestible form. Both types of analysis support decision making, and both can include numerics.

The power of numerical analysis appropriately applied can be enormous. On the other hand, unsound conclusions based on a hodgepodge of ill-conceived statistics can destroy credibility while in pursuit of "business intelligence." Selecting the right analytic tools and using them with high-quality data will strengthen your points.

After we've collected and organized hundreds or thousands of units of information, how can we add value to raw material to create an intelligence masterwork? This chapter will present several concepts that provide a point of departure for those readers who wish to analyze data and information to create intelligence products that yield insights or provide factual and statistical bases for conclusions.

Qualitative analysis seeks to infer knowledge from nonnumerical sources. For example, an opinion survey reveals stated attitudes toward the subject under study. Survey results often are expressed with a confidence interval. For example, 60 percent of the general population feels strongly about cutting back their fat intake. Depending upon sample size, a properly executed study might express that result with a confidence factor of 95 percent, plus or minus three percent. A surprisingly small sample size, say 2,000 to 3,000 respondents, could reflect the attitudes of the entire U.S. population if conducted with rigor.

Despite this level of confidence, the basis for the opinion or attitude is qualitative. This means that it is subjective and open to a degree of interpretation. Qualitative analysis is the province of interpretation. A literature search is performed, and the material is reviewed. The analytical product is a summary, in two or three pages, of perhaps 200 or 300 pages of source material. This type of subjective, qualitative analysis yields opinions and recommendations—the real stuff of executive decision making. These are the intuitive or subjective judgments so common in business intelligence. However, given today's information-rich environment, what is the best way to arrive at this intelligence product?

AutoSummarize in Microsoft Word

In the IBIS, collection relating to a project may have gathered these documents from dozens of Web sites. The first step in analyzing large quantities of text may be to summarize each text file. Microsoft Word's AutoSummarize feature will automatically summarize key points in a document. According to the Help text, "If you want to create a summary for others to read, use AutoSummarize to copy the key points and insert them into an executive summary or abstract. If you want to read a summary of an online document, you can display the document in AutoSummarize view. In this view, you can switch between displaying only the key points in a document and highlighting them in the document. As you read, you can also change the level of detail at any time.

"AutoSummarize analyzes the document and assigns a score to each sentence. (For example, it gives a higher score to sentences that contain words used frequently in the document.) You then choose a percentage of the highest-scoring sentences to display in the summary. AutoSummarize works best on well-structured documents, for example, reports, articles, and scientific papers. For the best quality summaries, make sure that the Find All Word Forms tool is installed."

Evaluation of subjective judgments

One way to quantify subjective judgments is to set up a spreadsheet to record scoring on each element under consideration. The spreadsheet can be used to assess subjective judgments with some relative degree of precision. Tables in word processing documents might serve the same purpose.

In plain documents and tables, Word sorts text alphabetically, numerically, or by date in ascending order (A to Z or 0 to 9) or descending order (Z to A or 9 to 0). Word uses paragraph marks () to separate items to be sorted. When sorting by text, items beginning with punctuation marks or symbols are sorted first, items beginning with numbers are sorted next, and items beginning with letters are sorted last. Word treats dates as three-digit numbers. When sorting by numbers, Word ignores all characters except numbers. The numbers can be in any location in a paragraph.

When sorting by date, Word recognizes the following as valid date separators: hyphens, forward slashes (/), commas, and periods. Word also recognizes colons (:) as valid time separators. If Word doesn't recognize a date or time, it places the item at the beginning or end of the list (depending on whether you're sorting in ascending or descending order).

If two or more items begin with the same character, Word evaluates subsequent characters in each item to determine which item should come first. When sorting by field results, if an entire field (such as a last name) is the same for two items, Word next evaluates subsequent fields (such as a first name) according to the specified sort options.

Market analysis

Market segmentation is another area where numerical analysis can be used. Geographic and personal demographics, correlated to consumer lifestyles, lead to a plan for selling a product or service. Population size and density, climate, and cost of living are some of the geographic numerics that can be analyzed, while age, education, income, and family size are personal numerics. Consumer lifestyles often are highly segmented and reported by ZIP code. Taken together these types of data can be analyzed to develop a marketing plan. Nearly all of the demographic information is available via the Internet. Some of the lifestyle segmentation numerics can be found in articles, books, and studies that can be located and sometimes accessed via the Internet.

Sales forecasting involves simple trend analysis, market share analysis (possibly linked to a Boston Consulting Group type matrix analysis of cash cow, star, problem child, and dog characterization), chain ratio, and other methods. Sales forecasts, like any other type of forecast, get people thinking about the future and help quantify elements to assist decision making in the face of uncertainty. Data from the Internet increasingly are available, and simple tools can be used to perform these forecasts.

Patent analysis

Technology is a very significant driver in many fields. Technology can play a role in general business strategy, development of new products or services, pricing, sales and marketing, operations, cost position, corporate image, and other aspects of the business. Patent analysis is increasingly used to determine the current and future configuration of the playing field.

The uniformity of patent records and their easy availability in data record format means that a variety of analyses are possible. Standard record layout includes inventor name(s), assignee (usually the employer), patents cited, and other information. These data can be aggregated and reports generated from relational databases or graphs plotted against other data imported into spreadsheet programs.

Benchmarking

During the 1980s, the "quality revolution" in America led to the establishment by the Department of Commerce of the Malcolm Baldrige National Quality Award (MBNQA). Part of the process of applying was a benchmarking exercise. This little gem became even more popular during the early 1990s and accelerated during the ISO 9000 certification phase of the consulting boom in that field. Spurred on by MBNQA winners that had to open up and explain how they won, would-be Baldrige companies found other "best in class" companies that would throw open their doors and allow benchmarkers to come in and inspect their operations. Some businesspeople quickly figured out that they might be giving away the store when it came to unintentionally revealing proprietary processes. However, benchmarking lives on.

Today the term benchmarking is more generic and generally involves studying a company to determine how it ticks. Deconstruction may provide strategic insights that could yield a competitive advantage or a new market opportunity. In fact there are local, national, and international organizations that to one degree or another have company-specific and industry benchmarking data available to their members.

Ratio analysis

Pure numerical analysis is common in business. One of the most frequently used forms is the development of ratios derived by dividing one number by another. The result is compared to some other quantity derived by applying the same process to another set of data from an earlier period or from another company or situation. Ratios can be used to measure performance of a firm against company goals or industry standards. There are many sources of numerical data that can be found on the Internet. These data range from government-compiled census and economic statistics to financial records of public companies. Other data files can be purchased or leased from a wide variety of sources.

Although detailed financial data from private companies are rarely found anywhere, some suggest that income statements and balance sheets can be derived by consensus of those in a position to accurately estimate figures that make up those financial reporting tools. By carefully compiling all of the bits and pieces of information available in the public domain (much of it now on the Internet), one can compile a very useful collection of numerical data that can be used for various analyses. For example, competitor monitoring might yield sales figures in one article, production figures in another, and expansion plans in still another article. Gathering these bits and pieces over time and steadily filling in the blanks as data become available can be more fun than putting together a jigsaw puzzle.

The income statement and balance sheet as well as financial reports yield numbers that can be used to determine ratios for financial analysis. Ratio analysis helps identify trends within the business, and they allow the user to compare financial performance with similar firms in the same line of business. Internet-accessible financial reports and data from CD-ROM systems (most notably the Moody's, available in many libraries)can be imported to a spreadsheet and compared to the target company's numbers.

The balance sheet is the primary source for developing ratios relating to liquidity and leverage. Liquidity measures the ability to pay bills. Leverage measures the extent to which the business depends upon debt financing. A few are detailed here to provide an understanding for the uninitiated.

Liquidity ratios

The current ratio shows whether the business has current assets that may be required to meet payments on current debt with a safety margin. It measures the business's financial strength.

Current Assets/Current Liabilities = Current Ratio

2 to 1 is a good target but a 1 to 1 ratio indicates less of a safety margin.

The quick ratio measures liquidity. It is sometimes referred to as the "acid test" because it does not include inventories, only liquid assets and available funds.

Current Assets Inventory/Current Liabilities = Quick Ratio

1 to 1 is conservative but should be viewed in the context of industry standards (60 to 90 usual accounts receivable, etc.).

Leverage ratios

Leverage ratios measure the extent to which borrowed funds have been used to finance the company's operations. Leverage ratios are indicators of a business's ability to meet principal and interest payments.

Total Liabilities/Shareholder's Equity = Debt to Equity Ratio

A debt to equity ratio of 0.4 or lower is a good signal for the average business, but higher ratios may be acceptable given management's financial strategy. Substituting long-term debt for total liabilities in the formula creates the long-term debt to equity ratio.

Debt ratio shows how much the firm has been financed with debt:

Total Liabilities/Total Assets = Debt Ratio

A lower ratio is better than a higher one, but again this must be compared to industry averages to judge a particular company's standing.

Income statement ratio analysis

These ratios use income and expense numbers to indicate leverage and profitability.

Gross margin ratio indicates relative profitability and shows management's ability to use assets to generate a profit.

Gross Profit/Net Sales = Gross Margin

Gross margin is highly dependent upon the particular industry in which the business operates. Analysis of profit margin over time shows important trends.

Net profit margin is the percentage of sales dollars left after subtracting the cost of goods sold as well as expenses:

Net Income/Sales = Net Profit Margin

Income taxes can be excluded from the Net Profit Margin calculation.

There are other management ratios, some of which are common in a particular industry. Common management ratios include average collection period, inventory turnover, return on assets, return on investment, and turnover ratios. Ratios derived from a specific business are compared to that derived from similar-size businesses in the same field. This basic analysis can be taken a step further with statistical analysis using Excel.

The 80/20 rule applied to spreadsheets

Throughout this book I have shown the reader how powerful functions of common office software can be used in uncommon ways. Most people get comfortable with just the functions they need to accomplish the task at hand. A few explore the capabilities beyond those needed for everyday tasks. These capabilities are, true to form in computer use, "solutions looking for problems." However, knowing about them can suggest new ways of using existing data to achieve high-level business intelligence products.

For example, Microsoft Excel is just one of the components of the Microsoft Office suite of tools. While there are others (e.g., Corel's Suite) this spreadsheet program has much more functionality than most people use in all but the most demanding tasks. Table 15.1 includes a partial list of components that can be installed.

Table 15.1

EXCEL ADD-INS	
AccessLinks Add-In	Creates Microsoft Access forms and reports to use with Microsoft Excel data, and imports Microsoft Excel data into Microsoft Access.
Analysis ToolPak	Adds financial, statistical, and engineering analysis functions.
Conditional Sum Wizard	Creates a formula that sums data in a list if the data matches criteria you specify.
File Conversion Wizard	Converts a group of files to Microsoft Excel workbook format.
Lookup Wizard	Creates a formula to look up data in a list using another known value in the list.
ODBC Add-In	Uses ODBC functions to connect to external data sources by using installed ODBC drivers.
Microsoft Excel Internet Assistant	Converts ranges of worksheet data and charts to Hypertext Markup Language (HTML) Web page files.
Solver Add-In	Calculates solutions to what-if scenarios based on adjustable cells and constraint cells.
Template Wizard with Data Tracking	Creates templates that record worksheet entries in a database for tracking and analysis.
Web Form Wizard	Sets up a form on a Web server so that data entered in the form is added to a database.

These functions represent just some of the many and varied capabilities you presently have at your fingertips to produce business intelligence from existing internal data or that which you retrieved from the Internet and organized in your IBI system. Because databases are so much a part of business intelligence, let's look in detail at this function.

Excel database and list management functions

In Microsoft Excel, a database is a list of related data in which rows of information are records and columns of data are fields. Excel includes 12 worksheet functions that analyze these data. Each of these functions, referred to as Dfunctions, uses three arguments: database, field, and criteria. Arguments refer to the worksheet ranges that are used by the function. Microsoft's illustration, shown here as Figure 15.1, is a database for a small orchard. Each record contains information about one tree. The range A5:E11 is named Database and the range A1:F3 is named Criteria. The first row of the list contains labels for each column. The reference can be entered as a cell range or as a name that represents the range that contains the list.

Field indicates which column is used in the function. Columns of data in the list must have an identifying label in the first row. Field can be given as text with the column label enclosed between double quotation marks, such as "Age" or "Yield" in the example list below, or as a number that represents the position of the column in the list: 1 for the first column (Tree in the example that follows), 2 for the second (Height), and so on.

Criteria is a reference to a range of cells that specify conditions for the function. The function returns information from the list that matches the conditions specified in the criteria range. The criteria range includes a copy of the column label in the list for the column you want the function to summarize. The criteria reference can be entered as a cell range, such as A1:F2 in the example database below, or as a name that represents the range, such as "Criteria."

DCOUNT (Database, "Age", A1:F2) equals 1. This function looks at the records of apple trees between a height of 10 and 16 and counts how many of the Age fields in those records contain numbers.

DCOUNTA (Database, "Profit", A1:F2) equals 1. This function looks at the records of apple trees between a height of 10 and 16 and counts how many of the Profit fields in those records are not blank.

DMAX (Database, "Profit", A1:A3) equals $105.00, the maximum profit of apple and pear trees.

DMIN (Database, "Profit", A1:B2) equals $75.00, the minimum profit of apple trees over 10.

DSUM (Database, "Profit", A1:A2) equals $225.00, the total profit from apple trees.

DSUM (Database, "Profit", A1:F2) equals $75.00, the total profit from apple trees with a height between 10 and 16.

DPRODUCT (Database, "Yield", A1:F2) equals 140, the product of the yields from apple trees with a height between 10 and 16.

DAVERAGE (Database, "Yield", A1:B2) equals 12, the average yield of apple trees over 10 feet in height.

DAVERAGE (Database, 3, Database) equals 13, the average age of all trees in the database.

DSTDEV (Database, "Yield", A1:A3) equals 2.97, the estimated standard deviation in the yield of apple and pear trees if the data in the database is only a sample of the total orchard population.

DSTDEVP (Database, "Yield", A1:A3) equals 2.65, the true standard deviation in the yield of apple and pear trees if the data in the database is the entire population.

DVAR (Database, "Yield", A1:A3) equals 8.8, the estimated variance in the yield of apple and pear trees if the data in the database is only a sample of the total orchard population.

DVARP (Database, "Yield", A1:A3) equals 7.04, the true variance in the yield of apple and pear trees if the data in the database is the entire orchard population.

DGET (Database, "Yield", Criteria) returns the #NUM! error value because more than one record meets the criteria.

	A	B	C	D	E	F
1	Tree	Height	Age	Yield	Profit	Height
2	Apple	>10				<16
3	Pear					
4						
5	Tree	Height	Age	Yield	Profit	
6	Apple	18	20	14	$ 105.00	
7	Pear	12	12	10	$ 96.00	
8	Cherry	13	14	9	$ 105.00	
9	Apple	14	15	10	$ 75.00	
10	Pear	9	8	8	$ 76.80	
11	Apple				$ 45.00	

Figure 15.1

Statistical analysis

According to Microsoft's literature, "Excel provides a set of data analysis tools called the Analysis ToolPak that you can use to save steps when you develop complex statistical or engineering analyses. You provide the data and parameters for each analysis; the tool uses the appropriate statistical or engineering macro functions and then displays the results in an output table. Some tools generate charts in addition to output tables. Excel provides many other statistical, financial, and engineering worksheet functions. A representative sampling of ToolPak's analytical capabilities includes the following functions:

"Correlation measures the relationship between two data sets that are scaled to be independent of the unit of measurement. The population correlation calculation returns the covariance of two data sets divided by the product of their standard deviations. You can use the correlation tool to determine whether two ranges of data move together. That is, whether large values of one set are associated with large values of the other (positive correlation), whether small values of one set are associated with large values of the other (negative correlation), or whether values in both sets are unrelated (correlation near zero).

"Regression analysis uses the least 'squares' method to fit a line through a set of observations. You can analyze how a single dependent variable is affected by the values of one or more independent variables; for example, how an athlete's performance is affected by such factors as age, height, and weight. You can apportion shares in the performance measure to each of these three factors, based on a set of performance data, and then use the results to predict the performance of a new, untested athlete.

"Histogram calculates individual and cumulative frequencies for a cell range of data and data bins. This tool generates data for the number of occurrences of a value in a data set. For example, in a class of 20 students, you could determine the distribution of scores in letter-grade categories. A histogram table presents the letter-grade boundaries and the number of scores between the lowest bound and the current bound. The single most-frequent score is the mode of the data.

"Descriptive statistics generates a report of univariate statistics for data in the input range, providing information about the central tendency and variability of your data. Options include: Confidence Level for Mean (for example, a value of 95 percent calculates the confidence level of the mean at a significance of 5 percent); Kth Largest and Kth Smallest (to include a row in the output table for the kth largest or smallest value for each range of data); Output Range (produces two columns of information for each data set, left column contains statistics labels and right column contains the statistics.); Summary statistics (to produce one field for each of the statistics in the output table: Mean, Standard Error, Median, Mode, Standard Deviation, Variance, Kurtosis, Skewness, Range, Minimum, Maximum, Sum, Count, Largest (#), Smallest (#), and Confidence Level).

"Sampling creates a sample from a population by treating the input range as a population. When the population is too large to process or chart, you can use a representative sample. You can also create a sample that contains only values from a particular part of a cycle if you believe that the input data is periodic. For example, if the input range contains quarterly sales figures, sampling with a periodic rate of four places values from the same quarter in the output range."

Relationship analysis

Originally an Atlanta-based software development firm, KnowledgeX provided a relationship analysis package. The company was purchased by IBM to incorporate the KnowledgeX technology in IBM's product line. The software provided a framework for creating, maintaining, refining, and distributing knowledge and intelligence. Various KnowledgeX windows were used to add members, define roles in relationships, discover relationships, connect members using object types, publish the discoveries in an HTML file, and distribute developed intelligence to others. Figure 15.2 is a screenshot of the KnowledgeX product.

KnowledgeX helped the user find relationships between and among related pieces of information. It linked members to other members and provided a way of establishing the strength of the relationship and the role that each member plays in the relationship. KnowledgeX created and tracked not only the relationships between members, but also their roles and strengths based on the user's perspective, revealing opportunities that may be relevant to the user.

KnowledgeX can be called a data mining tool. Its functionality is now a part of IBM's DB2 database product.

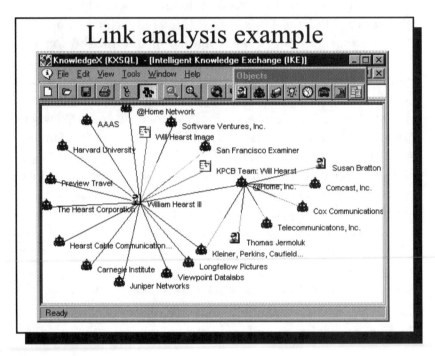

Figure 15.2

Data mining with DB2

Business decision-makers have vastly different levels of expertise and different needs for data analysis, ranging from tailored reports delivered over the company intranet to interactive mining to identify clusters, associations, and trends present but often hidden in the mass of unwashed data. IBM offers a wide range of approaches and tools to meet varied needs. Applications provide tailored user interfaces to address specific problems.

IBM's DB2 Universal Database is a relational database-management system that is fully Web-enabled, scalable from single processors to symmetric multiprocessors and to massively parallel clusters, and features multimedia capabilities with image, audio, video, text, and other advanced object-relational support. Various components can be combined to suit requirements.

DecisionEdge is IBM's complete, end-to-end business intelligence solution. This includes database, database servers, data mining, text mining, data analysis, industry data models, consulting, implementation services, and training. DecisionEdge is a solution from IBM for customer-relationship management, containing a number of standard and customized product and service options.

The IBM Intelligent Miner family helps you identify and extract high-value business intelligence from your data assets. Through a process of "knowledge discovery," your organization can leverage hidden information in its data, uncovering associations, patterns, and trends that can lead to competitive advantage.

Intelligent Miner for Data enables users to mine structured data stored in conventional databases or flat files. Its mining algorithms have been successfully used to address business problems in such areas as customer relationship marketing and fraud and abuse detection. It allows users to increasingly leverage the data warehouse and more quickly derive business value from that investment.

Intelligent Miner for Text harvests information from text sources such as customer correspondence, online news services, e-mail, and Web pages. It has the ability to extract patterns from text, organize documents by subject, find predominant themes in a collection of documents, and search for relevant documents using powerful and flexible queries.

Competitive analysis

The purpose of the competitive analysis (also known as competitor analysis) is to determine the strength and weaknesses of the competitors within your market, strategies that will provide you with a distinct advantage, the barriers that can be developed to prevent competition from entering your market, and any weaknesses that can be exploited within the product development cycle.[1]

According to David Acker,[2] the first step in a competitive analysis is to identify the current and potential competition. Once you have grouped your competitors, you can start to analyze their strategies and identify areas where they are most vulnerable. This can be done through an examination of your competitors' weaknesses and strengths. A competitor's strengths and weaknesses are usually based on the presence and absence of key assets and skills needed to be competitive in the market. To determine just what constitutes a key asset or skill within an industry, one expert suggests concentrating your efforts in four areas:

- Reasons behind successful and unsuccessful firms

- Prime customer motivators

- Major component costs

- Industry mobility barriers

This analysis, in conjunction with an examination of unsuccessful companies and the reasons behind their failure, should provide a good idea of just what key assets and skills are needed to be successful within a given industry and market segment. Through your competitor analysis you will also have to create a marketing strategy that will generate an asset or skill competitors do not have, which will provide you with a distinct and enduring competitive advantage.

Since competitive advantages are developed from key assets and skills, you should sit down and put together a competitive strength matrix by listing all the key assets and skills down the left margin of a piece of paper. Along the top, write down two column headers: weakness and strength. In each asset or skill category, place all the competitors that have weaknesses in that particular category under the weakness column, and all those that have strengths in that specific category in the strength column. After you've finished you'll be able to determine just where you stand in relation to the other firms competing in your industry.

Michael Porter, a leading management theorist, states that competitive strategy aims to establish a profitable and sustainable position against the forces that determine industry competition. According to Porter, two central questions underlie the choice of competitive strategy. The first is long-term profitability. The second is determining relative position within the field of competition.[3]

Competitor analysis is often the driver for IBIS. More knowledge of competitors can be helpful in formulating strategy. Determining competitive threats means assessing current and future competitors and their relationships to your current and future markets. This blends internal sales forecasting with projections of possible competitor impacts. Competitor analysis takes into account their goals, capabilities, and overall posture. Sensitivity analysis may be called for in some of these situations.

Because a model is only an approximation of reality, the sensitivity of the solution to changes in the model and input data is a very important part of analyzing the results. This type of analysis is called sensitivity analysis or postoptimality analysis. It determines how much the solution would change if there were changes in the model or the input data.[4]

These qualitative judgments can be transformed into a semi-qualitative scoring through the use of matrices set up in a spreadsheet. Categories to be ranked make up rows in the spreadsheet and columns represent companies being studied. A 1 to 10 ranking is used and spreadsheet cells can be programmed to yield a weight to differentiate the more important aspects of the ranking. This approach is portrayed in Figures 15.3 and 15.4.

An individual can work on these approaches, but better results can be obtained by having several disinterested experts provide rankings. The spreadsheet can be attached to an explanatory e-mail message and sent to various participants. An inducement to participate (for those not employed by the same company) can be offered. Often busy experts will respond if they are promised a copy of the resulting data.

Visualizing relationships with graphic representations

Visualization software is a bridge between analysis and communication. While visualization can help in organizing and analyzing quantities of disparate data, it can help in communicating important conclusions too. Visio Corporation flowchart and diagramming software uses drag-and-drop drawing to help users create diagrams that use shapes and tools keyed to standardized process methodologies. Total quality management (TQM), cause and effect, and diagrams that link to databases and spreadsheets can be augmented with other professional shapes and add-ons. These functions help the user visualize and communicate information infrastructures for data modeling. If you're familiar with architects' computer aided design (CAD) software, you can think of Visio as CAD for the business analyst.

Competitive Analysis Spreadsheet

```
=======================================================
                    COMPETITOR ANALYSIS
=======================================================
           (Rated on a scale of 1 to 5, 5 being high.)
```

No.	Category	US	Competitor A	Competitor B	Competitor C
1	Product Quality	4	5	3	4
2	Strategic/Mission Fit	4	5	4	4
3	Competitive Position	5	5	4	3
4	Market Position	3	4	5	3
5	Customer Support	4	3	4	2
6	Human Resources	4	5	2	4
7	Management Team	4	5	4	4
8	Financial Measures	5	5	2	3
9	Technology Issues	4	3	4	5
10	Accessibility of Srv.	5	4	3	4
11	Pricing	3	4	5	4
12	Consumer Awareness	4	5	4	3
13	Other_____	3	4	3	4
14	Other_____	4	5	3	4
15	Other_____	3	4	3	4
	Weighted Score	1,030	1,155	910	736

Figure 15.3

SPSS's allCLEAR software takes another path toward the communication of analyzed information. The package is claimed to be the only product that takes a text outline and turns it into a flowchart without drawing. It enables the user to create flowcharts, diagrams, process maps, fishbone diagrams, deployment charts, network diagrams, and other representations of textual material.

Consider the capabilities of word processing software to immediately convert HTML pages into text outlines. Figure 15.5 illustrates this powerful combination of tools consistent with the PROACtive process from Internet-derived information.

Competitive Analysis Spreadsheet Results

==
INPUT WEIGHTED VALUES BELOW
==

In the following tables, weight the relative value of each category, as well as the perceived weight of competitors A, B, and C. The weight assigned to "OUR ORGANIZATION" is 5.

	Category	Category Weighted Value	Competitor	Competitor Weight
==	====================	==========	==========	==========
1	Product Quality	4	A	5
2	Strategic/Mission Fit	4	B	5
3	Competitive Position	3	C	4
4	Market Position	4	------------	------------
5	Customer Support	5		
6	Human Resources	4		
7	Management Team	5		
8	Financial Measures	4		
9	Technology Issues	1	**Weighted**	
10	Accessibility of Srv.	4	**Ranked**	
11	Pricing	2		
12	Consumer Awareness	4		
13	Other_____	3		
14	Other_____	1		
15	Other_____	4		

Figure 15.4

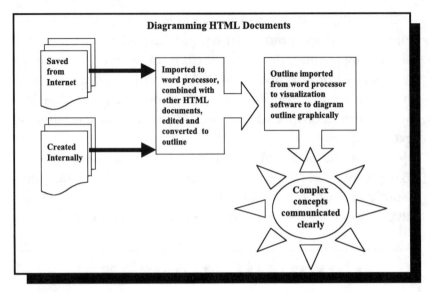

Diagramming HTML Documents

Figure 15.5

Relationship analysis with OrgChart

There are other, much less costly software products that help the user perform similar functions. One such software package is SoftKey's (**www.softkey.com**) OrgChart. In the context of Internet Business Intelligence, this software can be used to analyze information derived from a collection of HTML pages and other text downloaded from Internet sources. Use the word processor to convert these documents into an outline, which is then imported to OrgChart. The resulting diagram can quickly convey concepts that would not be apparent in a collection of many individual documents. The text is available for drill-down reference. The process is depicted in Figure 15.6.

Any org chart consists of four categories of components: the head of the organization (usually the president or CEO) or simply the name of the company; people (or departments) who are subordinate to someone on a higher level, but still have other people (or departments) who report to them; people (or departments) who are lowest in hierarchy and have no subordinates; and assistants or secretaries who report to a particular person (or department) in the organization, but otherwise do not belong on any of the hierarchy levels.

The head of the organization is always shown at the top center of the diagram. The org chart then branches out to the second category of components, which are represented at the appropriate levels of hierarchy. The third category of components is shown at the last level of each branch of the org chart. The assistants are shown in between the hierarchy levels, directly below the person to whom they report.

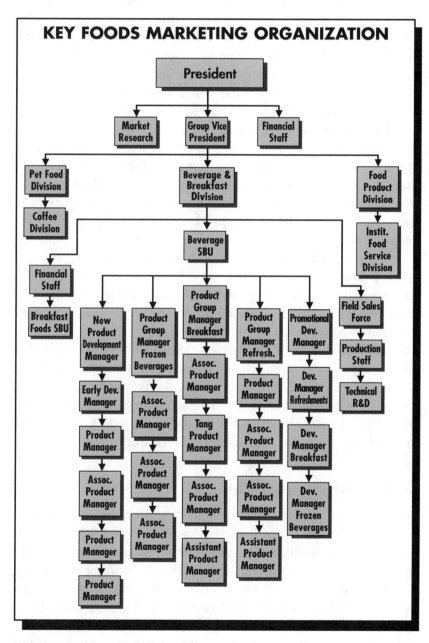

Figure 15.6

An OrgChart script file is the document that holds the text description of the information to be diagrammed or an outline. However, an OrgChart script also contains the punctuation marks (or the script symbols), such as "&" or "{}", which tell the program how to display the chart. When you create and save a script, also called an outline, OrgChart automatically gives it an >ACL extension.

When writing an outline, you can quickly create a certain part of the chart and even change the shape of a specific box by using outline commands. When OrgChart generates a diagram, it looks for cues in the script file that determines the flow of information. Indents and symbols, such as &, tell OrgChart how to format the text you type.

A diagram title must be entered at the very beginning of the script and followed by a blank line. If there is no blank line after the title, OrgChart will assume that it is the first box of the diagram. Subordinates are created by going to the line beneath the supervisor, pressing TAB to indent one level, and typing the text. People on the same level (for example, all vice presidents) should be indented the same amount of space on their own lines.

Any OrgChart diagram consists of boxes (complete with the text that is printed inside) lines (from one box to another, with arrows indicating the flow of information) and title (the diagram title). The program generates these elements automatically, from the information contained in the script.

An OrgChart diagram can also have elements that have been added through the graphic editing mode. These can be boxes, text, lines, or graphic images (copied from the clipboard). Unlike the diagram objects, these objects have no relationship to the script, are not generated automatically, and have to be created by the user. The product of all this is a chart that represents the relationships within the organization.

Geographic analysis

Another clever use of inexpensive software is illustrated in "geoplots" derived from inexpensive street mapping software with import capabilities. Delorme's Street Atlas USA enables the user to import a comma-delimited file containing name and location information. It then plots these data on a map. An example of its use is a geoplot of dealers in a particular state. This information is obtained from the product manufacturer's Web site, saved as text, "data-sculpted" into a comma-delimited file and imported to Street Atlas, then displayed. The process is portrayed in the series of Figures 15.7 through 15.9.

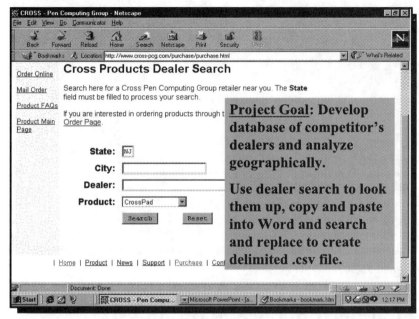

Figure 15.7

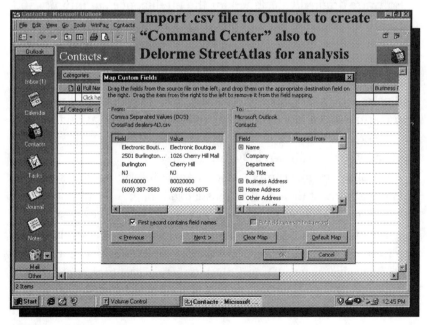

Figure 15.8

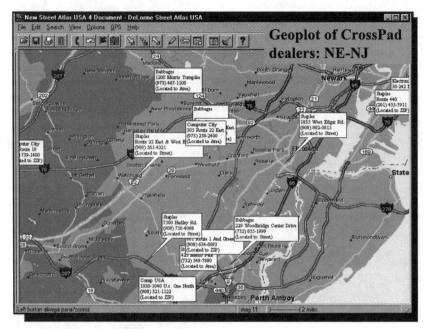

Figure 15.9

High-performance text analysis

Software originally designed for the intelligence community and currently in use is available to commercial users. The U.S. Army's National Ground Intelligence Center developed Pathfinder, which provides intelligence analysts and decision-makers with tools for analyzing and visualizing large, complex data sets to identify trends and patterns. These data analysis tools are used to extract information features from raw data, while fusion and visualization tools are used to create meaningful data aggregations and graphical displays, some of which are shown in Figure 15.10.

According to government documents describing the software, "Historically, most data analysis, visualization, and fusion tools used by intelligence analysts do not extend beyond simple business graphics, spreadsheet, and database applications. More recently, however, applications are exploiting visualization toolkits available today to provide sophisticated 2D and 3D interactive graphics and imaging techniques to produce images of complex information displays. Integration of data analysis and visualization built on data distributed across networks and data servers is providing powerful new ways to

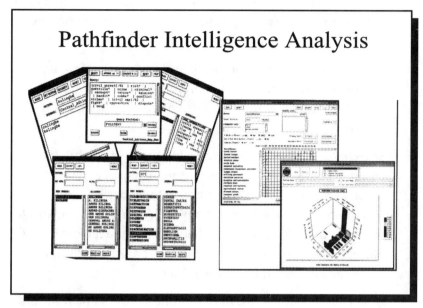

Pathfinder Intelligence Analysis

Figure 15.10

support user interaction with data (data zooming, data viewing, pro-files)." Specifically, Pathfinder tools include the following capabilities:

- **Analysis**—Allows the user to build Boolean queries to search Pathfinder databases for records of interest to the analysis task at hand.

- **Query Builder**—A tool to help users who are unfamiliar with Boolean logic build simple or complex queries for the Analysis Window.

- **Query History**—Allows users to create a library of often-used queries. Stores frequently used queries by name or category.

- **Words**—Allows the user to create queries from words that are actually in the database being searched. Also, has a soundex algorithm to find variations in spelling of words and words that sound alike contained in the database.

- **Master Thesaurus**—Uses the DTIC Scientific and Technical Thesaurus to find search terms for technologies and to auto-matically build queries using those terms.

- **User Thesaurus**—A user-defined thesaurus to compile search terms for topics that are pertinent to each user. Queries are automatically built from these terms.

- **Alias**—Allows a user to identify and save variations or aliases of a name under the correct or preferred name. Alias searching will find records with all variations of the preferred name.

- **Search Results/Search by Example/Search by Highlight**—Displays the records found as a result of a query. Allows refined searching (searching only on the records found by first query). Can search by example to find records statistically similar to the one selected. Records may be ranked by significance in Search Results window. All analytic tools operate on records in Search Results window.

- **Query Prism**—Runs two to five queries at the same time and returns the results of individual queries as all possible Boolean combination of the queries, e.g., A and not (B or C), (A and B) and not C, A and B and C, etc.

- **Cameo**—Allows users to construct models of their analytic problems using objects. Queries can be entered into each object to allow tailoring to the specific problem. Ranking and alert thresholds can be assigned. Cameo represents database contents visually using color intensity and acts as an alert tool.

- **Counts**—Displays the most frequently occurring words and two-, three- or four-word phrases that are in a set of records, and provides a chronograph showing the frequency of the word or phrase over time. Key terms reflecting events, technologies, or processes can be temporally evaluated in context over the database. Results may be graphed.

- **Galileo**—A visualization tool to examine records in a star-chart-like display and determine the overall meaning of the groupings of the records without having to read and manually integrate information in the records. Galileo was developed as a product by Presearch, Inc. based on research conducted by Pacific Northwest National Laboratories.

- **Field Matrix**—Provides a chronological listing of information in a selected field and shows groups of entities within the fields that are mentioned in the same records.

- **Group Matrix**—Shows the interaction between groups identified in Field Matrix and saved in a group file. Presentation is the same as Field Matrix.

- **Cross Field Matrix**—Shows the interaction between data in two fields in chronological format similar to Field Matrix.

- **Field Frequency Report**—Provides a report on the frequency of occurrence for each unique entry in the selected field. Results may be graphed.

- **Sort Fields**—Allows records to be sorted by up to five fields in any order and any number of fields to be displayed in the report.

- **Personal Information Manager (PIM)**—An object-oriented organizational tool allowing a user to use icons to link information for generating reports and intelligence products. Allows annotations to be stored with each icon and links to be established to records that support the analysis. Graphing capability is provided.

- **Geo**—Provides an integrated mapping capability. Selected records are searched for geo-coordinate information, and that information is then automatically plotted on maps. Records can be retrieved from plotted points.

Pathfinder is more than most business intelligence operations need for analysis. However, if you're serious about high-level analysis and are ready to commit the time and money to do it, Pathfinder can provide a competitive edge.

Endnotes

1. Entrepreneur's Guide To Raising Money CD-ROM.

2. David A. Aaker, *Developing Business Strategies* (John Wiley & Sons, New York, 1998).

3. Michael E. Porter, *Competitive Advantage: Creating and Sustaining Superior Performance* (The Free Press, New York, 1985).

4. Barry Render and Ralph Stair Jr., *Quantitative Analysis for Management, third edition* (Allyn and Bacon, Inc., Needham Heights, Massachusetts, 1988: 8-9).

CHAPTER 16

COMMUNICATING BUSINESS INTELLIGENCE

Business Intelligence (BI) is not really intelligence until it is properly communicated to the intended audience, usually decision-makers. If a successful action is taken based on the conclusion or recommendation derived from it, then the entire process is functioning as it should. This is the goal of the Internet Business Intelligence System (IBIS). Throughout the process we must be able to use persuasive communications to gather and develop BI, communicate it to the target audience, and cause action(s) to be carried out if called for.

The PROACtive process is the framework for planning, rapidly obtaining the required information, analyzing it, and finally communicating it to decision-makers. The form of communication is especially important today. It has never been easier, in all of the history of communications, to convey ideas, concepts, and facts to others. Even relatively unskilled people can create very sophisticated multimedia information products and make them available to, literally, the whole world.

The end product of the PROACtive process is, technically speaking, an output that can be formatted in one of three media: Internet/intranet; CD-ROM or diskette; and paper (see Figure 16.1). Many would think that the easiest-to-use format would be paper, and for the briefest of executive summaries this might be true. However, with the proliferation of notebook computers the "easiest to use" title might very well be conferred upon the CD-ROM. With a generation steeped in point-and-click and drill-down via HTML, the easiest to use (and most pleasing to experience) could be the executive summary with hypertext links to background information or other computer-based tools.

Imagine for a minute that the BI to be communicated involves a complex problem with multiple scenarios. If this is the case, a simple document, no matter how well put together and conveyed, may not be enough. The decision-maker may need to interactively explore the scenarios and input data to do so. Further, a simple yes or no may not suffice. With the use of an interactive information product, the decision-maker could very well make decisions that are more complex than a simple yes or no and communicate them back to one or more persons. This is the power of interactive computer communications.

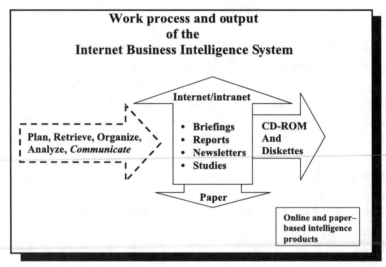

Figure 16.1

Persuasion

The mantra of "actionable intelligence" chanted by some business intelligence "professionals" usually neglects one very important aspect—persuading someone to take action. We can gather and analyze information till the cows come home, but if it isn't powerfully presented in the appropriate format and forum and persuasively perceived, it's just a waste of time. Even worse, it can lead to a common form of frustration where the BI professional works hard to create a good product that is not accepted. This lack of acceptance might not be due to the accuracy or judgment represented—it might be due to lack of persuasiveness. This is a double tragedy because it not only frustrates the BI professional, but it stymies the decision-maker who could propel the organization forward with truly actionable intelligence if it had been persuasive.

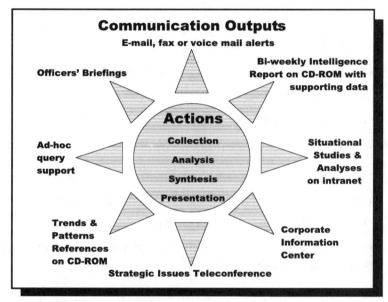

Figure 16.2

In his book *Power and Influence*, Robert L. Dilenschneider, then president and chief executive of Hill and Knowlton, Inc. International Public Relations Counsel, addresses the very real challenges of his subject. People with power often, but not always, have influence. He says, "In reality, influence is an indispensable part of everyday life. Used ethically, influence is a formidable skill. Without influence, organizations could not succeed, consensus and coalitions could not be built and attitudes would never change."

He explains the realities of influence and how influence works in society and especially in business. Second, it is to give everyone the opportunity to put proven influence tactics to work for themselves. Among the points he makes are these:

- The Power Triangle (connections between communication, recognition, and influence)

- Good communication is solid thinking translated into clear messages

- If you communicate effectively, you get positive recognition, which over time leads to influence

- A powerful person is competent, effective, and worthy of respect

- The art of influence is defining, realizing, and gradually strengthening your personal agenda

- Understand the many facets of "the favor bank" and use it wisely

- Be tough but in a constructive way

- Know how to operate with the proper style

- Step forward without being pushy

- The influential manager knows the value of and how to use his symbols for maximum effectiveness

- Never underestimate the usefulness of public data and study what you're already paying for

The true master of business intelligence helps people to accept a wrenching new look at the world. He helps people understand how the seemingly incredible could be true and why it is essential to act now.

First step: Organizing information to be communicated

Often the first step is straightforward. A superior asks for a report and the subordinate spends a few hours researching a topic, synthesizing the information, and writing a two-page summary memo. Sometimes there's an established format. At other times there may be a need to treat a complex subject in a detailed manner. Among the first questions that must be answered are: Who will read this report? Why is the report needed? What is needed in order to make a decision?

A good report conveys information, interprets it, and provides value. Going beyond basic information is important. Your conclusions point the way to solutions or the way to proceed. Good reports explain why or how and address a central issue while they interpret information in a way that enlightens the reader.[1]

Formats and templates

College courses teach basic formats for writing. Research papers are similar to a basic business intelligence product. As opposed to an essay (which is based on common knowledge and the writer's own experience), the research paper is based on a thorough review of information available on the subject with source acknowledgments. A report usually refers to a thorough record or description of the results of firsthand experiences. Steps involved in writing a research paper include the following:

1. Choosing a topic to be framed as a question to be answered or as an assertion of a possible conclusion (hypothesis)

2. Preparing a working bibliography (a list of relevant sources that may be added to or modified as the project progresses)

3. Collecting information including critical evaluation of sources

4. Outlining the paper

5. Writing the paper

In outlining the paper, the choice is to start right after the topic is determined or after information has been collected. The controlling idea dictates the content of the outline, but the way you organize it can vary. For example, a chronology explains each step in a sequence while comparison and contrast presents similarities or differences. A spatial pattern approach develops the physical dimensions of a topic. The cause-and-effect approach involves presentation of events or forces that produce certain results. Dividing a subject into its parts and classifying them is the analytical method of organization. A major research project could resemble a thesis or dissertation. It could include a table of contents, lists of tables or graphics, an abstract and appendix, and/or endnotes, as well as an index.[2]

There are many common formats and templates. See Table 16.1 for examples. Any reporter knows that who, what, when, where, why, and how must be covered in any news item. The classic newspaper article usually is written in an inverse pyramid style with nearly all of the essential points given in the "lead" sentence and then expanded upon throughout the article. The smallest details are presented toward the end of the article.

Table 16.1

REPORT TYPE	PURPOSE
Information	Conveys and explains facts
Study	Addresses problem, conveys alternative solutions with analysis and recommendations
Expert	Interprets facts from expert's perspective
Status	Update on current condition
Recommendation	Proposes something new

Formal report format

General Accounting Office reports are comprehensive documents that follow a standardized format that is a useful model for certain types of BI background reports. Any or all of these elements can be used:

- Title page

- Letter of transmittal to the report requester

- Results in brief section of several paragraphs

- Background section

- Scope and methodology explaining how the report was structured and conducted

- Body in sections and subsections presenting the bulk of the report

- Comment letters from those who reviewed the report

- Contents pages summarizing appendices, if required, and lists of tables and/or figures

- Listing of abbreviations used and their definitions

- Appendix

- Listing of major contributors to report

The Oxford Analytica (OA) is an international research and consulting firm drawing on the scholarship of Oxford and other major universities and research institutions around the world. Their Brief format is even simpler. The format includes event, significance, analysis, and conclusion. OA's Daily Brief is just one of several intelligence products. Other formats include briefings, short analyses, larger scale sectoral analyses, client critiques, and private seminars.

Other presentation templates are often used in specialized areas of business. For example, one reporting format always includes objectives, background, strategies, actions, and results.

Template Wizards

In addition to Word, another component of the Microsoft Office suite is PowerPoint. Used initially for creating transparencies for overhead projection and now for Internet slide shows, PowerPoint's AutoContent Wizard (Figure 16.3) can be helpful in organizing information to be communicated.

PowerPoint guides you to pre-built content templates such as those shown in Figure 16.4, and it provides ideas, starter text, formatting, and organization for your presentation. The templates cover a wide variety of topics. The wizard also contains templates from Dale Carnegie Training, which give tips on how to become a better presenter. There are many different color and style combinations available, but the most important aspect of communicating business intelligence is crafting the important points you wish to convey and persuasively presenting them to your audience.

An example of the AutoContent Wizard's guidance for organizing business presentations is the Recommending a Strategy template:

Vision Statement (vision and long-term direction)

Goal and Objective
    State the desired goal
    State the desired objective
    Use multiple points if necessary

Today's Situation
    Summary of the current situation
    Use brief bullets, discuss details verbally

How Did We Get Here?
    Any relevant historical information
    Original assumptions that are no longer valid

Available Options
    State the alternative strategies
    List advantages & disadvantages of each
    State cost of each option

Recommendation
   Recommend one or more of the strategies
   Summarize the results if things go as proposed

What to do next
   Identify Action Items

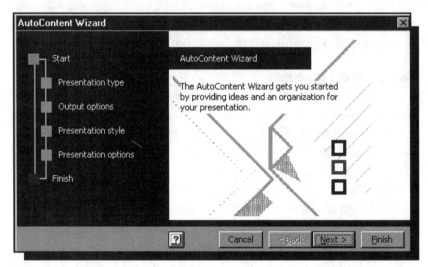

Figure 16.3

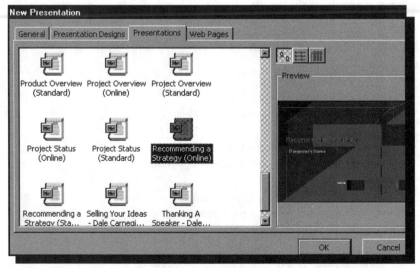

Figure 16.4

These fill-in-the-blank templates combined with pre-formatted graphics styles make it very easy to create a professional presentation. After delivering the presentation (or perhaps in lieu of a personal presentation) you may wish to publish it to the Internet or to an intranet site. This can be accomplished quickly and easily with the "publish to" HTML feature.

Microsoft Word features for communicating business intelligence

Now that we've looked at how to organize intelligence to be communicated, let's examine some of the mechanics of actually producing the product. Today, nearly everyone uses a word processor for business communication. However, the 80/20 rule of software utilization usually applies—that is, 80 percent (or more) of the people use 20 percent (or less) of a software package's total capability. Many of the extensive formatting, error correction, and graphics capabilities of high-end word processing software such as Microsoft Word are commonly used. However, some of the more uncommon features, applicable to facilitation of BI needs, can be put together to provide a foundation for the IBIS.

Annotating, finding, and opening text files

From File/Open, use the buttons to view files by List, Detail, Properties, or Preview. Using the Detail view you can use the commands and settings button to sort by file name, file type, size, or date modified. The Advanced find bar opens a full-featured dialog box with several search capabilities to find files across your entire system, including a network setup.

From File/Versions you can save various versions with explanatory notes. This is helpful in maintaining a working history of a document, particularly important when several people are working on the same report. You can see who did what on a document and when, as well as enter descriptive text about the changes made in each version. Tools/Track Changes also is relevant in versioning of documents.

From File/Properties, access several dialog boxes to annotate the document with details about a file that help identify it. Title, author name, subject, and keywords are searchable via File/Open/

Advanced Search topics or other important information in the file. Create custom file properties and link them to specific items in your active file.

From Edit/Find/More, use additional advanced features to search through a document for a specified target. Another option here is the Find and Replace function that also permits you to use special characters for search and replace functions that help in data sculpting.

Collaboration

With business travel prices exceeding $350 per diem for food and lodging alone in some of the more expensive destinations, remote collaboration in lieu of meetings can be a real money-saving tactic. This may not be so important in casual day-to-day collaboration as in latter stages of draft review and discussion. Nonetheless, building up expertise with remote collaboration may assist in overall cost reduction for the larger enterprise. It may allow small businesses with limited budgets to work in ways the owners had never imagined. The Internet is the common denominator, and software features make it possible.

For example, in Word, from File/Send you can communicate the writing to someone via e-mail or fax. You can route a document through e-mail, rather than send it, when you want others to review a copy of it online, one after another. You can send the document to one recipient after another, so that each recipient can see the previous revisions and annotations, or to all recipients at once. You can allow only certain parts of the document to be modified. As the document is routed, you can track its status. After all of the recipients have reviewed the document, it will automatically be returned to you. You also can post a document to a Microsoft Exchange public folder when you want to make the document available to others but you don't want to send it through e-mail. You can also post a document to a Microsoft Outlook folder.

When sending an e-mail you can include a link to an external resource on the Internet. When you type one of the following Internet protocols in the text box of a mail message, Outlook creates a hyperlink for you from the text. If recipients of the message have an Internet browser installed on their computers that supports the protocol, they can click the hyperlink to quickly go to the destination. The following Internet protocols are supported:

- **file://**—A protocol used to open a file on an intranet.

- **ftp://**—File Transfer Protocol (FTP), the most common method used to transfer files over the Internet.

- **gopher://**—Gopher protocol, by which hyperlinks and text are stored separately.

- **http://**—Hypertext Transfer Protocol (HTTP).

- **mailto**—A protocol used to send mail to an e-mail address. When the recipient clicks this hyperlink, a new message opens with the mailto e-mail address filled in.

- **news**—A protocol used to open an Internet newsgroup, for recipients who are connected to an NNTP server.

- **nntp://**—Network News Transfer Protocol—a protocol used to distribute, inquire, retrieve, and post Usenet news articles over the Internet.

- **Outlook: or Outlook://**—A protocol used to open an Outlook folder or an item or file in Outlook. This protocol is supported only in Outlook.

- **telnet://**—The Internet standard protocol for logging on from remote locations.

- **wais://**—Wide Area Information Servers protocol—a distributed information retrieval system used to retrieve documents based on keywords you supply.

Simplifying complex functions

Toolbars allow you to organize the commands in Word the way you want to so you can find and use them quickly. You can easily customize toolbars. For example, you can add and remove menus and buttons, create your own custom toolbars, hide or display toolbars, and move toolbars. In previous versions of Office, toolbars only contained buttons. Now toolbars can contain buttons, menus, or a combination of both.

The menu bar is a special toolbar at the top of the screen that contains menus such as File, Edit, and View. You can customize the menu bar the same way you customize any built-in toolbar; for example, you can quickly add and remove buttons and menus on the menu bar, but you can't hide the menu bar.

From view/toolbars you can pick functions that help you go way beyond document creation. In addition to advanced formatting including form creation, you can program routines and pull into your document information from various external databases.

Selecting the drawing toolbar presents a number of sophisticated features. This one toolbar can open up a whole range of communications possibilities that can assist you in reducing much detail to simple concepts, portrayed graphically. For example, one item on the drawing toolbar is autoshapes; a sampling is shown in Figure 16.5. This provides direct access to several predefined shapes that can be placed in the document, moved around, and manipulated as to size and shape. Of particular note are the block arrows, flow chart symbols, and call-outs.

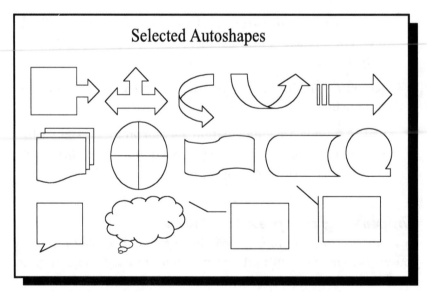

Figure 16.5

Other tools in Word

Many books have been written about the Microsoft Word portion of the Microsoft Office suite of software. All of these Microsoft products, and many others including Netscape's offerings, can form the core of the IBIS. While there are hundreds or thousands of features useful for IBIS, covering some of them provides a selection that should help the reader discover the capabilities and spark thought on how to use them in a specific situation.

From Insert/Autotext or Insert/Field, automatically insert complex information and/or links to other document sections, other documents, or other files. Insert/Cross Reference is used to end text with a field in the document that directs the reader to another location. A cross-reference can be inserted as a hyperlink, so presumably it can be used in text for a Web page.

Use Tools/AutoSummarize to automatically summarize the key points in a document that could be helpful in creating an executive summary or abstract. With online documents, you can switch between displaying only the key points in a document and highlighting them in the document. As you read, you can also change the level of detail. AutoSummarize analyzes the document and assigns a score to each sentence. You choose a percentage of the highest-scoring sentences to display in the summary. AutoSummarize works best on well-structured documents, but it is still a relatively new feature that holds great promise to help reduce workload.

Communicating via Newsgroups and mail lists

Many of the foregoing features can be used in Newsgroup communication. The same is true with e-mail sent via mail lists. You can embed various enhancements to these types of communications. This allows you to enhance text-only messages to communicate with one person or a group. See Figure 16.6 for an electronic mail message with attached Microsoft Word file enhanced with graphics.

In a world where meetings of any type require the scheduling of multiple individuals at various locations, perhaps across several time zones, a virtual meeting without real-time interaction often might be the best choice. Particularly if there is an ongoing nature to the communication, Newsgroups and mail lists, used to their fullest potential, can serve as a convenient substitute for meetings, often proving more effective.

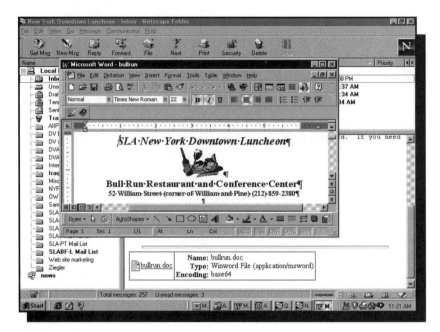

Figure 16.6

Publishing presentations on the Internet

If you have access rights and File Transfer Protocol (FTP) support for saving files, you can save presentations to the Internet from the Save As dialog box (File menu). PowerPoint comes with an Internet Assistant that creates HTML documents from your presentation. The Internet Assistant helps you customize your presentation. For example, you can include animations, use frames, choose the way you move to other slides or documents, and select different button styles. The Internet Assistant maintains the interactive settings in PowerPoint that jump to other slides or documents.

Hyperlinks in your presentation allow the viewer to jump to a variety of locations. A hyperlink could whisk the viewer to a specific slide within the presentation, a different presentation altogether, a Word document or Microsoft Excel spreadsheet, a company intranet, or an address on the Internet. You can create a hyperlink from any text or object, and then you can either click the hyperlink or hold the mouse over it to start its action. You can also associate two actions with the text or object. For example, you can move the mouse over an object to play a sound and then click the object to jump to another slide. If you have text within a shape, you can set up separate hyperlinks for the shape and the text. You insert hyperlinks by using the Action Settings dialog box (Slide Show menu), or you can click Insert Hyperlink on the Standard toolbar.

Lights, camera, action!

Sometimes, you need to approach a particular audience with a low-tech solution. This might be the case with certain individuals who might only view an information product at their leisure or in a few minutes of spare time. Also, while it is technically possible to take any type image and re-create it in the digital world, overall it might be more effective to consider VHS videotape for communication in some circumstances.

Although it might sound a bit tacky and outdated, film output transferred to video tape might be useful in some situations. Many service bureaus can make slides from your PowerPoint files without requiring special file preparation. These bureaus let you send your files electronically. The service bureau uses your PowerPoint file to image 35mm slides, digital color overheads, large display prints, or posters.

Quite a bit of potential BI material resides as photographic images. These images could include photographic film from any number of corporate photography sessions and assignments. Aerial photographs, executive portraits, and even product photography probably first saw light through the lens of a standard camera. Using the original film (negative or photographic slide) gives the highest quality reproduction and usually is the easiest format to work from requiring the fewest conversion steps.

Most standard photographic processors (custom labs and even chain stores) provide a low-cost service for transferring 35mm photographic slides to VHS video tape. A soundtrack can be added to the videotape for narration and/or background music. Higher quality productions can be made with a correspondingly higher price tag.

Powering up PowerPoint

The real multimedia power of a PowerPoint presentation is only possible when it is kept in the digital environment. An extensive set of PowerPoint features enables you to create highly interactive multimedia presentations. Buttons on the Animation Effects toolbar can be used to animate text and objects. Animation effects are set in a dialog box, from which you can define the animation effect, rearrange the animation order, set the length of time before each animation begins playing, and preview the animation. For added multimedia impact, you can animate bars, data points, or other chart data.

You can record the presenter's voice to deliver a presentation in a self-running slide show, and then send it online or on disk to remote audiences. The Music Tracks feature can be used in a PowerPoint slide show to accentuate animation effects or to add customized background music and sound effects to your presentation. You select the style, length, and tempo you want for the music, and Music Tracks composes it to match your criteria. You can set the background music to automatically fade at the end of a presentation or to transition slightly as you advance your slides.

PowerPoint includes a set of built-in 3-D buttons (Figure 16.7) for actions including Forward, Back, Home, Help, Information, Sound, and Movie. You can click these buttons during a slide show to start another program, play a sound or movie, or link to other slides, files, and Web pages. All of this can be presented on a Web site.

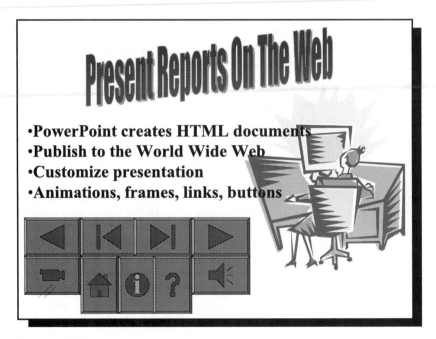

Figure 16.7

The Action Settings command (Slide Show menu) makes it easy for you to define an interactive action for an object. You can specify the destination of a hyperlink, select a program to start, or specify a sound or movie to play. PowerPoint supports the ability to attach an action setting to a particular spot on a slide. One such setting can be to a URL for a Web site. When you save the slide as an HTML document, the interactive "hot spots" on the slide become image maps that can link to different locations on the Web.

Adobe Acrobat

A considerable amount of serious business information on the Internet, especially formal documents and government reports, is in the Adobe Acrobat format. Acrobat software can be used to create and distribute documents that communicate finished business intelligence. After it is created with commercial software, it can be distributed with the freeware reader. This can be especially useful for road warriors who want to carry extensive reference materials on a CD-ROM. These "libraries" can be written back at the office and distributed globally if needed.

Adobe (**www.adobe.com/acrobat**) is well known for its type fonts and such software as PhotoShop and Page Maker publishing software. The Acrobat Reader allows anyone to view, navigate, and print documents in the Adobe Portable Document Format (PDF). PDF documents can be published on the World Wide Web and read in Web browsers, or in Acrobat viewers used as helper applications with Web browsers.

According to Adobe, "Each document or other resource on the Web is identified by a unique uniform resource locator (URL) address. Clicking a URL link to a PDF document on the Web can open the document identified by the URL in your Web browser for inline viewing, or in Acrobat Reader if the Reader has been set up as a helper application for your browser. You can also read PDF files that have been embedded in HTML documents on the Web. To open a linked PDF document in a browser, simply click the link. The PDF document is downloaded to your machine either one page at a time or completely before displaying on-screen, depending on your browser, the Web server, and whether the PDF document has been optimized."

If your Web browser does not support inline viewing of PDF documents or you prefer not to view PDF inline, you can set up Acrobat

Reader as a helper application with your browser's preferences. With Reader set up as a helper, Reader will launch and display any PDF file linked on the Web. When you use Reader as a helper application, page at-a-time downloading, form submittal, search highlighting on the Web, and viewing embedded PDF files are not available.

The free Acrobat Reader has a number of powerful features for document viewing and management. A general info dialog box provides several pertinent items about the document. Preferences can be set for several operations in the Reader, including a text note reading feature. There is a good Find function as well as many page display and navigation options for viewing the document in the Reader.

Netscape Composer

According to Netscape's NetHelp, "The document creation capabilities in Netscape provide both experienced and beginning content creators with a simple yet powerful solution for editing and publishing online documents. What-you-see-is-what-you-get (WYSIWYG) editing allows first-time users to create dynamic online documents easily and publish them to local file systems and remote servers with ease. Some of the many functions you can execute with Netscape Composer (see Figure 16.8) are listed below:

"Work in a WYSIWYG environment. You can see the results of paragraph and font tags applied as you type.

"Add, remove and modify text. Click on any part of a downloaded Web page and immediately work with text and images.

"Drag-and-drop hyperlinks and images from the bookmark, mail, news, or browse windows, to a document in the editor.

"Drag an HTML or image file from the Windows Explorer and drop it in an edit window.

"Publish your documents on Internet. Simplify the process of posting pages to a server by using one button to copy your files from your local hard disk to a remote directory or server.

"Format text to suit your needs. You can apply paragraph and character styles to text just as you would in your favorite word-processing application.

"Change font, font size and color. Use these features to create pages that focus a reader's attention where you want.

"Work with inline images, where the picture appears as part of the Web page or a separate external link that you need to download apart from Web pages. Composer supports GIF (CompuServe Graphics Interchange Format .GIF extension) and JPEG (Joint Photographic Experts Group .JPG extension) formats.

"Tables, useful for presenting information you want to display in a grid."

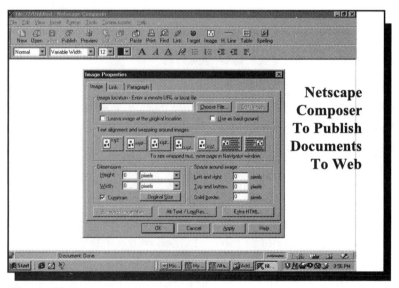

Figure 16.8

Free classes on communication

Netscape Composer's Help provides a wonderful little tutorial on communicating information via Web page creation. In addition to step-by-step help for specific functions, the Help provides explanations of formatting style and HTML basics that not only tell you how to do something in Composer but also what actually can be done that might bear on your specific needs. It even provides an interesting and informative Page Design Basics section. For example, this clear and illuminating item is contained in the HTML Basics portion of Composer Help:

Formatting in HTML documents consists of tags of plain ASCII text instructions enclosed in angle brackets <>. A format area typically uses two tags: one at the beginning and another at the end. For example, to designate a particular line as a heading, you enclose the heading text inside tags that mark the beginning and end:

<H3>Hello World Wide Web!</H3>

The <H3> tag marks the beginning of text to be considered a level 3 heading (Heading 3); the </H3> tag marks the end of the text heading. Instead of the usual manual way of inserting this tag, the Composer lets you automatically apply an H1 format using the drop-down style list on the Paragraph toolbar, or by choosing Paragraph from the Format menu.

Communicating Business Intelligence via CD-ROM

Distribution via the Internet is always preferable to physical distribution of any type of computer file. Speed, cost, and ease of use are the main reasons why the Internet beats other forms of distribution. However, real life being what it is, we don't yet live in an Internet perfect world. CD-ROM distribution of larger files, groups of hypertext linked documents, and even multimedia file is practical, and it may be the only way to widely distribute large amounts of information to out-of-the way corners of the world. And don't forget that you can put audio and video onto a CD-ROM too without the network transmission delays sometimes encountered on the Internet. Figure 16.9 shows an inexpensive CD-ROM writer typical of those costing a few hundred dollars. Mass duplication can be accomplished for as little as $1 per disc.

For the larger organization (or for the small business that needs to distribute information widely) the CD-ROM is a very cost-effective communications tool. It is somewhat secure in that each disc can be physically numbered and a record kept of its distribution. If there are Adobe Acrobat files on the disc the information contained within them is also somewhat secure. Acrobat has basic security features that include password protection for each PDF file. This allows authors to prevent end-users from doing more than read the content. Third-party programs and extensions now are available to enhance the security of Acrobat documents.

CD-ROM writers are now routinely available. Internal devices or external units (good for use with a notebook computer or for mobility) can be purchased for as little as $300. Software is required to "burn" CD-ROMs and work with data on them. Adaptec's DirectCD is a way to write files directly to a CD-Recordable (CD-R) or CD-ReWritable (CD-RW) disc much like you would to a floppy diskette or removable drive. DirectCD provides a file system based on UDF v.1.5 and writes data to the CD-R or CD-RW disc using packet writing technology. This file system gives you drive letter access to your CD-RW drive. The system can format the disc to the ISO 9660 standard. Selecting this option will allow you to read the disc on most standard CD-ROM drives.

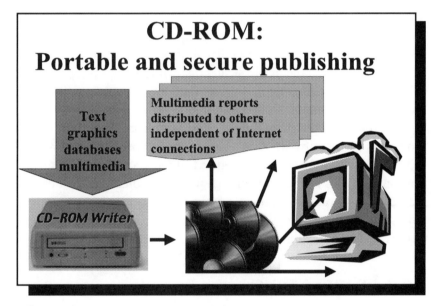

Figure 16.9

Some CD-R duplicators can duplicate up to 24 650-MB data discs in one hour. Add-on towers can extend this capability. Typical prices for a four-CD-ROM duplicator are between $1,500 and $3,000. Printing label information on the CD-ROM can be accomplished with special color printers ranging in price from $500 to $1,000. Standard printers can be used to print special round labels that permit "home-brew" labeling of CD-ROMs. A variety of storage options (plastic jewel case, polypropylene pocket, paper envelope) are available.

If you need large-scale duplication of CD-ROM discs (more than 10 to 15) it's best to use a commercial duplicating service. They charge about $1 to $5 per copy in quantity (100-plus) and duplicators can provide labeling and jewel cases for just a little bit more. Additionally, data conversion vendors provide keyboarding, OCR, imaging, and indexing services. Depending upon the contract you negotiate, large quantities of documents (20,000-plus pages) can be stored on one CD-ROM for business intelligence purposes for a reasonable price.

Reports on diskette

If you want to run a slide show on another computer, you can use PowerPoint's Pack and Go Wizard. The wizard packages together, on a disk, all the files and fonts used in the presentation. When you intend to run your show on a computer that doesn't have PowerPoint installed, it also packages the PowerPoint Viewer on the disk. This can be useful in wide distribution of a presentation by e-mailing the packed file or physically distributing it on floppy disk or CD-ROM. The latter might be required to store a larger file with graphics and multiple hyperlinked documents.

A standard diskette can hold a considerable amount of information even if it is formatted as a self-running PowerPoint presentation. However, the use of embedded objects such as graphics or multimedia files will rapidly enlarge file size. Judicious use of essential graphics, and relying more on hyperlinks and tables, as well as typographic enhancement, will go a long way toward optimizing the report on diskette while keeping its size manageable.

Fax broadcasting

Fax modems and associated software can be used to communicate important information uniformly to a widely dispersed group. This mode of communication is especially useful in reaching people who may not have access to the Internet or even an internal e-mail system. Nearly all computer modems now incorporate fax functions that turn your computer into a fax machine.

One of the leading fax software programs is WinFax PRO from Symantec Corporation. Using WinFax, you can assemble one or more documents (attaching files created in a word processor) on your computer into a single outgoing fax, or create a one-page fax using a cover page. The easiest way to send a fax is to "print" to the fax software and fax modem by setting the printer to Print to Fax in any Windows application. You can send the document as a fax or save it as a fax attachment for future use. One of the most common business intelligence communications tools is the newsletter. You can use your word processor to create the newsletter and WinFax to distribute it.

WinFax reduces faxing time by using compression technology. It also helps you save money on your phone bill by scheduling faxes for off-peak hours or by sending them over the Internet. For the mobile business intelligence professional, the ability to send and receive faxes using a laptop may be very convenient. WinFax PRO permits retrieval of new faxes from the office using WinFax remote retrieval. You also can forward faxes automatically from your office to any fax number. To print a fax or a document you created in a Windows program (for example, a letter), fax it to the hotel front desk, obviating the need to carry a printer for infrequent use.

Here are some of the features that are most suited to business intelligence:

- Combine multiple documents from various programs into one fax.

- Scan a paper document into your computer and fax it.

- Send the same fax to multiple recipients.

- Schedule faxes so they are sent during off-peak hours.

- Send faxes over the Internet using an Internet Fax Service.

- Receive faxes automatically without interrupting your work.

- Forward faxes automatically to your next destination or use remote retrieval.

- Edit faxes you receive by circling text and adding review comments, or by converting them to text you can edit.

- Organize faxes by creating folders, then drag and drop faxes into them.

- Create phonebooks for tracking information about individuals and groups.

- Organize phonebook records for individuals into folders for easy access.

• Use phonebooks from contact managers such as ACT!

According to Symantec, "If you have set up the Internet Fax option in WinFax, you can send faxes over the Internet. When you send faxes to a long distance fax number, this feature may reduce or eliminate the long distance charges you would normally pay. In many cases, the service charges associated with an Internet fax are less expensive than the long distance charges involved with sending a fax. In addition, if you connect to the Internet using a LAN, you do not need a modem to send faxes.

"To send faxes over the Internet, you must establish an Internet connection, either LAN (no modem required) or dial-up (modem required). Set up an Internet Fax Service account using the Internet Fax Setup wizard. You must have a credit card to register for an account as fees are charged to your card when you use this service.

"When you send a fax over the Internet, WinFax connects to the Internet using your account, sends the fax to the Internet fax server closest to the destination of your fax, then sends the fax to the recipient from that location. Billing for Internet Fax services is similar to billing for Internet service providers. You are charged a flat rate for a block of time each month. Each time you send a fax, transmission time is deducted from your monthly allotment."

WinFax Help states, "To check for current fees for Internet Fax services, click the Web Browser button on the WinFax toolbar. If you have a Web browser installed on your computer, the Web browser starts, connects to the appropriate Web site, then displays the current prices. If your modem supports file transfer, you can use WinFax to send the actual data files directly to the recipient, without converting the files to fax images. This type of fax communication is known as Binary File Transfer (BFT). With BFT, WinFax processes and sends events faster to save you time and, in some cases, connection charges. In addition, since your event is not sent as fax images, the recipient does not need to use OCR to work with editable copies of the original files."

If you are really paranoid about who got what and when, you will be happy to know that WinFax keeps track of each fax you send and receive by creating a log record in the logs window. A log record contains the message as well as information about the message. The information available for each log record includes identification of the recipient/sender, delivery date and time, message type (regular fax, Internet fax, BFT, e-mail or voice), transmission status, and other details. These logs can be searched and sorted on-screen and printed or saved as a file. You can also view information about a log record in the display area at the bottom of the logs window.

"WinFax is compliant with extended MAPI 1.0 to provide complete access to Exchange features. From within WinFax, you can send and receive e-mail messages, use your Exchange address book and work in the folders of your Exchange message store. To use Exchange in WinFax, you must enable Exchange in your WinFax setup. From Exchange, you can view your WinFax logs and events, send faxes from the WinFax send dialog and open the Attachments, Cover Pages and Phonebooks windows. To use WinFax in Exchange, add WinFax to your Exchange profile."

There are three types of WinFax phonebooks: WinFax phonebooks allow you to create and manage recipient records directly in WinFax; Linked phonebooks provide read-only access to recipient records created in other programs; Imported phonebooks provide access to recipient records created in other programs or previous versions of WinFax.

Once you have compiled a phonebook of fax recipients, you can create a recipient group by selecting the phonebook in which you want to create the group and using the Create Group dialog. Depending upon the speed of the recipients' fax systems, you can send about 100 one-page faxes in about two hours.

Windows native communications capabilities

Bill Gates wants you to know that Windows is more than a platform for launching computer programs. He'd be proud if you knew about the wide range of functional capability in dozens of useful programs. In the realm of communications, you will find several features that may be of use for your business intelligence communications requirements.

Since we've talked about faxing with WinFAX Pro, we should give Microsoft equal time. Windows comes with a fax program that is much simpler than the full-featured WinFAX. For some, this may be a benefit. If the program is too complicated, many users feel frustrated, particularly those with less time to fiddle than others who can take the time to learn a complicated program or take advantage of numerous features.

Microsoft Fax helps you send and receive fax messages in a simple stand-alone program. You can also send faxes directly from programs you create them in, such as Microsoft Word, utilizing a personal address book with fax numbers and other information. A handy Compose New Fax Wizard (accessible from Start/Accessories/Fax) steps you through the creation of a fax message with or without a cover page. You can select prepared cover pages or create your own.

Another small utility program in Windows is Phone Dialer. It enables you to place telephone calls from your computer by using your modem or another Windows telephony device. In addition to speed-dial buttons, Phone Dialer also maintains a log of who and when you dialed. To select the types of calls to log, click the Log menu and then click Other. You can dial a number from the log and purge log entries.

HyperTerminal is a utility that enables remote access and file transfer, and it can be used to troubleshoot a modem connection. Also, HyperTerminal allows you to capture text or send text to another computer after connecting to it using the program. Another option is "capture to printer," which prints text as it is received.

Briefcase helps keep your files updated when you use two computers. To use Briefcase, you copy the files you want to work on into your laptop Briefcase. Work on the files from your laptop or secondary computer. When you reconnect to your main computer, click Update All, and Briefcase will update the original copies of the files. For information about how to use Briefcase, look up "Briefcase, synchronizing files" in the Help index.

Exchange

Another communications component of Windows is Microsoft Exchange. This feature helps you organize, access, and share all types of information. With Microsoft Exchange, you can:

- Send electronic mail
- Include files and objects created in other applications in your messages

- Use the Address Book to select recipient names

- Create folders where you can store related messages, files, and other items

To open Microsoft Exchange, click the Inbox icon on the desktop. There are many formatting options to help you make your message most effective, including bold, italic, and a choice of fonts. The people you correspond with must also be using Microsoft Exchange or another electronic mail system that is connected to your network.

Before you can use Microsoft Exchange, you must create a profile. Your profile contains essential information, such as the delivery location for your incoming mail and the location of your Address Book. When you start Microsoft Exchange for the first time, you are prompted to create a profile.

To open Microsoft Exchange, click the Start button, point to Programs, and then click Microsoft Exchange. This action displays your folder list. If you open Microsoft Exchange by double clicking the Inbox icon on the desktop, your folder list will not be displayed unless you click Folders on the View menu. When you restart Microsoft Exchange, the last view you selected is displayed.

The Microsoft Exchange Viewer has two display panes. The left side of the Viewer lists your personal folders, and the right side lists the contents of the selected folder. Folders can contain e-mail messages, files created in other applications, faxes, and even messages from other messaging systems, such as online services. The ability to place all types of items in a folder enables you to store related documents, spreadsheets, and messages in a common location. As you read the items in your Inbox, you can reply to, forward, or delete them, or file them in other folders.

Remote communications can be accomplished in Exchange. When working at home or on the road, you can read and reply to mail off-line. Then, if you have a modem and access to a telephone line, you can establish a remote connection to your network, and send and receive e-mail as if you were at your office.

Networking

For those who are concerned with network computing, Windows provides some important components. According to Windows

Help, "A network is a group of two or more computers connected to each other by a cable, over telephone lines, or through wireless communication. When you are connected to a network, you can share resources on your computer, such as documents, programs, printers, and modems, and use resources that other people have shared."

You will need the following network components to set up your computer to use a network: Client software enables you to use resources that have been shared by other people on the network. Service software enables you to share your resources with other network users. File and printer sharing for Microsoft Networks is an example of service software. A network adapter is an expansion card or other device that physically connects your computer to the network. A protocol is the "language" your computer uses to communicate with other computers on the network.

To share a folder or a printer, you can use your right mouse button to click the folder or printer, and then click Sharing on the menu. When you share folders and printers, you can set up a password as the key to opening them, or you can create a list of users that you want to have access to them. If sharing is not enabled, you can turn it on by double clicking the Network icon in Control Panel. There are two ways to control access to your shared resources. Share-level access control enables you to protect your shared resources with a password. User-level access control enables you to specify exactly who has access to your shared resources.

You can use the shortcut keys listed in Table 16.2 to perform common tasks in Microsoft Exchange. Many of these useful, time-saving shortcuts also can be used in other Windows programs.

Sharing corporate knowledge

Until relatively recently, corporate knowledge resided in the minds of executives and on paper filed away in the drawers of filing cabinets. This was an efficient system prior to the information explosion of the past few decades. Today corporate knowledge is stored on diskettes, hard drives, tapes, and optical discs. Making the right information available to the people who need it is one facet of business intelligence. Another important aspect is sharing information among those responsible for generating and using business intelligence.

Table 16.2

TASK	KEYBOARD SHORTCUT
Address Book (open)	CTRL+SHIFT+B
Bold text	CTRL+B
Bullets (on or off)	CTRL+SHIFT+L
Cancel	ESC
Center text	CTRL+E
Check names	CTRL+K
Close the active window, or Microsoft Exchange if the Viewer window is active	ALT+F4
Collapse the selected folder	LEFT ARROW
Copy an item	CTRL+SHIFT+C
Copy text or graphics	CTRL+C
Cut text or graphics	CTRL+X
Delete an item	CTRL+D
Delete character on the left or the selected object	BACKSPACE
Delete character on the right or the selected object	DELETE
Delete word on the left	CTRL+BACKSPACE
Delete word on the right	CTRL+DELETE
Deliver mail	CTRL+M
Expand the selected folder	RIGHT ARROW
Find text	CTRL+SHIFT+F
Forward a message	CTRL+F
Inbox (open)	CTRL+SHIFT+I
Indent text less	CTRL+SHIFT+T
Indent text more	CTRL+T
Italicize text	CTRL+I
Left align text	CTRL+L
Message (new)	CTRL+N
Message (open)	CTRL+O
Move an item	CTRL+SHIFT+M
Move the insertion point one word left	CTRL+LEFT ARROW
Move the insertion point one word right	CTRL+RIGHT ARROW
Move the insertion point to the bottom of the screen	CTRL+PAGE DOWN
Move the insertion point to the end of a message	CTRL+END
Move the insertion point to the end of a paragraph	CTRL+DOWN ARROW
Move the insertion point to the start of a message	CTRL+HOME
Move the insertion point to the start of a paragraph	CTRL+UP ARROW
Move the insertion point to the top of the screen	CTRL+PAGE UP
Move up one folder level in the Viewer	BACKSPACE
Next item (open)	CTRL+>
Outbox (open)	CTRL+SHIFT+O
Paste text or graphics	CTRL+V
Previous item (open)	CTRL+<

Print item	CTRL+P
Properties (display or modify)	ALT+ENTER
Remove text formatting	CTRL+SPACEBAR
Repeat the last find	SHIFT+F4
Replace text	CTRL+H
Reply to all	CTRL+SHIFT+R
Reply to sender of an item	CTRL+R
Right align text	CTRL+G
Save an item	CTRL+S
Save as	F12
Select all	CTRL+A
Send a message	ALT+S
Spelling (checking)	F7
Underline text	CTRL+U
Undo last available action	CTRL+Z

It's been said throughout this book that business intelligence really isn't intelligence unless it is communicated. This means transferring information from one person's head to another. The most traditional of these methods is to present the information face to face.

In-person briefings

Communicating business intelligence via an in-person briefing is best accomplished using a computer-generated presentation via a data projector. Microsoft's PowerPoint is the de facto standard for presentations. PowerPoint gives you the tools to create slides that can be viewed on a computer monitor, projected via a data projector, printed in a variety of formats, or published as a slide show in HTML format.

In other parts of this book, information has been presented to help you better understand some of the more pertinent features of PowerPoint. There are a variety of other excellent programs that help you generate complete slide shows.

Data projector prices have dropped dramatically as dozens of manufacturers jumped into the market in the late 1990s. Today a good data projector for small-group presentations can be purchased for under $3,000 and more powerful projectors (500-plus ANSI lumens) with very high resolution and sophisticated features can be purchased for well under $5,000. Technological advancements likely will continue to push down prices on lower-end or older models of data projectors.

As digital video recorders proliferate and blend with the capabilities of corporate communications, in-person briefings also will include on-screen presentations that have been video taped and inserted into traditional slide shows. Miniaturization and hybridization will eventually move these high performance digital video devices to the desktop, further diminishing the need for in-person meetings.

Live conferencing

The Internet provides incredible capability for communications. E-mail has been the most popular form of communication, but much more is possible. As transmission speeds have increased two-hundred-fold in the past decade from 300 bps in the early 1980s to 56,000 bps, the capability for live conferencing with audio and video has become a reality. Even higher speeds are now common. Residential Integrated Services Digital Network (ISDN) connections provide 128,000 bps for $25 per month in many localities. Digital Subscriber Lines (DSL), where available, turn POTS (plain old telephone service) into high-speed data circuits for a bit more than ISDN. DirectPC satellite dish users can achieve 500,000 bps, while those users with access to cable television system Internet service providers enjoy near T1 speed of 1.5 million bps. With these higher speeds a complex stream of multimedia communication is possible.

We have come to expect rich graphics as an embellishment to our communications. As modem speeds have increased, so too have the sophistication of the images that accompany text. Rich interactive multimedia is becoming the norm. Business intelligence products often require charts or graphs to fully convey important information in an easily digestible manner. As represented in Figure 16.10, the technical capabilities of our Internet connections as well as associated hardware and software are increasing while the overall cost is decreasing. We are able to think in terms of previously cost-prohibitive communications elements. This now includes live video conferencing.

There are thousands of live "Web cam" sites throughout the world. This is an interesting curiosity, but it can serve the business intelligence professional with an added dimension of communications capability. For example, there are dozens of computer cameras that cost between $100 and $200 each. All come with some type of software to operate the camera, and some come with full-featured video conferencing programs such as Microsoft NetMeeting.

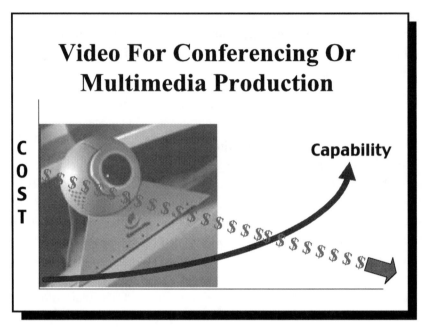

Figure 16.10

Microsoft NetMeeting

One of the earliest conferencing software providers was Microsoft with their NetMeeting package. Microsoft states, "Video is just one of the powerful features of NetMeeting. Its data conferencing features let you collaborate with a group of people from within any 32-bit Windows application—drawing on a shared whiteboard, sending text messages, and transferring files. With many of the same features as Netscape Conference, NetMeeting's realtime audio lets you talk to other people over the Internet or converse while watching live video from one of the conference sites. NetMeeting's video, audio, and data conferencing are all based on industry standards, so you can communicate with people using compatible products."

By default, you are logged on to a directory server when NetMeeting starts. You can change the default directory server. You can also view different directory servers without logging on to a different server or changing your default server.

Only the first two people to participate in the NetMeeting conference will have an audiovisual connection. You can have multiple participants in a NetMeeting conference, but only two can share the audio and video connection at the same time. Only participants who are currently viewing video can switch to another participant. This enhances the security of the Internet portion of the connection.

You can make your address handy for colleagues by sending them a SpeedDial for your computer. On the SpeedDial menu, click Add SpeedDial, type your computer's address, and then select the protocol you want people to use to call you. To send a SpeedDial to people, you can send a message with the SpeedDial embedded. You can put a SpeedDial someone has sent you in your SpeedDial folder within the NetMeeting folder.

You can run NetMeeting in the background so it will run when Windows starts and notify you of incoming calls. This could be handy if you want to hold a meeting but, as always, everyone shows up at different times. You can monitor for calls too, and in some cases, particularly in the case of far-flung collaborators overseas, you are available for no-cost casual contact calls.

Conference ware

While Netscape and Microsoft have confronted each other in many areas, including conferencing, other developers have been working on similar software. WebBoard by O'Reilly Software (**www.webboard.oreilly.com**) is a Web conferencing package. WebBoard is an enterprise-class threaded discussion and chat server with 1,000-user IRC Chat, SQL database support, and per-board traffic logs.

Another approach is to build a virtual office via a private intranet hosted by a third-party service provider. Netscape Virtual Office by Concentric enables individuals, small businesses, and project teams to quickly, easily, and economically establish and run private intranets regardless of location, computer type, or operating system. Excite launched an audio conferencing feature in mid-1999.

Business intelligence briefing procedure

Just what constitutes a regular program of business intelligence communication? The following is a general overview of the possibilities.

A major report could consist of 40 to 60 slides in a Microsoft PowerPoint presentation that covers the subject(s) as directed by top management. In addition to the standard black and white printout in binder, the PowerPoint format .ppt file on diskette also can be included with the handout. For those without PowerPoint on their computers, a CD-ROM version with the Microsoft PowerPoint Viewer (a 1.8-MB stand-alone viewer for free distribution) can be distributed.

This same presentation can be delivered at multiple locations simultaneously through the use of Netscape Conference or NetMeeting via the Internet. This software allows the meeting facilitator to conduct Q&A during and after the program. This can be recorded and used in training videos or other multimedia productions, including posting to the intranet.

Building on the initial PowerPoint file, additional presentations of recorded material can be scheduled and "broadcast" via the Internet. Also, development of interactive CD-ROM briefing can be put together at very low cost. Material from the briefing also could be used for training purposes (e.g., employee orientation) as appropriate.

Many organizations have personnel at various locations. A CD-ROM or Internet-accessible .ppt file provides them the capability to view updates of corporate policy or new developments at their leisure. In fact these can be scheduled for production and distribution on a regular basis—weekly, monthly, bimonthly, or quarterly—to augment employee, dealer, representative, or even customer communications.

Wireless communications

Staying in touch has never been easier. During the later 1990s, a proliferation of wireless alphanumeric devices flooded the consumer marketplace. Mass-market volume drove prices down and in some cases stimulated the development and introduction of new types of communications tools. With wireless services and the Internet, it's now possible to video conference from anywhere to anywhere without wires. Figure 16.11 illustrates hardware (radio and modem PCMCIA cards and tiny video camera) as well as a block diagram of Bell Atlantic's Cellular Digital Packet Data wireless Internet service.

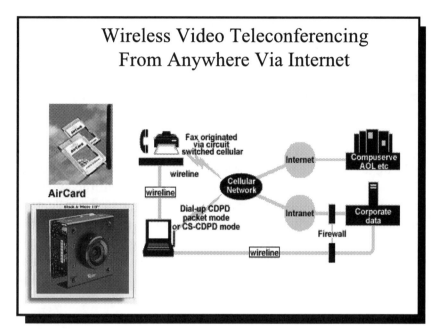

Figure 16.11

AT&T Wireless Services, like many other telecom services, provides a Web page for anyone to send a message to a digital PCS phone, alphanumeric pager, or other mobile computing communications devices offered by AT&T. Messages typed into a field on the Web page are routed through the Internet to the device the customer is carrying. Usually the phone number of the receiving device is the first part of the address with the second part something like @mobile.att.net. Short messages (usually up to 100 characters) can be transmitted directly from any computer. Some systems even let you create an address book. This leads us to the potential Internet Business Intelligence application.

Nationwide paging services can send the same message to all subscribers addressed by a message sent via the system. This means that one-half of a two-way communications link can be established at very low cost. The other half of the link is free, except for the price of a phone call. Consider the situation of an executive who realizes that much business intelligence is locked up inside his employees' heads. How do you access this wealth of knowledge, particularly during periods of intense need for details that may be well known to one or two individuals?

Setting up a system in which an Internet-dispatched message is sent to some or all of the executive's employees may be the answer. If you have 50 field reps scattered across the country, why not issue them an alphanumeric pager or alphanumeric-capable digital wireless phone? One query can be sent to some or all instantly, and one or more field reps could respond to the question by calling in to the executive's office via a toll-free telephone line.

One of the biggest obstacles to this type of system is some peoples' distaste for the particular technology or the reluctance to use the system. A solution to that problem could be in the award of money or other prizes weekly or monthly for the best application of the system. Further, all members of this intelligence network could participate, not just the top-down queries from mahogany row. Finally, a weekly broadcast e-mail could be sent to all network members to summarize the best applications during the past week.

Wireless Internet video

Wireless Internet video combines long-range wireless transmission and the Internet to remotely view video from anywhere in the world. It is a low-cost combination of computer hardware, software, and Internet service enabling you to set up and operate a small battery-powered, remotely viewable video camera in just about any situation ranging from a conference room to a hotel room—even the back seat of an automobile.

Logitech's family of digital video cameras, along with a variety of other manufacturers' offerings, are available for all popular personal computer platforms and interface standards. A well-known, low-cost unit is QuickCam. Most are priced under $200. With this type of video source connected to the computer, usually through the parallel port, the computer is connected to the Internet. Normally this is accomplished by plugging a phone line into the computer's modem. In this case, for mobility, we're using radio to make the link.

The Sierra Wireless AirCard combo is representative of the hardware necessary for a wireless connection. This set of two Type II PCMCIA cards is packaged to offer circuit switched cellular and packet data (CDPD) functions. The wireless CDPD PCMCIA card links a notebook computer directly to the Internet via a CDPD Internet service provider. The AirCard radio specifications include transmit 824 to 849 MHz; receive 869 to 894 MHz; power output 600 mW; power consumption: 5v, sleep typical <0.5 mA, maximum 5mA, transmit typical 500 mA, maximum 650 mA, sleep 3 mA.

The AirCard's software, Watcher, is a Windows application that configures and monitors the modems for CDPD, circuit switched cellular, and wireline operation. Watcher has a setup dialog that lets you verify the modem connection to the COM port and the basic configuration strings for circuit-switched cellular and wireline operation. AirCard is plug-and-play CDPD and also allows you to access your regular e-mail (Microsoft Exchange, cc:Mail, Eudora, etc.) without different "wireless" e-mail addresses.

Bell Atlantic Mobile (BAM) is a Regional Bell Operating Company in the Northeast U.S. that provides a wireless service called Airbridge. This CDPD System overlays the cellular voice network to provide a wireless extension of existing packet data networks. It provides secure wireless packet data connectivity (19.2 kilobits/sec) and is based on industry-standard Internet Protocol (IP). CDPD encodes all data into digital transmission bursts (packets) and transfers these bursts over the air securely and efficiently using a forward error-correction scheme in all data transmissions.

BAM was the first cellular carrier to offer commercial CDPD service in April 1994. The company now has commercial service in the New York metropolitan area, New Jersey, Connecticut, Massachusetts, Pittsburgh, the greater Philadelphia area, the Washington and Baltimore metropolitan areas, and North and South Carolina. They are establishing relationships with other CDPD carriers to provide clients with nationwide CDPD services. At 19.2 kbps, CDPD is considerably faster than other packet radio data network operators that offer Internet access. However, CDPD availability is not complete. In addition to BAM, Ameritech, AT&T, Cellular One, and GTE Mobilnet also provide the service, and others, such as RadioMail Corp. in San Jose, likely will in the future.

Once you've actually connected the transmission point computer and camera to the Internet, you need to connect to the receiving computer. This can be accomplished using Microsoft NetMeeting on both computers.

This chapter has encompassed a great deal of material ranging from clarity of written communications through various means with which to communicate the information. The Internet has opened the door to endless communications possibilities. New technology will continue to advance the technical capabilities, but business intelligence is, has been, and always will be founded on ages-old principles of logic, analysis, and communication.

Endnotes

1. Michael C. Thomsett, *The Little Black Book of Business Reports* (Amacom, New York,1988).

2. Campbell, Ballou, Slade, *Form and Style*, sixth edition (Houghton Mifflin Company, Boston,1982).

CHAPTER 17

POTENTIAL PROBLEMS AND PITFALLS

The United States became a world power because of its ability to produce tangible things, but the 21st century will see an emphasis on creating information products—whether they are stories or images, insurance policies or brokerage accounts, manufacturing operations software or package tracking databases. These information products and the knowledge behind them are computerized and, in many cases, connected to the Internet. Theoretically at least, it is possible for anyone anywhere to steal these assets using computer technology.

Most larger companies have a formal, clearly articulated internal policy designed to protect against loss of their own privileged information. This usually applies to employees as well as management and may include former employees and managers. Some apply the same standards to suppliers. Policies can cover such situations as media interviews and association memberships. Companies that employ scientists have an even greater challenge when it comes to publication of research in journals. While this is necessary, it is often tempered by demands of lawyers protecting the company's intellectual property or others who see a competitive threat to revealing certain types of scientific information.

Because of privacy concerns and possible litigation, few companies routinely monitor their employee communications. However, letters, e-mail, and faxes not only have potential for information leaks, they also can create liability for the company if the employee runs afoul of the law, especially in the realm of harassment.

Much has been written about the Internet's alleged "dark side." Tabloid hysteria hypes a few isolated incidents to sell more papers or boost ratings. There are pornographic pictures and words in great abundance. But, there are many corner stores selling similar magazines and videos. There are Internet connections that enable law breakers to link up electronically. This bears monitoring by the appropriate authorities. There are various commercial offerings in the caveat emptor category, the most irritating of which is mounting "junk e-mail." Finally, there are issues of privacy that may even bear on use of the Internet for investigations. Prudent use of this powerful tool can yield dramatic results in a legal and ethical way.

When establishing an Internet Business Intelligence System (IBIS), part of the process should include consideration of information protection. Given the overwhelming emphasis on "competitor intelligence" during the 1990s, there is little hope that we will see a "kinder and gentler" business environment emerging any time soon. In fact, the United States government has for some time been preparing for "information warfare." Policies are not enough. Active measures including awareness programs and physical security also are required because the threat is real.

Author James F. Dunnigan writes, "You, your bank and the Department of Defense use the same phone lines. Sure, you can send the data in a secret code (encrypted), but these codes can be broken. Everyone who uses networked computers is vulnerable. Exploiting that vulnerability is largely what information warfare is all about."[1]

In 1811 Francis Cabot Lowell of Massachusetts visited England and walked off with a very big piece of the Industrial Revolution: the Cartwright loom.[2] Today's battlefield is economic and, similar to what the United States as an emerging did in the early 19th century, our friends and former enemies may now be hollowing out our economy.

Despite our inauspicious start as typified by Lowell, Americans lead the world in high technology. From Russia's alleged shopping tours for U.S. secrets to China's clever use of U.S. campuses, companies, and consumers to modernize its military, we may be facing a slow but steady bleeding of knowledge needed to remain competitive in the world marketplace. Some experts assert that an economic war is underway.[3]

In 1997 the U.S. Department of Justice, United States Attorney for the Eastern District of Pennsylvania prosecuted a case relating to the attempted theft of trade secrets from Bristol-Myers Squibb. The trade secrets involved the manufacturing processes for Tactual, a cancer-fighting pharmaceutical. This case involved mail fraud, conspiracy to commit commercial bribery, foreign travel to commit commercial bribery, conspiracy to steal trade secrets, and attempted theft of trade secrets. This was just one of many cases investigated or prosecuted by the United States government.

FBI director Louis J. Freeh testified before the Senate Select Committee on Intelligence and Senate Committee on the Judiciary, Subcommittee on Terrorism, Technology and Government Information hearing on Economic Espionage, February 28, 1996. In part, he said, "The development and production of proprietary economic information is an integral part of virtually every aspect of United States trade, commerce and business and, hence, is essential to maintaining the health and competitiveness of critical segments of the United States economy. The theft, misappropriation, and wrongful receipt, transfer, and use of United States proprietary economic information, particularly by foreign governments and their agents and instrumentalities, but also by domestic malefactors, directly threatens the development and production of that information and, hence, directly imperils the health and competitiveness of our economy.

"The ever increasing value of proprietary economic information in the global and domestic marketplaces, and the corresponding spread of technology, have combined to significantly increase both the opportunities and motives for conducting economic espionage. As a consequence, foreign governments, through a variety of means, actively target U.S. persons, firms, industries and the U.S. government itself, to steal or wrongfully obtain critical technologies, data, and information in order to provide their own industrial sectors with a competitive advantage. Similarly, theft or misappropriation of proprietary economic information by domestic thieves has also increased.

"Since the initiation of the FBI's Economic Counterintelligence Program, the FBI has seen a 100 percent increase in the number of economic espionage-related investigative matters, involving 23 countries. This increase is primarily due to recent changes in the FBI's counterintelligence program and the concomitant emphasis on resources and initiatives, but it also demonstrates that the problem is not a small one." In mid-1999 the FBI announced a reorganization of its intelligence functions.

FBI's ANSIR

For the past several years the FBI has coordinated with the private sector a program called Awareness of National Security Issues and Response (ANSIR). It is the FBI's National Security Awareness Program, the "public voice" of the FBI for espionage, counterintelligence, counterterrorism, economic espionage, cyber and physical infrastructure protection, and all national security issues.

According to the FBI, the program is designed to provide unclassified national security threat and warning information to U.S. corporate security directors and executives, law enforcement, and other government agencies. It also focuses on the "response" capability unique to the FBI's jurisdiction in both law enforcement and counterintelligence investigations. Information is disseminated nationwide via the ANSIR-Email and ANSIR-FAX networks. Each of the FBI's 56 field offices has an ANSIR coordinator and is equipped to provide national security threat and awareness information on a regular basis to corporate recipients within their jurisdiction. Theft of U.S. technology and sensitive economic information by foreign intelligence services and competitors has been estimated by the White House and others to be valued up to a hundred billion dollars annually. Critical infrastructure protection, both cyber and physical, is also a major focus of the FBI, and the ANSIR program helps to identify these infrastructures and ensure that communication with the FBI is established.

Each ANSIR coordinator in the FBI's 56 field offices is a member of the American Society for Industrial Security. This membership enhances public/private sector communication and cooperation for the mutual benefit of both. FBI ANSIR coordinators meet regularly with industry leaders and security directors for updates on current national security issues.

The ANSIR program focuses on the "techniques of espionage" when relating national security awareness information to industry. Discussing techniques allows us to be very specific in giving industry representatives tangible information to help them decide their own vulnerabilities. These techniques include compromise of industry information through "dumpster diving" where Foreign Intelligence

Services and competitors may try to obtain corporate proprietary information, or listening devices that may be as simple as using a police scanner to tune in the frequency of the wireless microphone being used in the corporate boardroom. Through the ANSIR program and the discussion of techniques of espionage, corporations are able to learn from the experiences of others enabling them to avoid adverse results.

Along with awareness, the ANSIR program provides information about the FBI's unique "response" capability with regard to issues of national security. The FBI has primary jurisdiction for a variety of criminal and counterintelligence investigations that impact on national security. For instance, the recent passage of the Economic Espionage Act of 1996 opened up new areas of FBI response to the wrongful acquisition of intellectual property. It also encourages corporations to consider how best to protect their proprietary information or trade secrets from both domestic and foreign theft.

National security threat list

The FBI's foreign counterintelligence mission has set out a strategy known as the National Security Threat List (NSTL). The NSTL combines two elements: First, it includes national security threat issues regardless of the country of origin. Second, it includes a classified list of foreign powers that pose a strategic intelligence threat to U.S. security interests.

Economic espionage concerns foreign-power-sponsored or foreign-power-coordinated intelligence activity directed at the U.S. government or U.S. corporations, establishments, or persons, which involves the unlawful or clandestine targeting or acquisition of sensitive financial, trade, or economic policy information; proprietary economic information; critical technologies; or the unlawful or clandestine targeting or influencing of sensitive economic policy decisions.

Targeting the National Information Infrastructure concerns facilities, personnel, information, or computer, cable, satellite, or telecommunications systems that are associated with the National Information Infrastructure. Proscribed intelligence activities include denial or disruption of computer, cable, satellite, or telecommunications services; unauthorized monitoring or disclosure of proprietary or classified information and unauthorized modification or destruction of computer programming codes, computer network databases, stored information or computer capabilities; or manipulation of computer, cable, satellite or telecommunications services resulting in fraud, financial loss, or other federal criminal violations.

Targeting the U.S. government concerns foreign-power-sponsored or foreign-power-coordinated intelligence activity directed at the U.S. government or U.S. corporations, establishments, or persons, which involves the targeting of government programs, information, or facilities or the targeting of personnel of the U.S. intelligence community; foreign affairs or economic affairs community; or defense establishment and related activities of national preparedness.

Another area is "perception management." This issue concerns foreign-power-sponsored or foreign-power-coordinated intelligence activity directed at the U.S. government or U.S. corporations, establishments, or persons, which involves manipulating information, communicating false information, or propagating deceptive information and communications designed to distort the perception of the public (domestically or internationally) or of U.S. government officials regarding U.S. policies, ranging from foreign policy to economic strategies.

Foreign Intelligence Activities concerns actions against the United States government or U.S. corporations, establishments, or persons, which is not described by or included in the other issue threats.

An amendment to Title 18, U.S.C., Section 3071, authorizes the Attorney General to make payment for information of espionage activity in any country, which leads to the arrest and conviction of any person(s) for commission of an act of espionage against the United States, for conspiring or attempting to commit an act of espionage against the United States, or which leads to the prevention or frustration of an act of espionage against the United States.

Economic espionage

Our allies have spied on us in various sectors, so our adversaries undoubtedly have done so even more than them. This too is supported by facts, some in the form of successful federal prosecutions under the Economic Espionage Act (Figure 17.1).

Although it's been around in some form since at least Old Testament times, economic espionage has proliferated because of the importance of technological data and its ease of transport. There are many factors in the rise of this illegal activity, not the least is U.S. policy with regard to visas that allow foreign students to dominate the technological side of our academic institutions. However, it's clear that the ease with which information flows today facilitates the transfer of any type of information including trade secrets.

The Economic Espionage Act of 1996

- **Title 18 USC amended to protect proprietary economic information**
- **Insertion of Chapter 90, Protection of Trade Secrets**
- **Sections cover economic espionage, theft of trade secrets, exceptions, criminal forfeiture, orders to preserve confidentiality and other elements**
- **Penalty is up to 15 years imprisonment, up to $10 million fine for corporations**

Figure 17.1

A significant development, no doubt brought about by increasingly intense competition from foreign competitors, is the passage of the Economic Espionage Act of 1996. It amended title 18 of the United States Code to protect proprietary economic information. Title 18 was amended by inserting Chapter 90—Protection of Trade Secrets.

The law states, "Whoever, intending or knowing that the offense will benefit any foreign government, foreign instrumentality, or foreign agent, knowingly steals, or without authorization appropriates, takes, carries away, or conceals, or by fraud, artifice, or deception obtains a trade secret; without authorization copies, duplicates, sketches, draws, photographs, downloads, uploads, alters, destroys, photocopies, replicates, transmits, delivers, sends, mails, communicates, or conveys a trade secret; receives, buys, or possesses a trade secret, knowing the same to have been stolen or appropriated, obtained, or converted without authorization; attempts to commit any offense described in any of paragraphs (1) through (3); or (5) conspires with one or more other persons to commit any offense described in any of paragraphs (1) through (3), and one or more of such persons do any act to effect the object of the conspiracy, shall, except as provided in subsection (b), be fined not more than $500,000 or imprisoned not more than 15 years, or both. Any organization that commits any offense described in subsection (a) shall be fined not more than $10,000,000."

In essence, the law appears to prohibit the acquisition of many types of trade secrets and perhaps other closely held business information. The impact of this law on the practice of illegal forms of BI will be examined in the courts during the next few years. An enormous amount of information is publicly available and, if developed and used intelligently, can provide effective business intelligence without the need to resort to illegal practices.

Information security

There are three main aspects of information security: confidentiality, integrity, and availability. These protect against the unauthorized disclosure, modification, or destruction of information. The focus of a background paper and the OTA report "Information Security and Privacy in Network Environments" (September 1994) that it supplements, is technical and institutional measures to ensure the confidentiality and integrity of unclassified electronic information in networks, not the security of the networks themselves.

The term confidentiality refers to disclosure of information only to authorized individuals, entities, and so forth. Privacy refers to the social balance between an individual's right to keep information confidential and the societal benefit derived from sharing information, and how this balance is codified to give individuals the means to control personal information. The terms are not mutually exclusive: safeguards that help ensure confidentiality of information can be used to protect personal privacy.

The term safeguard, as in "information safeguards" or "to safeguard information," should be differentiated from security. This is to avoid misunderstandings regarding use of the term "security," which some readers may interpret in terms of classified information or as excluding measures to protect personal privacy. In discussion of information safeguards, the focus is on technical and institutional measures to ensure the confidentiality and integrity of the information, and also the authenticity of its origin.

Codes and ciphers

Cryptography can be used to fulfill these functions for electronic information. Modern encryption techniques, for example, can be used to safeguard the confidentiality of the contents of a message (or a stored file). Integrity is used to refer to the property that the information has not been subject to unauthorized or unexpected changes. Authenticity refers to the property that the message or information comes from the stated source or origin. Message authentication techniques and digital signatures based on cryptography can be used to ensure the integrity of the message (that it has been received exactly as it was sent) and the authenticity of its origin (that it comes from the stated source).

During the long history of paper-based "information systems" for commerce and communication, a number of safeguards were developed to ensure the confidentiality, integrity, and authenticity of documents and messages. These traditional safeguards included secret code books and passwords, physical "seals" to authenticate signatures, and auditable bookkeeping procedures. Mathematical analogs of these safeguards are implemented in the electronic environment. The most powerful of these are based on cryptography.

The recorded history of cryptography is more than 4,000 years old. Manual encryption methods using code books, letter and number substitutions, and transpositions have been used for hundreds of years—for example, the Library of Congress has letters from Thomas Jefferson to James Madison containing encrypted passages. Modern, computer-based cryptography and cryptanalysts began in the World War II era, with the successful Allied computational efforts to break the ciphers generated by the German Enigma machines, and with the British Colossus computing machines used to analyze a crucial cipher used in the most sensitive German teletype messages.

In the post-WWII era, the premiere locus of U.S. cryptographic has been the Defense Department's National Security Agency (NSA). NSA's preeminent position results from its extensive role in U.S. signals intelligence and in securing classified communications, and the resulting need to understand cryptography as a tool to protect information and as a tool used by adversaries. In its modern setting, cryptography is a field of applied mathematics/computer science. Cryptographic algorithms—specific techniques for transforming the original input into a form that is unintelligible without special knowledge of some secret (closely held) information—are used to encrypt and decrypt messages, data, or other text. The encrypted text is often referred to as ciphertext; the original or decrypted text is often referred to as plaintext or cleartext.

In modern cryptography, the secret information is the cryptographic key that "unlocks" the ciphertext and reveals the plaintext. The encryption algorithms and decryption keys are different and one of them can be made public. With the advent of "public-key" techniques, cryptography also came into use for digital signatures that are of widespread interest as a means for electronically authenticating and signing commercial transactions like purchase orders, tax returns, and funds transfers, as well as ensuring that unauthorized changes or errors are detected.

Cryptanalysis is the study and development of various "code-breaking" methods to deduce the contents of the original plaintext message. The strength of an encryption algorithm is a function of the number of steps, storage, and time required to break the cipher and read any encrypted message, without prior knowledge of the key. Mathematical advances, advances in cryptanalysts, and advances in computing all can reduce the security afforded by a cryptosystem that was previously considered "unbreakable" in practice. The strength of a modern encryption scheme is determined by the algorithm itself and the length of the key.[4]

Rules of conduct

Victorian values of a profound social conscience and a formal adherence to strict standards of personal and social morality began forming around 1800.[5] Ethics, or agreements about codes of personal and interpersonal conduct, has been a subject of philosophers since time immemorial. Business transactions, so deeply imbedded in trust and confidence in one's fellows, have been an integral part of this search for guides to conduct beyond the question of legal boundaries.[6] In our time, professional societies have created commonly accepted codes of conduct.

For example, the Society of Competitive Intelligence Professionals promulgates the following Code of Ethics for CI Professionals:

- To continually strive to increase recognition and respect for the profession

- To comply with all applicable laws, domestic and international

- To accurately disclose all relevant information, including one's identity and organization, prior to all interviews

- To fully respect all requests for confidentiality of information

- To avoid conflicts of interest in fulfilling one's duties

- To provide honest and realistic recommendations and conclusions in the execution of one's duties

- To promote this code of ethics within one's company, with third-party contractors, and within the entire profession

- To faithfully adhere to and abide by one's company's policies, objectives, and guidelines

According to SCIP, "Espionage is the use of illegal means to gather information. In fact, economic espionage represents a failure of CI. Almost all the information a CI professional needs can be collected by examining published information sources, conducting interviews, and using other legal, ethical methods. Using a variety of analytical tools, a skilled CI professional can fill by deduction any gaps in information already gathered. Promoting CI as a discipline bound by a strict code of ethics and practiced by trained professionals is the paramount goal of the Society.

"The term counterintelligence describes the steps an organization takes to protect information sought by 'hostile' intelligence gatherers. One of the most effective counterintelligence measures is to define 'trade secret' information relevant to the company and control its dissemination.

"CI is not spying. It isn't necessary to use illegal or unethical methods in CI. In fact, doing so is a failure of CI, because almost everything decision makers need to know about the competitive environment can be discovered using legal, ethical means. The information that can't be found with research can be deduced with good analysis, which is just one of the ways CI adds value to an organization. By joining SCIP, a member agrees to abide by the Society's code of ethics. The code of ethics forbids breaching an employer's guidelines, breaking the law, or misrepresentation."

Endnotes

1. James F. Dunnigan, *Digital Soldiers: The Evolution of High-Tech Weaponry and Tomorrow's Brave New Battlefield* (St. Martin's Press, New York, 1966:277).

2. John J. Fialka, *War by Other Means: Economic Espionage in America* (W.W. Norton & Company, New York, 1997).

3. Fialka.

4. U.S. Congress, Office of Technology Assessment, "Issue Update on Information Security and Privacy in Network Environments," Boxes 1-1 and 2-1, OTA-BP-ITC-147 (Washington, DC: U.S. Government Printing Office, June 1995).

5. Wren, Daniel A., *The Evolution of Management Thought*, second edition (John Wiley & Sons, New York, 1979:67).

6. Fialka, page 452.

CHAPTER 18

REFLECTIONS

The Internet as a technological facilitator of knowledge management goes nowhere without motivation. The spark of intuition or insight drives us forward in pursuit of a goal, and in business at least one of those goals is usually to make a profit. Despite what we may have learned in the later half of the 20th century, making a profit is not sinful. God helps us to be successful so that we can execute His will here on earth. That means having the resources to do things like employ people (directly and indirectly), create quality products and services, and to share His Word with others.

Societal forces subtly shape and direct motivation, but certain truisms remain. There is a powerful magnetism that draws large chunks of society in specific directions. Those who artfully resist the pull may or may not be lucky enough to be rewarded with success in life beyond the ordinary. The 21st century begins with a revolution in the capability to create, use, and share knowledge. If we assume that the nature of man is good, we can rejoice in the knowledge that we can do this to express ourselves and to connect with others for good purposes. In business this means finding resources (to produce) and markets (to sell).

The journey from initial idea or concept to success in business can today be accomplished in the new world of cyberspace. As the 20th century drew to a close, millions of new enterprises all over the globe were setting up shop in this new world. Many more millions of individuals were venturing into this new world to find entertainment, knowledge, and human connection, as well as goods and services. Perhaps two-thirds of the world's population in developed countries has yet to take part in this new experience.

There is a bit of the explorer in nearly all of us. To one degree or another many of us are willing to trod the unfamiliar path. The inherent conflict is that we also want to consistently make the right decisions at the right times. Wrong decisions from time to time are an opportunity to learn and re-target our processes. For us this process must be facilitated with a fresh supply of ideas from which insights can be derived.

This may be one of the greatest contributions of the Internet in support of commerce. Both buyer and seller need to be able to understand the world and interact in a mutually beneficial way. In the process, markets are created. This analogy can be used to imagine the future of the Internet in the context of business intelligence.

As technology has advanced, the sophistication of information flow has increased. Samuel F. B. Morse tapped out signals that were transmitted by electrical impulses to the receiver. Those electrons traveled at the speed of light, the same speed they travel via the Internet. Our ever-more-sophisticated methods of sending and receiving those impulses leads us, nearly two centuries later, from simple clicks to more complex clicks. The telegrapher's key has been replaced with a "mouse" and a point-and-click technique that likely will be with us for a long time. The finger action today unleashes a more potent stream of information. Where it took many clicks of the telegraph key to transmit a single sentence, a single click of the mouse button can initiate the transfer of volumes of multimedia information limited only by our ability to comprehend, understand, and use it. So, there are essentially two areas for potential advancement: One is the technological and the other is human ability.

Technologically speaking, we can be certain that "more-better-faster" will continue to be the operative phrase. Computer processors, Internet connections, and related hardware and software will advance to beckon us forward. Two-way video is becoming commonplace, and record companies are moving from racks of plastic in expensive stores to stacks of CD-ROMs on consumers' computer tables. In many cases the middleman is disappearing, and in some cases he is reappearing in cyberspace.

In some cases this is a good thing, but in others, where little real value is added, it is not and probably will be transitory. It takes an entrepreneur to stake out a location in cyberspace and convince others to take up residence there. The creation of a market like this is a good thing and this middleman is to be congratulated. However, there are those who do little more than resell at a high profit. Effective use of the Internet is making this harder to do as producer and consumer are being brought together more efficiently in cyberspace.

As this new world becomes more populated, the human capacity to find things within it diminishes and requires technological means to locate the desired address in cyberspace. New and better methods of finding things will be one of the bigger challenges in the 21st century. But simply finding things is just half of the battle. The other is digesting the information so that it can be used in a meaningful way. Here too, technological advances similar in importance to the introduction of HTML and browsers will enable people to acquire and use larger quantities of more dense information.

All of these technological advances are to no good end if they are not utilized, however. It all comes back to motivation and desire. These most basic of human characteristics drive our seeking, and we must think about the world in meaningful ways. There are at least two reactions to advancing technology. One is to embrace it and the other is to not embrace it, for a variety of reasons. There are those who are flatly afraid of it, others who are intimidated by it, and still others are suspicious of it. The latter may have good reason to be suspicious, as there will always be bad people wanting to take advantage of others by whatever means are available to them.

The first two reasons not to embrace new technology can and should be addressed. Why are people afraid and intimidated? Could it be that someone has told them they are not smart enough to harness technology, or do they simply feel inferior to others that do? Those who avoid the Internet and related computer technologies may do so out of choice, seeking to simplify their lives. They of course have this right, but others whose choice is made for them by outside influences or negative self-esteem must understand that they will be at a disadvantage unless they take the necessary steps to exploit new capabilities.

This may be the most important notion of all when considering the Internet and business intelligence or, more broadly, knowledge management. Understanding and addressing the human needs of individuals whose lives can benefit, in all sorts of ways, from the Internet's vast sources and methods of knowledge management may itself become an important discipline. Involving more people in the educational, informational, and commercial aspects of the Internet can only benefit business and society in general.

GLOSSARY

10K. Annual report filed with the U.S. Securities and Exchange Commission by companies with publicly traded stock. It provides a comprehensive overview of the registrant's business. The report must be filed within 90 days after the end of the company's fiscal year. (For a complete list of the many required forms and reports that public companies must file, see the SEC's Web site.)

Abstract. One or two concise paragraphs that describe a much longer article.

Activity-based costing. Focuses on activities as the fundamental cost objects.

American Standard Code for Information Interchange (ASCII). Character set consisting of 96 upper- and lowercase letters plus 32 non-printing control characters to achieve uniformity in communication between differing computers. An extended 256-character set is stored in read-only memory.

Asynchronous Transfer Mode (ATM). Data is transmitted in the form of 53-byte units called cells. Each cell consists of a 5-byte header and a 48-byte payload. Cells from any one source need not be periodically spaced within the overall cell stream. Users are not assigned a set position in a recurring frame as is common in circuit switching.

Awareness of National Security Issues and Response (ANSIR). A Federal Bureau of Investigation program to combat industrial espionage by foreign powers.

Bandwidth. A measurement of speed or capacity of a communications channel measured in frequency (cycles per second expressed as Hertz) or amount (bits per second).

Benchmarking. A formal process used to study a similar company to understand best practices. Used in total quality management and applicable to business intelligence.

408 Internet Business Intelligence

Bit. Basic unit of information in binary numbering system. The binary digits 1 and 0 correspond to electrical on or off conditions. See Byte.

Bookmarks. A convenient means of filing Web page addresses for retrieval. Bookmarks are stored in a list within the browser by clicking on Favorites (Internet Explorer) or dragging the Netsite bookmark icon to Bookmark Quick File icon (Netscape Navigator).

Boolean logic. An algebraic system of logic named after the 19th-century English mathematician George Boole. Operators include NEAR, then NOT, then AND, then OR. Usually used to create search queries.

Bulletin Board System. When modem-equipped microcomputers became available to the general public, software was written that allowed a computer to automatically connect to another via telephone line for the purpose of reading text or exchanging files.

Business Intelligence (BI). The activity of monitoring the environment external to the firm for relevant information for incorporation into decision making. A broad term that includes areas of endeavor such as competitive intelligence, market research, economic analysis, operations research, and other disciplines to assist management in decision making and strategy development.

Byte. A string of bits that make up one keystroke in a personal computer. See Bit.

CD-Recordable (CD-R). A thin 4.75-inch plastic disc that can be written to one or more times but cannot be rewritten. Holds up to 650 MB of data.

CD-ReWritable (CD-RW). A thin 4.75-inch plastic disc that can be written to one or more times. It can be rewritten, holding up to 650 MB of data.

CD-ROM. Compact Disc, Read Only Memory permits reading and writing via laser light of about 650 megabytes of information on an inexpensive disc.

Circuit switched cellular and packet data (CDPD). One format for data via wireless communication.

Comma delimited file (CSV). Also known as comma separated values file, a standard ASCII file used to form records that can be imported into most database programs.

Competitive (Competitor) Intelligence (CI). A subset of business intelligence that closely examines the history and current capabilities of competitors to predict their behavior from which strategy can be developed.

Conference Board. Headquartered in New York City, a membership association made up primarily of executives from large corporations.

Conference ware. Software that enables several users in remote locations to communicate simultaneously. In its simplest form, users type information for each other to see and respond to, but more complex functions such as sharing document editing or video conferencing are possible.

Control key. In the IBM-compatible world this is a separate key usually marked "Ctrl" and pressed in conjunction with another key to initiate a function.

Copyright Fair Use. In United States Code Title 17—Copyrights, Chapter 1—Subject Matter And Scope Of Copyright, Section 107—Limitations on exclusive rights. Fair Use states: The fair use of a copyrighted work, including such use by reproduction in copies or phonorecords or by any other means specified by that section, for purposes such as criticism, comment, news reporting, teaching (including multiple copies for classroom use), scholarship, or research, is not an infringement of copyright.

Cryptography. Encryption techniques used to safeguard the confidentiality of information and data. Cryptography is a field of applied mathematics/computer science that uses cryptographic algorithms to transform the original input into a form that is unintelligible without special knowledge of secret (closely held) information. Used to encrypt and decrypt messages, data, or other text.

Customer intelligence. Useful information garnered from customers that relates to the marketplace or their reactions to one's own company and its products or services.

Cyberspace. A popular term for the online Internet environment in which communications take place globally.

Data aggregation. The process of pulling together disparate elements of data to create a database or data file.

Data market. A broad marketplace in which the Internet competes with other information products delivered via print and electronic formats.

Data mining. Often refers to specific systems for developing new knowledge from existing databases but can be used in a generic sense.

Data sculpting. A process of reconfiguring characters within a data file usually to enable text to be used as a database in the form of a comma delimited file.

Deming Prize. Established in 1950 and administered by the Union of Japanese.

Demographic targeting. Uses characteristics such as age, income, education level, or ethnicity of a population to specify a particular market segment made up of people.

Desktop. The screen with program icons usually showing when a personal computer operating in Windows starts.

Digital Video Recorders. Camcorder or recording decks that use IEEE 1394 standard (Firewire) technology for very-high-speed, high-quality recording and editing of video by computer.

Download. The process of transferring data from one computer to another.

Drag and drop. The ability to drag icons and other software objects from one location and file or link them to another location.

DSL. Digital subscriber line, a newer form of Internet connection that optimizes copper wire and telephone circuitry for high-speed data transmission. DSL technology has various forms including ADSL, HDSL, IDSL, R-ADSL, SDSL, and VDSL, offering users a choice of speeds ranging from 32 Kbps to, in laboratory settings, more than 50 Mbps.

Due diligence. A legal term involving careful investigation of a business, usually during the process of a merger or acquisition.

DVD. Digital video disc player technology began appearing in 1999 with capacity to play movies on computers, with capacity of at least 4.7 gigabytes of data.

Economic Census. Profiles prepared by the U.S. Census Bureau every 5 years, from the national to the local level. The Advance Report presents national statistics for every sector and subsector of the economy.

Economic espionage. Economic espionage concerns foreign power-sponsored or foreign-power-coordinated intelligence activity directed at the U.S. government or U.S. corporations, establishments, or persons, which involves the unlawful or clandestine targeting or acquisition of sensitive financial, trade or economic policy information, proprietary economic information, or critical technologies; or the unlawful or clandestine targeting or influencing of sensitive economic policy decisions. Codified in The Economic Espionage Act of 1996, Title 18, Chapter 90 of the United States Code.

E-mail discussion groups. Also known as mail lists or LISTSERV.

Environmental scanning. The process of continuously and thoroughly researching the business landscape with particular attention to markets, regulatory affairs, and technology developments.

Executive Information Systems. A 1980s term used to categorize easy-to-use computer information systems designed for top executives in large organizations.

Exporting. To move data from a database or other program into a new file. The opposite of importing.

Firewire. See digital video recorders.

FlashSessions. America Online's software that helps the subscriber schedule downloading of e-mail so it can be read off-line.

Fluff. Promotional literature casting the subject in a good light regardless of the real situation.

Freeform database. A database without an entry form for data. See structured and unstructured information.

Freeware. Software distributed at no charge. It may contain copyright restrictions.

Frequently Asked Questions (FAQ). Archived information, usually in newsgroups, that answers common questions.

Front end. Usually refers to a graphical user interface, which is a simplified "control panel" for a more complicated computer function.

Geographic targeting. Uses a ZIP code, latitude/longitude, or center point and radius or non-circular boundary to define a land area.

Geosynchronous Earth Orbiting Satellites (GEOS). GEOS are placed in a geosynchronous orbit at 22,300 miles above the equator and are major components of the global telecommunications system.

Gigabyte. A billion bytes.

Groupware. Software that enables individuals to share information and communicate. As a specific category of software, the field is dominated by IBM's Notes product but can include such conferencing products as Microsoft's Netmeeting.

Hierarchical. In searching, going from broad concept to specific term in steps. In organization, chief executive at the top going downward to the least skilled person.

HTML. Hypertext markup language is the authoring language used to create hypertext documents on the World Wide Web, created at the European Laboratory for Particle Physics (CERN) by Tim Berners-Lee who later became director of W3C based at MIT. He wrote the first WWW client and communications software, defining URLs, HTTP (Hypertext Transfer Protocol), and HTML.

Humint. Personal contacts are the sources of human intelligence.

Hyperlink. A word or graphic that, when clicked on by action of a mouse button, generates movement within a page or document.

HyperText Transfer Protocol (HTTP). See HTML.

IBIS. See Internet Business Intelligence System.

Importing. To move data into a database or other program. The opposite of exporting.

Incorporation. A legal registration of an entity to do business, usually filed with a secretary of state. Sole proprietorships do not need to file such registrations, although some jurisdictions require a business license or fictitious name filing.

Information architecture (IA). The overall blueprint for computer technology in an organization.

Information warfare. Usually used in the context of national security, an overt or covert attack against military or civilian (National Information Infrastructure) targets for destructive purposes.

Intellectual capital. A scarce resource contained within the minds of employees, worthy of valuable asset status.

Intellectual property. A general term used for inventions, trademarks, or copyrighted materials.

Intelligence Cycle. As defined the Central Intelligence Agency, the process by which raw information is acquired, gathered, transmitted, analyzed, and made available as finished intelligence for policymakers to use in decision making and action.

Interactive multimedia. Beyond simply playing it, multimedia can be manipulated by the user; for example, altering the storyline or getting customized instruction.

Internet. Interconnected network usually referring to a globally connected server using TCP/IP.

Internet Business Intelligence System (IBIS). A comprehensive system of wide-ranging information sources (Internet and other supporting resources) and methods providing a tool for exploiting information and creating a knowledge advantage.

Internet Service Providers (ISP). A commercial service that provides access to the Internet through points of presence (POP) via telephone line.

ISDN. An international standard for transmitting voice, video, and data over digital lines at 64 Kbps. ISDN uses 64-Kbps circuit-switched channels, called B channels, or "bearer" channels, to carry voice and data. Data users can bond two channels to achieve 128 Kbps service.

Joint venture. A partnership of two or more separate companies, usually limited to one project.

Keyword. A word or words assigned as representative of text either for the purpose of categorizing the text or searching for it.

Knowledge Management (KM). Efficient utilization of intellectual capital and an overarching concept that includes business intelligence. The process of gathering and using data and information from within an organization and outside of it in an effort to better manage the enterprise.

LAN. Local area network.

LISTSERV. A registered trademark licensed to L-Soft international, Inc. LISTSERV is a system that makes it possible to create, manage, and control electronic mailing lists.

Low Earth Orbiting Satellites (LEOS). LEOS are placed in orbit 310 to 870 miles (See GEOS) so they can be operated with less power and reduced time delays. LEOS likely will form the network for wireless Internet via satellite.

M&A. Merger and acquisition is a general term for combination of two or more businesses.

Mailing lists. A generic term for a system that permits one person to send e-mail to more than one person in one operation. See LISTSERV.

Management information systems (MIS). An older term that has given way to Information Technology (IT).

Market research. Function that links the consumer, customer, and public to the marketer through information about opportunities and problems that can be solved or fulfilled by products or services.

Matrix. An array of elements usually contained in rows and columns.

Metadata. Includes mass storage, large-scale distributed computing, document management, and multimedia processing.

Metasearch. On the Internet, usually is performed by entering a search term into a form that submits the term to multiple search engines.

Modem. Device usually used to connect a digital computer to an analog telephone line. While TV-Cable Internet services and telephone company ISDN service use hardware referred to as "modems," these do not modulate or demodulate signals so they are more accurately described as network devices or terminal adapters.

Multimedia. Computer information that incorporates more than text and static graphics. Can include sound and video.

Myers-Briggs Type Indicator (MBTI). A mental measurement system that categorizes personalities for the purpose of matching an individual to job function.

National Information Infrastructure (NII). The phrase has an expansive meaning and includes more than just the physical facilities used to transmit, store, process, and display voice, data, and images. Beyond physical components, the value of the NII depends on the quality of many other elements, such as applications and software, to name but a few.

National Security Threat List (NSTL). NSTL includes security issues regardless of the country of origin and a classified list of foreign powers that pose a strategic intelligence threat to U.S. security interests.

Natural Language Query (NLQ). A database query in plain English usually framed as a question.

Netiquette. Appropriate behavior when posting to Newsgroups.

Newsgroups. See Usenet.

Object linking and embedding (OLE). Microsoft standards for creating dynamic links between documents, spreadsheets, graphs, and databases in different application software.

OCR. Optical character recognition. A process that optically scans printed documents and creates a text file that can be manipulated in a word processor.

ODBC. Open Database Connectivity (ODBC) is a standard or application programming interface (API) for accessing a database.

Off-line browsing. To view information after it has been downloaded from another computer when there is no active connection to the other computer.

Online service. A value-added provider of computer connection services, usually an Internet Service Provider (ISP) like America Online or CompuServe. Also includes some premium business information services with dial-up connections.

Packet. See packet switching.

Packet switching. A method of transmitting information in packets that contain addresses of sender and recipient, error-checking data, and information. Packets may travel via different routes from sender to recipient and are collected by a router.

PCMCIA. Personal Computer Memory Card International Association standard for a credit-card size device that slips into a slot, usually to provide a modem for notebook computers, although cards are available for other functions.

PDF. Adobe's Portable Document Format.Files that maintain the original layout and graphic design of the published documents. This format allows users to search, copy, display, and print the reports on a variety of computer platforms using the Adobe Acrobat software available free of charge at the Adobe Web site.

Points of presence (POPs). Local telephone exchange where dial-up connections terminate into modems.

Portal. On the Internet, a domain in cyberspace that provides such services as searching capability, news, aggregated information, and e-mail, usually accompanied by advertising.

POTS. Plain old telephone service, without enhancements such as voice mail or call waiting.

Premium business information. High-cost information usually accessed via a subscription service.

Premium databases. See premium business information.

Primary research. Data gathered directly from individuals.

PROACtive. The process of planning, rapidly obtaining required information, organizing, analyzing, and communicating it for business advantage.

Proprietary content. See proprietary information.

Proprietary information. Information owned by an entity and considered private and/or valuable.

Public records. Records of any sort that are created by local, state, or federal government agencies and are required by law to be available for public inspection.

Publicly Accessible Mailing Lists. See e-mail discussion groups.

Qualitative analysis. Nonnumerical analysis often involving intuitive or subjective judgments.

Quantitative analysis. Mathematical analysis often using statistical techniques.

Registration/subscription services. Mostly free services on the Internet, often portals, which provide value-added in exchange for user registration.

Regression analysis. The "least squares" method to fit a line through a set of numerical observation to analyze how a single dependent variable is affected by the values of one or more independent variables.

Relationship analysis. Usually a graphic portrayal of the relationships among entities.

Relevance ranking. A ranking algorithm to determine the order in which matching documents are returned on a search results page, usually from a search engine.

Rigor. Proven by repeated checks or investigation. As in "scientific rigor."

RJ type phone jack. RJ (registered jacks, sometimes described as RJ-XX) telephone connection interfaces (receptacle and plug) registered with the Federal Communications Commission (FCC). 47CFR68—Connection Of Terminal Equipment To The Telephone Network provides for uniform standards for the protection of the telephone network from harms caused by the connection of terminal equipment and associated wiring. The RJ-11 is the most common plug for connecting modems to telephone lines and is used in many countries.

Satellite imagery. Previously a very expensive and difficult-to-locate product, satellite pictures with one-meter resolution now are available from sources on the Internet by credit card transaction.

Scenario planning. A popular strategic-planning process that avoids the dangers of single-point forecasts by allowing users to explore the implications of several alternative futures.

SCIP. Society of Competitive Intelligence Professionals, headquartered in Alexandria, Virginia.

Search expression. See Boolean logic.

Secondary research. Data gathered by reviewing published literature.

Shareware. A "try for free before you buy" marketing method.

SIC. Standard Industrial Classification. Numerical codes developed by U.S. government to classify businesses according to primary activity.

Spam. Junk e-mail often sent to thousands of people at one time. Now less frequent due to filtering, lawsuits, and regulations.

SQL. Structured query language used on personal computers to access data on larger mini- or mainframe computers.

Strategic alliance. An ongoing partnership of two or more separate companies.

Strategic planning. A wide-view, holistic approach to business that begins with vision and mission and broadly considers markets and resources, planning from one to five years ahead.

Strategy. In business, the art and science of managing organizations in competitive situations.

Structured information. Like names and addresses in a database, structured information is maintained in consistent format records. See unstructured information and freeform database.

SWOT. Strengths, Weaknesses, Opportunities, and Threats, classic considerations in strategy development.

T1. A digital connection capable of transmitting data at a rate of approximately 1.5 million bps (bits per second). Although generally this has been associated with costly special telephone line connections, TV-Cable Internet and DSL services increasingly provide this level of speed at a much lower price.

Tactical information. Used to solve a problem at hand.

TCP/IP. Transfer Control Protocol/Internet Protocol. The standard for common computer communication and error correction.

Template wizards. A software feature that assists the user in its operation in a step-by-step manner.

Templates. A fill-in-the-blank form or other construction of a similar nature.

TIFF. Tagged Image File Format, a common image file format.

Uniform Resource Locator (URL). The address for a resource or site on the Internet. For example, you might tell your browser to find a hypertext document for David Vine Associates by typing into your browser **http://www.davidvineassociates. com** (increasingly, the http:// is not necessary).

UNIX. An operating system written in the programming language C at Bell Laboratories. It is the foundation upon which the Internet was built.

Unstructured information. A database that does not require pre-defined field lengths or field types.

Usenet newsgroups. A user network of bulletin board like postings widely available via the Internet.

Visualization. The general process of graphical representation of complex data.

Web cam. Video camera connected to the Internet so anyone can use it to view a scene. Sometimes can be panned or zoomed remotely by the user.

Wireless communications. Communication by radio, usually at cellular telephone frequencies or higher.

Wireless Internet video. Video transmission by radio with a connection to the Internet, usually at cellular telephone frequencies or higher.

ABOUT THE AUTHOR

Since 1982, David Vine has used personal computers in his consulting practice for business research and many other unique functions, ranging from keeping clients informed about critically relevant breaking news to prospecting for new business to communicating with important publics. He has consistently pushed the "edge of the envelope" in applications of electronic information for research and communication on behalf of clients, ranging from multinational corporations to small businesses and various governmental organizations.

Vine began his career as a journalist in the late 1960s and moved into the public relations field during the late 1970s. A former part-time flight instructor, he has written extensively for aviation and computer trade press as well as management publications. He and his wife enjoy bird-watching and cruising, and he is an avid reader and shortwave radio listener. He has served on the boards of local, state, and international civic and professional associations.

Vine holds a master's degree in business administration with a concentration in strategic planning from Rowan University and an undergraduate business degree from Thomas Edison State College. He is married to Mar-Lee McKean, Ph.D. Dr. McKean, a former senior research scientist in the pharmaceutical industry, now consults in this field. They reside in Princeton, New Jersey.

David Vine invites you to visit his Web site at **www.davidvine associates.com**.

INDEX

A

accountants, 103
accounting software, 93–95
Acker, David, 339
Acrobat Reader, 369–370
ACT!, 80, 119
Action Settings in PowerPoint, 368–369
Adaptec's DirectCD, 373
address books, 188, 191, 296, 302
address manager software, 257
Adobe Acrobat, 369–370
    security features, 372
Adobe's Portable Document Format
        (PDF), 265
AdTalk, 83
advertising, 83–85
Advertising Age, 83
AEC InfoCenter, 251
Airbridge, 389
AirCard, 388–389
allCLEAR, 343
Alliance for Converging Technologies,10
AlphaConnect, 117
AltaVista, 117, 205–206, 212–213
American Business Information, 262
American Express, 241–244
American Institute of Certified Public
        Accountants, 103
American Library Association, 144,
        261–262
American Marketing Association's
    Strategic Leadership Forum, 8
American Psychological Association, 261
America Online
    AOL International, 173
    AOLnet, 173
    AOL Studios, 173
    Channel Line-Up, 174
    CompuServe, 180–181
    databases, 176
    Favorite Places, 176
    FlashSessions, 179–180
    Instant Messenger, 175

    merger with Time-Warner, 172
    My News, 175
    NetFind, 174–175
    news clipping service, 175–176
    newsgroups, 220–221
    News Profiles, 176–180
    Online Community, 174
    Personal Filing Cabinets, 175–176
    personalization and control, 174–175
analysis
    competitive, 145–150, 339–341,
        342–343 (figs.) (*See also*
        intelligence, business)
        business plan template, 146–147
        methodologies, 145–146
        new product development,
            147–148
        template, 148–149
    correlation, 336
    financial, 93–95, 330–332
    information
        AutoSummarize function,
            327–328, 365
        benchmarking, 330
        competitive analysis, 145–150,
            339–341, 342–343 (figs.)
        database management,
            333–335, 338–339
        DB2, 338–339
        financial analysis, 330–332
        geographic analysis, 346–347
        intelligence analysis, 348–351
        KnowledgeX, 337–338
        market analysis, 329
        patent analysis, 329
        Pathfinder, 348–351
        qualitative and quantitative
            analysis, 326–327
        ratio analysis, 330–332
        relationship analysis, 337–338,
            344–346
        sales forecasting, 329
        spreadsheet use, 328

analysis (*continued*)
  statistical analysis, 336–337
  text analysis, 348–351
  use of Excel, 333–337
  visualization software, 341,
    343–346
market, 329
numerical, 326
patent, 329
portfolio, 82
postoptimality, 341
regression, 336
relationship, 337–338, 344–346
sensitivity, 341
shareholder value, 98
software, 138–139
statistical, 336–337
subscriptions, information, 157–158
text, 348–351
Analysis ToolPak, 51, 336–337
Andreesen, Marc, 162
Andriot, Laurie, 279
animation effects, 367–368
ANSIR Program, 394–395
AOL. *See* America Online
Argus Clearinghouse, 203–204
article citation databases, 275–276
Art of War, 4
ASCII, 195
  conversion of audio files to, 318–319
askSam, 138, 197, 314–316
Association for Psychological Type, 25
association link sites, 217–218
AT&T, 13, 387
Audible, Inc., 318
audio file conversion to ASCII, 318–319
AutoContent Wizard, 359–361
autoshapes, 364 (fig.)
AutoSummarize function, 327–328, 365
avoidance, technological, 405
Awareness of National Security Issues
    and Response (ANSIR), 394–395

B

balanced scorecard, 97
Bankrate.com, 113
Bell Atlantic
  Bell Atlantic Mobile (BAM), 389
  Cellular Digital Packet Data, 386
Bell System, 5

benchmarking, 330
Berners-Lee, Tim, 162
Bertelsmann AG, 173, 274
bid software, 258
Big LEOS systems, 184–185
BioMedNet, 251–252
BoardView, 98–102
bookmarks, 189–190
  importing HTML files, 306–307
  organizing, 304–309
  software for managing, 308–309
Boolean searching, 206
Briefcase, 378
briefings, in-person, 382–383
Briggs, Katherine Cook, 25
Bristol-Myers Squibb, 392–393
browsers, Internet, 163, 187–188
Bureau of Economic Analysis, 51, 53
Bureau of National Affairs (BNA), 277
business
  directories, 265–273, 278–282, 283 (fig)
  information
    commoditization of, 157
    online, 240
    providers, 30–31, 277–278
    publicly traded companies,
      241–245
    sources, 179–180
  news, 239, 245–248
  planning, 49–53, 258
    financial information, 53
    marketing information, 52
    template, 146–147
  valuation, 106–108
Business Analyst, 94
business intelligence. *See* intelligence,
    business
Businessman's Checklist for Success, 142
Business Researcher's Interest, 104
business-to-business marketing, 77–78,
    86–87
Business Trends Analysts, 73
Business Wire, 49, 81, 179

C

cable modem service, 168
calendar software, 302
cameras
  computer, 383–384
  digital video, 388

Capital-Connection, 116
capital, raising Small Business, 258
card file software, 302–303
case studies
  business intelligence, 87–88
  business-to-business marketing,
    86–87
  consumer marketing, 85–86
  gathering company information,
    108–109
  Internet use in due diligence, 64–66
  Internet use in threat assessment,
    66–67
  investor's study of temporary staffing
    industry, 122–126
  proprietary information security,
    67–68
CDPD systems, 388–389
CD-ROM
  business directories, 265–273
  communicating business intelligence
    via, 372–374
  contracting data, government,
    263–264
  copyright issues, 272–273
  databases available in libraries,
    265–273
  duplication, 372–374
  Energy InfoDisc, 265
  exporting data from, 272
  Gale Group, 269–270
  government produced, 264–265
  Kompass, 269
  magazine indexes, 270–272
  NewsBank, 277
  newspapers on, 277
  OTA Legacy, 265
  security features, 372
  Standard & Poor, 267
  statistics, government, 265
  storage of Web pages, 192–195
  telephone books, 262
  writers, 373
  Yellow Pages, 262
CEOs, information for, 60, 61
channels, Web, 193–194
chat, Internet, 21–22
civilian intelligence, 11–12
Coates, Joseph F., 58
code of ethics, 400–402

collaboration, electronic, 362–363
Comcast, 168
commoditization of business
    information, 157
communications
  low cost services, 238
  wireless, 181–185
Communicator, Netscape, 188, 191–192
compensation, employee, 97
competitive advantage, 39
competitive analysis. *See* analysis,
    competitive
competitive gaming, 82
Composer, Netscape, 188, 370–371
compression technology, 375
CompuServe, 172–173, 180–181
computer cameras, 383–384
computer communication channels,
    internal, 155
ComputerSelect, 270
conduct, rules of, 400–402
Conference Board, The, 98–102
conferencing, Internet, 383–385
confidentiality of information, 398
consumer confidence data, 98–99
consumer marketing case study, 85–86
consumer price index, 99
contact management, 78–80, 119,
    120–122, 257, 296
contacts, developing, 45–46
control key functions, 196
Cooperative Association for Internet
    Data Analysis (CAIDA), 166
copy and paste functions, 192, 196
copyright issues, 272–273
CorelCENTRAL, 301–303
corporate knowledge sharing, 380, 382
corporate profits after tax, 99–100
corporate-provided information,
    252–253
Corporate ResourceNet, 277
CorpTech, 78
correlation analysis, 336
cost considerations for information
    sources, 289
costing, activity-based, 97
cost of Internet business intelligence
    systems system, 134–135
courses, online, 258–259
Cox Communications, 168

Crain's New York Business, 81
credit cards, small business, 113
credit information, 89–90
CrossPad, 319
cryptography, 399–400
customer development. *See under*
    marketing
customer information. *See* contact
    management
customizing toolbars, 363–364
cyberplaces, 45
cybertribes, 70

D
Daily Brief, OA's, 359
Dale Carnegie Training, 359
databases
    AOL, 176
    article citation, 275–276
    CD-ROM, 261–275, 265–273
    converting text to, 197–198
    customer, 78
    directory, 278
    importing Web page information,
        197–198
    management, 141, 314–318, 333–335,
        338–339
    premium online, 275–276
    See also spreadsheets
data market, 44–45
Data Over Cable Service Interface
    Specifications (DOCSIS), 168
data sculpting, 195–198
data set directories, 282–287
Dataware Technologies, Inc., 252–253
Day, G.J., 142
DB2, 338–339
Decision Edge, 141, 339
Deja.com, 221–224
Deja News, 208
Delorme's Street Atlas USA, 346–347
Deming, W. Edwards, 5
Department of Commerce, 330
deregulation, telecommunications,
    185–186
descriptive statistics, 337
Dfuntions, 334–335
diagramming software, 341, 343–346
Dialog Information Services, Inc., 273
Diebold, John, 292

digests, list, 227–228
Digital City, Inc., 173
digital satellite service, 170–172
Digital Subscriber Line (DSL)
    technology, 169–170
DigitalWork, 81
Dilenschneider, Robert L., 355
Dimensional Insight, 138
DirecPC, 171
DirectCD, 373
directories, business, 265–273, 278–282,
    283 (fig)
diskettes, saving presentations on, 374
dissemination of information, 321–324
Division of Advanced Computational
    Infrastructure and Research (ACIR),
    166
documents
    PDF, 369–370
    scanning, 316–318
    screening, 321–323
    security, 372
    storing, 316–318
    summaries, 327–328, 365
domain names, 19–20
Douglass, Benjamin, 90
Dow Jones & Company, 274
drag and drop, 190–191
dtSearch, 316–318
DT Software, Inc., 316–317
due diligence, 57–58, 64–66, 103–106
Dun & Bradstreet, 90, 121, 240, 275
Dunnigan, James F., 392
Dun, Robert Graham, 90
duplication, CD-ROM, 372–374
DVD Web page storage, 192–195

E
EBSCO Information Services, 277
ECCO, 185
Economic Counterintelligence Program,
    393–394
economic data, 98–102
economic espionage, 395–398
Economic Espionage Act, 396–397
EDGAR, 254
editors, mail list, 228–229
electronic collaboration, 362–363
Electronic Communications Privacy Act
    (ECPA), 219–220

electronic mail lists. *See* mail lists,
    electronic
Ellipso, 185
e-mail, 44
    address books, 119
    communicating business intelligence
        via, 362–363
    enhanced communication, 365–366
    filtering, 300
    organization, 296–300
    portal-based accounts, 238
    privacy protection, 219–220
    See also mail lists, electronic
employment data, 100
encryption, 399–400
Encyclopaedia Britannica, 291
Energy InfoDisc, 265
Energy Information Agency, 265
environmental factors in Internet
        business intelligence, 48
espionage, economic, 395–398
estimation software, 258
ethics, competitive intelligence, 401–402
European Center for Nuclear Research
        (CERN), 162
evaluating information quality, 144–145
Excel, 137, 197, 333–337
        Analysis Toolpak, 51
Exchange, Microsoft, 378–380, 381–382
        (figs.)
Excite, 201, 207, 213, 239
external information, gathering, 40–41
e-zines, 23–24

F

Favorite Places, AOL, 176
faxes, 374–378
FBI, 393–397
Federal Express, 13–14
Federal Internet Exchange, 165
Federal Reserve System, 51
FedWorld, 30
files
    advanced functions, 361–362
    LISTSERV functions, 234
File Transfer Protocol (FTP), 163, 189
filtering e-mail, 300
financial management
    business valuation, 106–108
    collecting economic data, 98–102
    data for business plans, 53

due diligence, 103–106
financial analysis, 93–95, 330–332
financial functions and information
        sources, 91–93
financial information online, 201
government reports and, 95–97
information for, 60–62, 91–94
internal audits, 103–108
reports, 94–95, 330–332
small business, 113–116
software, 93–95
staging, 115–116
strategic, 95–98
Financial Times Group, 30
"find" functions, 294–296
Finding Statistics Online, 279
FlashSessions, AOL, 179–180
flowcharts, 341, 343–346
folders, managing, 293–296
foreign exchange rate, 100
formal reports, 358–359
Forrester Research, Inc., 24
forums, mail list, 231–232
Free Agent, 225
Freeh, Louis J., 393
freeware. *See* software
FTP (File Transfer Protocol), 163, 189
Fulltext Sources Online, 279
future of business intelligence, 404–405
futurists, 58–59

G

Gale Directory of Databases, 278
Gale Group, The, 269–270, 278
Galvin, Robert W., 6
GAO. *See* General Accounting Office
Gates, Bill, 377
General Accounting Office (GAO),
        95–97, 253–254, 358
    GAO Reports, 95–97, 254, 358
General Survey Outline, 149
geographic analysis, 346–347
geographic information systems (GIS),
        287–289
geoplots, 346–347
GEOS systems, 183–184
Geosynchronous Earth Orbiting
        Satellites (GEOS) systems,
        183–184
Global Business Network, 30
global positioning system (GPS), 288
Globalstar, 185
glossary of terms, 407–418
goals of Internet business intelligence, 2
Goldmine, 119

gopher, 163, 189
"Government Giveaways for
    Entrepreneurs," 263
government information
    CD-ROM, 264–265
    contract data, 263–264
    documents online, 32–34, 253–254
    financial management using, 95–97
    link sites, 217–218
    security, 394–396
    statistics, 265
Government Printing Office, 253
graphics enhanced communication,
    365–366
gross domestic product (GDP), 100
groupware, 319–321

H
Hacker Quarterly, 23
hackers, Internet, 23–24
handwriting recognition devices, 319
Harbor Telco, 253
hardware, wireless communications,
    386–389
Hatvany, Bela, 261
histogram, 336
history of business intelligence, 3–4
Hoover's Online, 30
HotBot, 207
HotOffice, 238
HTML, 20–21, 162
    creating HTML-linked documents,
        creating, 309–313
    formatting documents, 371–372
    importing HTML files as bookmarks,
        306–307
    page analysis with visualization
        software, 343–346
Hughes Network Systems, 170
human resources information, 61, 63
"humint" sources, 296
HyperTerminal, 378
HyperText Transfer Protocol (HTTP), 189

I
I-Barter, 230
identifying competitors, 53–56
IDIS (Internet-Derived Intelligence
    Systems, 192–195
images, saving, 192
income statement ratio analysis, 332
indexes to magazine articles, 270–272
Index of Publicly Accessible Mailing
    Lists, 229
industrial parks, Internet, 251–252

industrial production index, 100
industry specific Internet resources,
    251–252
influence, use in business intelligence,
    354–356
InfoBusiness, 263
information
    architecture, 292–293
    conglomerates, 273–275
    corporate-provided, 252–253
    dissemination, 321–324
    evaluation, 144–145
    needs for strategy development,
        46–47
    professionals, periodicals for, 280
    quality/quantity, 142–145
    security, 391–402
        ANSIR program, 394–395
        aspects of, 398
        cryptography, 399–400
        Economic Counterintelligence
            Program, 393–394
        FBI involvement in, 394–396
        intelligence activity, foreign-
            power-sponsored, 395–396
        Internet, 67–68
        National Security Threat List,
            395–396
        safeguards, 398–400
        trade secrets theft, 392–393
    sharing, 154–158, 380, 382
    sources
        business, 179–180
        cost considerations, 289
        for managers, 61–63
    subscription analysis, 157–158
    systems, 2–3
Information Access Company (IAC),
    269–270
Information Today, 280
Information Today, Inc., 278–280
Infoseek, 207
InfoSpace, 121, 202
InfoTrac, 270
in-house information sharing, 154–158
Instant Messenger, AOL, 175
instructional videotapes, 155
Intellectual Property Gold, 277–278
intelligence, business
    for business plans, 49–53
    case studies, 87–88
    communicating
        Adobe Acrobat, 369–370
        advanced file functions, 361–362
        CD-ROM, 372–374

electronic collaboration, 362–363
e-mail, 365–366
fax broadcasting, 374–378
forms of output, 353–354
graphics enhanced
    communication, 365–366
in-person briefings, 382–383
Internet conferencing, 383–385
Internet presentations, 366–367
Microsoft Exchange, 378–380,
    381–382 (figs.)
multimedia presentations,
    367–369
networked computers, 379–380,
    381–382 (figs.)
Newsgroups, 365–366
organizing information, 356–361
paging, 387
presentations on diskette, 374
program overview, 385–386
reports, 356–361
videotape, 367
Web page creation, 370–372
wireless communications,
    386–390
competitive, 2, 9 (*See also* analysis,
    competitive)
competitor identification, 53–56
components, 7
costs, 134–135
defined, 1
due diligence and, 57–58
early trends, 5–6
environmental factors, 48
ethics, 401–402
future of, 404–405
goals, 2, 131–132
history, 3–4
identifying competitors, 53–56
influence, use of, 354–356
information advantages, 13–14
information quality and quantity,
    142–143
information requirements by
    management functions,
    60–61
needs assessment, 132–134
organizations, 7–9
predictive, 12–13
predictive intelligence, 12–13
press releases, 80–81
program implementation outline,
    152–153
public records, 32–35, 34 (fig)
research, 143, 154

software tools, 135–142
staffing, 25–26
strategy development, 14–17, 42,
    46–47
survey of most valuable, 42–43
system cost, 134–135
system features, 153–154
teams, 150–152
Twelve Themes of the New
    Economy, 10–11
types of competitor information
    sought, 7
cycle, 11, 15
predictive, 12–13
Intelligence Community (IC), 12
Intelligent Concept Extraction, 209
Intelligent Miner, 141, 339
international business news, 245–248
international operations managers,
    information for, 62
International Press Release Tool, 81
Internet, 20–23
access, 167–172
accessing external information,
    40–41
accountants and, 103
address books, 191
advertising links, 82–83
bookmarks, 189–190
browsers, 163, 187–188
as business tool, 13
cable modem service, 168
channels, 193–194
chat, 21–22
components of Internet-centered BI
    system, 156–157
conferencing, 383–385
copy and paste functions, 192, 196
culture, 23–25
customer databases, 78
developing contacts on, 45–46
digital satellite service, 170–172
Digital Subscriber Lines, 169–170
domain names, 19–20
downloading Web pages automatically,
    192–195
drag and drop, 190–191
due diligence and, 57–58, 64–66
as early warning system, 44–45
editorial content, 29–36
exporting information to databases,
    197–198
fax options, 376–377
financial information sources, 91–93
future of, 36, 181–185, 404–405

Internet (*continued*)
  hackers, 23–24
  history, 161–162
  industrial parks, 251–252
  industry-specific resources, 251–252
  information packets, 164
  Internet-Derived Intelligence
    Systems (IDIS), 192–195
  ISDN, 167–168
  keyword searches, 205–206
  knowledge transfer facilitation,
    36–37
  maps, 121
  Messenger, 192
  multimedia, 22, 383–385
  Netcaster, 193–195
  Netscape tips, 191–192
  newspaper databases, 81
  packet-switched data, 20
  pay-per-view, 31, 32 (fig)
  personality types of users, 27–29
  professional forums, 180–181
  protocol, 20, 163–164
  publishing presentations on,
    366–367
  research and development
    resources, 75–77
  satellite access technology, 183–185
  saving images, 192
  searching techniques, 71–72
  security, 385
  security of proprietary information,
    67–68
  service providers, 21, 163, 166–167
  shopping malls, 251–252
  small business resource guides,
    116–118
  speed, 167–168
  statistics and demographics, 24
  subscription services, 237–238
  switching to word processing, 192,
    196
  technical information, 19–20,
    163–166
  threat assessment, 66–67
  tools, 188
  traffic flow, 164–166
  transmission speed, 22, 383
  URLs, 19–20, 188–189
  wireless Internet video, 388–389
  wireless service, 181–185, 386–390
  Yellow Pages sites, 121
  See also search engines;
    Web pages; Web sites
Internet Assistant, 366–367

Internet Blue Pages, 279–280
Internet-Derived Intelligence Systems
    (IDIS), 192–195
Internet Service Providers, 21, 166–167
Internet Society, 21, 166
InterNotes, 320
intranets, 154
  HotOffice, 238
  low-cost setup, 238
  Web pages, 155
Investor's Business Daily, 118
Iridium system, 184–185
ISDN, 167–168
ISPs, 21, 163, 166–167
iVALS survey, 27–29

J
Jefferson, Thomas, 399
joining e-mail lists, 230–231
Jumbo shareware/freeware site, 308
Jung, C.G., 25

K
Kahn, Herman, 4–5
key business issues focus of competitor
    analysis, 145–146
Knight-Ridder, Inc., 179, 273–275
knowledge building, 154–158
knowledge management
  Dataware resources on, 252–253
  defined, 9
  Internet's knowledge transfer
    facilitation, 36–37
  methodology, 9–10
knowledge sharing, 154–158, 380, 382
KnowledgeX, 337–338
Kompass, 269

L
labor force data, 100
LEOS systems, 183–185
leverage ratios, 332
libraries, databases in, 265–273, 275–276
Library of Congress, 399
link sites, 217–218
liquidity, 91
  ratios, 331–332
lists, e-mail. *See* mail lists, electronic
LISTSERV, 226–228, 230–232
  file functions, 234
listwarehouse.com, 80
Liszt Directory of E-Mail Discussion
    Groups, 229
Little LEOS systems, 184–185
Lockheed, 273

Logicon's Message Dissemination
    System (LMDS), 321–324
Logitech, 388
Lotus Freelance Graphics, 148–149
Lotus Notes, 130, 238, 319–321, 323
Low Earth Orbiting Satellites (LEOS)
    systems, 183–185
Lowell, Francis Cabon, 392
Lycos, 117, 207, 214, 238

M

Mackay, Harvey, 79
Madison, James, 399
MAE facilities, 165
magazine article indexes, 270–272
Magellan, 209
mailing lists, business, 157
mail lists, electronic
    basics, 227–228
    defined, 226
    digests, 227–228
    editors, 228
    file functions, 234
    joining/leaving, 230–231
    knowledge development through,
        234–235
    list of subscribers, 232
    LISTSERV, 226, 228, 230–232, 234
    locating, 229–230
    management software, 230
    membership, 228
    moderators, 228
    options, 232–233
    posting messages, 231–232
    public/private, 228–229
    searching, 229
    subscriptions, 228
    topics, 233
    See also e-mail
Malcolm Baldrige National Quality
    Award, 6, 330
management, 4–6, 11
management information
    accessing the data market, 44–45
    for business planning, 49–53
    developing contacts, 45–46
    due diligence, 57–58
    e-mail use, 44
    external environmental factors, 48
    for identifying competitors, 53–56
    Internet, 40–41
    marketing information, 60, 62
    mission statements, 49–50
    mobile computing, 44
    needs, 46–47

    organizational vision, 47–48
    requirements, 60–61
    sources, 61–63
    strategy development, 46–47
    time managing, 44
mapping software, 346–347
maps, Internet, 121
marketing, 78–80
    advertising, 83–85
    business plan information, 52
    business-to-business sales, 77–78
    case studies, 85–88
    CD-ROM products for, 262–263
    competitive gaming, 82
    contact management software, 80
    customer development, 118–119
    customer intelligence, 78–80
    defined, 69
    information gathering templates,
        79–80
    Internet use in, 77–78
    management, 83–85
    managers' information, 60, 62
    market analysis, 329
    market research, 69, 71–75
    portfolio analysis, 82
    press releases for background
        information, 80–81
    product development, 75–77
    research and development
        resources, Internet, 75–77
    sales forecasting, 329
    scenario planning, 82
    small business, 120–122
    strategies, 82
    trends, 83
MarketPlace, 52
matrix use
    in competitive analysis, 341, 342–343
        (figs.)
    in organizing information, 309–312
Maximizer, 80, 119
McKinsey & Company, 149
Mentor's Last Words, 23
message management, 323–324
message posting to mail lists, 231–232
message systems, network, 155–156
Messenger, Netscape, 188, 192
metasearch resources, 210–212
Microsoft
    Excel, 51, 137, 197, 333–337
    Exchange, 378–380, 381–382 (figs.)
    Fax, 378
    Internet Explorer, 163, 187–188
        organizing bookmarks in, 304–305

Microsoft (*continued*)
  NetMeeting, 384–385, 389
  Outlook, 119, 300–301
  Word
    AutoSummarize function,
      327–328
    creating HTML documents using,
      312–313
    toolbars, 363–364
military intelligence, 3–4, 11–12
Milles, James, 230
mission statements, 49–50
Mitsui & Co., Ltd., 173
mobile computing, 44
modem speeds, 383
moderated digest, 228
moderators, mail list, 228–229
Moochers.com, 204–205
Mosaic, 162
Motorola, 6, 168
MultiActive Maximizer, 80
multimedia
  Internet offerings, 22
  music, 368
  presentations, 367–369
  search engines, 215–216
Music Tracks, 368
Myers-Briggs Type Indicator, 25–27
Myers, Isabel Briggs, 25
My News, AOL, 175
My Yahoo!, 239

N
NASA's Global Change Master Directory
    (GCMD), 282–287
National Association of Business
    Economists, 98
National Association of State
    Information Resource Executives
    (NASIRE), 32–33, 217
National Center for Supercomputer
    Applications, 162
National Information Infrastructure,
    395–396
National Laboratory for Applied
    Network Research (NLANR), 166
National Science Foundation, 163, 164,
    166
National Security Agency, 399
national security issues, 394–396
National Security Threat List (NSTL),
    395–396
Neou, Vivian, 229–230
Netcaster, 193–195
Netcenter, 240

Netcraft, 21
NetFind, 174–175
NetMeeting, 384–385, 389
Netscape
  Communicator, 188, 191–192
  Composer, 188, 370–371
  creating HTML documents using,
    312–313
  Navigator, 163, 187–189
    organizing bookmarks in,
      305–307
  Netcaster, 193–195
  Netcenter, 240
  search feature, 216
  Virtual Office, 385
networked computers, 379–380,
    381–382 (figs.)
network message systems, 155–156
Network News Transfer Protocol
    (NNTP), 220
Network Wizards, 24
Neucomb, John, 149
news
  article types available on AOL,
    179–180
  business, 239, 245–248
  clipping services, 175–176, 180, 239
  custom news pages, 240
  newspapers
    on CD-ROM, 277
    databases, 81
    online, 277
    publishers, 274–275
  newsreaders, 224
  online, 201
  sources, link sites to, 218
NewsBank, 277
newsgroups, 220–226
  business, 157
  enhanced communication, 365–366
  managing, 320
  searching, 221–226
  software, 225–226
NewsHound, 275
newsletters, 155
News Profiles, AOL, 176–180
News Rover, 225–226
NewsTracker, 207, 239
Nihon Keizai Shimbun, Inc. (Nikkei),
    173
North American Network Operator's
    Group (NANOG), 166
NSFNET, 163, 164
NUA Internet Surveys, 24
numerical analysis, 326

O

OCR software, 317
Odyssey, 185
Office of Technology Assessment, 265
online business information providers, 277–278
Online Manual, 279
operations managers, information for, 60, 62–63
Optical Character Recognition (OCR) software, 154
orbimage, 289
organizational vision and mission, 47–50
organization charts, 344–346
organizations, business intelligence, 7–9
organizing information, 356–361
    address books, 296, 302
    bookmarks, 304–309
    card file, 302–303
    contact management, 296
    CorelCENTRAL use, 301–303
    database management, 314–318
    e-mail organization, 296–300
    filtering e-mail, 300
    "find" functions, 294–296
    hyperlink use in, 309–313
    information architecture, 292–293
    information dissemination, 321–324
    Internet information management, 320
    linking information, 303
    Logicon's Message Dissemination System (LMDS), 321–324
    Lotus Notes Groupware, 319–321
    managing folders, 293–296
    matrix use, 309–312
    message management, 323–324
    Microsoft Outlook use, 300–301
    need for, 291–292
    personal organizer software, 257
    storing Web pages, 298–300
OrgChart, 344–346
Oshadata, 57
OTA Legacy, 265
outline of business intelligence program implementation, 152–153
Outline of Knowledge, 291
outlines, report, 357
Outlook Express, 220
Oxford Analytica (OA), 358–359

P

packet radio data networks, 388–389

packet-switched data, 20
paging systems, 387
Partnerships for Advanced Computational Infrastructure (PACI), 166
patent analysis, 329
Pathfinder Intelligence Software, 140, 348–351
Paula, Berinstein, 279
perception management, 396
personal consumption expenditures, 99
Personal Filing Cabinets, AOL, 175–176
personality
    and Internet business intelligence staffing, 25–26
    iVALS type grouping, 27–29
    Myers-Briggs type grouping, 25–27
personal organizer software, 257
persuasion, use of in business intelligence, 354–356
phonebooks, WinFax, 377
phone dialer software, 302–303, 378
phone service. *see* telecommunications
phreaking, 23–24
Planet Connect, 221
PointCast Network, 239
Portable Document Format (PDF), 369–370
Porter, Michael, 340
portfolio analysis, 82
postoptimality analysis, 341
Power and Influence, 355
PowerPoint, 359–361, 366–369, 374, 382–383
    Action Settings, 368–369
predictive intelligence, 12–13
presentations
    diskettes, 374
    in-person briefings using, 382–383
    Internet publishing, 366–367
    multimedia, 367–369
    videotaped, 367, 383
    See also multimedia; reports
press releases, 80–81
primary research software, 257–258
privacy protection, e-mail, 219–220
    See also security
private pod, 238
PR Newswire, 81
PROACtive process, 9
    components, 15–16
    small business marketing, 120–121
    steps involved, 130–131
producer price index (PPI), 100
product development, 75–77, 147–148

product information, 253
production managers, information for, 60, 62–63
productivity data, 101–102
professional Internet forums, 180–181
profits, corporate after-tax, 99–100
PROMT, 270
proposals software, 258
proprietary information security, 67–68, 391–402
protocol, Internet, 163–164
psychology and Internet business intelligence staffing, 25–26
public companies information, 241–244
public documents, 32–34, 241, 253–254
public records online, 31–35
publishers, business information, 30–31
purge features of business intelligence products, 153

Q
qualitative and quantitative analysis, 326–327
quality improvement, 5
Questel•Orbit, 277–278
QuickCam, 388
Quicken, 113

R
radio stations using RealAudio, 248–251
ratio analysis, 330–332
RealAudio outlets, 248–251
Real Cities, 274–275
recordable discs, 373
RedFlag's Business Analyst, 94
Reed Elsevier plc, 273
regression analysis, 336
relationship analysis, 337–338, 344–346
relevance rankings, search engine, 209, 213–215
remote communications, 375, 379
remote sensing programs, 287–289
reporting and analysis software, 138–139
reports
    financial, 94–95, 330–332
    formal, 358–359
    GAO, 95–97, 254, 358
    generating, 153
    research, 356–361
    See also presentations
research
    stages, 143
    topics for business intelligence, 154
research and development resources, 60, 62, 75–77

Reuters news reports, 179–180
rewritable discs, 373
Rigby, Darrell K., 9
Robert Morris Associates, 53

S
safeguards, information, 398–400
sales. *See* marketing
sampling, statistical, 337
satellite communications technology, 183–185
satellite imagery, 288
satellite service, digital, 170–172
saving images, 192
scanning documents, 154, 316–318
scenario planning, 82
scientific management, 4
search and replace functions, 195
search engines
    AltaVista, 205–206
    Argus Clearinghouse, 203–204
    browser, 216
    compared, 208–209
    Deja News, 208
    e-mail accounts, 238
    Excite, 201, 207, 213, 239
    features, 212–215
    financial information, 201
    hierarchical, 203–205
    HotBot, 207
    Infoseek, 207
    InfoSpace, 202
    internal site, 215–216
    Lycos, 207
    Magellan, 209
    metasearch resources, 210–212
    multimedia, 215–216
    news, 201
    newsgroup search capabilities, 221–224
    NewsTracker, 207
    personalities, 202–203
    portals, 200
    relevance rankings, 209, 213–215
    telephone books, 202
    topical guides, 203–205
    Yahoo!, 200, 204
Searcher: The Magazine for Database Professionals, 280
searching, 255–256
    AOL databases, 176
    Boolean, 206
    features of business intelligence products, 153
    full-text, 295

keyword searches, 205–206
newsgroups, 221–226
News Profiles, 176–180
techniques, 71–72
Windows "find" functions, 294–296
Securities and Exchange Commission,
    30, 124, 241, 254
security
    features of CD-ROM, 372
    information, 391–402
    Internet, 385
    proprietary information, 67–68
selective dissemination of information
    (SDI), 322–323
sensitivity analysis, 341
shareholder value analysis, 98
shareware. *See* software
Shaw, W.C., 142
shopping malls, Internet, 251–252
SIC Codes, 52
Sierra Wireless AirCard, 388–389
Silver, Jonathan, 104–106
SilverPlatter, 261–262
slide show presentations, 367–368, 382
Small Business Administration,
    114–115, 258–259
small businesses
    contact management systems, 119,
        120–122
    credit cards, 113
    customer contact, 120–122
    customer development, 118–119
    financial staging, 115–116
    financing, 113–116
    marketing, 120–122
    online courses for, 258–259
    PROACtive marketing process,
        120–121
    SBA financing programs, 114–115
    software, 117–118
    startup resources, 116–117
    strategy, 112
    venture capital, 114, 116
    Web guides, 116–118
Small Business Investment Company
    (SBIC), 114
Society of Competitive Intelligence
    Professionals, 7, 401
Sociological Abstracts, 261
SoftKey, 344
software
    80/20 rule, 361
    accounting, 93–95
    address manager, 257
    Adobe Acrobat, 265, 369–370

allCLEAR, 343
Analysis ToolPak, 51, 336–337
askSam, 138, 197, 314–316
AutoContent Wizard, 359–361
bidding, 258
bookmark management, 308–309
browsers, 187–189
Business Analyst, 94
business intelligence, 135–142
calendar, 302
contact management, 80, 119, 257
Corel/Microsoft compared, 137
costs, 137–142
database management, 141,
    197–198, 314–318
DB2, 141, 338–339
Decision Edge, 141, 339
Delorme's Street Atlas USA, 346–347
DI-Diver, 138–139
DirectCD, 373
dtSearch, 316–318
estimating, 258
Excel, 51, 137, 197, 333–337
financial analysis, 93–95
Free Agent, 225
freeware, 204–205, 254–258
groupware, 319–321
IBIS tools, 135–142
Intelligent Miner, 141, 339
Internet Assistant, 366–367
InterNotes, 320
KnowledgeX, 337–338
LISTSERV, 226–228, 230–232, 234
Logicon's Message Dissemination
    System (LMDS), 321–324
Lotus Freelance Graphics, 148–149
Lotus Notes, 319–321
mail list management, 230
mapping, 346–347
MarketPlace, 52
Microsoft Exchange, 378–380,
    381–382 (figs.)
Microsoft Fax, 378
Microsoft NetMeeting, 384–385, 389
Microsoft Office, 137
Microsoft Outlook, 119, 300–301
Microsoft Word, 312–313, 327–328,
    363–364
Netcaster, 193–195
Netscape Composer, 370–371
newsgroup, 225–226
News Rover, 225–226
OCR (Optical Character
    Recognition), 154
OrgChart, 344–346

software (*continued*)
Pathfinder, 140, 348–351
personal organizer, 257
phone dialer, 302–303, 378
PowerPoint, 359–361, 366–369, 374, 382–383
primary research, 257–258
proposals, 258
reporting, 138–139
scanning, 317
shareware, 94–95, 253, 254–258, 255–258
small business, 117–118
spreadsheet, 137
TexBridge Pro OCR, 317
utilization rule, 361
Virtual Office, 385
Visio, 341
visualization, 341, 343–346
voice recognition, 318
Watcher, 389
WebFerret, 255–256
WinFax PRO, 374–377
WordPerfect Office, 137
ZDNET, 255
solvency, 91
sorting in Word, 328
Special Libraries Association, 8
SpeedDial, 385
SPIN-2, 289
SPOT system, 288
spreadsheets, 328, 333–335, 341, 342 –343 (figs.)
See also databases
SRI International, 27–29
Standard Industrial Classification (SIC) Codes, 52
Standard & Poor, 267
statistical analysis of information, 336–337
statistical quality control, 5
statistical sampling, 337
statistics, 279
government, 265
Internet, 24
StockVue2000, 117–118
storing documents, 316–318
strategic intelligence, 42
Strategic Leadership Forum, 8, 59
strategy development, 46–47
subscription analysis, information, 157–158
subscription services, Internet, 237–238
subsidiaries, information on, 241–244
summaries of documents, 327–328

Sun Tzu, 4
Survey of Current Business, 51
Swim with the Sharks Without Being Eaten Alive, 79
SWOT (Strengths, Weaknesses, Opportunities and Threats), 14, 49
Symantec Corporation, 80, 119, 374
system features of business intelligence program, 153–154

T
Tactual, 393
Tagged Image File Format (TIFF), 154
Tappan, Lewis, 90
Tapscott, Don, 10
target organization focus of competitor analysis, 145
Taylor, Frederick W., 4
TCI, 168
teams, business intelligence, 150–152
technological avoidance, 405
technology transfer, 119
telecommunications, 181–186
telephone books, online, 202
Teligent, 185
Telnet, 163
templates, report, 357–361
TerraSat Geomatics, Inc., 289
terraserver.com, 289
text analysis, 348–351
TextBridge Pro OCR software, 317
text files, manipulating, 361–363
theft of trade secrets, 392–393
Thomson Corporation, 273
threat assessment, 66–67
Tile.Net, 229
time management, 44
Time-Warner, 168, 172
toolbars, 363–364
topics, mail list, 233
Trade and Industry Database, 270
trade secrets theft, 392–393
transmission speed, Internet, 22, 383
Tribune Business News, 179
Tripod, 238
tutorials, Web page creation, 371–372
Twelve Themes of the New Economy, 10–11

U
Uniform Resource Locators (URLs), 188–189
UNIX, 163
URLs, 19–20, 188–189

V

vBNS, 164, 166
venture capital, 114, 116
Veronica, 163
videotapes, 367
    instructional, 155
    presentations, 383
video, wireless Internet, 388
virtual offices, 385
Visio Corporation, 341
vision, organizational, 47–48
visualization software, 341, 343–346
voice recognition software, 318–319

W

Wall Street Journal, The, 274
Washington Business Journal, 104
Watcher, 389
WebBoard, 385
WebFerret, 255–256
Web pages
    creating, 370–372
    intranet, 155
    storing, 298–300
    See also HTML
Web sites
    2600 The Hacker Quarterly, 23
    AdAge, 83
    Adobe Acrobat, 369–370
    AdTalk, 83
    AEC InfoCenter, 251
    American Institute of Certified
        Public Accountants, 103
    AOL, 175
    Argus Clearinghouse, 203
    askSam, 138
    Audible, Inc., 318
    Bankrate.com, 113
    BioMedNet, 251
    Business Researcher's Interest, 104
    Business Trends Analysts, 73
    Business Wire, 49
    Capital-Connection, 116
    Conference Board, 98
    CorpTech, 78
    Crain's New York Business, 81
    Dataware Technologies, Inc., 252
    Deja, 221
    Deja News, 208
    DigitalWork, 81
    Dimensional Insight, 138
    DirecPC, 171
    DT Software, 316
    Dun & Bradstreet, 78, 121, 240
    Energy Information Agency, 265
    Federal Reserve, 95
    FedWorld, 30
    Financial Times Group, 30
    Forrester Research, Inc., 24
    Gale Group, The, 270
    General Accounting Office, 97, 253
    Global Business Network, 30
    Government Printing Office, 253
    Harbor Telco, 253
    Hoover's Online, 30
    HotBot, 207
    HotOffice, 238
    I-Barter, 230
    Index of Publicly Accessible Mailing
        Lists, 229
    Information Today, 280
    Infoseek, 207
    InfoSpace, 121, 202
    International Press Release Tool, 81
    Jumbo shareware/freeware site, 308
    Kompass, 269
    listwarehouse.com, 80
    Liszt Directory of E-Mail Discussion
        Groups, 229
    Lycos, 207
    Magellan, 209
    Moochers.com, 204–205
    My Yahoo!, 239
    NASA's Global Change Master
        Directory (GCMD), 282
    National Association of State
        Information Resource
        Executives (NASIRE), 217
    Netcraft, 21
    Network Wizards, 24
    newsreaders, 224
    NewsTracker, 207, 239
    NUA Internet Surveys, 24
    orbimage, 289
    Oshadata, 57
    PointCast Network, 239
    PR Newswire, 49
    Quicken, 113
    RedFlag's Business Analyst, 94
    Securities and Exchange
        Commission, 30, 124, 241, 254
    Small Business Administration, 114,
        259
    SoftKey, 344
    SPIN-2, 289
    SPOT system, 288
    technology transfer site, 119
    Teligent, 185
    TerraSat Geomatics, Inc., 289

Web sites (*continued*)
  terraserver.com, 289
  Tile.Net, 229
  Vivian Neou, 229
  Web Board, 385
  Yaffa Publishing, 83
  Yahoo!, 204
  Yellow Pages, 121
  ZDNet Software Library, 255
Web, World Wide. *See* Internet
Wide Area Networks (WANs), 154
WinFax PRO, 374–377
wireless communication, 181–185,
      386–390
WordPerfect, 137
word processing, 137, 312–313, 327–328,
      363–364
  switching to from Web pages, 192,
      196
WorldCom, 164

X

Xerox Corporation, 317

Y

Yaffa Publishing, 83
Yahoo!, 116–117, 200, 204, 210, 214–215,
      224
Yellow Pages
  CD-ROM directories, 262
  Web sites, 121

Z

ZDNet Software Library, 255
Zona Research, Inc., 27–29

More Great Books
from Information Today, Inc.

MILLENNIUM INTELLIGENCE
Understanding and Conducting Competitive Intelligence in the Digital Age
Jerry Miller and the Business Intelligence Braintrust
With contributions from the world's leading business intelligence practitioners, here is a tremendously informative and practical look at the CI process, how it is changing, and how it can be managed effectively in the Digital Age. Loaded with case studies, tips, and techniques, chapters include: What Is Intelligence?; The Skills Needed to Execute Intelligence Effectively; Information Sources Used for Intelligence; The Legal and Ethical Aspects of Intelligence; Corporate Security and Intelligence...and much more!

Softbound • ISBN 0-910965-28-5 • $29.95

KNOWLEDGE MANAGEMENT
FOR THE INFORMATION PROFESSIONAL
T. Kanti Srikantaiah and Michael E.D Koenig, eds.
Written from the perspective of the information community, this book examines the business community's recent enthusiasm for "Knowledge Management." With contributions from 26 leading KM practitioners, academicians, and information professionals, editors Srikantaiah and Koenig bridge the gap between two distinct perspectives, equipping information professionals with the tools to make a broader and more effective contribution in developing KM systems and creating a knowledge management culture within their organizations.

Hardbound • ISBN 1-57387-079-X
ASIS Members $35.60   **Non-Members $44.50**

SUPER SEARCHERS DO BUSINESS
The Online Secrets of Top Business Researchers
Mary Ellen Bates • Edited by Reva Basch
Super Searchers Do Business probes the minds of 11 leading researchers who use the Internet and online services to find critical business information. Through her in-depth interviews, Mary Ellen Bates—a business super searcher herself—gets the pros to reveal how they choose online sources, evaluate search results, and tackle the most challenging business research projects. Loaded with expert tips, techniques, and strategies, this is the first title in the exciting new "Super Searchers" series, edited by Reva Basch. If you do business research online, or plan to, let the Super Searchers be your guides.

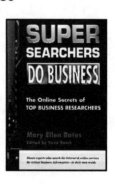

Softbound • ISBN 0-910965-33-1 • $24.95

LAW OF THE SUPER SEARCHERS
The Online Secrets of Top Legal Researchers
T.R. Halvorson • Edited by Reva Basch

In their own words, eight of the world's leading legal researchers explain how they use the Internet and online services to approach, analyze, and carry through a legal research project. In interviewing the experts, practicing attorney and online searcher T.R. Halvorson avoids the typical introductory approach to online research and focuses on topics critical to lawyers and legal research professionals: documenting the search, organizing a strategy, what to consider before logging on, efficient ways to build a search, and much more. *Law of the Super Searchers*—the second title in the new "Super Searchers" series edited by Reva Basch—offers fundamental strategies for legal researchers who need to take advantage of the wealth of information available online.

Softbound • ISBN 0-910965-34-X • $24.95

SECRETS OF THE SUPER NET SEARCHERS
The Reflections, Revelations and Hard-Won Wisdom of 35 of the World's Top Internet Researchers
Reva Basch • Edited by Mary Ellen Bates

Reva Basch, whom *WIRED* Magazine has called "The Ultimate Intelligent Agent," delivers insights, anecdotes, tips, techniques, and case studies through her interviews with 35 of the world's top Internet hunters and gatherers. The Super Net Searchers explain how to find valuable information on the Internet, distinguish cyber-gems from cyber-junk, avoid "Internet Overload," and much more.

Softbound • ISBN 0-910965-22-6 • $29.95

DESIGN WISE
A Guide for Evaluating the Interface Design of Information Resources
Alison Head

"*Design Wise* takes us beyond what's cool and what's hot and shows us what works and what doesn't."

—Elizabeth Osder, *The New York Times on the Web*

The increased usage of computers and the Internet for accessing information has resulted in a torrent of new multimedia products. For an information user, the question used to be: "What's the name of the provider that carries so-and-so?" Today, the question is: "Of all the versions of so-and-so, which one is the easiest to use?" The result is that knowing how to size up user-centered interface design is becoming as important for people who choose and use information resources as for those who design them. *Design Wise* introduces readers to the basics of interface design, and explains why and how a design evaluation should be undertaken before you buy or license Web- and disk-based information products.

Softbound • ISBN 0-910965-31-5 • $29.95

NET.PEOPLE
The Personalities and Passions
Behind the Web Sites
Thomas E. Bleier and Eric C. Steinert

With the explosive growth of the Internet, people from all walks of life are bringing their dreams and schemes to life as Web sites. In *net.people*, authors Bleier and Steinert take you up close and personal with the creators of 35 of the world's most intriguing online ventures. For the first time, these entrepreneurs and visionaries share their personal stories and hard-won secrets of Webmastering. You'll learn how each of them launched a home page, increased site traffic, geared up for e-commerce, found financing, dealt with failure and success, built new relationships—and discovered that a Web site had changed their life forever.

Softbound • ISBN 0-910965-37-4 • $19.95

GREAT SCOUTS!
CyberGuides for Subject Searching on the Web
Nora Paul and Margot Williams • Edited by
Paula Hane • Foreword by Barbara Quint

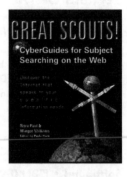

Great Scouts! is a cure for information overload. Authors Nora Paul (The Poynter Institute) and Margot Williams (*The Washington Post*) direct readers to the very best subject-specific, Web-based information resources. Thirty chapters cover specialized "CyberGuides" selected as the premier Internet sources of information on business, education, arts and entertainment, science and technology, health and medicine, politics and government, law, sports, and much more. With its expert advice and evaluations of information and link content, value, currency, stability, and usability, Great Scouts! takes you "beyond search engines"—and directly to the top sources of information for your topic. As a bonus, a Web page features updated links to all the sites covered in the book.

Softbound • ISBN 0-910965-27-7 • $24.95

INTERNET BLUE PAGES, 1999 Edition
The Guide to Federal Government Web Sites
Laurie Andriot

With over 900 Web addresses, this guide is designed to help you find any agency easily. Arranged in accordance with the US Government Manual, each entry includes the name of the agency, the Web address (URL), a brief description of the agency, and links to the agency or subagency's home page. For helpful cross-referencing, an alphabetical agency listing and a comprehensive index for subject searching are also included. Regularly updated information and links are provided on the author's Web site.

Softbound • ISBN 0-910965-29-3 • $34.95

ELECTRONIC STYLES
A Handbook for Citing Electronic Information
Xia Li and Nancy Crane

The second edition of the best-selling guide to referencing electronic information and citing the complete range of electronic formats includes text-based information, electronic journals and discussion lists, Web sites, CD-ROM and multimedia products, and commercial online documents.

Softbound • ISBN 1-57387-027-7 • $19.99

NET CURRICULUM
An Educator's Guide to Using the Internet
Linda C. Joseph

Linda Joseph, popular columnist for *MultiMedia Schools* magazine, puts her K-12 and Internet know-how to work in this must-have book for teachers and school media specialists. This is a practical guide that provides dozens of exciting project ideas, plus information on accessing information, electronic publishing, building Web pages, researching online, copyright and fair use, student safety, and much more.

Softbound • ISBN 0-910965-30-7 • $29.95

THE MODEM REFERENCE, 4th Edition
The Complete Guide to PC Communications
Michael A. Banks

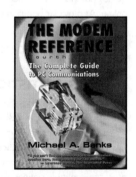

"If you can't find the answer to a telecommunications problem here, there probably isn't an answer."

—Lawrence Blasko, *The Associated Press*

Now in its 4th edition, this popular handbook explains the concepts behind computer data, data encoding, and transmission; providing practical advice for PC users who want to get the most from their online operations. In his uniquely readable style, author and techno-guru Mike Banks (*The Internet Unplugged*) takes readers on a tour of PC data communications technology, explaining how modems, fax machines, computer networks, and the Internet work. He provides an in-depth look at how data is communicated between computers all around the world, demystifying the terminology, hardware, and software. *The Modem Reference* is a must-read for students, professional online users, and all computer users who want to maximize their PC fax and data communications capability.

Available: May 2000 • Softbound • ISBN 0-910965-36-6 • $29.95

The Extreme Searcher's Guide To
WEB SEARCH ENGINES
A Handbook for the Serious Searcher
Randolph Hock

"Extreme searcher" Randolph (Ran) Hock—internationally respected Internet trainer and authority on Web search engines—offers advice designed to help you get immediate results. Ran not only shows you what's "under the hood" of the major search engines, but explains their relative strengths and weaknesses, reveals their many (and often overlooked) special features, and offers tips and techniques for searching the Web more efficiently and effectively than ever. Updates and links are provided at the author's Web site.

Softbound • ISBN 0-910965-26-9 • $24.95

UNCLE SAM'S K-12 WEB
Government Internet Resources for Educators, Students, and Parents
Laurie Andriot

Uncle Sam's K-12 Web is the only comprehensive print reference to federal government Web sites of educational interest. Three major sections provide easy access for students, parents, and teachers. Annotated entries include site name, URL, description of site content, and target grade level for student sites. *Uncle Sam's K-12 Web* helps children safely surf the Web while enjoying the many fun and educational Web sites Uncle Sam offers—and guides parents and teachers to the vast amount of government educational material available online. As a reader bonus, regularly updated information and links are provided on the author's Web site, fedweb.com.

Softbound • ISBN 0-910965-32-3 • $24.95

FINDING STATISTICS ONLINE
How to Locate the Elusive Numbers You Need
Paula Berinstein • Edited by Susanne Bjørner

Need statistics? Find them more quickly and easily than ever—online! Finding good statistics is a challenge for even the most experienced researcher. Today, it's likely that the statistics you need are available online—but where? This book explains how to effectively use the Internet and professional online systems to find the statistics you need to succeed.

Softbound • 0-910 65-25-0 • $29.95

Ask for CyberAge Books at your local bookstore or order online at
www.infotoday.com
For a complete catalog, contact:
Information Today, Inc.
143 Old Marlton Pike, Medford, NJ 08055 • 609/654-6266
email: custserv@infotoday.com